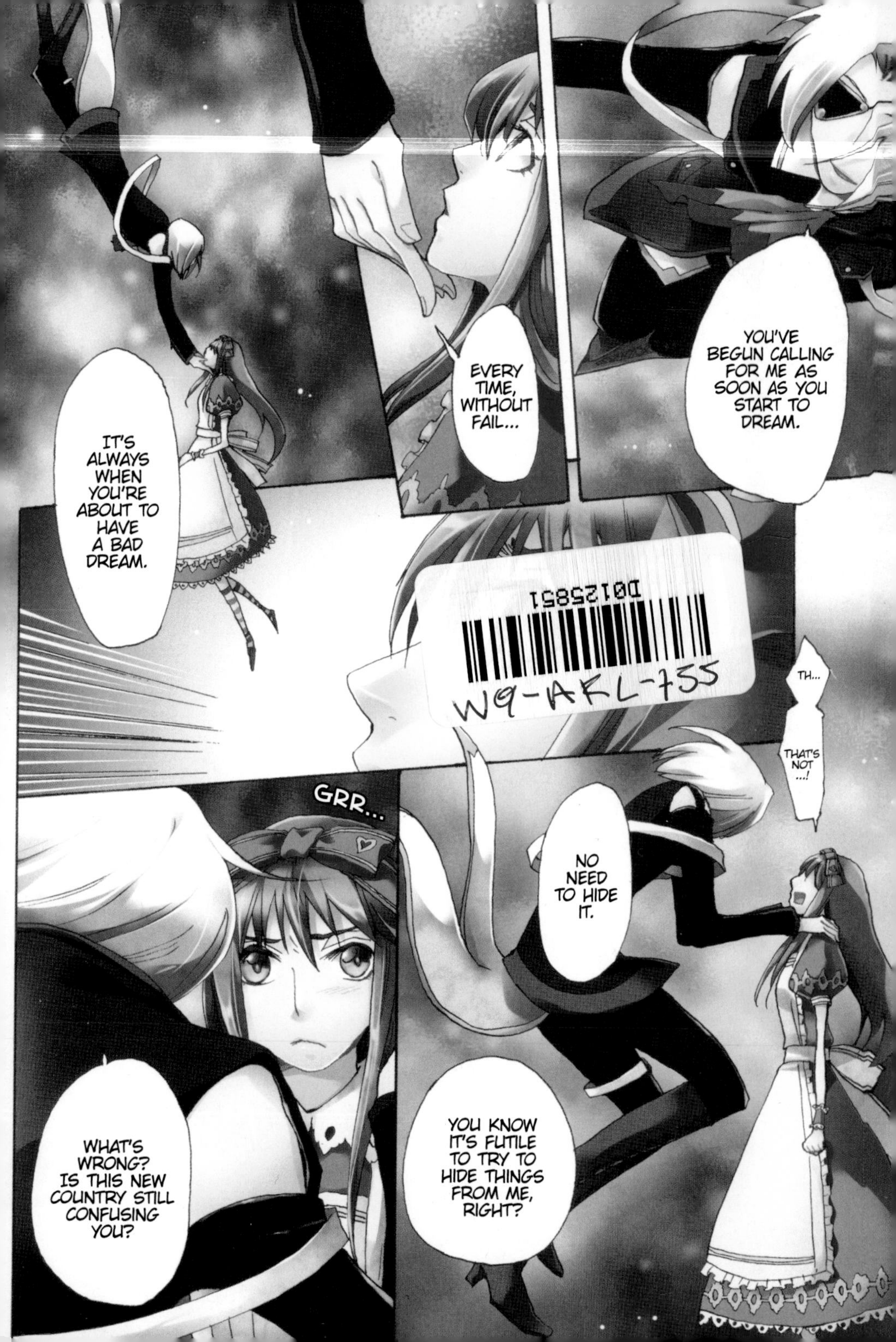
YOU'VE BEGUN CALLING FOR ME AS SOON AS YOU START TO DREAM.
EVERY TIME, WITHOUT FAIL...
IT'S ALWAYS WHEN YOU'RE ABOUT TO HAVE A BAD DREAM.
TH...
THAT'S NOT ...!
NO NEED TO HIDE IT.
YOU KNOW IT'S FUTILE TO TRY TO HIDE THINGS FROM ME, RIGHT?
GRR...
WHAT'S WRONG? IS THIS NEW COUNTRY STILL CONFUSING YOU?

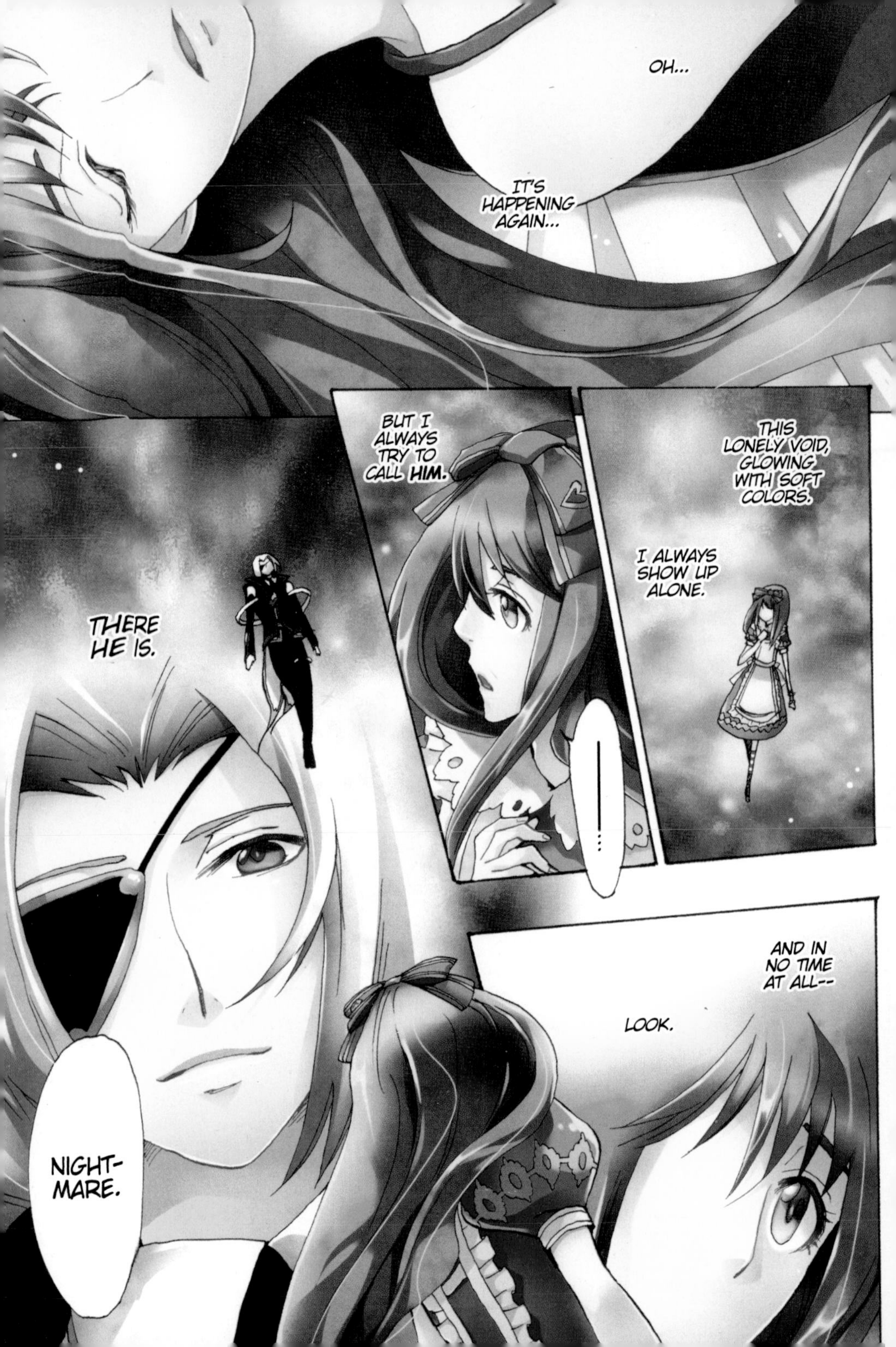
OH...
IT'S HAPPENING AGAIN...
THIS LONELY VOID, GLOWING WITH SOFT COLORS.
I ALWAYS SHOW UP ALONE.
BUT I ALWAYS TRY TO CALL **HIM**.
AND IN NO TIME AT ALL--
LOOK.
THERE HE IS.
NIGHT-MARE.

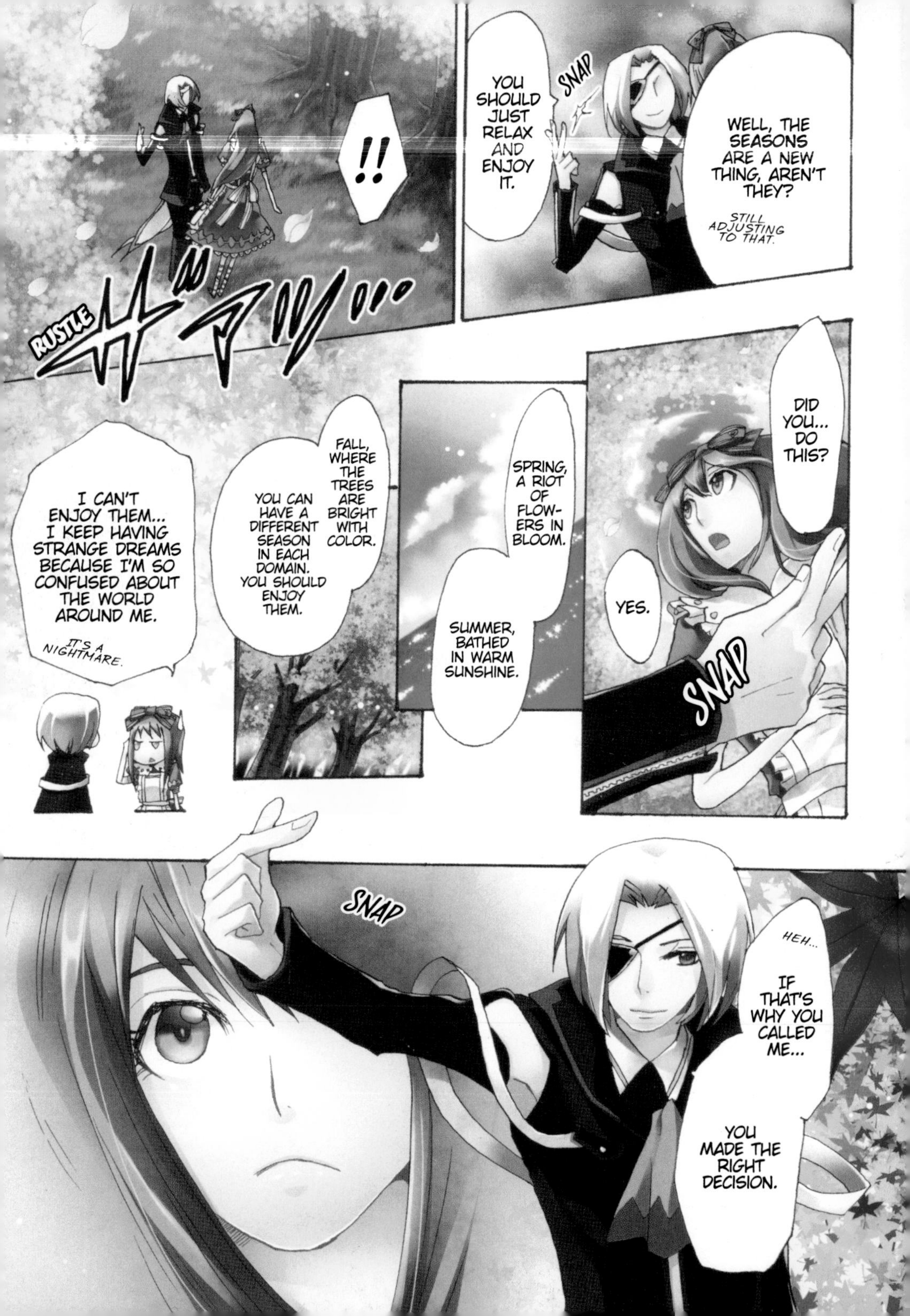
WELL, THE SEASONS ARE A NEW THING, AREN'T THEY?
STILL ADJUSTING TO THAT.
SNAP
YOU SHOULD JUST RELAX AND ENJOY IT.
!!
RUSTLE
DID YOU... DO THIS?
YES.
SNAP
SPRING, A RIOT OF FLOWERS IN BLOOM.
SUMMER, BATHED IN WARM SUNSHINE.
FALL, WHERE THE TREES ARE BRIGHT WITH COLOR.
YOU CAN HAVE A DIFFERENT SEASON IN EACH DOMAIN. YOU SHOULD ENJOY THEM.
I CAN'T ENJOY THEM... I KEEP HAVING STRANGE DREAMS BECAUSE I'M SO CONFUSED ABOUT THE WORLD AROUND ME.
IT'S A NIGHTMARE.
HEH...
IF THAT'S WHY YOU CALLED ME...
SNAP
YOU MADE THE RIGHT DECISION.

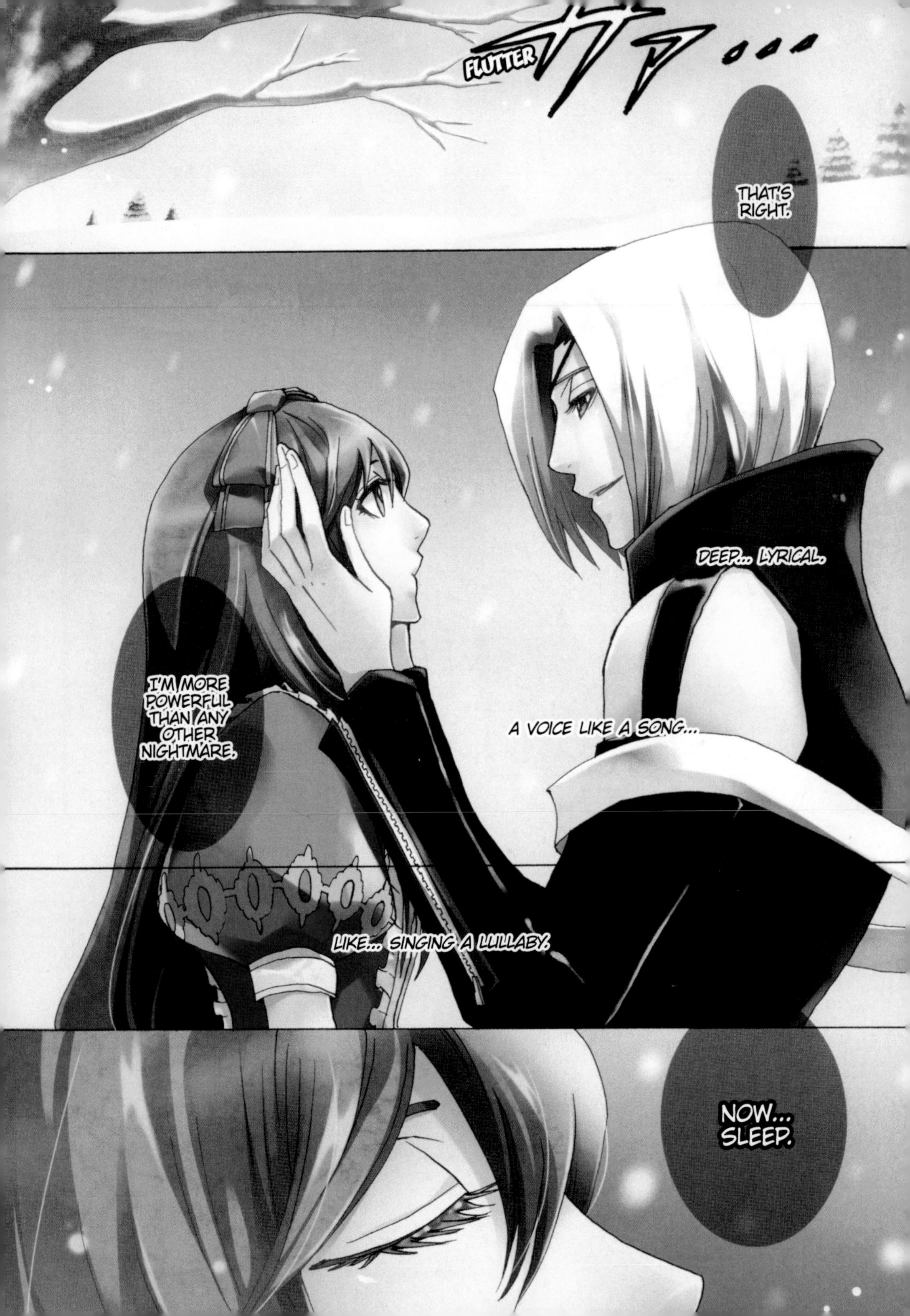
FLUTTER
THAT'S RIGHT.
DEEP... LYRICAL.
A VOICE LIKE A SONG...
I'M MORE POWERFUL THAN ANY OTHER NIGHTMARE.
LIKE... SINGING A LULLABY.
NOW... SLEEP.

ALICE IN THE COUNTRY OF JOKER
The Nightmare Trilogy Vol. 1
~Dream Before Dawn~

JOB
よぶ

SEVEN SEAS ENTERTAINMENT PRESENTS

Alice IN THE COUNTRY OF Joker

THE NIGHTMARE TRILOGY VOL. 1

art by JOB / story by QUINROSE

TRANSLATION
Angela Liu

ADAPTATION
Shanti Whitesides

LETTERING AND LAYOUT
Laura Scoville

LOGO DESIGN
Courtney Williams

COVER DESIGN
Nicky Lim

PROOFREADER
Lianne Sentar

MANAGING EDITOR
Adam Arnold

PUBLISHER
Jason DeAngelis

ALICE IN THE COUNTRY OF JOKER: DREAM BEFORE DAWN

First published in Japan in 2010 by ICHIJINSHA Inc., Tokyo.
English translation rights arranged with ICHIJINSHA Inc., Tokyo, Japan.

ISBN: 978-1-626920-60-6

Printed in Canada

First Printing: August 2014

10 9 8 7 6 5 4 3 2 1

READING DIRECTIONS

This book reads from ***right to left***, Japanese style. If this is your first time reading manga, you start reading from the top right panel on each page and take it from there. If you get lost, just follow the numbered diagram here. It may seem backwards at first, but you□ll get the hang of it! Have fun!!

3
1
2
5
4
6
8
7
9

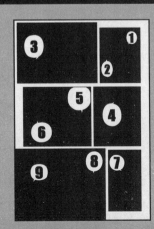

Alice in the Country of Joker

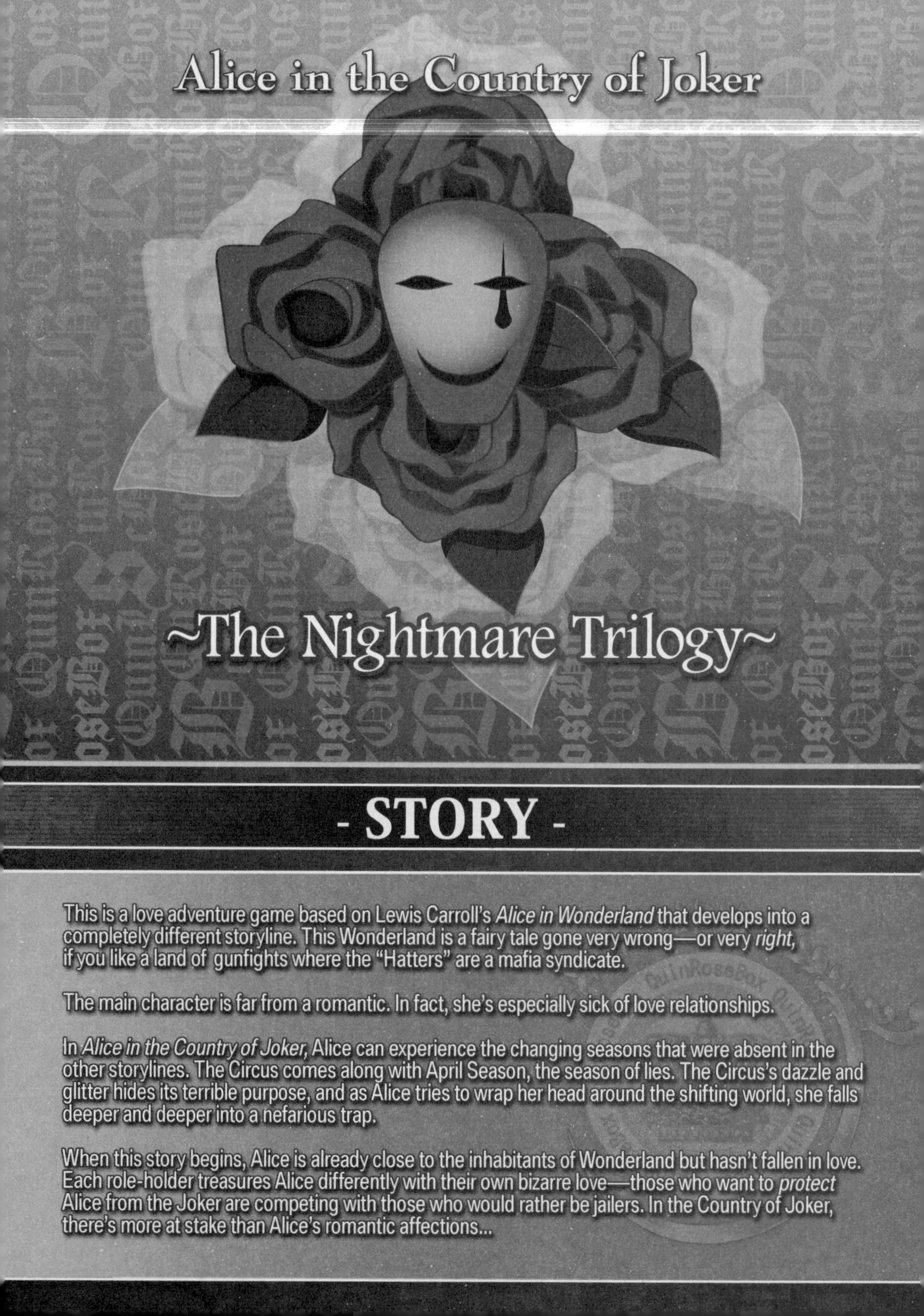

~The Nightmare Trilogy~

- STORY -

This is a love adventure game based on Lewis Carroll's *Alice in Wonderland* that develops into a completely different storyline. This Wonderland is a fairy tale gone very wrong—or very *right*, if you like a land of gunfights where the "Hatters" are a mafia syndicate.

The main character is far from a romantic. In fact, she's especially sick of love relationships.

In *Alice in the Country of Joker,* Alice can experience the changing seasons that were absent in the other storylines. The Circus comes along with April Season, the season of lies. The Circus's dazzle and glitter hides its terrible purpose, and as Alice tries to wrap her head around the shifting world, she falls deeper and deeper into a nefarious trap.

When this story begins, Alice is already close to the inhabitants of Wonderland but hasn't fallen in love. Each role-holder treasures Alice differently with their own bizarre love—those who want to *protect* Alice from the Joker are competing with those who would rather be jailers. In the Country of Joker, there's more at stake than Alice's romantic affections...

◆◆◆ Character ◆◆◆

Alice Liddell

An average teenage girl...with a heavy complex. After being dragged to Wonderland by the White Rabbit, she's managed to adapt and even enjoy her bizarre surroundings.

Blood Dupre

The dangerous, shadowy leader of the mafia group known as the Hatter Family. He's incredibly smart, but due to his temperamental moods and his desire to keep things "interesting," he often digs his own grave— and the graves of many others.

Elliot March

The No. 2 of the Hatter Family and Blood's right-hand man, Elliot is an ex-criminal and an escaped convict. After partnering with Blood, he improved his violent nature and thinks for several seconds before shooting. In his mind, this is a vast improvement.

Tweedle Dum

The other Bloody Twin, Dum loves money. He can also become an adult when he feels like it.

Vivaldi

Ruthless and cruel, Vivaldi is an arrogant beauty with a wild temper. She takes her fury out on everyone around her, including her poor subordinates. Although a picture-perfect Mad Queen, she cares for Alice as if Alice were her little sister... or a very interesting plaything.

Peter White

Prime Minister of Heart Castle who has rabbit ears growing out of his head. He loves Alice and hates everything else. His cruel, irrational actions are disturbing, but he acts like a completely different person— er, rabbit?—when in the throes of his love for Alice.

Ace

The Knight of Hearts and subordinate of Vivaldi. He's a very unlucky (yet strangely positive) man...who tends to plow forward and only worsen his situation. Ace is one of the Clockmaker's few friends and visits Julius frequently—usually getting lost on the way.

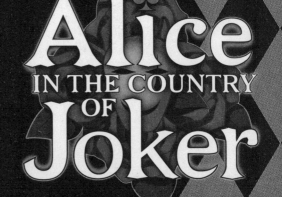

Alice
IN THE COUNTRY OF
Joker

Boris Airay

A riddle-loving cat with a signature smirk, he has a tendency to pose questions and never answer them. Since seeing the Sleepy Mouse whets his appetite, he carries a fork and knife at all times.

Pierce Villiers

An insomniac mouse who drinks too much coffee. He's terrified of Boris but loves Nightmare, who brings precious sleep. He used to be a part of the Hatter family, but after relentless bullying from the cat and twins, he's become a runaway.

Tweedle Dee

Gatekeeper of the Hatter territory, Dee loves days off. He and his brother can be innocent at times, but their (frequent) malice and unsavory activities earned them the nickname "Bloody Twins." He can shifts his body between a child and an adult version of itself.

Gray Ringmarc

Nightmare's subordinate. This sound thinker with a strong work ethic is surprisingly good with a blade. Elliot considers Gray a comrade, since they share a strong dedication to their bosses...which annoys Gray.

Julius Monrey

This gloomy Clockmaker is also known as the Undertaker. Despite being a sarcastic workaholic, he gets along with Ace. He had some part in the imprisonment of Elliot, the March Hare, and is thus the target for hatred.

Mary Gowland

The owner of the Amusement Park. He hides his hated first name, Mary, but pretty much everyone already knows it. His full name is a play on words that sounds like "Merry Go Round" when said quickly. He's a terrible, terrible musician.

Nightmare

A sickly nightmare who often coughs up blood. He has the power to read people's thoughts and enter dreams. He technically holds a high position and has many subordinates, but since he can't even take care of his own health, he leaves most things to Gray.

Joker

In the Circus, Joker is the leader... and the warden. He exists in two forms: White and Black, which take turns controlling either his body or his mask. This poor card loves to entertain his uninterested peers, but can't seem tounderstand why his friendly affections are rarely returned.

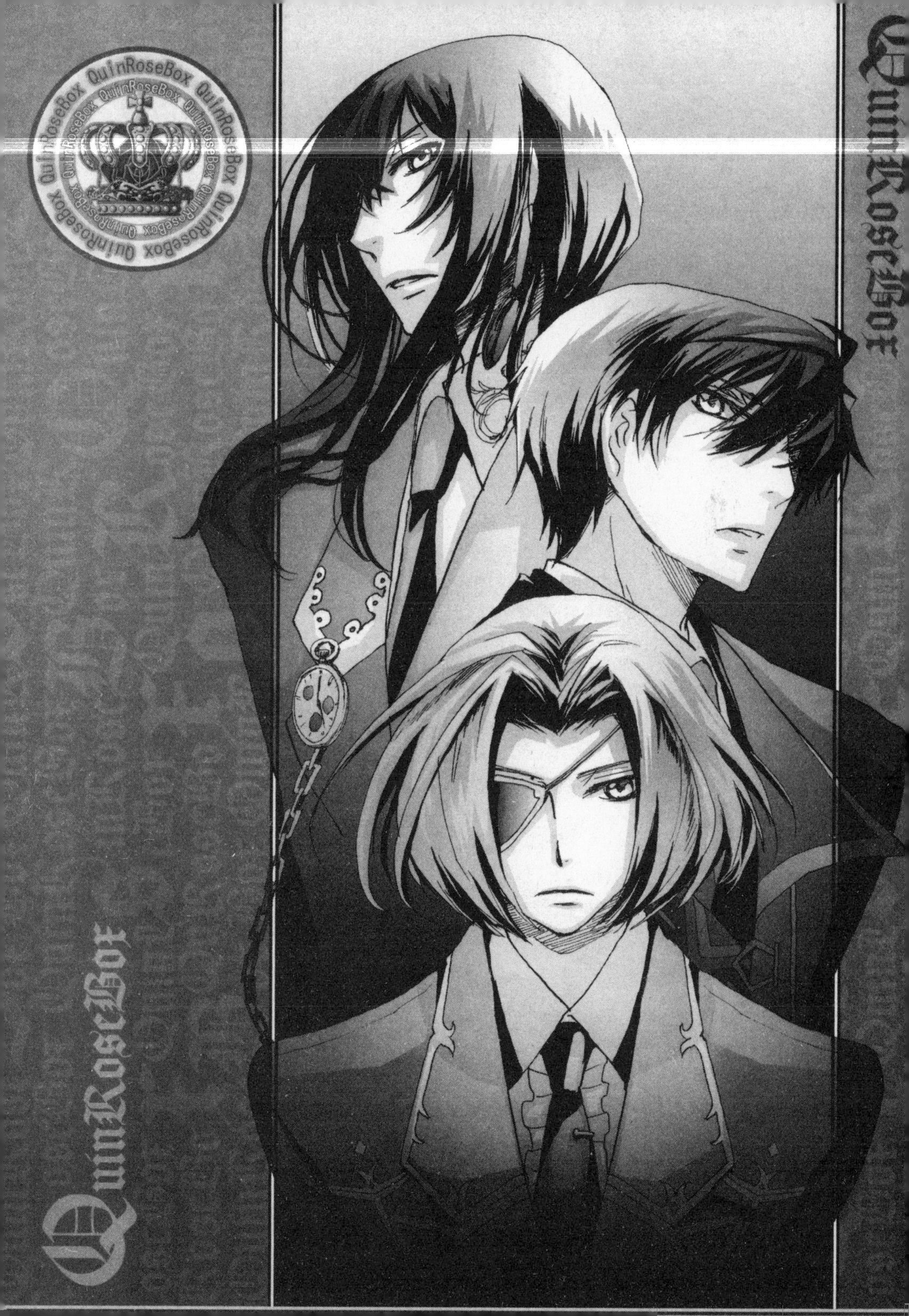
QuinRoseBox
QuinRoseBox
QuinRoseBox

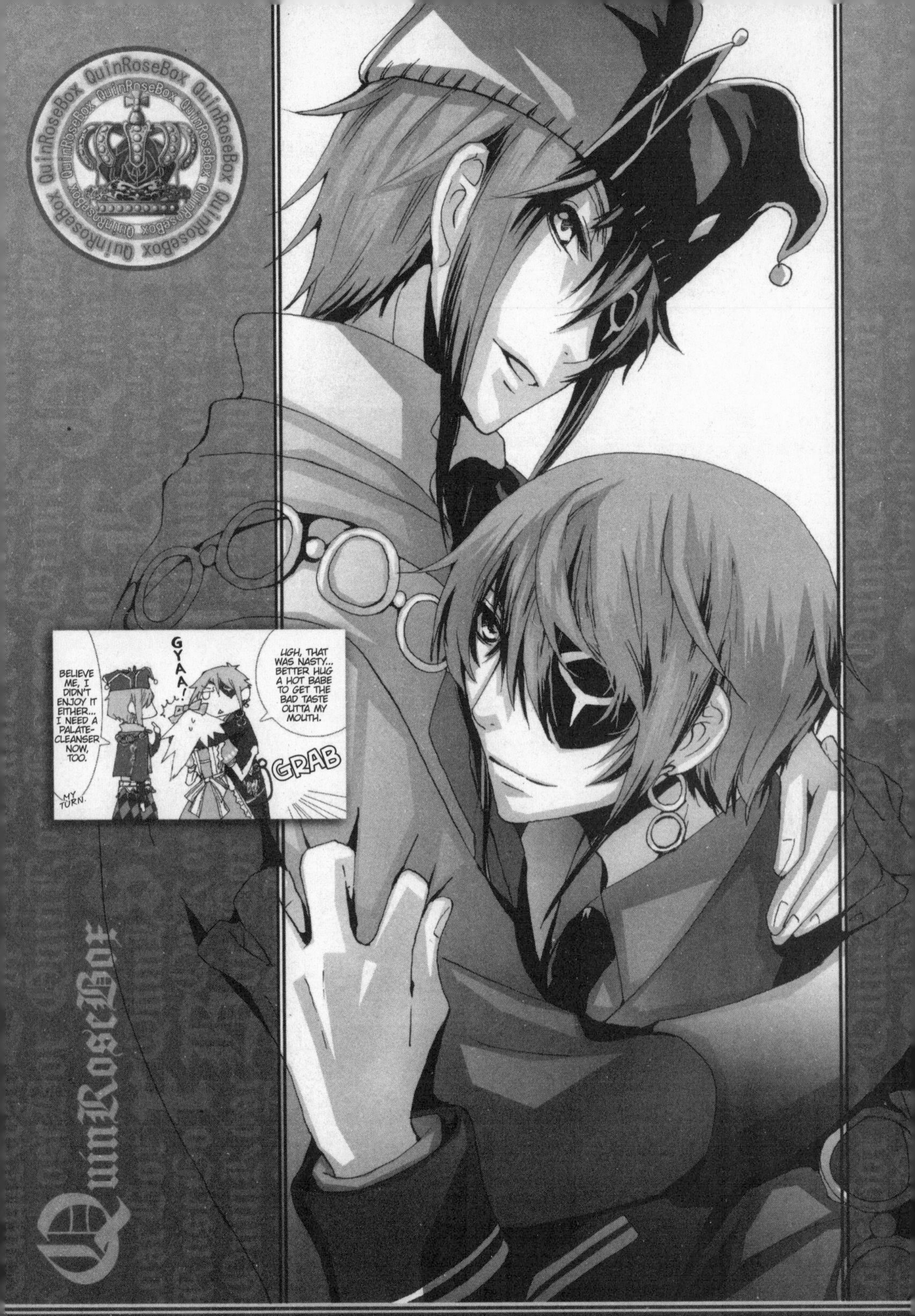
QuinRoseBox
UGH, THAT WAS NASTY... BETTER HUG A HOT BABE TO GET THE BAD TASTE OUTTA MY MOUTH.
GYAA!
GRAB
BELIEVE ME, I DIDN'T ENJOY IT EITHER... I NEED A PALATE-CLEANSER NOW, TOO.
MY TURN.
QuinRoseBox

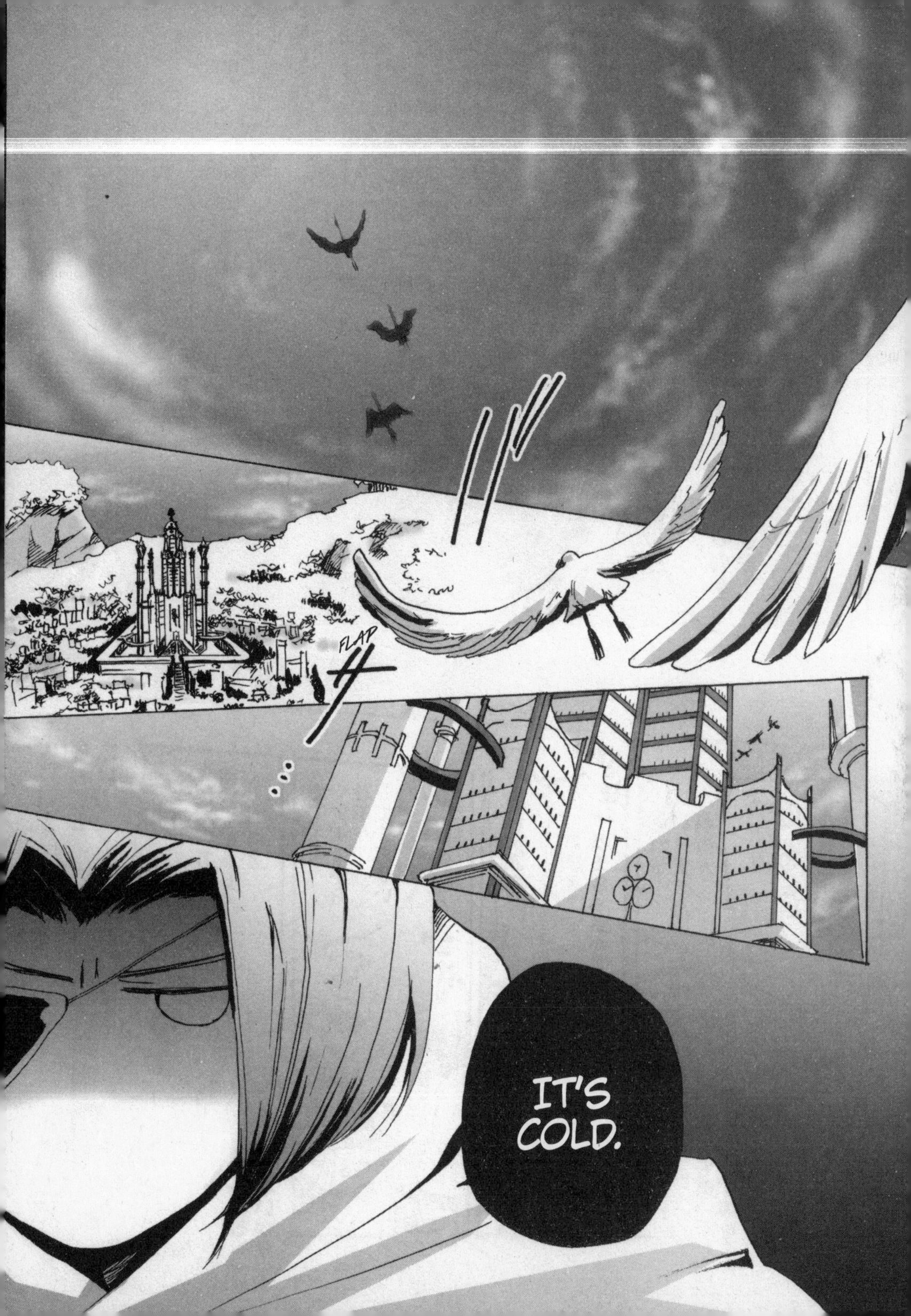
FLAP
...
IT'S COLD.

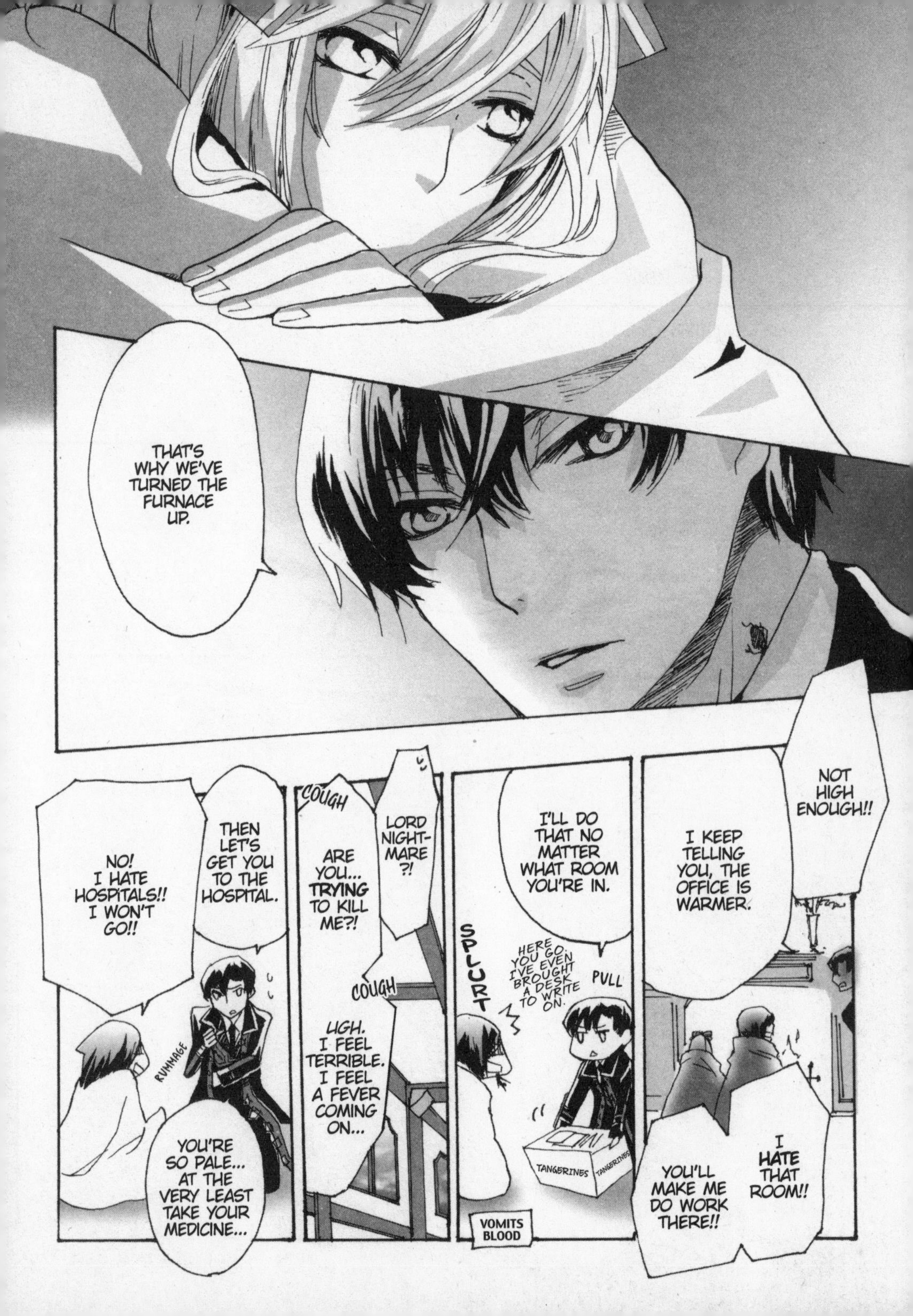
THAT'S WHY WE'VE TURNED THE FURNACE UP.
NOT HIGH ENOUGH!!
I KEEP TELLING YOU, THE OFFICE IS WARMER.
I HATE THAT ROOM!!
YOU'LL MAKE ME DO WORK THERE!!
I'LL DO THAT NO MATTER WHAT ROOM YOU'RE IN.
PULL
HERE YOU GO. I'VE EVEN BROUGHT A DESK TO WRITE ON.
SPLURT
TANGERINES
TANGERINES
VOMITS BLOOD
LORD NIGHTMARE?!
COUGH
ARE YOU... TRYING TO KILL ME?!
COUGH
UGH. I FEEL TERRIBLE. I FEEL A FEVER COMING ON...
THEN LET'S GET YOU TO THE HOSPITAL.
NO! I HATE HOSPITALS!! I WON'T GO!!
RUMMAGE
YOU'RE SO PALE... AT THE VERY LEAST TAKE YOUR MEDICINE...

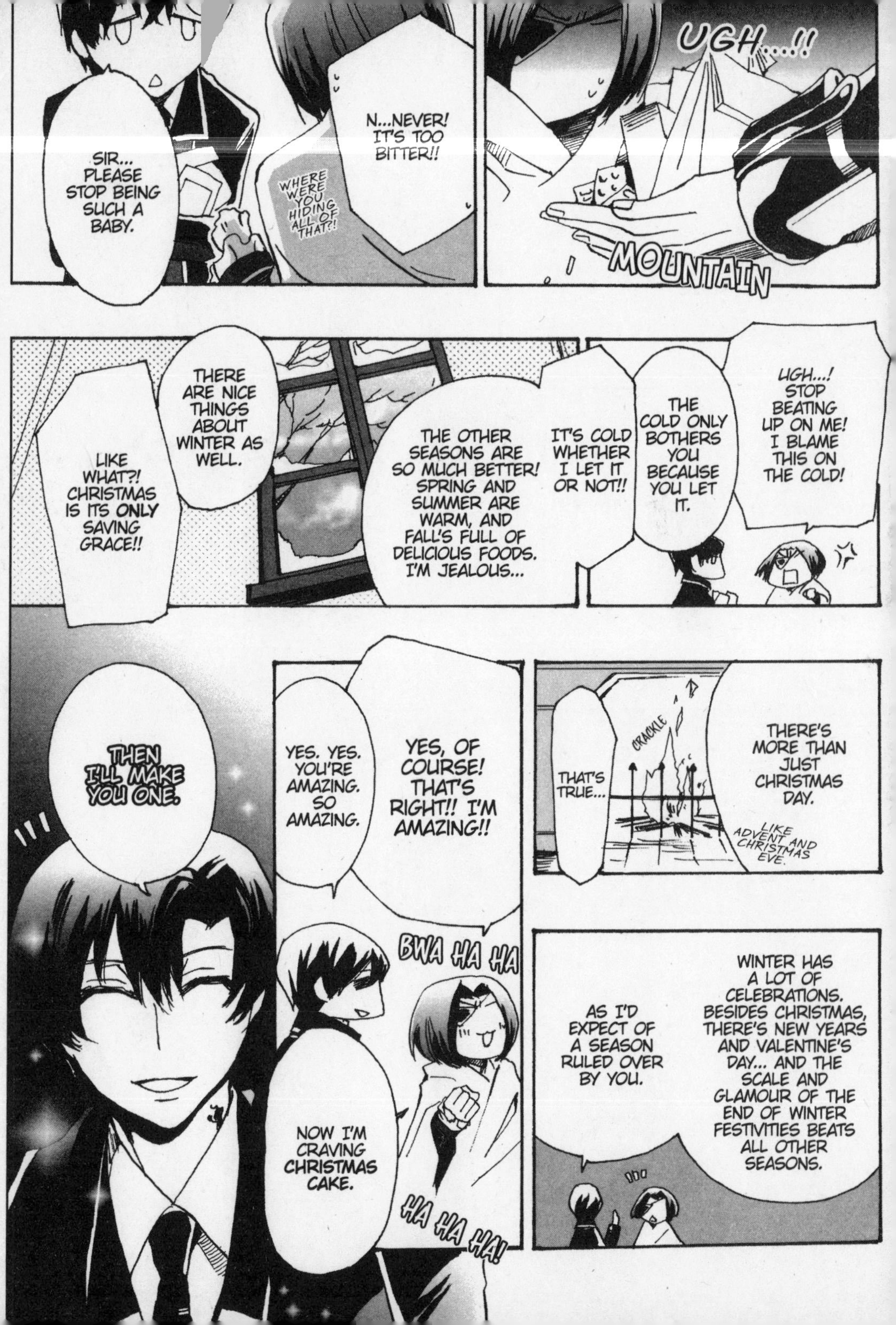
UGH...!!
MOUNTAIN
N...NEVER! IT'S TOO BITTER!!
WHERE WERE YOU HIDING ALL OF THAT?!
SIR... PLEASE STOP BEING SUCH A BABY.
UGH...! STOP BEATING UP ON ME! I BLAME THIS ON THE COLD!
THE COLD ONLY BOTHERS YOU BECAUSE YOU LET IT.
IT'S COLD WHETHER I LET IT OR NOT!!
THE OTHER SEASONS ARE SO MUCH BETTER! SPRING AND SUMMER ARE WARM, AND FALL'S FULL OF DELICIOUS FOODS. I'M JEALOUS...
THERE ARE NICE THINGS ABOUT WINTER AS WELL.
LIKE WHAT?! CHRISTMAS IS ITS ONLY SAVING GRACE!!
THERE'S MORE THAN JUST CHRISTMAS DAY.
LIKE ADVENT AND CHRISTMAS EVE.
CRACKLE
THAT'S TRUE...
WINTER HAS A LOT OF CELEBRATIONS. BESIDES CHRISTMAS, THERE'S NEW YEARS AND VALENTINE'S DAY... AND THE SCALE AND GLAMOUR OF THE END OF WINTER FESTIVITIES BEATS ALL OTHER SEASONS.
AS I'D EXPECT OF A SEASON RULED OVER BY YOU.
YES, OF COURSE! THAT'S RIGHT!! I'M AMAZING!!
YES. YES. YOU'RE AMAZING. SO AMAZING.
BWA HA HA
HA HA HA!
NOW I'M CRAVING CHRISTMAS CAKE.
THEN I'LL MAKE YOU ONE.

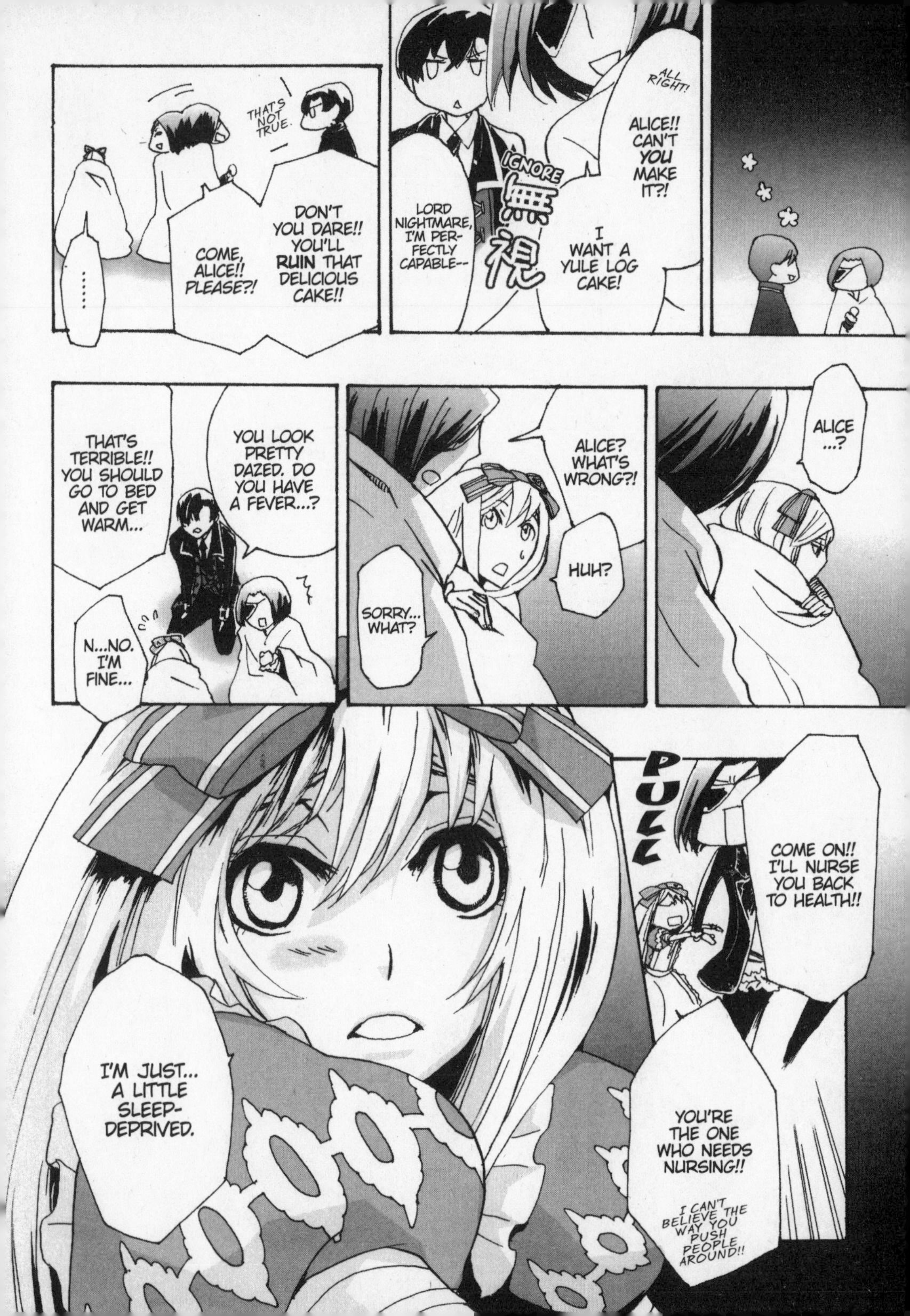
ALL RIGHT!
ALICE!! CAN'T YOU MAKE IT?!
I WANT A YULE LOG CAKE!
IGNORE 無視
LORD NIGHTMARE, I'M PERFECTLY CAPABLE--
THAT'S NOT TRUE.
DON'T YOU DARE!! YOU'LL RUIN THAT DELICIOUS CAKE!!
COME, ALICE!! PLEASE?!
......
ALICE ...?
ALICE? WHAT'S WRONG?!
HUH?
SORRY... WHAT?
YOU LOOK PRETTY DAZED. DO YOU HAVE A FEVER...?
THAT'S TERRIBLE!! YOU SHOULD GO TO BED AND GET WARM...
N...NO. I'M FINE...
PULL
COME ON!! I'LL NURSE YOU BACK TO HEALTH!!
YOU'RE THE ONE WHO NEEDS NURSING!!
I CAN'T BELIEVE THE WAY YOU PUSH PEOPLE AROUND!!
I'M JUST... A LITTLE SLEEP-DEPRIVED.

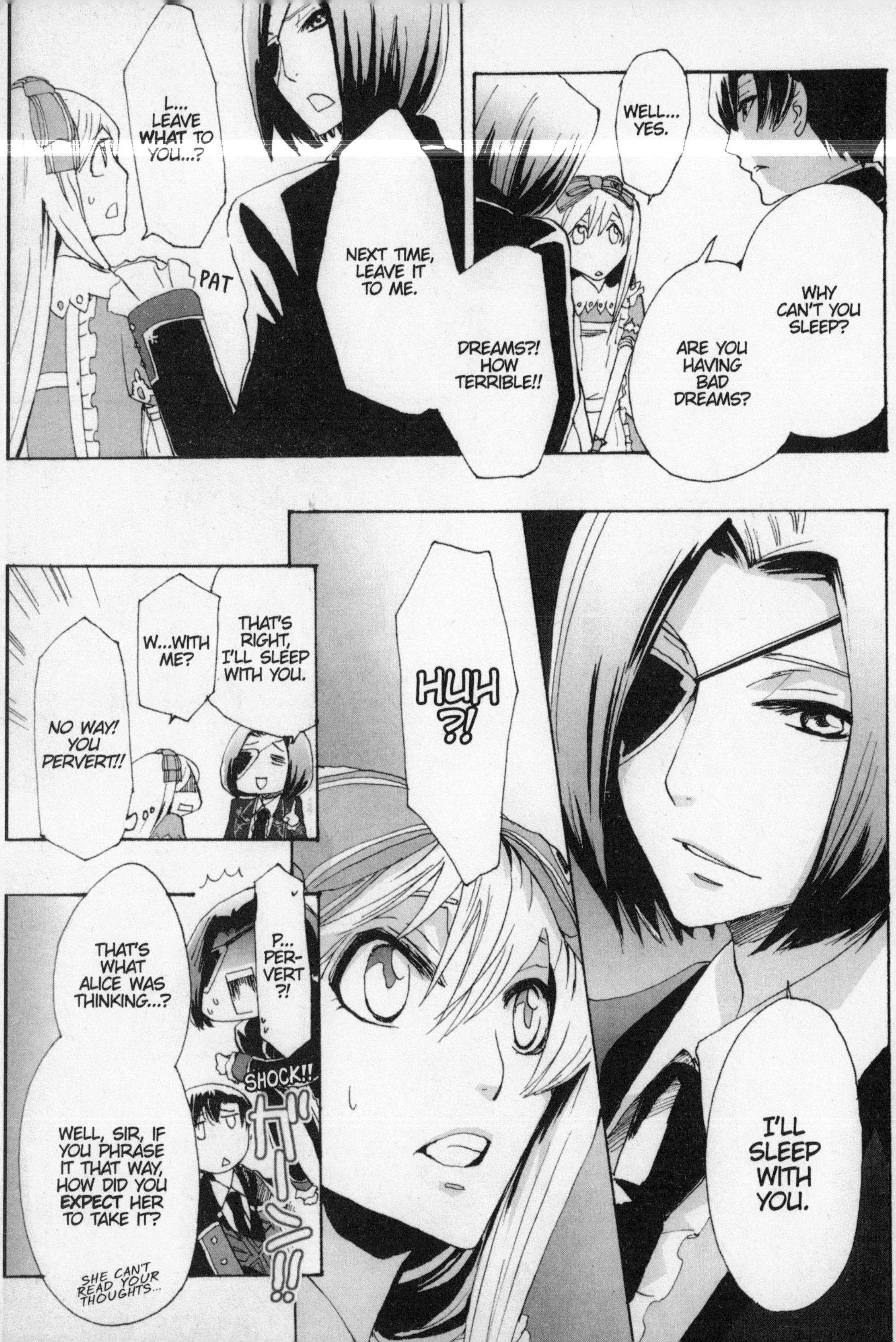
WHY CAN'T YOU SLEEP?
ARE YOU HAVING BAD DREAMS?
WELL... YES.
DREAMS?! HOW TERRIBLE!!
NEXT TIME, LEAVE IT TO ME.
PAT
L... LEAVE WHAT TO YOU...?
I'LL SLEEP WITH YOU.
HUH ?!
THAT'S RIGHT, I'LL SLEEP WITH YOU.
W...WITH ME?
NO WAY! YOU PERVERT!!
P... PER-VERT ?!
THAT'S WHAT ALICE WAS THINKING...?
SHOCK!!
WELL, SIR, IF YOU PHRASE IT THAT WAY, HOW DID YOU EXPECT HER TO TAKE IT?
SHE CAN'T READ YOUR THOUGHTS...

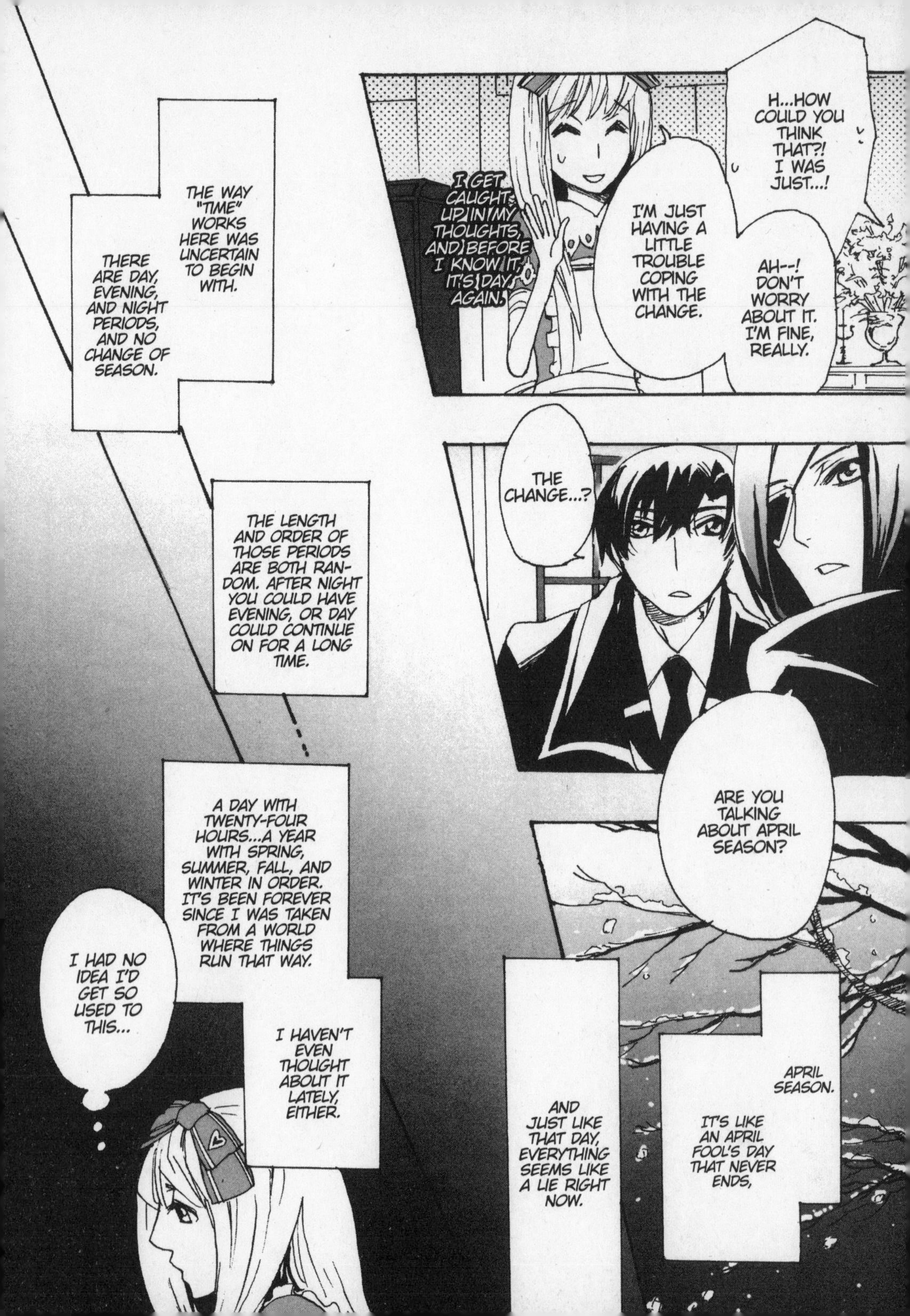
H...HOW COULD YOU THINK THAT?! I WAS JUST...!
AH--! DON'T WORRY ABOUT IT. I'M FINE, REALLY.
I'M JUST HAVING A LITTLE TROUBLE COPING WITH THE CHANGE.
I GET CAUGHT UP IN MY THOUGHTS, AND BEFORE I KNOW IT, IT'S DAY AGAIN.
THE WAY "TIME" WORKS HERE WAS UNCERTAIN TO BEGIN WITH.
THERE ARE DAY, EVENING, AND NIGHT PERIODS, AND NO CHANGE OF SEASON.
THE CHANGE...?
ARE YOU TALKING ABOUT APRIL SEASON?
THE LENGTH AND ORDER OF THOSE PERIODS ARE BOTH RAN-DOM. AFTER NIGHT YOU COULD HAVE EVENING, OR DAY COULD CONTINUE ON FOR A LONG TIME.
APRIL SEASON.
IT'S LIKE AN APRIL FOOL'S DAY THAT NEVER ENDS,
AND JUST LIKE THAT DAY, EVERYTHING SEEMS LIKE A LIE RIGHT NOW.
A DAY WITH TWENTY-FOUR HOURS...A YEAR WITH SPRING, SUMMER, FALL, AND WINTER IN ORDER. IT'S BEEN FOREVER SINCE I WAS TAKEN FROM A WORLD WHERE THINGS RUN THAT WAY.
I HAVEN'T EVEN THOUGHT ABOUT IT LATELY, EITHER.
I HAD NO IDEA I'D GET SO USED TO THIS...

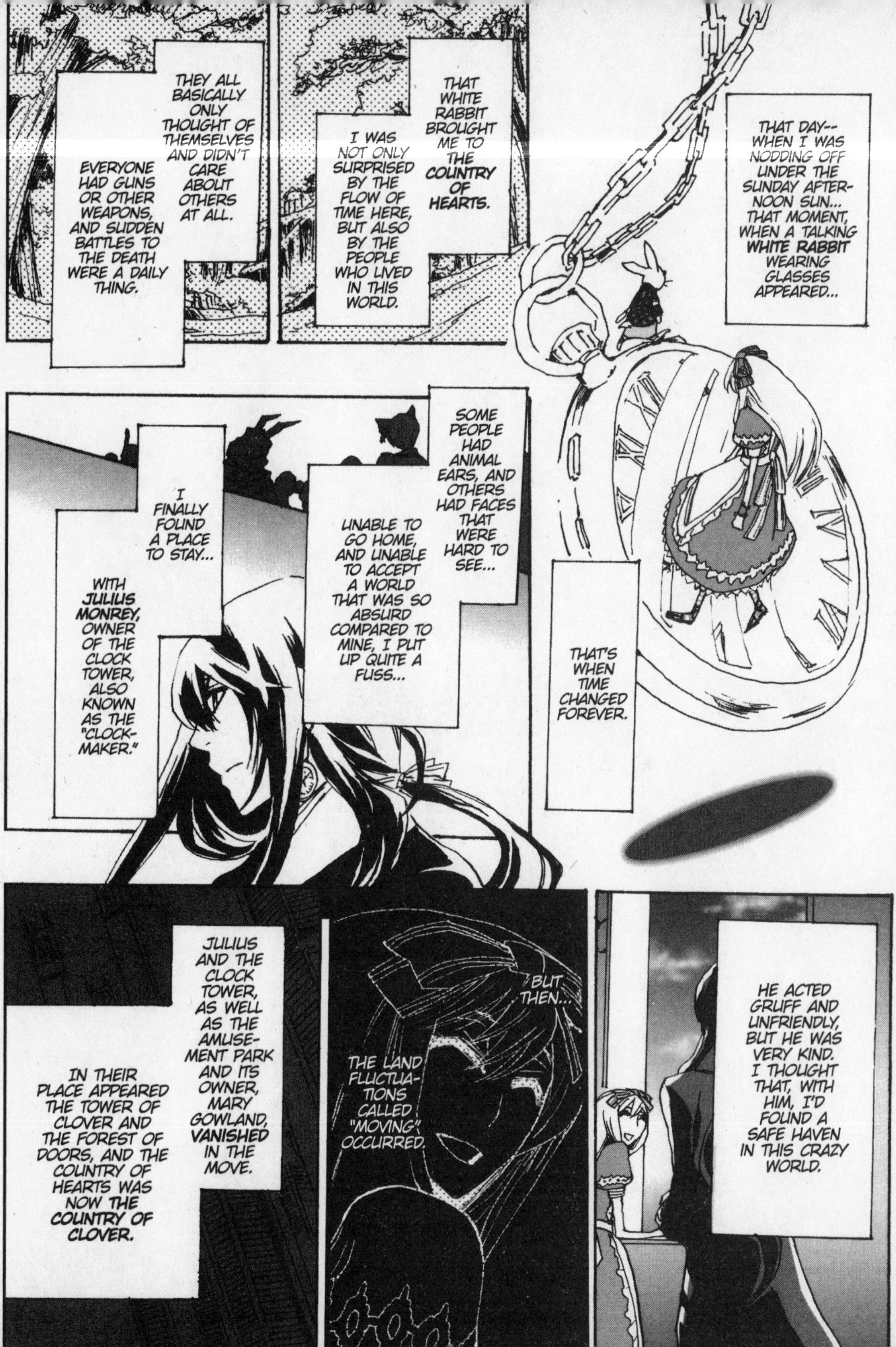

THAT DAY-- WHEN I WAS NODDING OFF UNDER THE SUNDAY AFTER-NOON SUN... THAT MOMENT, WHEN A TALKING **WHITE RABBIT** WEARING GLASSES APPEARED...
THAT'S WHEN TIME CHANGED FOREVER.
THAT WHITE RABBIT BROUGHT ME TO **THE COUNTRY OF HEARTS.**
I WAS NOT ONLY SURPRISED BY THE FLOW OF TIME HERE, BUT ALSO BY THE PEOPLE WHO LIVED IN THIS WORLD.
THEY ALL BASICALLY ONLY THOUGHT OF THEMSELVES AND DIDN'T CARE ABOUT OTHERS AT ALL.
EVERYONE HAD GUNS OR OTHER WEAPONS, AND SUDDEN BATTLES TO THE DEATH WERE A DAILY THING.
SOME PEOPLE HAD ANIMAL EARS, AND OTHERS HAD FACES THAT WERE HARD TO SEE...
UNABLE TO GO HOME, AND UNABLE TO ACCEPT A WORLD THAT WAS SO ABSURD COMPARED TO MINE, I PUT UP QUITE A FUSS...
I FINALLY FOUND A PLACE TO STAY...
WITH **JULIUS MONREY,** OWNER OF THE CLOCK TOWER, ALSO KNOWN AS THE "CLOCK-MAKER."
HE ACTED GRUFF AND UNFRIENDLY, BUT HE WAS VERY KIND. I THOUGHT THAT, WITH HIM, I'D FOUND A SAFE HAVEN IN THIS CRAZY WORLD.
BUT THEN...
THE LAND FLUCTUA-TIONS CALLED "MOVING" OCCURRED.
JULIUS AND THE CLOCK TOWER, AS WELL AS THE AMUSE-MENT PARK AND ITS OWNER, MARY GOWLAND, **VANISHED** IN THE MOVE.
IN THEIR PLACE APPEARED THE TOWER OF CLOVER AND THE FOREST OF DOORS, AND THE COUNTRY OF HEARTS WAS NOW **THE COUNTRY OF CLOVER.**

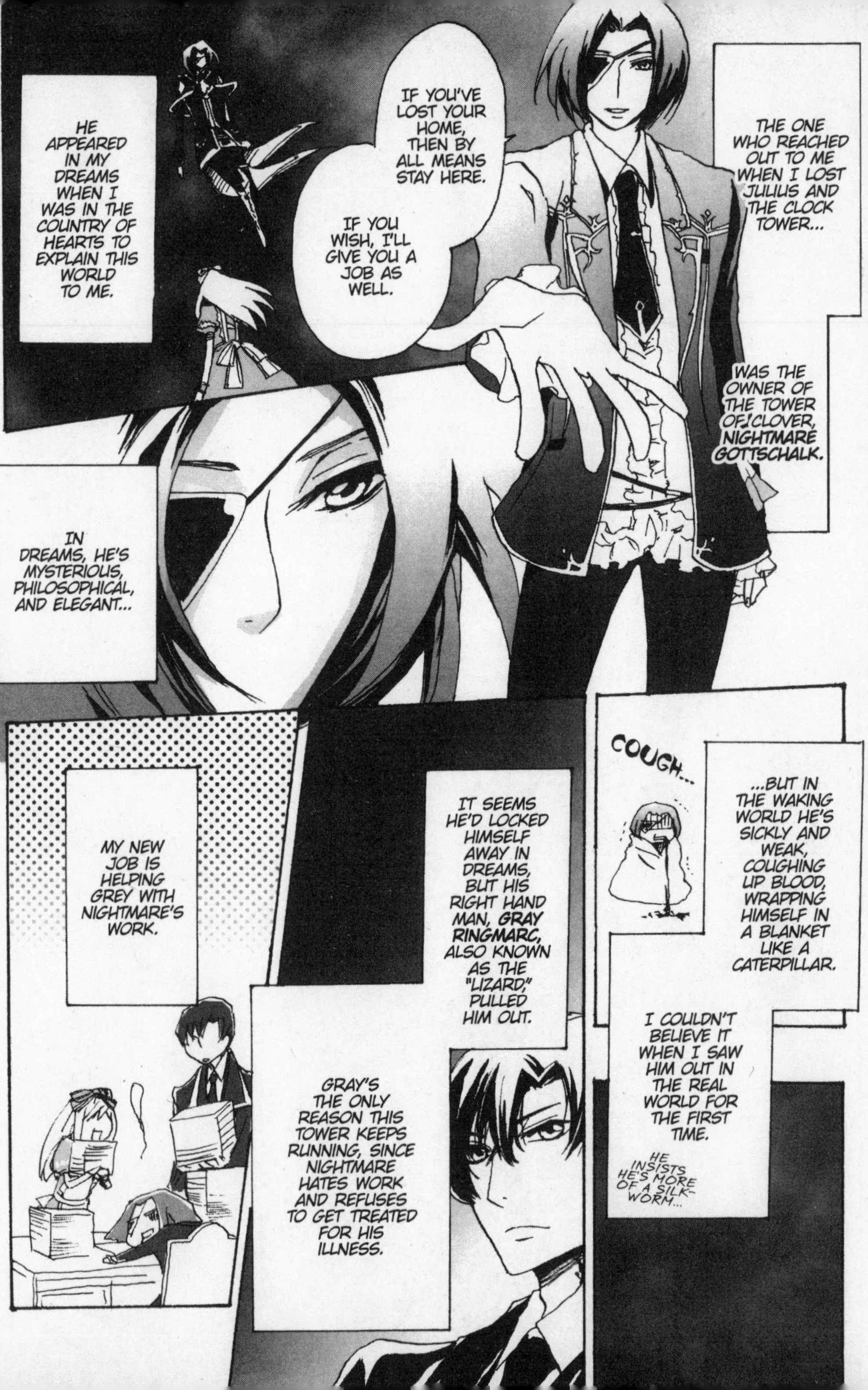
THE ONE WHO REACHED OUT TO ME WHEN I LOST JULIUS AND THE CLOCK TOWER...
IF YOU'VE LOST YOUR HOME, THEN BY ALL MEANS STAY HERE.
IF YOU WISH, I'LL GIVE YOU A JOB AS WELL.
HE APPEARED IN MY DREAMS WHEN I WAS IN THE COUNTRY OF HEARTS TO EXPLAIN THIS WORLD TO ME.
WAS THE OWNER OF THE TOWER OF CLOVER, NIGHTMARE GOTTSCHALK.
IN DREAMS, HE'S MYSTERIOUS, PHILOSOPHICAL, AND ELEGANT...
COUGH...
...BUT IN THE WAKING WORLD HE'S SICKLY AND WEAK, COUGHING UP BLOOD, WRAPPING HIMSELF IN A BLANKET LIKE A CATERPILLAR.
I COULDN'T BELIEVE IT WHEN I SAW HIM OUT IN THE REAL WORLD FOR THE FIRST TIME.
HE INSISTS HE'S MORE OF A SILKWORM...
IT SEEMS HE'D LOCKED HIMSELF AWAY IN DREAMS, BUT HIS RIGHT HAND MAN, GRAY RINGMARC, ALSO KNOWN AS THE "LIZARD," PULLED HIM OUT.
GRAY'S THE ONLY REASON THIS TOWER KEEPS RUNNING, SINCE NIGHTMARE HATES WORK AND REFUSES TO GET TREATED FOR HIS ILLNESS.
MY NEW JOB IS HELPING GREY WITH NIGHTMARE'S WORK.

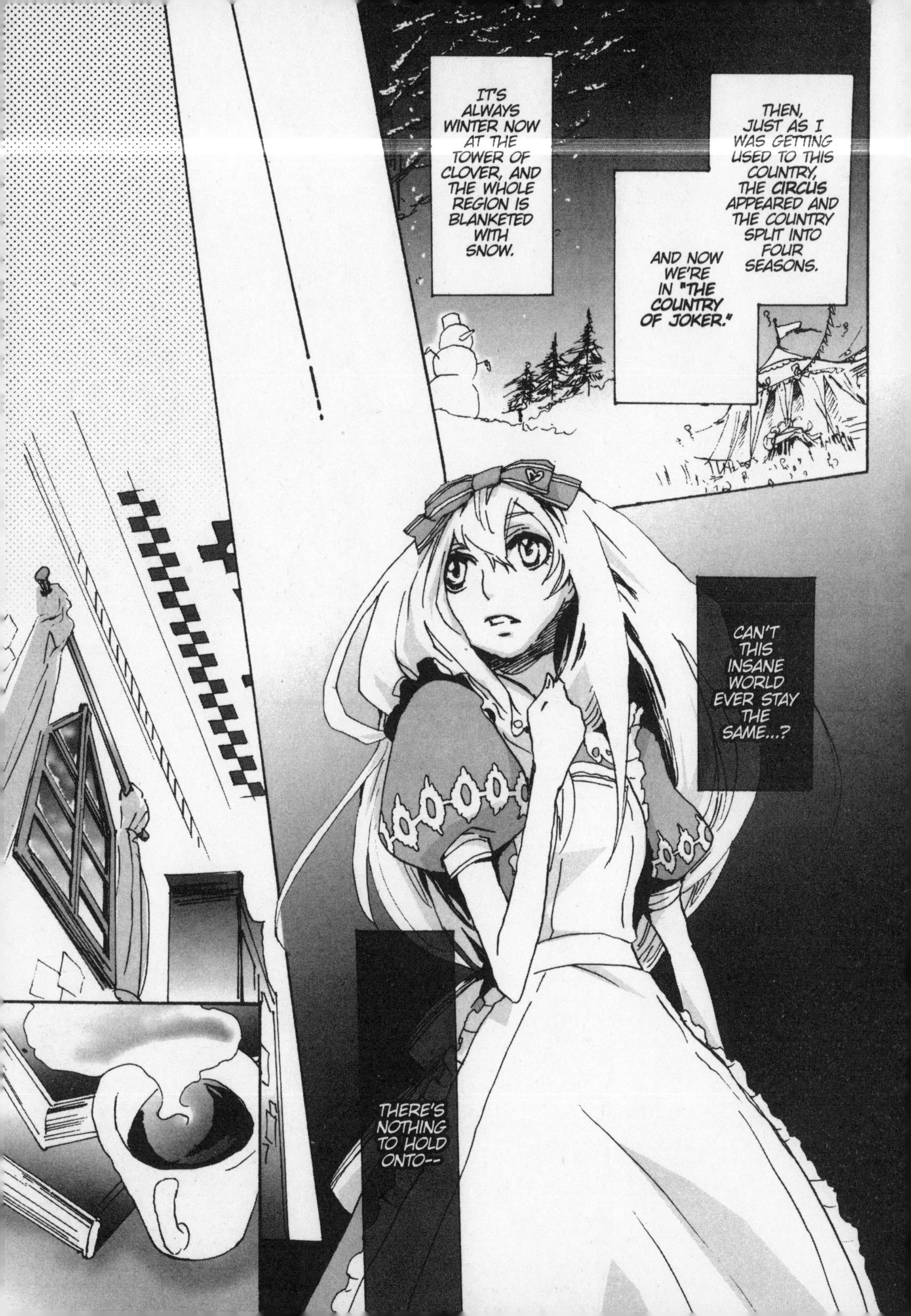
IT'S ALWAYS WINTER NOW AT THE TOWER OF CLOVER, AND THE WHOLE REGION IS BLANKETED WITH SNOW.
THEN, JUST AS I WAS GETTING USED TO THIS COUNTRY, THE CIRCUS APPEARED AND THE COUNTRY SPLIT INTO FOUR SEASONS.
AND NOW WE'RE IN "THE COUNTRY OF JOKER."
CAN'T THIS INSANE WORLD EVER STAY THE SAME...?
THERE'S NOTHING TO HOLD ONTO--

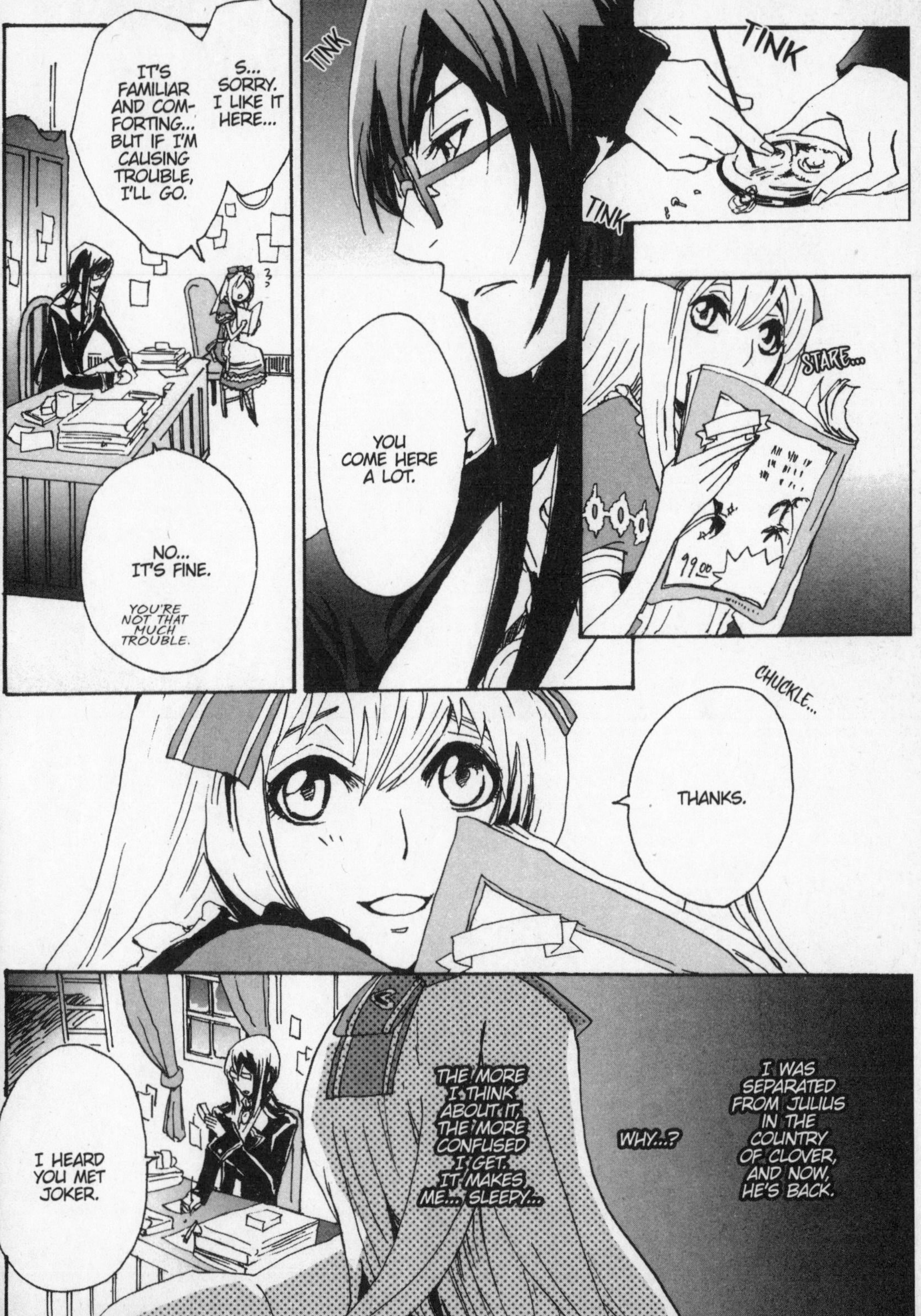
TINK
TINK
TINK
STARE...
TINK
YOU COME HERE A LOT.
S... SORRY. I LIKE IT HERE...
IT'S FAMILIAR AND COMFORTING... BUT IF I'M CAUSING TROUBLE, I'LL GO.
NO... IT'S FINE.
YOU'RE NOT THAT MUCH TROUBLE.
CHUCKLE...
THANKS.
I WAS SEPARATED FROM JULIUS IN THE COUNTRY OF CLOVER, AND NOW, HE'S BACK.
WHY...?
THE MORE I THINK ABOUT IT, THE MORE CONFUSED I GET. IT MAKES ME... SLEEPY...
I HEARD YOU MET JOKER.

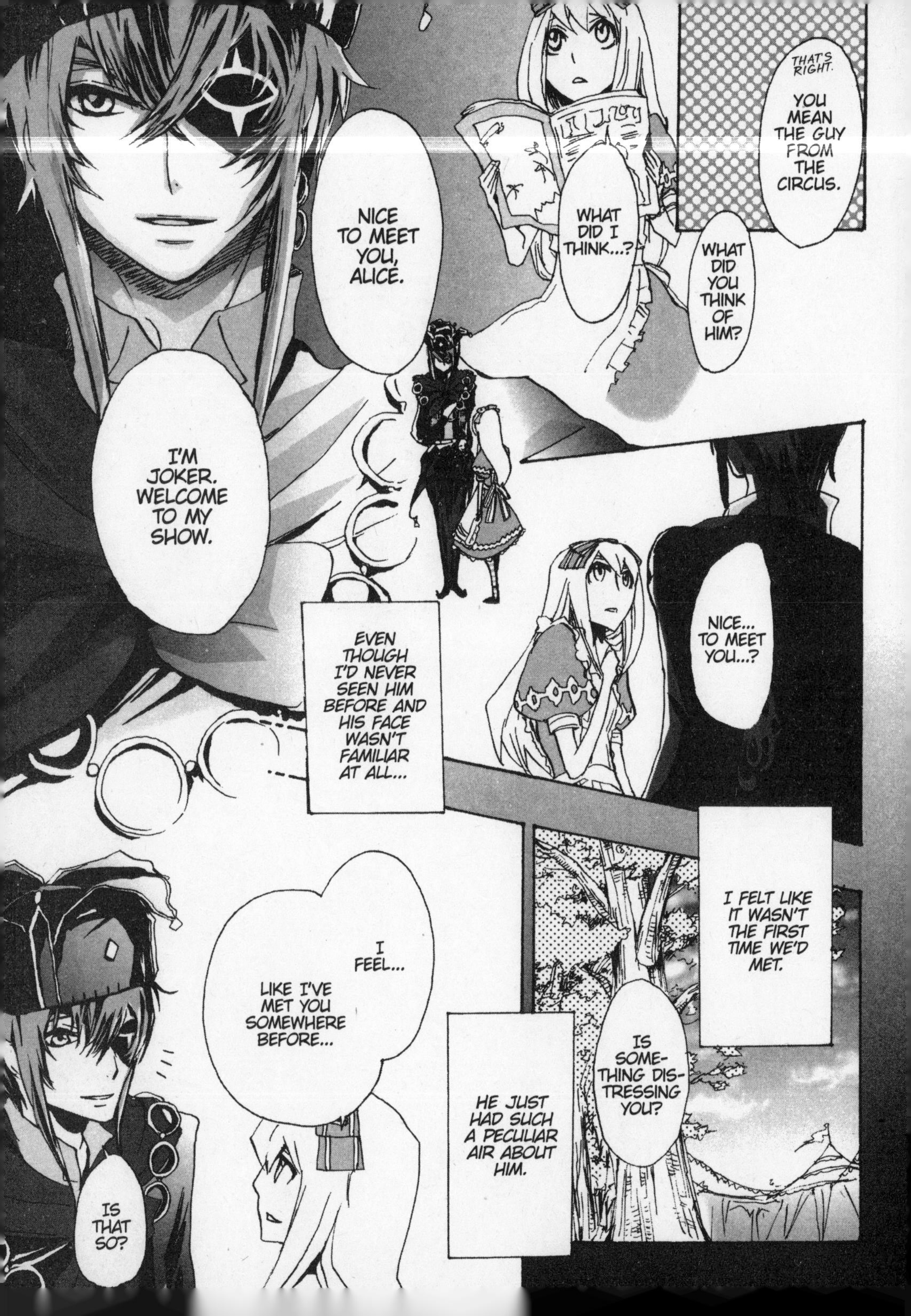
THAT'S RIGHT.
YOU MEAN THE GUY FROM THE CIRCUS.
WHAT DID YOU THINK OF HIM?
WHAT DID I THINK...?
NICE... TO MEET YOU...?
EVEN THOUGH I'D NEVER SEEN HIM BEFORE AND HIS FACE WASN'T FAMILIAR AT ALL...
NICE TO MEET YOU, ALICE.
I'M JOKER. WELCOME TO MY SHOW.
I FELT LIKE IT WASN'T THE FIRST TIME WE'D MET.
IS SOMETHING DISTRESSING YOU?
HE JUST HAD SUCH A PECULIAR AIR ABOUT HIM.
I FEEL...
LIKE I'VE MET YOU SOMEWHERE BEFORE...
IS THAT SO?

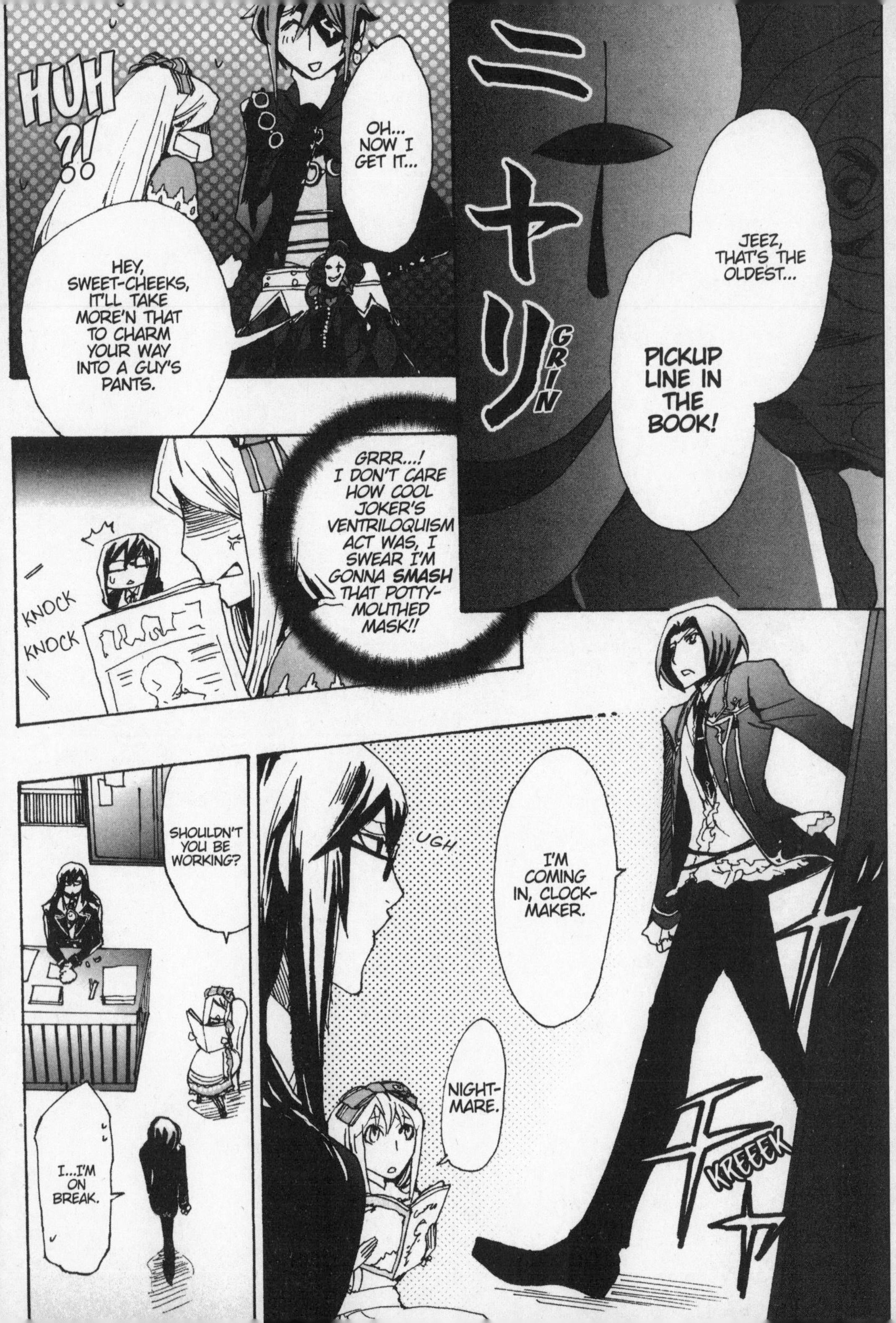
ニヤリ
GRIN
JEEZ, THAT'S THE OLDEST...
PICKUP LINE IN THE BOOK!
HUH ?!
OH... NOW I GET IT...
HEY, SWEET-CHEEKS, IT'LL TAKE MORE'N THAT TO CHARM YOUR WAY INTO A GUY'S PANTS.
GRRR...! I DON'T CARE HOW COOL JOKER'S VENTRILOQUISM ACT WAS, I SWEAR I'M GONNA SMASH THAT POTTY-MOUTHED MASK!!
KNOCK
KNOCK
KREEEK
I'M COMING IN, CLOCK-MAKER.
UGH
NIGHT-MARE.
SHOULDN'T YOU BE WORKING?
I...I'M ON BREAK.

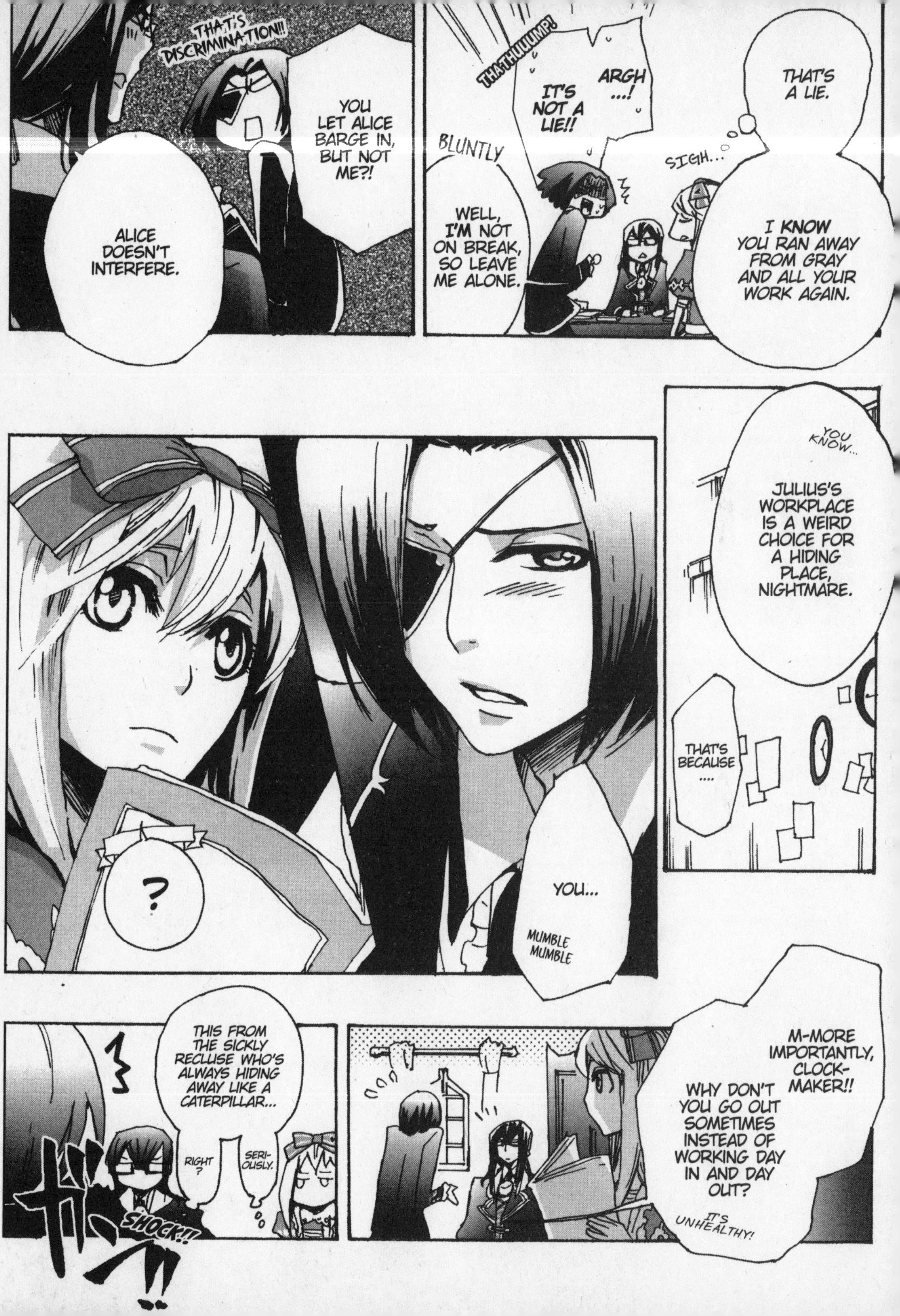
THAT'S A LIE.
I KNOW YOU RAN AWAY FROM GRAY AND ALL YOUR WORK AGAIN.
SIGH...
THATHUUUMP!
ARGH ...!
IT'S NOT A LIE!!
BLUNTLY
WELL, I'M NOT ON BREAK, SO LEAVE ME ALONE.
THAT'S DISCRIMINATION!!
YOU LET ALICE BARGE IN, BUT NOT ME?!
ALICE DOESN'T INTERFERE.
YOU KNOW...
JULIUS'S WORKPLACE IS A WEIRD CHOICE FOR A HIDING PLACE, NIGHTMARE.
THAT'S BECAUSE ....
YOU...
MUMBLE MUMBLE
?
M-MORE IMPORTANTLY, CLOCK-MAKER!!
WHY DON'T YOU GO OUT SOMETIMES INSTEAD OF WORKING DAY IN AND DAY OUT?
IT'S UNHEALTHY!
THIS FROM THE SICKLY RECLUSE WHO'S ALWAYS HIDING AWAY LIKE A CATERPILLAR...
SERI-OUSLY.
RIGHT?
SHOCK!!

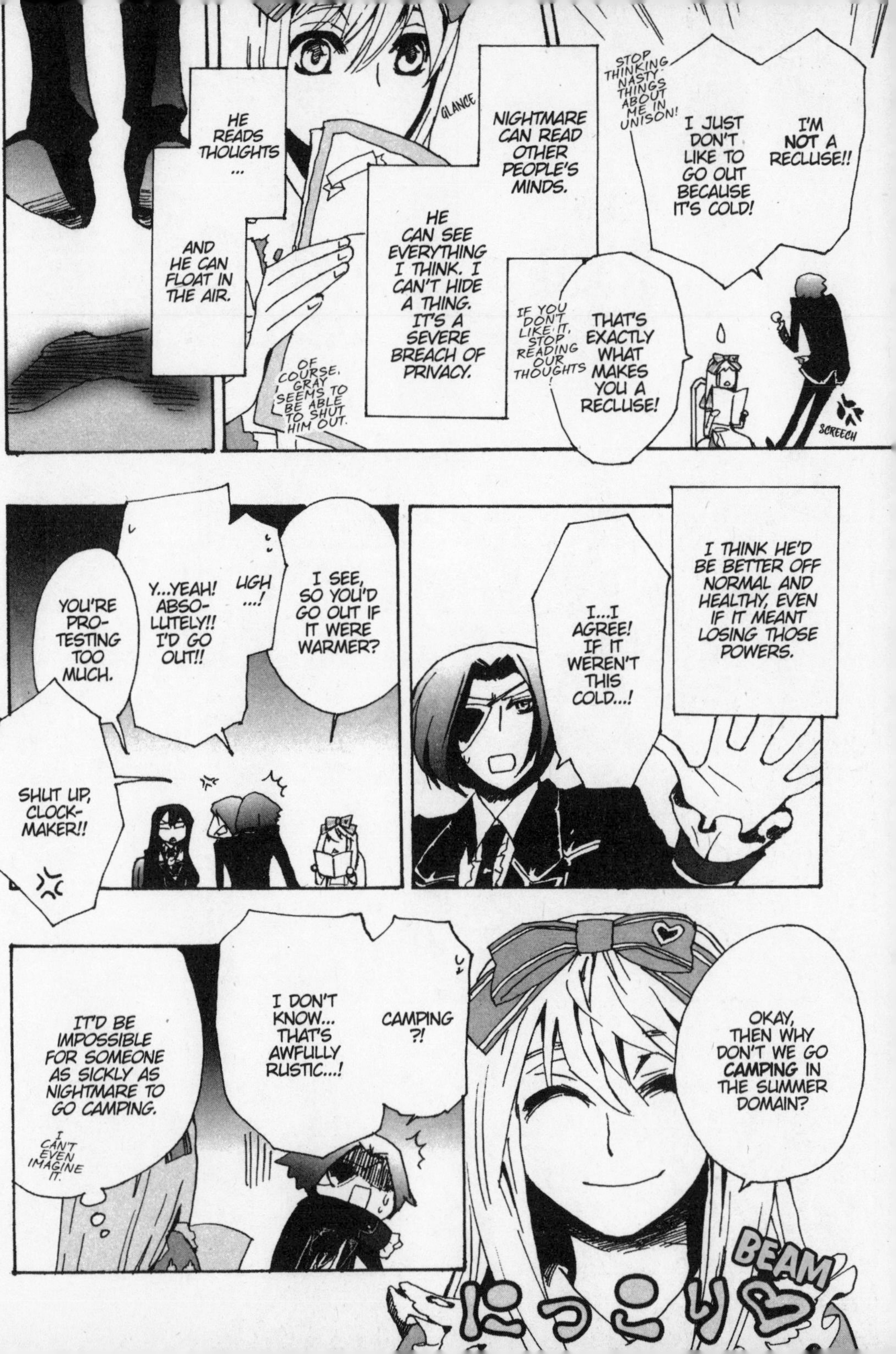
I'M NOT A RECLUSE!!
I JUST DON'T LIKE TO GO OUT BECAUSE IT'S COLD!
STOP THINKING NASTY THINGS ABOUT ME IN UNISON!
THAT'S EXACTLY WHAT MAKES YOU A RECLUSE!
IF YOU DON'T LIKE IT, STOP READING OUR THOUGHTS!
SCREECH
NIGHTMARE CAN READ OTHER PEOPLE'S MINDS.
HE CAN SEE EVERYTHING I THINK. I CAN'T HIDE A THING. IT'S A SEVERE BREACH OF PRIVACY.
OF COURSE, GRAY SEEMS TO BE ABLE TO SHUT HIM OUT.
GLANCE
HE READS THOUGHTS...
AND HE CAN FLOAT IN THE AIR.
I THINK HE'D BE BETTER OFF NORMAL AND HEALTHY, EVEN IF IT MEANT LOSING THOSE POWERS.
I...I AGREE! IF IT WEREN'T THIS COLD...!
I SEE, SO YOU'D GO OUT IF IT WERE WARMER?
UGH ...!
Y...YEAH! ABSOLUTELY!! I'D GO OUT!!
YOU'RE PROTESTING TOO MUCH.
SHUT UP, CLOCKMAKER!!
OKAY, THEN WHY DON'T WE GO CAMPING IN THE SUMMER DOMAIN?
CAMPING ?!
I DON'T KNOW... THAT'S AWFULLY RUSTIC...!
IT'D BE IMPOSSIBLE FOR SOMEONE AS SICKLY AS NIGHTMARE TO GO CAMPING.
I CAN'T EVEN IMAGINE IT.
BEAM
にっこり

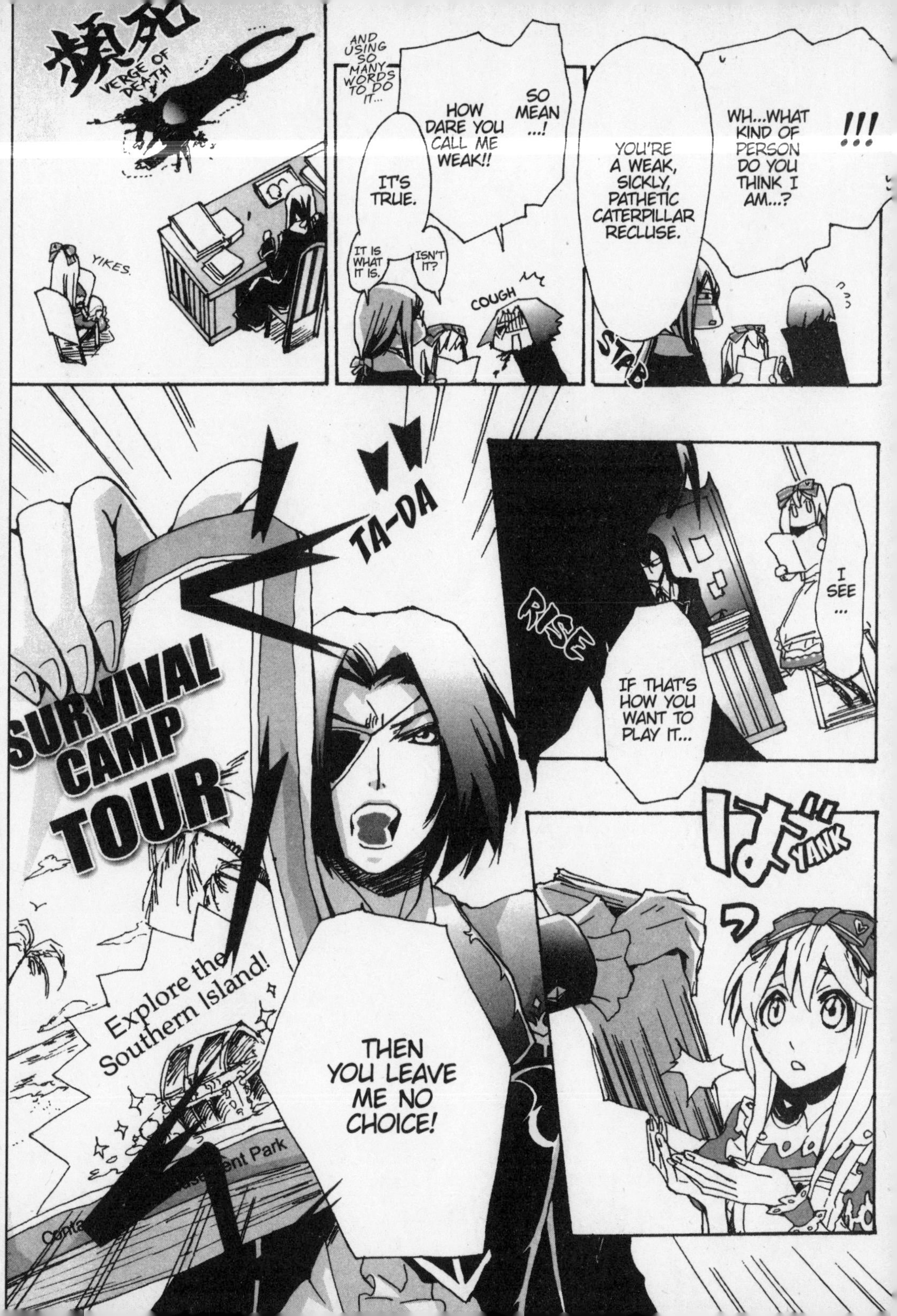
!!!
WH...WHAT KIND OF PERSON DO YOU THINK I AM...?
YOU'RE A WEAK, SICKLY, PATHETIC CATERPILLAR RECLUSE.
STAB
AND USING SO MANY WORDS TO DO IT...
SO MEAN ...!
HOW DARE YOU CALL ME WEAK!!
IT'S TRUE.
ISN'T IT?
IT IS WHAT IT IS.
COUGH
瀕死
VERGE OF DEATH
YIKES.
I SEE ...
RISE
IF THAT'S HOW YOU WANT TO PLAY IT...
YANK
TA-DA
SURVIVAL CAMP TOUR
Explore the Southern Island!
THEN YOU LEAVE ME NO CHOICE!

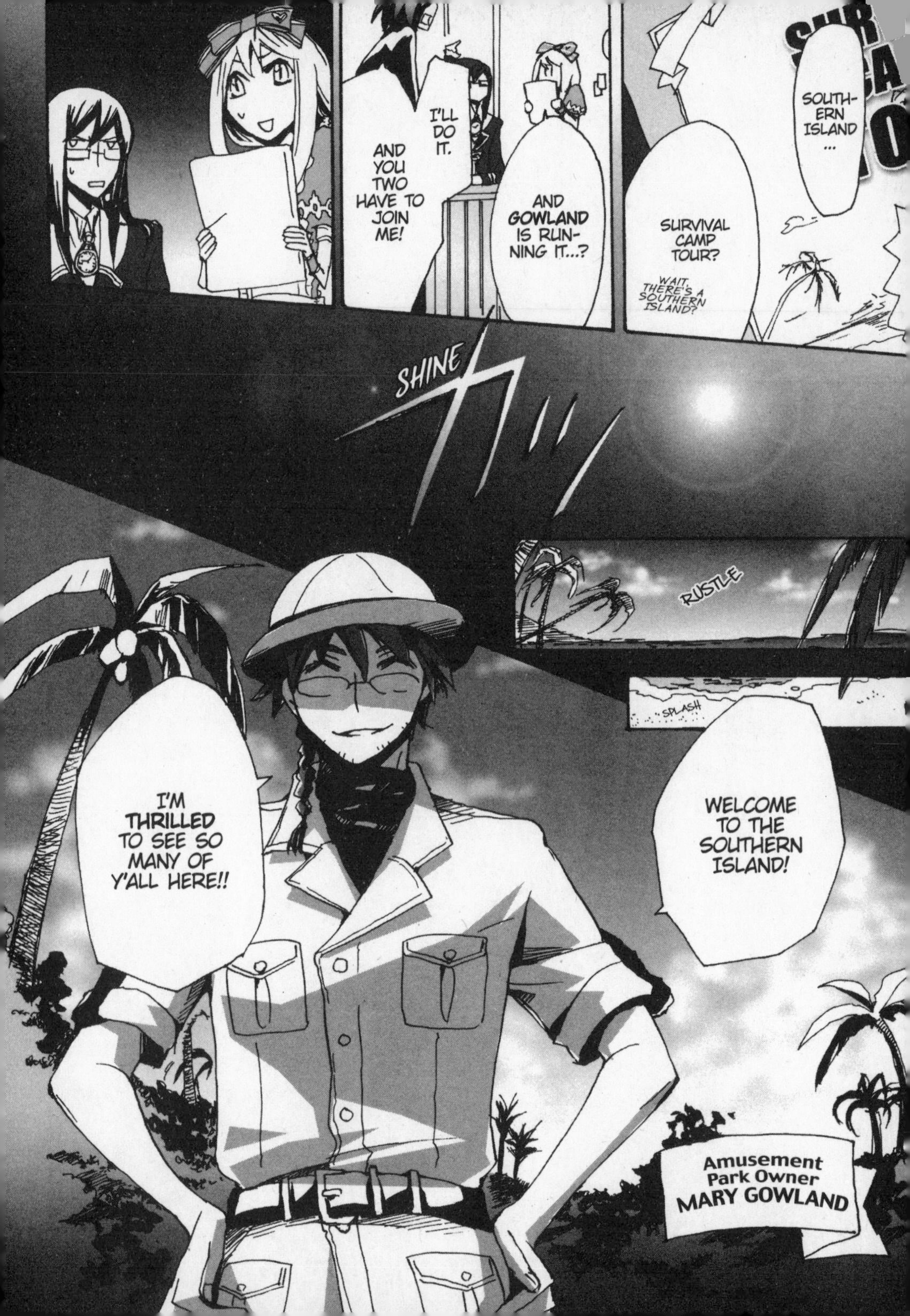
SOUTHERN ISLAND...
SURVIVAL CAMP TOUR?
WAIT, THERE'S A SOUTHERN ISLAND?
AND GOWLAND IS RUNNING IT...?
I'LL DO IT.
AND YOU TWO HAVE TO JOIN ME!
SHINE
RUSTLE
SPLASH
WELCOME TO THE SOUTHERN ISLAND!
I'M THRILLED TO SEE SO MANY OF Y'ALL HERE!!
Amusement Park Owner MARY GOWLAND

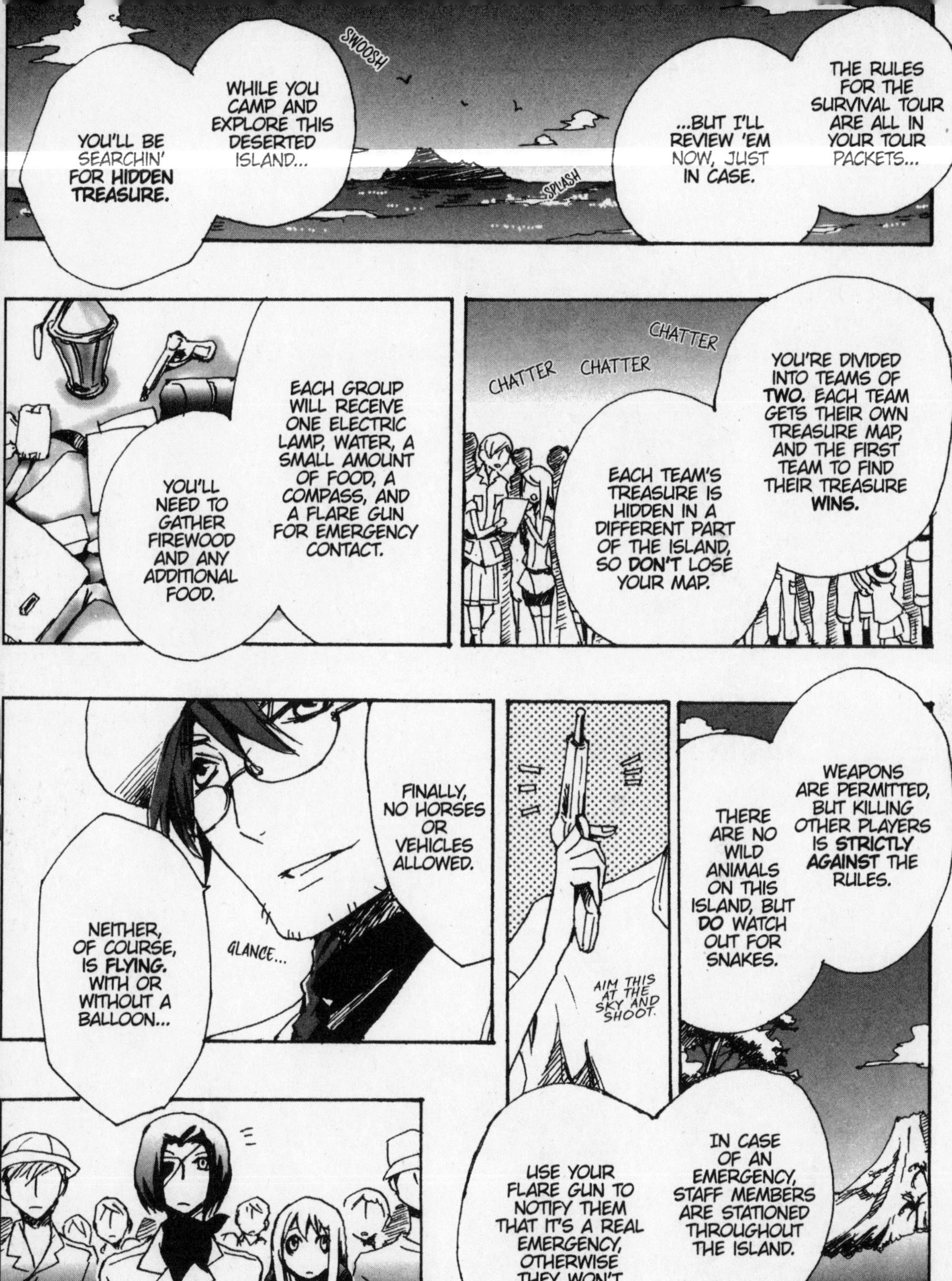
THE RULES FOR THE SURVIVAL TOUR ARE ALL IN YOUR TOUR PACKETS...
...BUT I'LL REVIEW 'EM NOW, JUST IN CASE.
SWOOSH
SPLASH
WHILE YOU CAMP AND EXPLORE THIS DESERTED ISLAND...
YOU'LL BE SEARCHIN' FOR HIDDEN TREASURE.
CHATTER
YOU'RE DIVIDED INTO TEAMS OF TWO. EACH TEAM GETS THEIR OWN TREASURE MAP, AND THE FIRST TEAM TO FIND THEIR TREASURE WINS.
EACH TEAM'S TREASURE IS HIDDEN IN A DIFFERENT PART OF THE ISLAND, SO DON'T LOSE YOUR MAP.
CHATTER
CHATTER
EACH GROUP WILL RECEIVE ONE ELECTRIC LAMP, WATER, A SMALL AMOUNT OF FOOD, A COMPASS, AND A FLARE GUN FOR EMERGENCY CONTACT.
YOU'LL NEED TO GATHER FIREWOOD AND ANY ADDITIONAL FOOD.
WEAPONS ARE PERMITTED, BUT KILLING OTHER PLAYERS IS STRICTLY AGAINST THE RULES.
THERE ARE NO WILD ANIMALS ON THIS ISLAND, BUT DO WATCH OUT FOR SNAKES.
AIM THIS AT THE SKY AND SHOOT.
IN CASE OF AN EMERGENCY, STAFF MEMBERS ARE STATIONED THROUGHOUT THE ISLAND.
USE YOUR FLARE GUN TO NOTIFY THEM THAT IT'S A REAL EMERGENCY, OTHERWISE THEY WON'T INTERFERE.
FINALLY, NO HORSES OR VEHICLES ALLOWED.
NEITHER, OF COURSE, IS FLYING. WITH OR WITHOUT A BALLOON...
GLANCE...

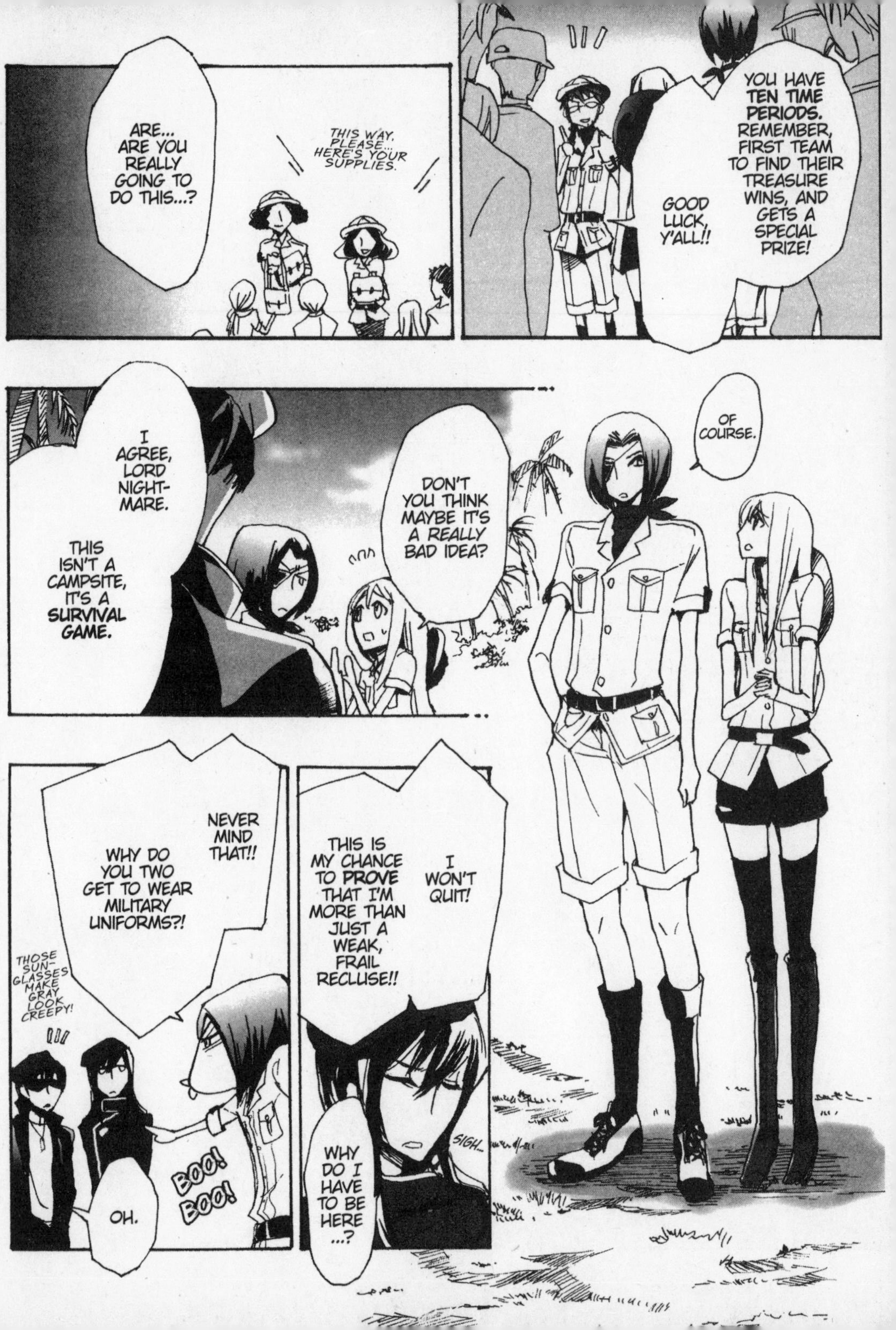
YOU HAVE TEN TIME PERIODS. REMEMBER, FIRST TEAM TO FIND THEIR TREASURE WINS, AND GETS A SPECIAL PRIZE!
GOOD LUCK, Y'ALL!!
THIS WAY, PLEASE... HERE'S YOUR SUPPLIES.
ARE... ARE YOU REALLY GOING TO DO THIS...?
OF COURSE.
DON'T YOU THINK MAYBE IT'S A REALLY BAD IDEA?
I AGREE, LORD NIGHTMARE.
THIS ISN'T A CAMPSITE, IT'S A SURVIVAL GAME.
I WON'T QUIT!
THIS IS MY CHANCE TO PROVE THAT I'M MORE THAN JUST A WEAK, FRAIL RECLUSE!!
SIGH...
WHY DO I HAVE TO BE HERE ...?
NEVER MIND THAT!!
WHY DO YOU TWO GET TO WEAR MILITARY UNIFORMS?!
THOSE SUN-GLASSES MAKE GRAY LOOK CREEPY!
BOO! BOO!
OH.

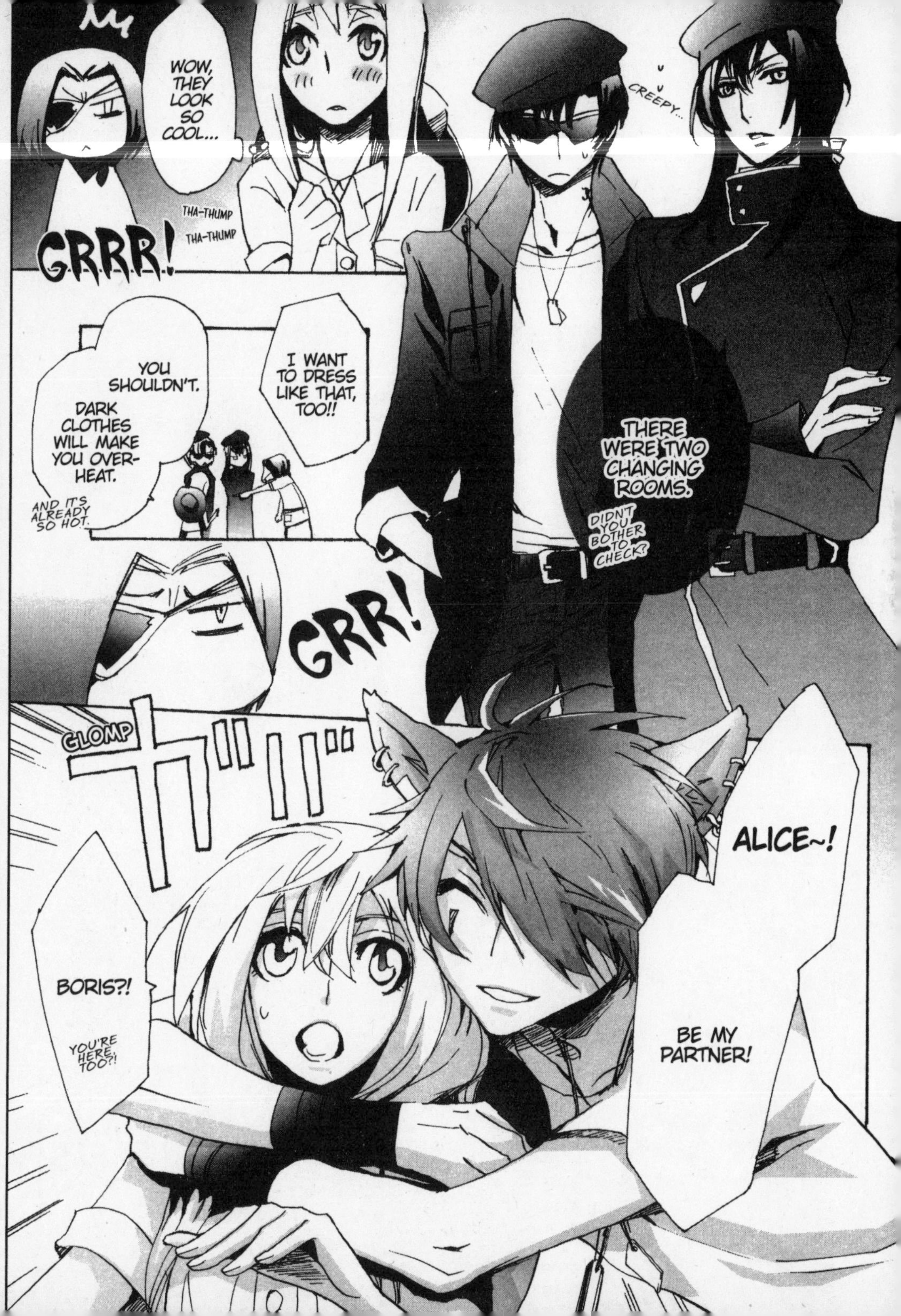
CREEPY...
THERE WERE TWO CHANGING ROOMS.
DIDN'T YOU BOTHER TO CHECK?
WOW, THEY LOOK SO COOL...
THA-THUMP
THA-THUMP
GRRR!
I WANT TO DRESS LIKE THAT, TOO!!
YOU SHOULDN'T.
DARK CLOTHES WILL MAKE YOU OVER-HEAT.
AND IT'S ALREADY SO HOT.
GRR!
GLOMP
ALICE~!
BE MY PARTNER!
BORIS?!
YOU'RE HERE, TOO?!

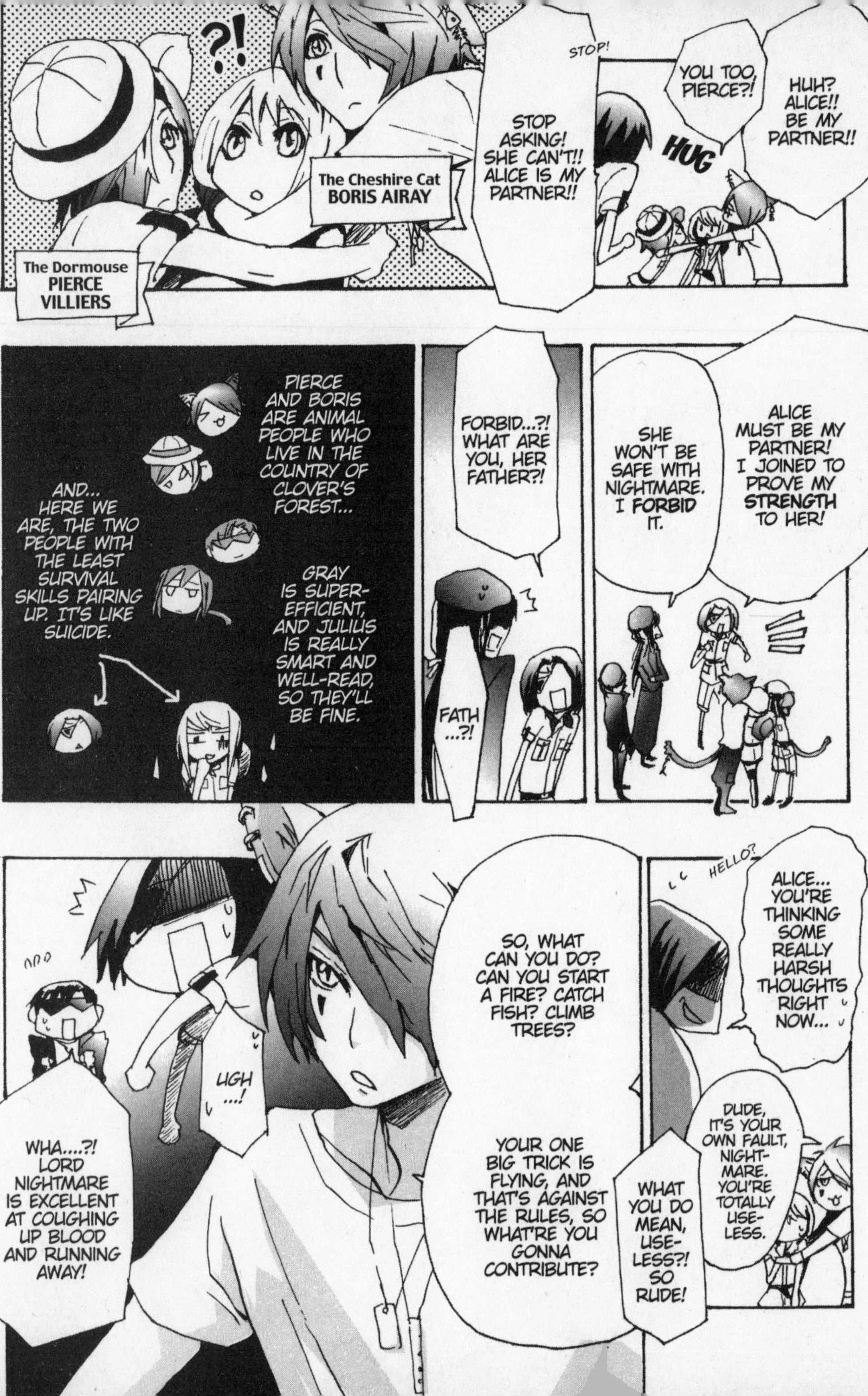
HUH? ALICE!! BE MY PARTNER!!
YOU TOO, PIERCE?!
HUG
STOP!
STOP ASKING! SHE CAN'T!! ALICE IS MY PARTNER!!
?!
The Cheshire Cat BORIS AIRAY
The Dormouse PIERCE VILLIERS
ALICE MUST BE MY PARTNER! I JOINED TO PROVE MY STRENGTH TO HER!
SHE WON'T BE SAFE WITH NIGHTMARE. I FORBID IT.
FORBID...?! WHAT ARE YOU, HER FATHER?!
FATH ...?!
PIERCE AND BORIS ARE ANIMAL PEOPLE WHO LIVE IN THE COUNTRY OF CLOVER'S FOREST...
GRAY IS SUPER-EFFICIENT, AND JULIUS IS REALLY SMART AND WELL-READ, SO THEY'LL BE FINE.
AND... HERE WE ARE, THE TWO PEOPLE WITH THE LEAST SURVIVAL SKILLS PAIRING UP. IT'S LIKE SUICIDE.
HELLO?
ALICE... YOU'RE THINKING SOME REALLY HARSH THOUGHTS RIGHT NOW...
DUDE, IT'S YOUR OWN FAULT, NIGHT-MARE. YOU'RE TOTALLY USE-LESS.
WHAT YOU DO MEAN, USE-LESS?! SO RUDE!
SO, WHAT CAN YOU DO? CAN YOU START A FIRE? CATCH FISH? CLIMB TREES?
YOUR ONE BIG TRICK IS FLYING, AND THAT'S AGAINST THE RULES, SO WHAT'RE YOU GONNA CONTRIBUTE?
UGH ...!
WHA....?! LORD NIGHTMARE IS EXCELLENT AT COUGHING UP BLOOD AND RUNNING AWAY!

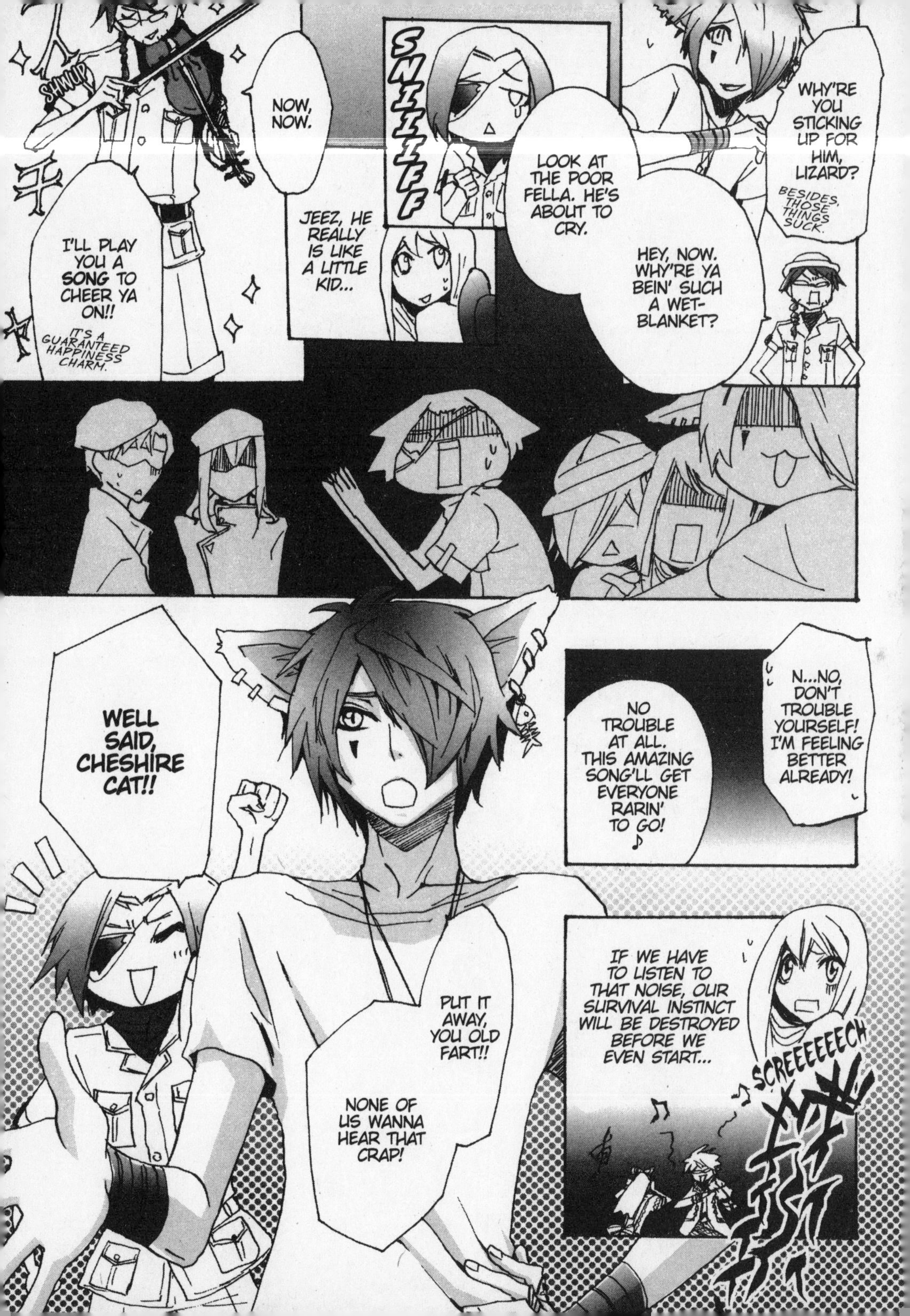
WHY'RE YOU STICKING UP FOR HIM, LIZARD?
BESIDES, THOSE THINGS SUCK.
HEY, NOW. WHY'RE YA BEIN' SUCH A WET-BLANKET?
SNIIFF
LOOK AT THE POOR FELLA. HE'S ABOUT TO CRY.
JEEZ, HE REALLY IS LIKE A LITTLE KID...
SHWUP
NOW, NOW.
I'LL PLAY YOU A SONG TO CHEER YA ON!!
IT'S A GUARANTEED HAPPINESS CHARM.
N...NO, DON'T TROUBLE YOURSELF! I'M FEELING BETTER ALREADY!
NO TROUBLE AT ALL. THIS AMAZING SONG'LL GET EVERYONE RARIN' TO GO! ♪
WELL SAID, CHESHIRE CAT!!
IF WE HAVE TO LISTEN TO THAT NOISE, OUR SURVIVAL INSTINCT WILL BE DESTROYED BEFORE WE EVEN START...
SCREEEEEEECH
PUT IT AWAY, YOU OLD FART!!
NONE OF US WANNA HEAR THAT CRAP!

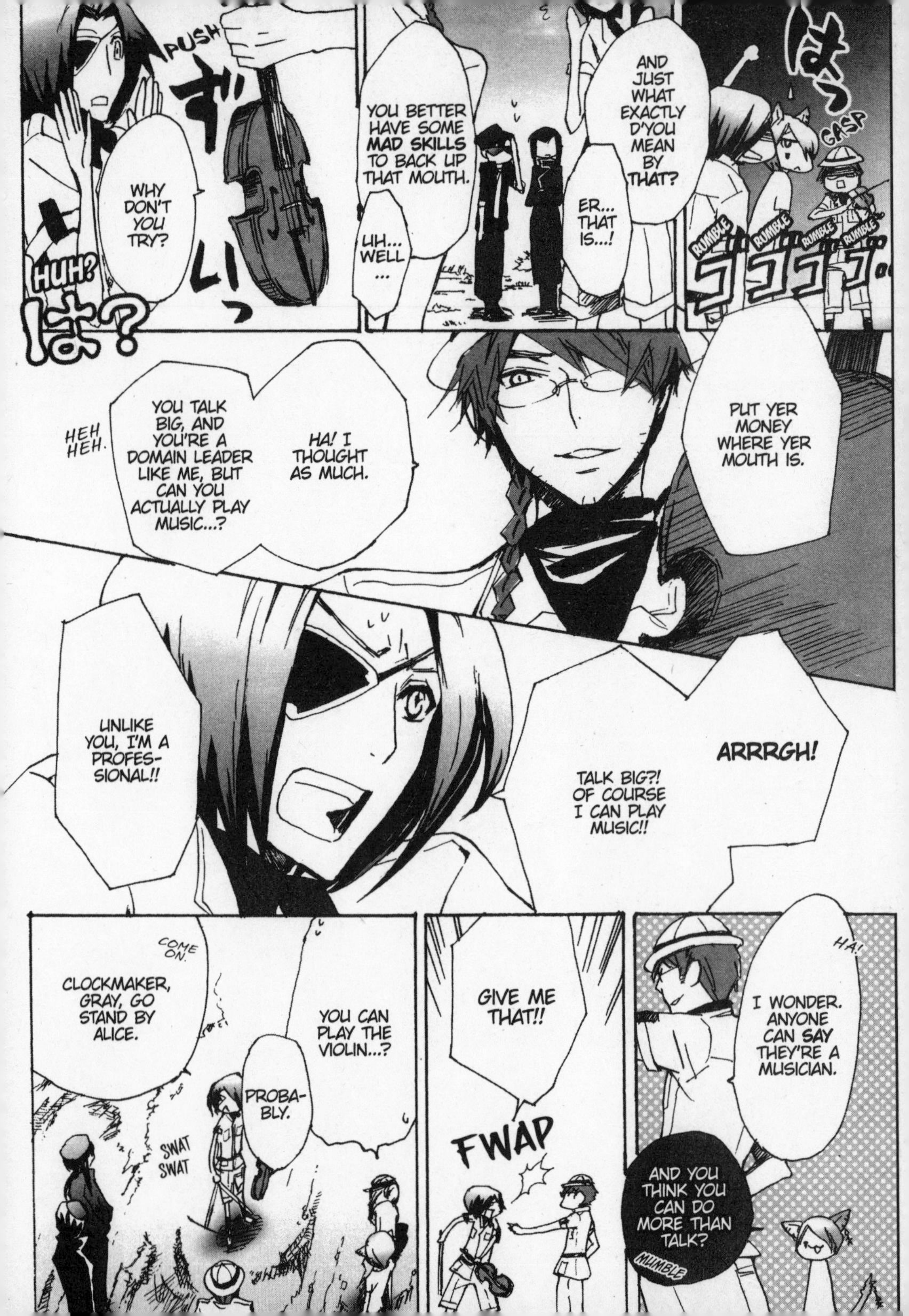

はっ
GASP
AND JUST WHAT EXACTLY D'YOU MEAN BY THAT?
ER... THAT IS...!
RUMBLE RUMBLE RUMBLE RUMBLE
ゴゴゴ
YOU BETTER HAVE SOME MAD SKILLS TO BACK UP THAT MOUTH.
UH... WELL ...
PUSH
ず
WHY DON'T YOU TRY?
HUH?
は?
PUT YER MONEY WHERE YER MOUTH IS.
HA! I THOUGHT AS MUCH.
YOU TALK BIG, AND YOU'RE A DOMAIN LEADER LIKE ME, BUT CAN YOU ACTUALLY PLAY MUSIC...?
HEH HEH.
ARRRGH!
TALK BIG?! OF COURSE I CAN PLAY MUSIC!!
UNLIKE YOU, I'M A PROFES-SIONAL!!
HA!
I WONDER. ANYONE CAN SAY THEY'RE A MUSICIAN.
AND YOU THINK YOU CAN DO MORE THAN TALK?
MUMBLE
GIVE ME THAT!!
FWAP
YOU CAN PLAY THE VIOLIN...?
PROBA-BLY.
COME ON.
CLOCKMAKER, GRAY, GO STAND BY ALICE.
SWAT SWAT

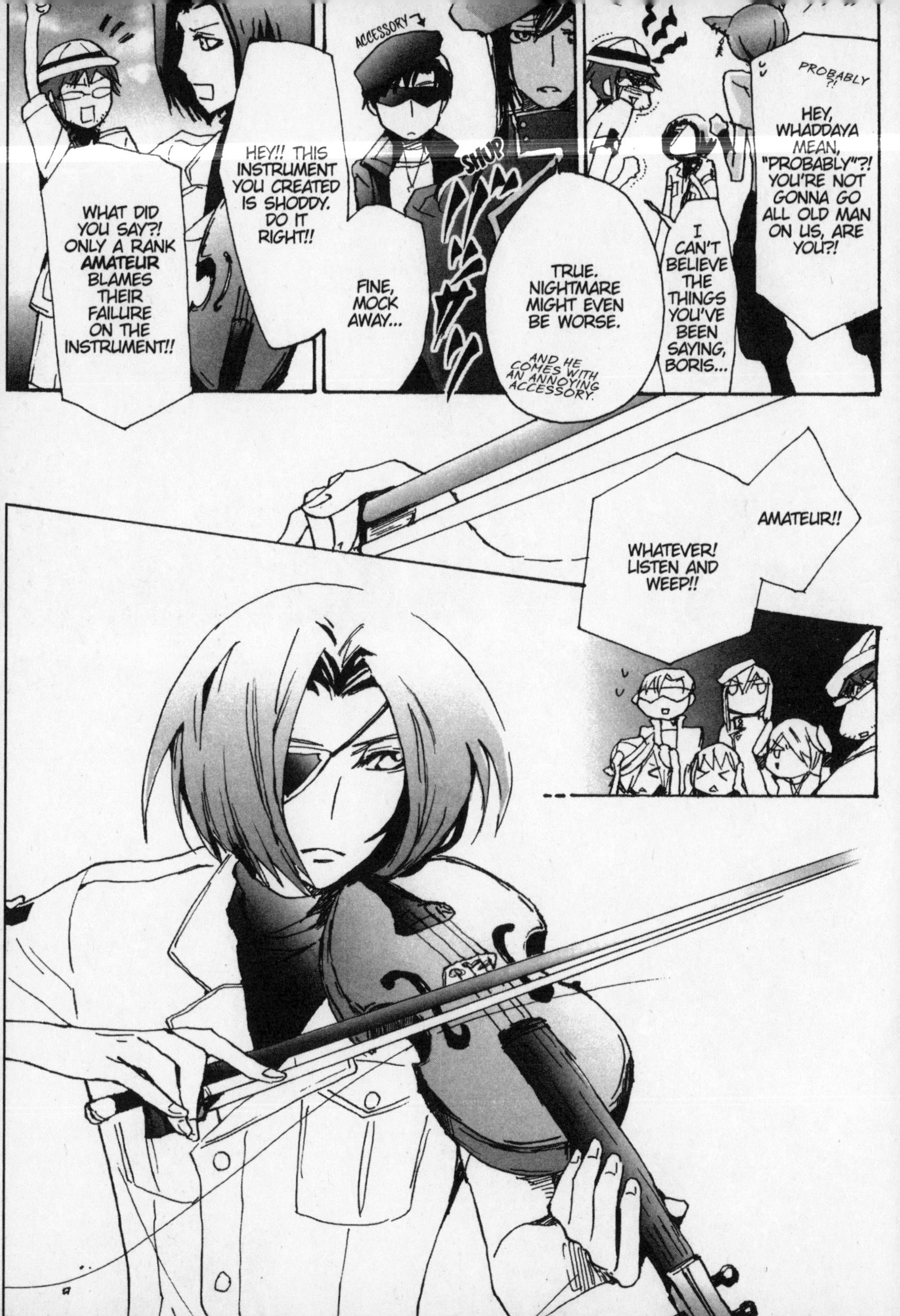
PROBABLY ?!
HEY, WHADDAYA MEAN, "PROBABLY"?! YOU'RE NOT GONNA GO ALL OLD MAN ON US, ARE YOU?!
I CAN'T BELIEVE THE THINGS YOU'VE BEEN SAYING, BORIS...
ACCESSORY
SHUP
TRUE. NIGHTMARE MIGHT EVEN BE WORSE.
AND HE COMES WITH AN ANNOYING ACCESSORY.
FINE, MOCK AWAY...
HEY!! THIS INSTRUMENT YOU CREATED IS SHODDY. DO IT RIGHT!!
WHAT DID YOU SAY?! ONLY A RANK **AMATEUR** BLAMES THEIR FAILURE ON THE INSTRUMENT!!
AMATEUR!!
WHATEVER! LISTEN AND WEEP!!

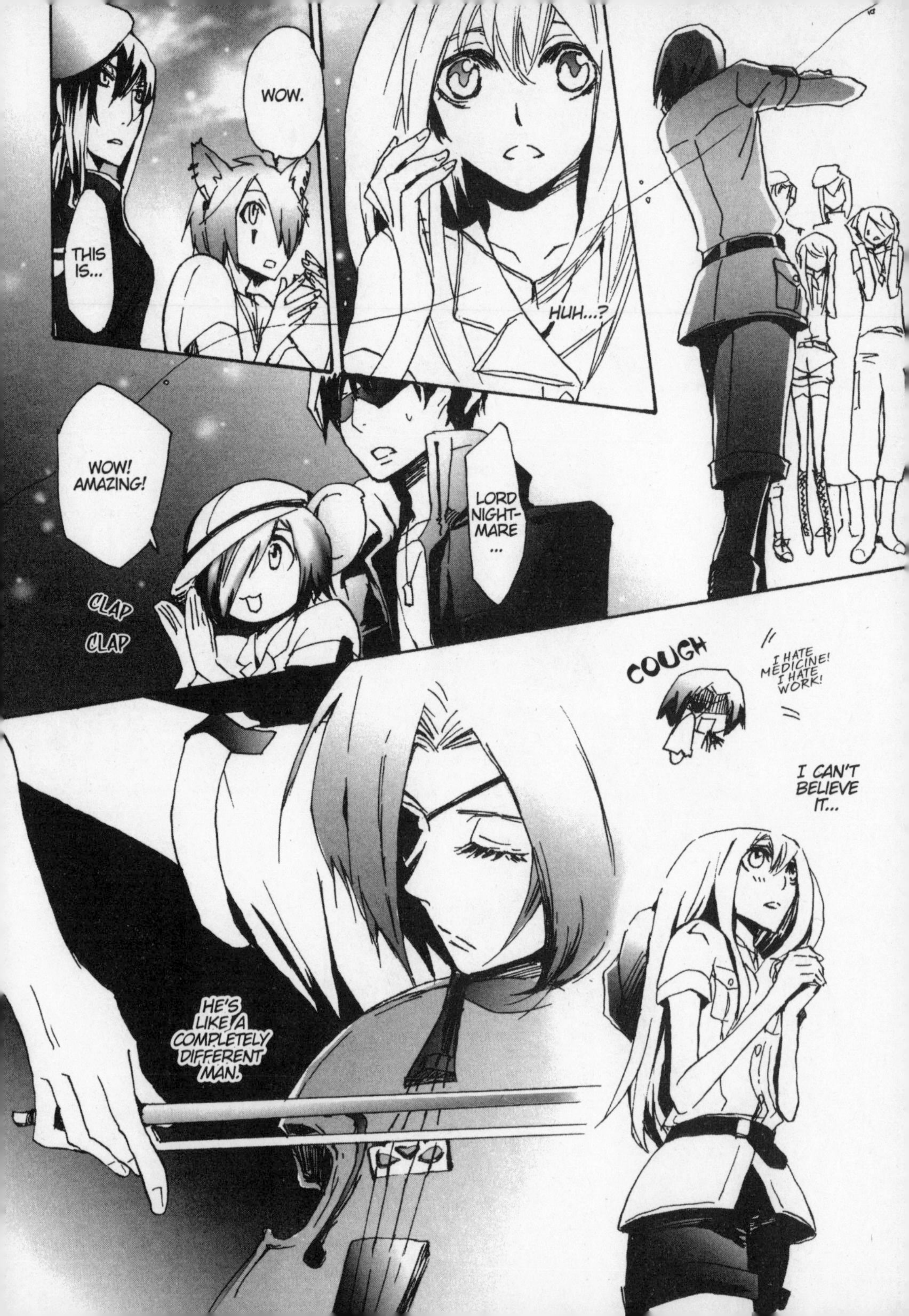
HUH...?
WOW.
THIS IS...
LORD NIGHT-MARE ...
WOW! AMAZING!
CLAP
CLAP
COUGH
I HATE MEDICINE! I HATE WORK!
I CAN'T BELIEVE IT...
HE'S LIKE A COMPLETELY DIFFERENT MAN.

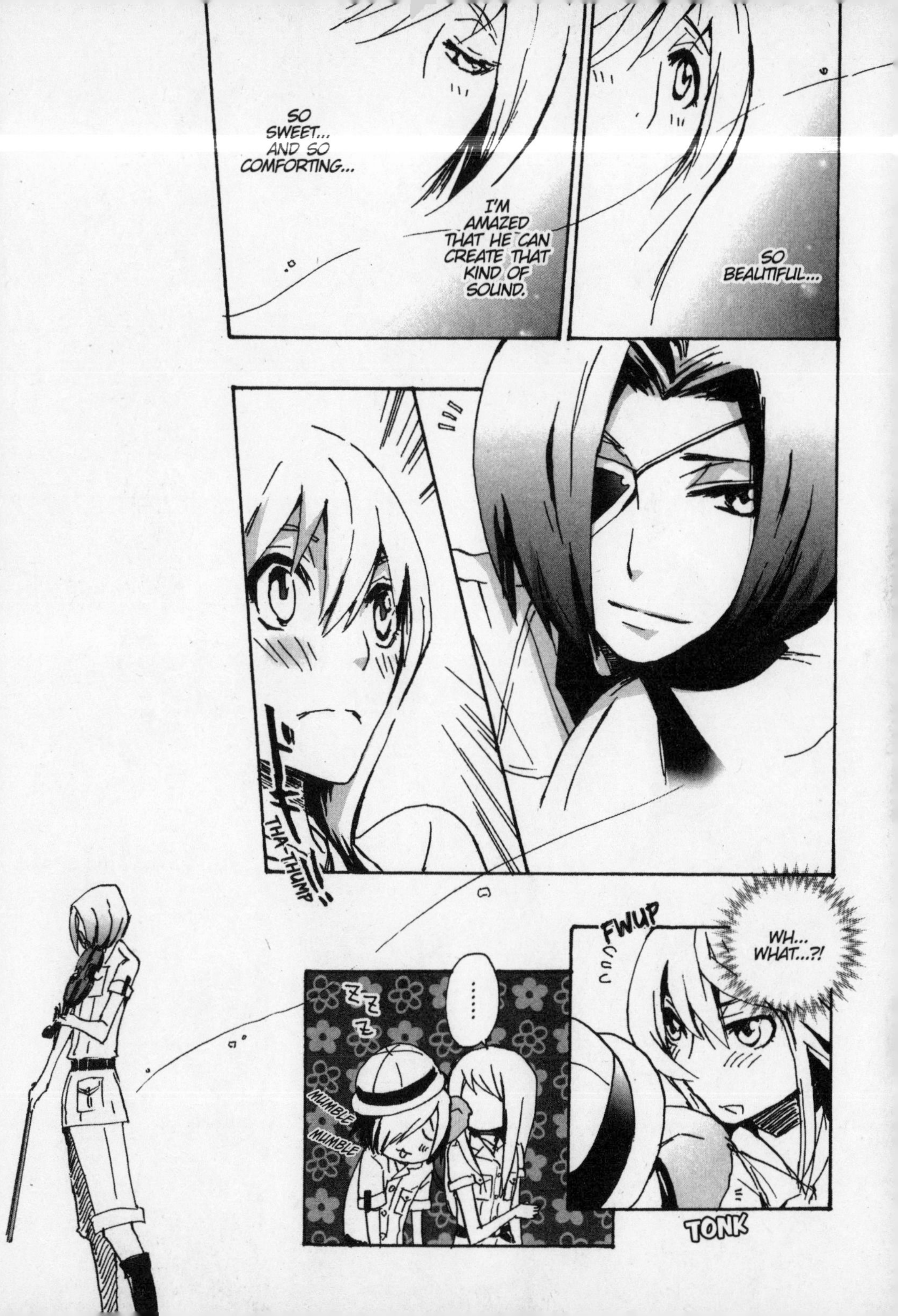
SO BEAUTIFUL...
I'M AMAZED THAT HE CAN CREATE THAT KIND OF SOUND.
SO SWEET... AND SO COMFORTING...
THA-THUMP
WH... WHAT...?!
FWUP
TONK
......
Z Z Z
MUMBLE MUMBLE

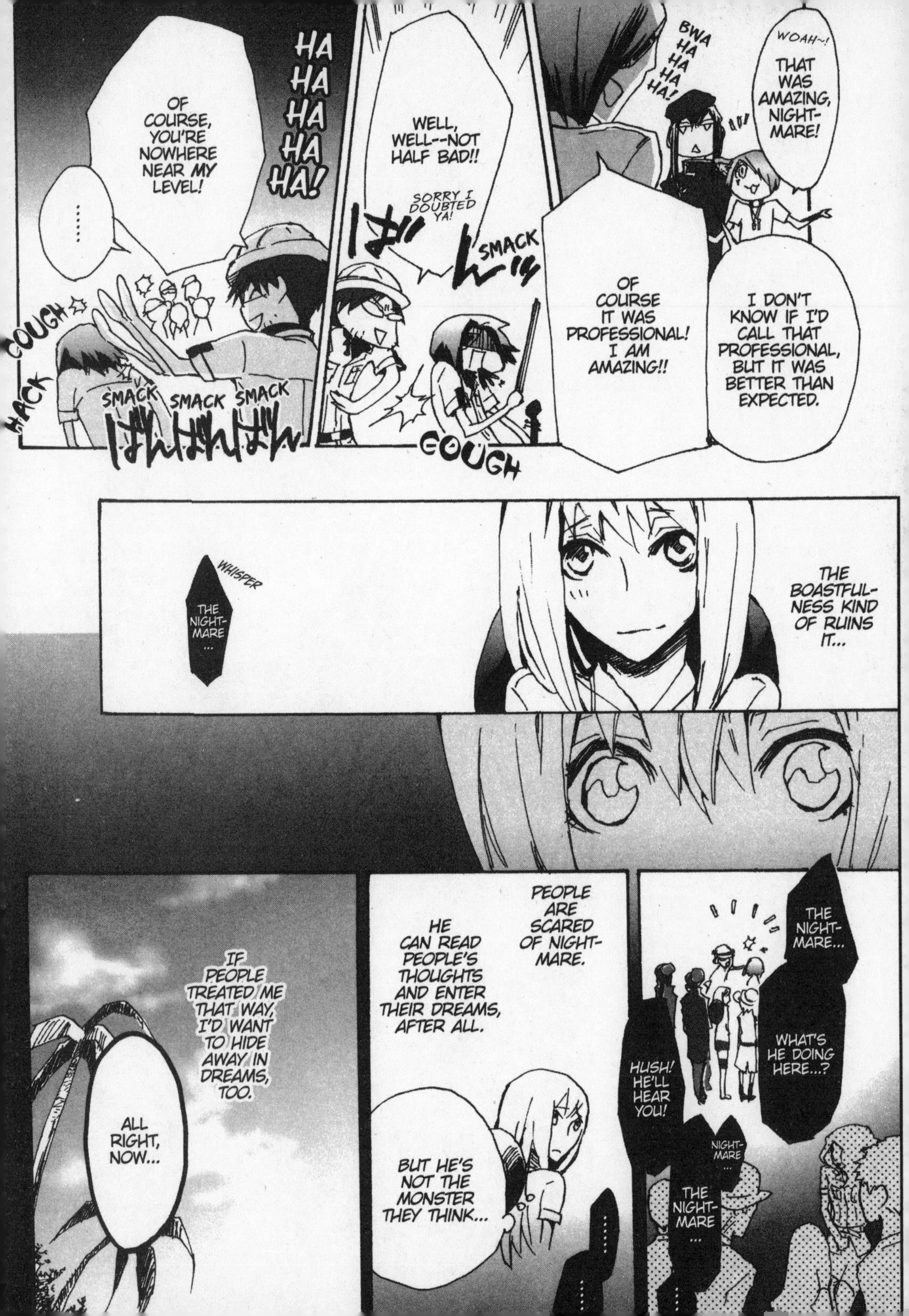
BWA HA HA HA HA!
WOAH~! THAT WAS AMAZING, NIGHTMARE!
I DON'T KNOW IF I'D CALL THAT PROFESSIONAL, BUT IT WAS BETTER THAN EXPECTED.
OF COURSE IT WAS PROFESSIONAL! I AM AMAZING!!
WELL, WELL--NOT HALF BAD!!
SORRY I DOUBTED YA!
ばん
SMACK
COUGH
HA HA HA HA HA!
OF COURSE, YOU'RE NOWHERE NEAR MY LEVEL!
......
COUGH
HACK
SMACK SMACK SMACK
ばんばんばん
THE BOASTFULNESS KIND OF RUINS IT...
WHISPER
THE NIGHTMARE...
THE NIGHTMARE...
WHAT'S HE DOING HERE...?
HUSH! HE'LL HEAR YOU!
NIGHTMARE...
THE NIGHTMARE...
PEOPLE ARE SCARED OF NIGHTMARE.
HE CAN READ PEOPLE'S THOUGHTS AND ENTER THEIR DREAMS, AFTER ALL.
BUT HE'S NOT THE MONSTER THEY THINK...
......
IF PEOPLE TREATED ME THAT WAY, I'D WANT TO HIDE AWAY IN DREAMS, TOO.
ALL RIGHT, NOW...

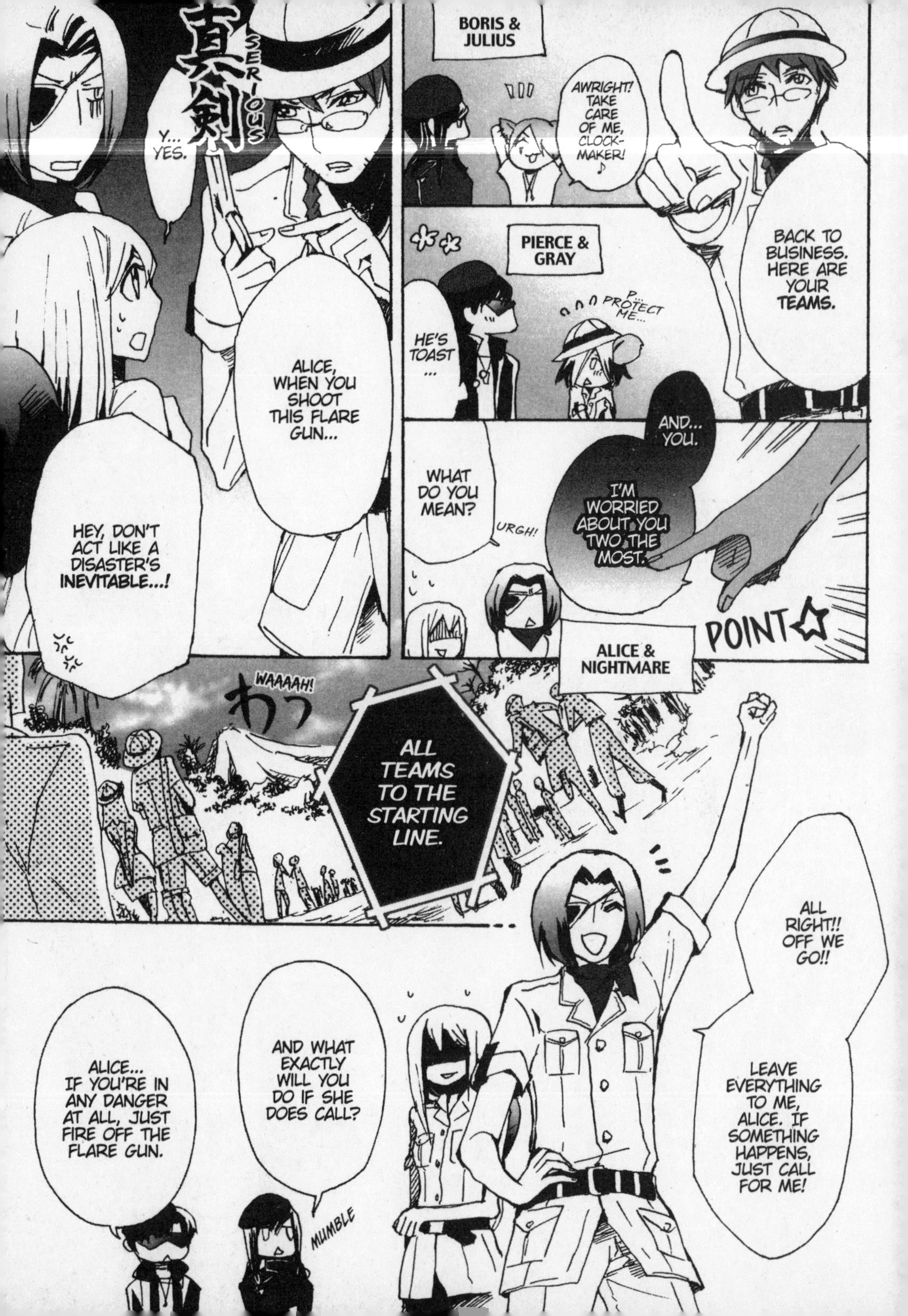
BACK TO BUSINESS. HERE ARE YOUR TEAMS.
BORIS & JULIUS
AWRIGHT! TAKE CARE OF ME, CLOCKMAKER! ♪
PIERCE & GRAY
P... PROTECT ME...
HE'S TOAST...
AND... YOU.
I'M WORRIED ABOUT YOU TWO THE MOST.
POINT☆
ALICE & NIGHTMARE
URGH!
WHAT DO YOU MEAN?
SERIOUS
ALICE, WHEN YOU SHOOT THIS FLARE GUN...
Y... YES.
HEY, DON'T ACT LIKE A DISASTER'S INEVITABLE...!
ALL TEAMS TO THE STARTING LINE.
WAAAAH!
ALL RIGHT!! OFF WE GO!!
LEAVE EVERYTHING TO ME, ALICE. IF SOMETHING HAPPENS, JUST CALL FOR ME!
AND WHAT EXACTLY WILL YOU DO IF SHE DOES CALL?
ALICE... IF YOU'RE IN ANY DANGER AT ALL, JUST FIRE OFF THE FLARE GUN.
MUMBLE

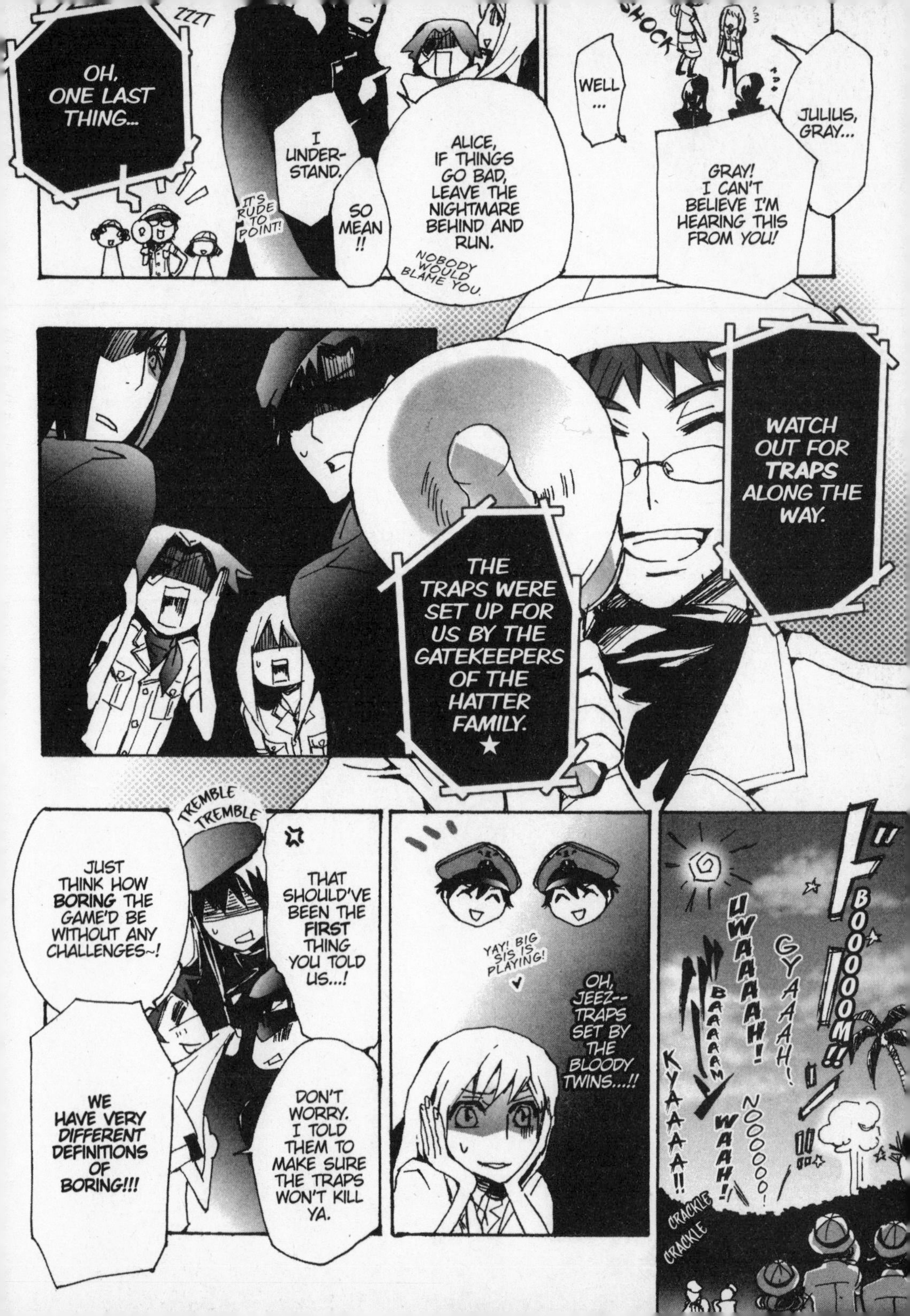
SHOCK
JULIUS, GRAY...
WELL ...
GRAY! I CAN'T BELIEVE I'M HEARING THIS FROM YOU!
ALICE, IF THINGS GO BAD, LEAVE THE NIGHTMARE BEHIND AND RUN.
NOBODY WOULD BLAME YOU.
I UNDER-STAND.
SO MEAN !!
IT'S RUDE TO POINT!
ZZZT
OH, ONE LAST THING...
WATCH OUT FOR TRAPS ALONG THE WAY.
THE TRAPS WERE SET UP FOR US BY THE GATEKEEPERS OF THE HATTER FAMILY. ★
BOOOOOOM!!
UWAAAAAH!
GYAAAH!
BAAAAAAM
NOOOOOO!
WAAAH!
KYAAAAA!!
CRACKLE CRACKLE
YAY! BIG SIS IS PLAYING!
OH, JEEZ-- TRAPS SET BY THE BLOODY TWINS...!!
TREMBLE TREMBLE
THAT SHOULD'VE BEEN THE FIRST THING YOU TOLD US...!
JUST THINK HOW BORING THE GAME'D BE WITHOUT ANY CHALLENGES~!
DON'T WORRY. I TOLD THEM TO MAKE SURE THE TRAPS WON'T KILL YA.
WE HAVE VERY DIFFERENT DEFINITIONS OF BORING!!!

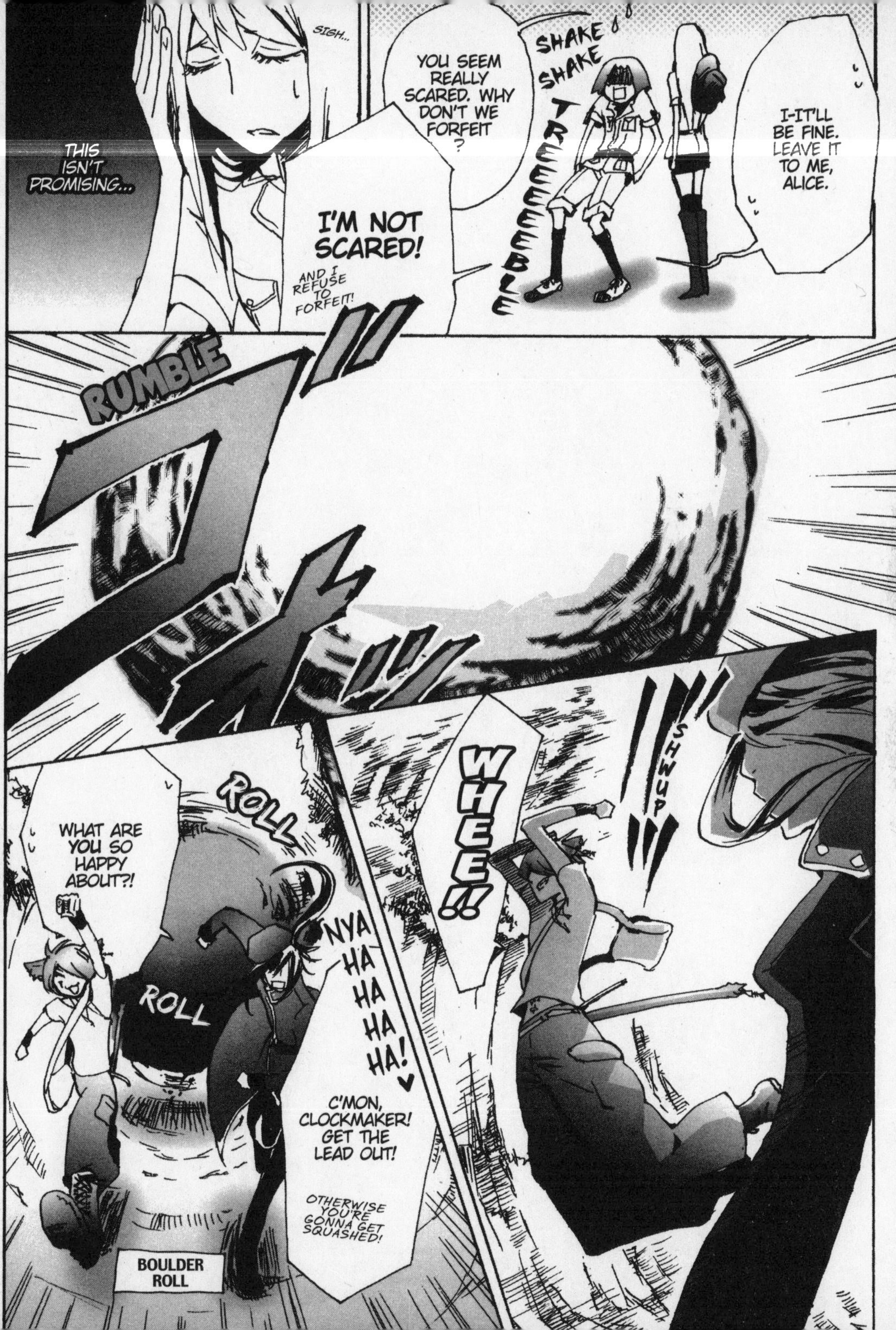
SHAKE
SHAKE
TREEEEEBLE
I-IT'LL BE FINE. LEAVE IT TO ME, ALICE.
YOU SEEM REALLY SCARED. WHY DON'T WE FORFEIT?
I'M NOT SCARED!
AND I REFUSE TO FORFEIT!
SIGH...
THIS ISN'T PROMISING...
RUMBLE
SHWUP!!
WHEE!!
NYA HA HA HA HA HA!♥
C'MON, CLOCKMAKER! GET THE LEAD OUT!
OTHERWISE YOU'RE GONNA GET SQUASHED!
WHAT ARE YOU SO HAPPY ABOUT?!
ROLL
ROLL
BOULDER ROLL

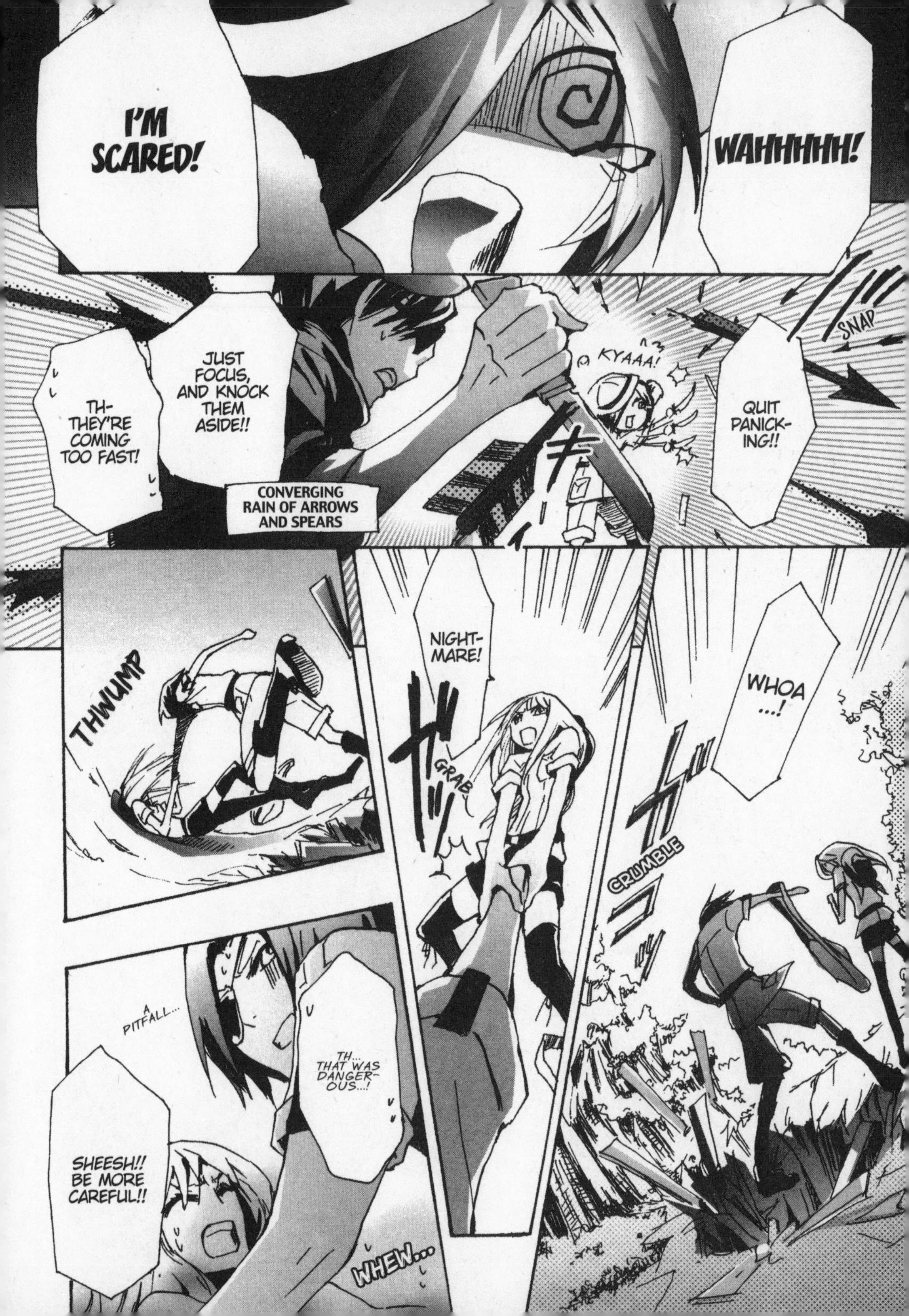
WAHHHHH!
I'M SCARED!
SNAP
QUIT PANICKING!!
KYAAA!
JUST FOCUS, AND KNOCK THEM ASIDE!!
TH- THEY'RE COMING TOO FAST!
CONVERGING RAIN OF ARROWS AND SPEARS
WHOA ...!
CRUMBLE
NIGHTMARE!
GRAB
THWUMP
A PITFALL...
TH... THAT WAS DANGEROUS...!
SHEESH!! BE MORE CAREFUL!!
WHEW...

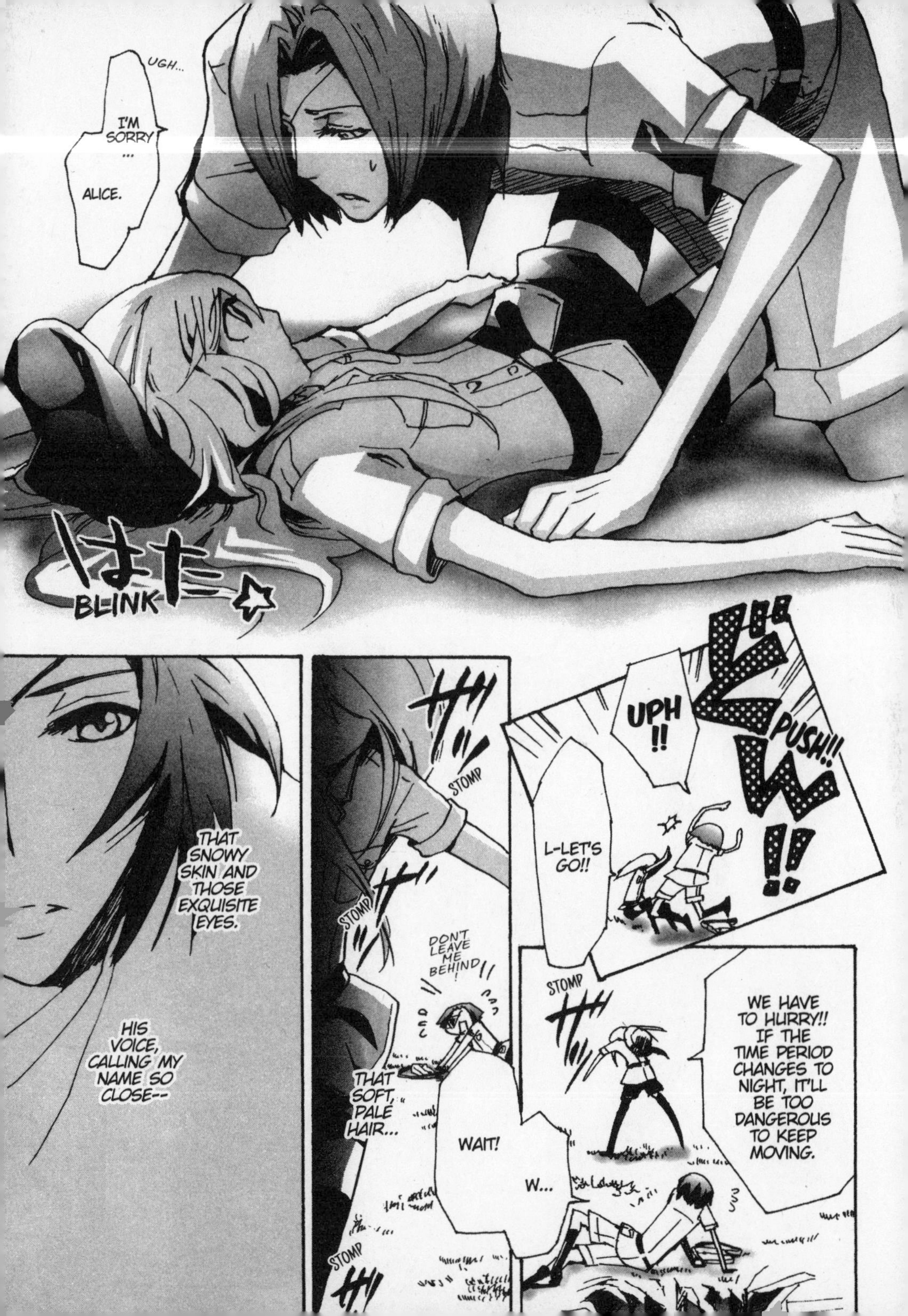
UGH...
I'M SORRY ... ALICE.
はた
BLINK
UPH!!
PUSH!!
L-LET'S GO!!
STOMP
WE HAVE TO HURRY!! IF THE TIME PERIOD CHANGES TO NIGHT, IT'LL BE TOO DANGEROUS TO KEEP MOVING.
W...
WAIT!
STOMP
STOMP
DON'T LEAVE ME BEHIND!
THAT SOFT, PALE HAIR...
STOMP
THAT SNOWY SKIN AND THOSE EXQUISITE EYES.
HIS VOICE, CALLING MY NAME SO CLOSE--

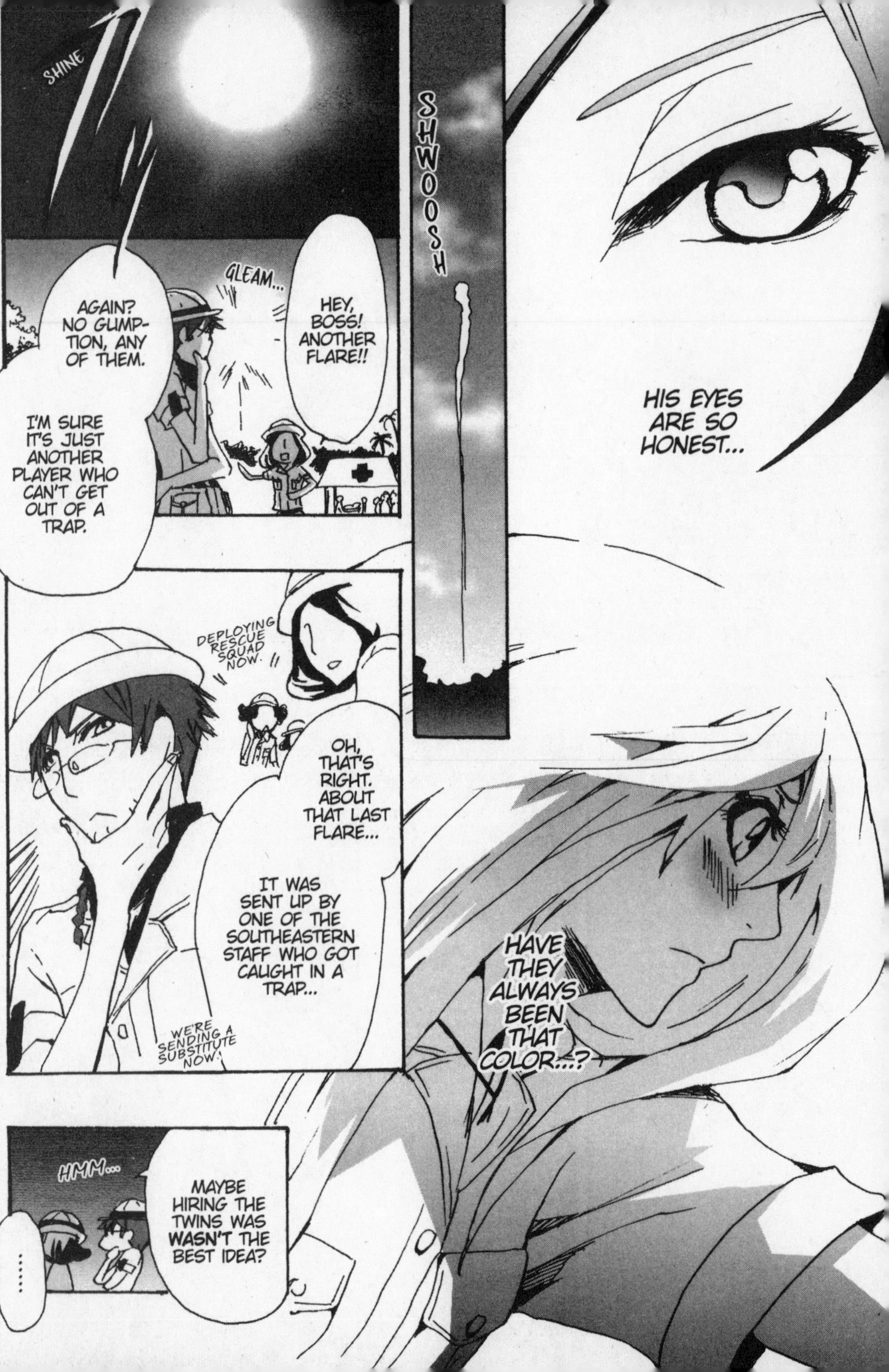
HIS EYES ARE SO HONEST...
HAVE THEY ALWAYS BEEN THAT COLOR...?
SHWOOSH
SHINE
HEY, BOSS! ANOTHER FLARE!!
GLEAM...
AGAIN? NO GUMPTION, ANY OF THEM.
I'M SURE IT'S JUST ANOTHER PLAYER WHO CAN'T GET OUT OF A TRAP.
DEPLOYING RESCUE SQUAD NOW.
OH, THAT'S RIGHT. ABOUT THAT LAST FLARE...
IT WAS SENT UP BY ONE OF THE SOUTHEASTERN STAFF WHO GOT CAUGHT IN A TRAP...
WE'RE SENDING A SUBSTITUTE NOW.
HMM...
MAYBE HIRING THE TWINS WAS WASN'T THE BEST IDEA?
......

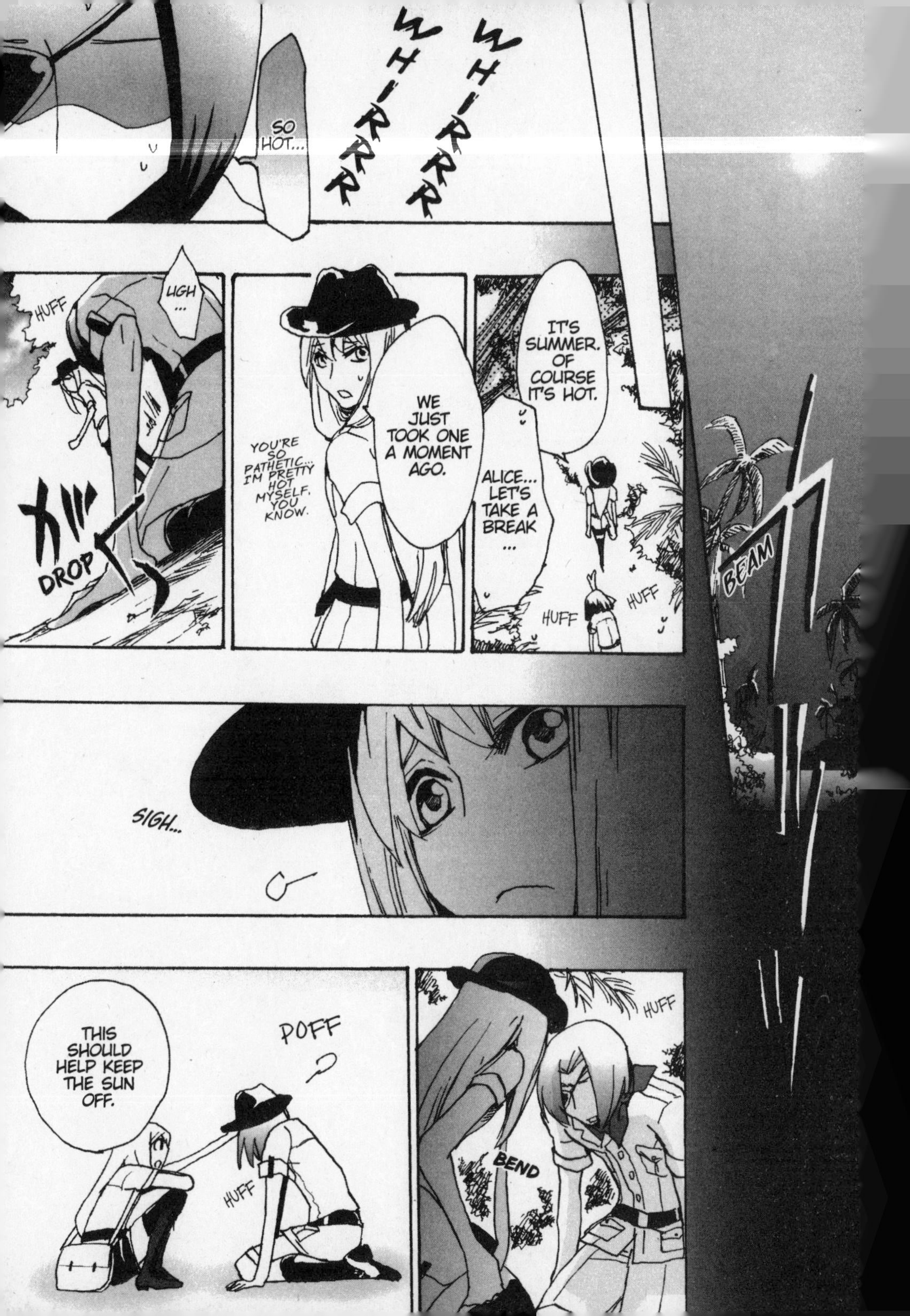
WHIRRR
WHIRRR
SO HOT...
BEAM
IT'S SUMMER. OF COURSE IT'S HOT.
ALICE... LET'S TAKE A BREAK...
HUFF
HUFF
WE JUST TOOK ONE A MOMENT AGO.
YOU'RE SO PATHETIC... I'M PRETTY HOT MYSELF, YOU KNOW.
UGH...
HUFF
ガッ
DROP
SIGH...
HUFF
BEND
POFF
THIS SHOULD HELP KEEP THE SUN OFF.
HUFF

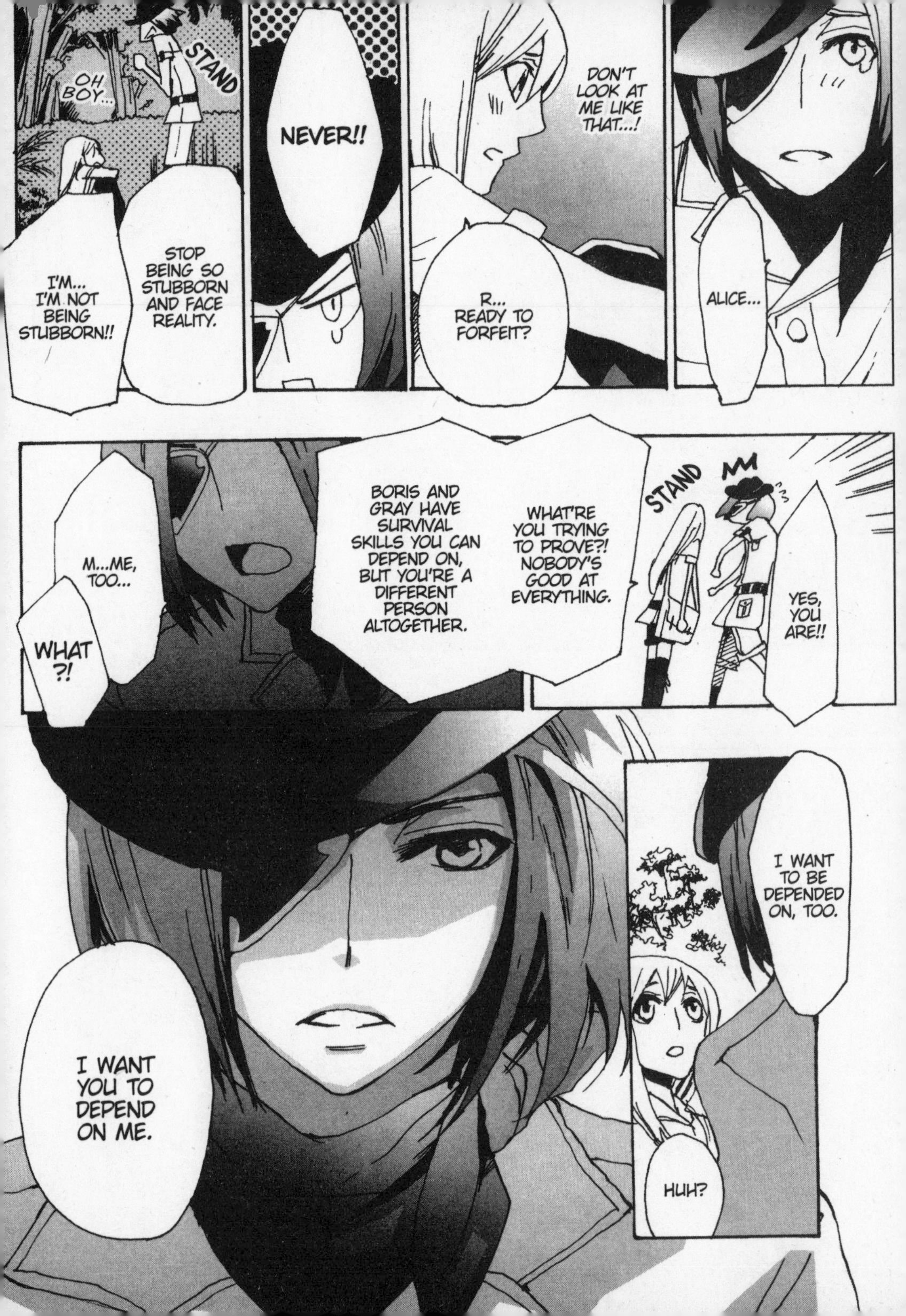
ALICE...
DON'T LOOK AT ME LIKE THAT...!
R... READY TO FORFEIT?
NEVER!!
STAND
OH BOY...
STOP BEING SO STUBBORN AND FACE REALITY.
I'M... I'M NOT BEING STUBBORN!!
YES, YOU ARE!!
STAND
WHAT'RE YOU TRYING TO PROVE?! NOBODY'S GOOD AT EVERYTHING.
BORIS AND GRAY HAVE SURVIVAL SKILLS YOU CAN DEPEND ON, BUT YOU'RE A DIFFERENT PERSON ALTOGETHER.
M...ME, TOO...
WHAT?!
I WANT TO BE DEPENDED ON, TOO.
HUH?
I WANT YOU TO DEPEND ON ME.

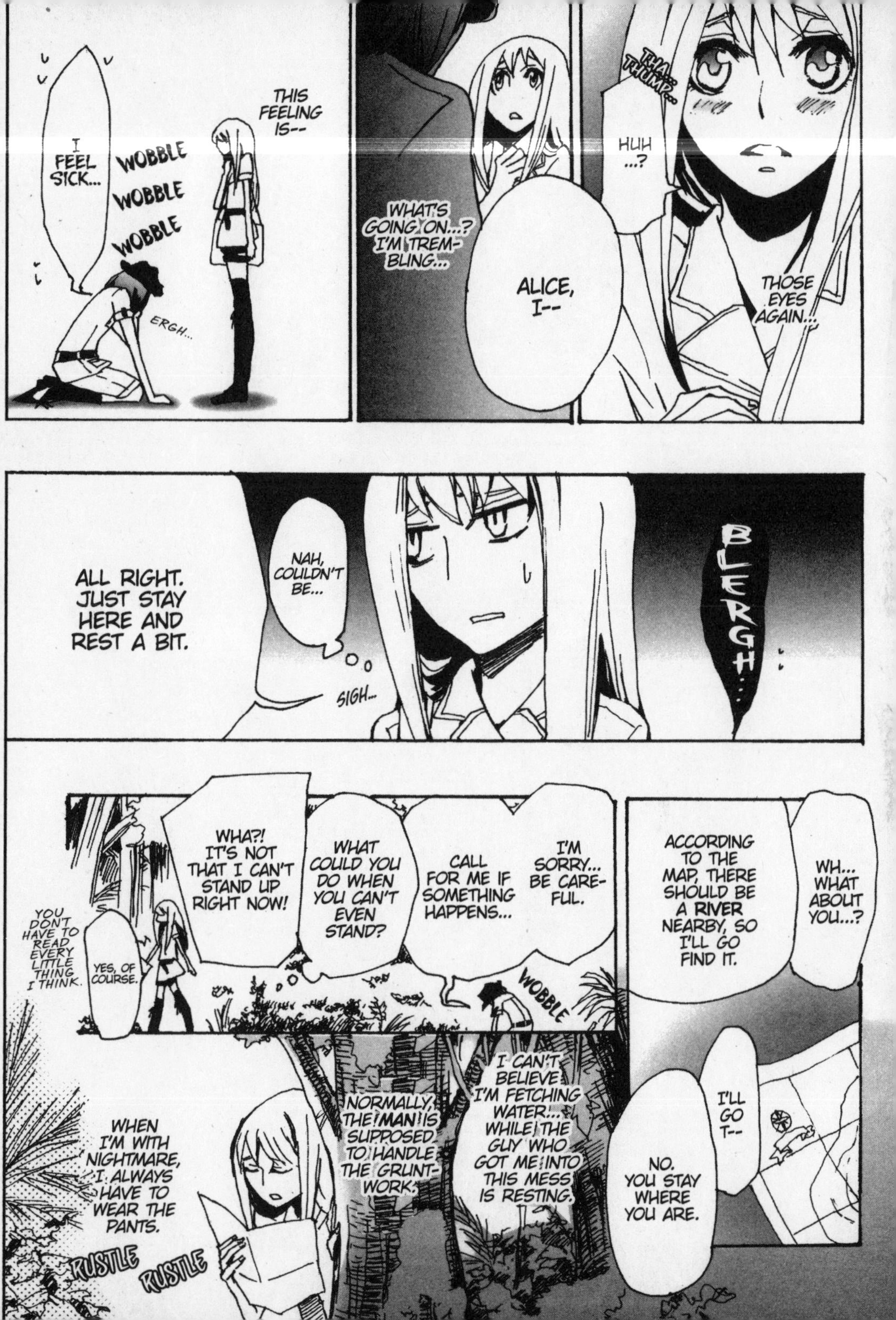
THA... THUMP...
HUH ...?
THOSE EYES AGAIN...
WHAT'S GOING ON...? I'M TREMBLING...
ALICE, I--
THIS FEELING IS--
I FEEL SICK...
WOBBLE
WOBBLE
WOBBLE
ERGH...
BLERGH...
NAH, COULDN'T BE...
SIGH...
ALL RIGHT. JUST STAY HERE AND REST A BIT.
ACCORDING TO THE MAP, THERE SHOULD BE A RIVER NEARBY, SO I'LL GO FIND IT.
WH... WHAT ABOUT YOU...?
I'M SORRY... BE CAREFUL.
CALL FOR ME IF SOMETHING HAPPENS...
WHAT COULD YOU DO WHEN YOU CAN'T EVEN STAND?
WHA?! IT'S NOT THAT I CAN'T STAND UP RIGHT NOW!
WOBBLE
YES, OF COURSE.
YOU DON'T HAVE TO READ EVERY LITTLE THING I THINK.
I'LL GO T--
NO. YOU STAY WHERE YOU ARE.
I CAN'T BELIEVE I'M FETCHING WATER... WHILE THE GUY WHO GOT ME INTO THIS MESS IS RESTING.
NORMALLY, THE MAN IS SUPPOSED TO HANDLE THE GRUNTWORK.
WHEN I'M WITH NIGHTMARE, I ALWAYS HAVE TO WEAR THE PANTS.
RUSTLE
RUSTLE

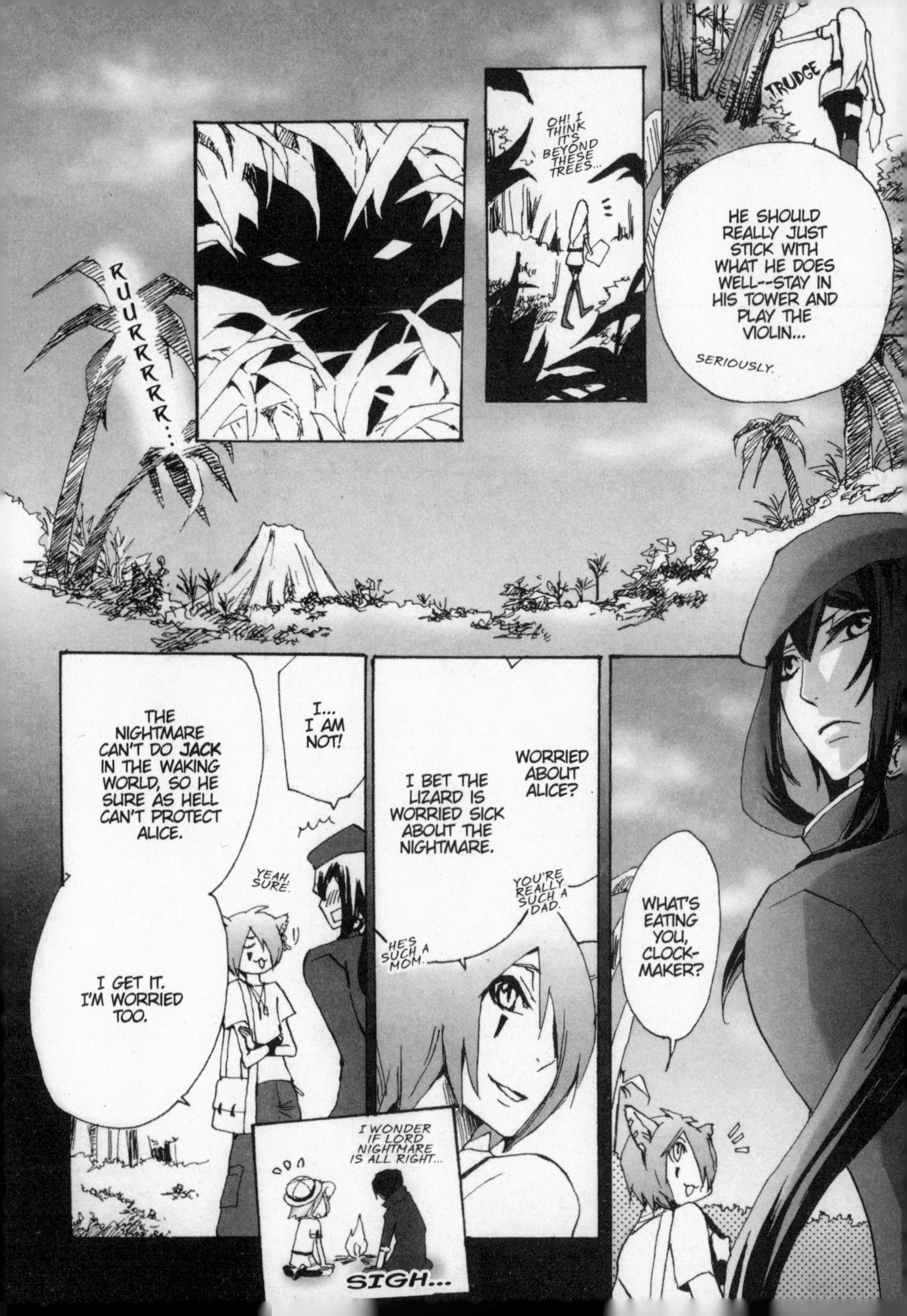
TRUDGE
HE SHOULD REALLY JUST STICK WITH WHAT HE DOES WELL--STAY IN HIS TOWER AND PLAY THE VIOLIN...
SERIOUSLY.
OH! I THINK IT'S BEYOND THESE TREES...
RUURRRRR...
WHAT'S EATING YOU, CLOCK-MAKER?
WORRIED ABOUT ALICE?
I BET THE LIZARD IS WORRIED SICK ABOUT THE NIGHTMARE.
YOU'RE REALLY SUCH A DAD.
HE'S SUCH A MOM.
I... I AM NOT!
THE NIGHTMARE CAN'T DO JACK IN THE WAKING WORLD, SO HE SURE AS HELL CAN'T PROTECT ALICE.
YEAH, SURE.
I GET IT. I'M WORRIED TOO.
I WONDER IF LORD NIGHTMARE IS ALL RIGHT...
SIGH...

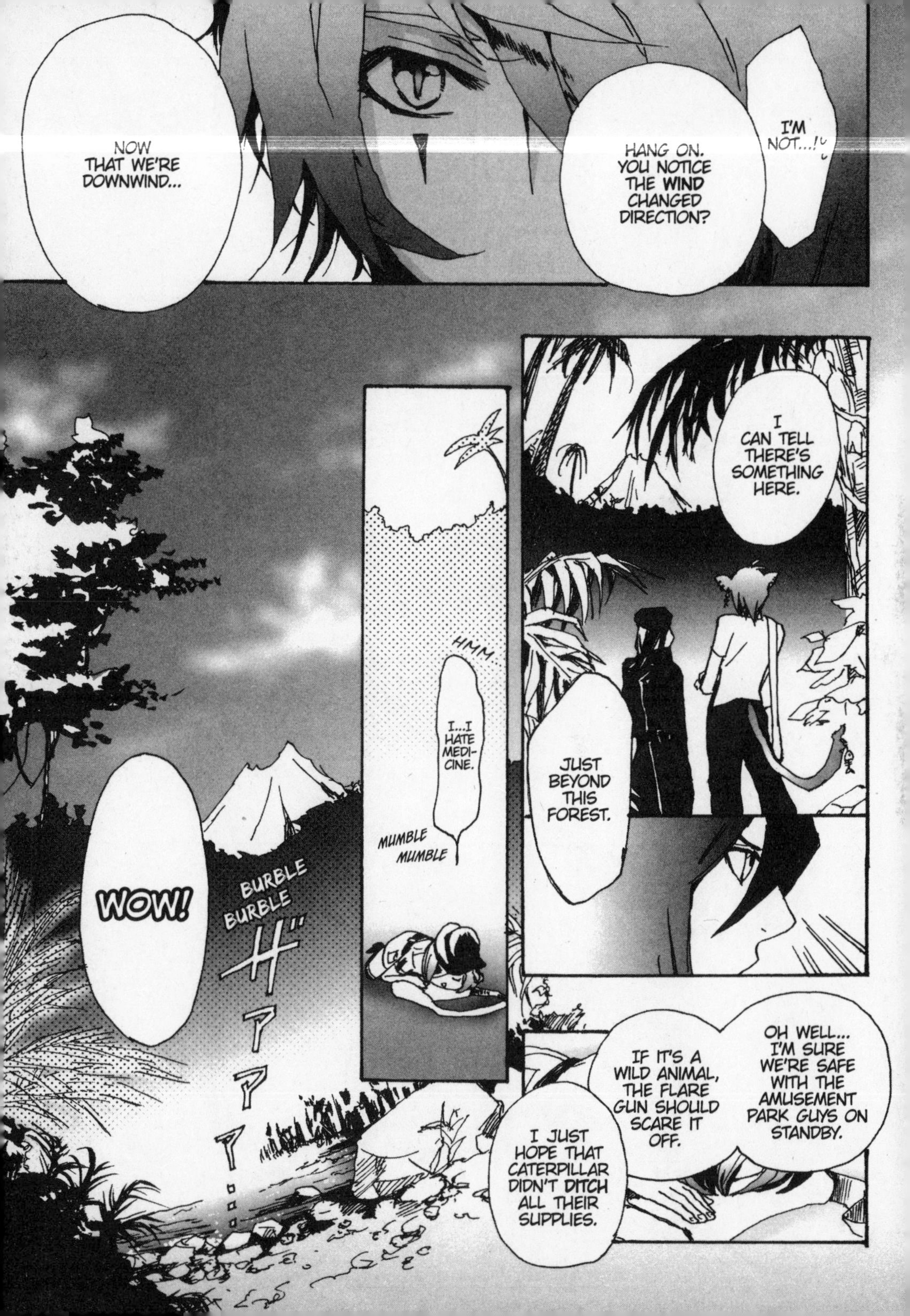
I'M NOT...!!
HANG ON. YOU NOTICE THE WIND CHANGED DIRECTION?
NOW THAT WE'RE DOWNWIND...
I CAN TELL THERE'S SOMETHING HERE.
JUST BEYOND THIS FOREST.
HMM.
I...I HATE MEDICINE.
MUMBLE MUMBLE
WOW!
BURBLE BURBLE
ザアアア…
OH WELL... I'M SURE WE'RE SAFE WITH THE AMUSEMENT PARK GUYS ON STANDBY.
IF IT'S A WILD ANIMAL, THE FLARE GUN SHOULD SCARE IT OFF.
I JUST HOPE THAT CATERPILLAR DIDN'T DITCH ALL THEIR SUPPLIES.

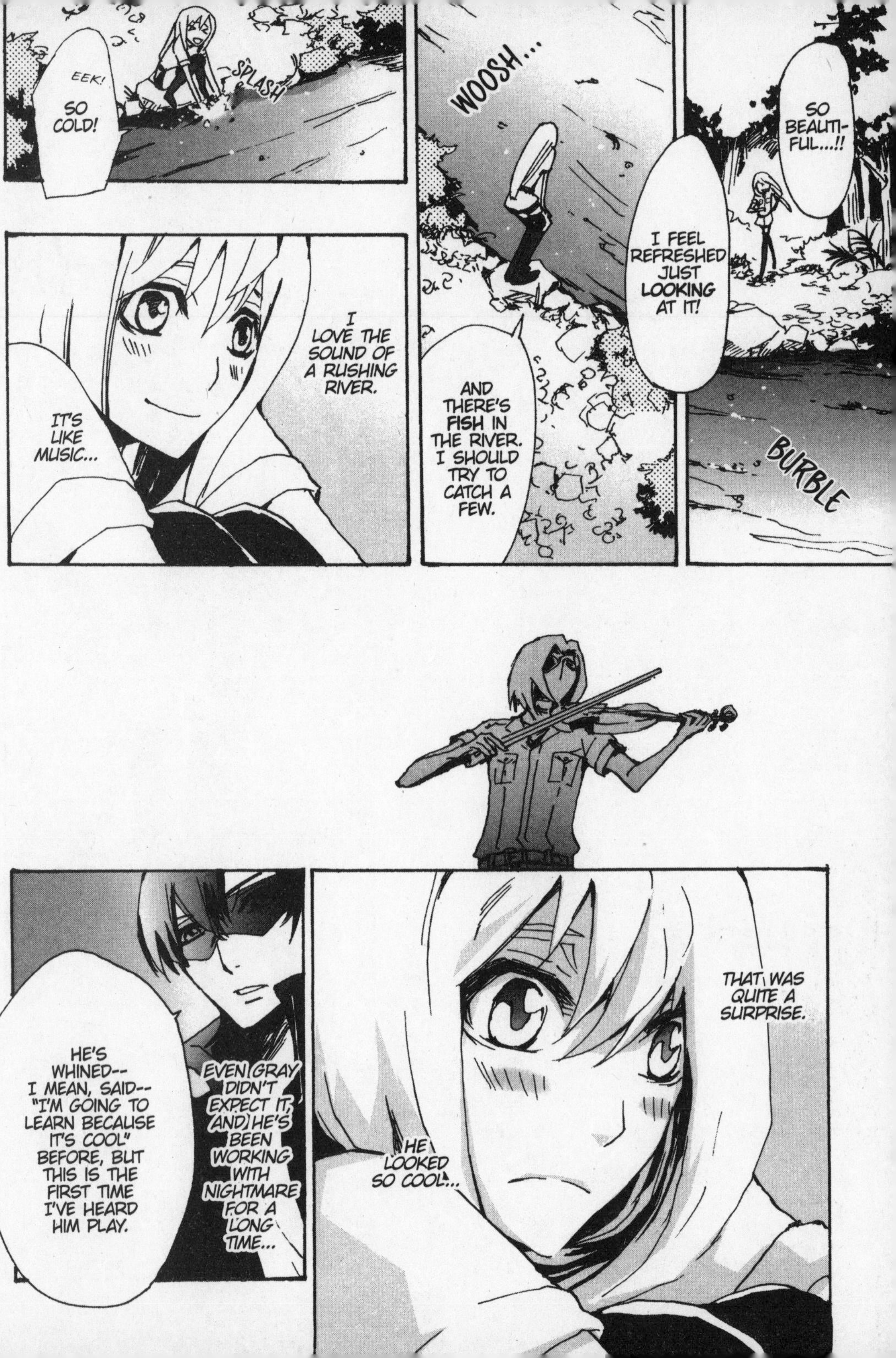
SO BEAUTIFUL...!!
I FEEL REFRESHED JUST LOOKING AT IT!
BURBLE
WOOSH...
AND THERE'S FISH IN THE RIVER. I SHOULD TRY TO CATCH A FEW.
SPLASH
EEK! SO COLD!
I LOVE THE SOUND OF A RUSHING RIVER.
IT'S LIKE MUSIC...
THAT WAS QUITE A SURPRISE.
HE LOOKED SO COOL...
EVEN GRAY DIDN'T EXPECT IT, AND HE'S BEEN WORKING WITH NIGHTMARE FOR A LONG TIME...
HE'S WHINED-- I MEAN, SAID-- "I'M GOING TO LEARN BECAUSE IT'S COOL" BEFORE, BUT THIS IS THE FIRST TIME I'VE HEARD HIM PLAY.

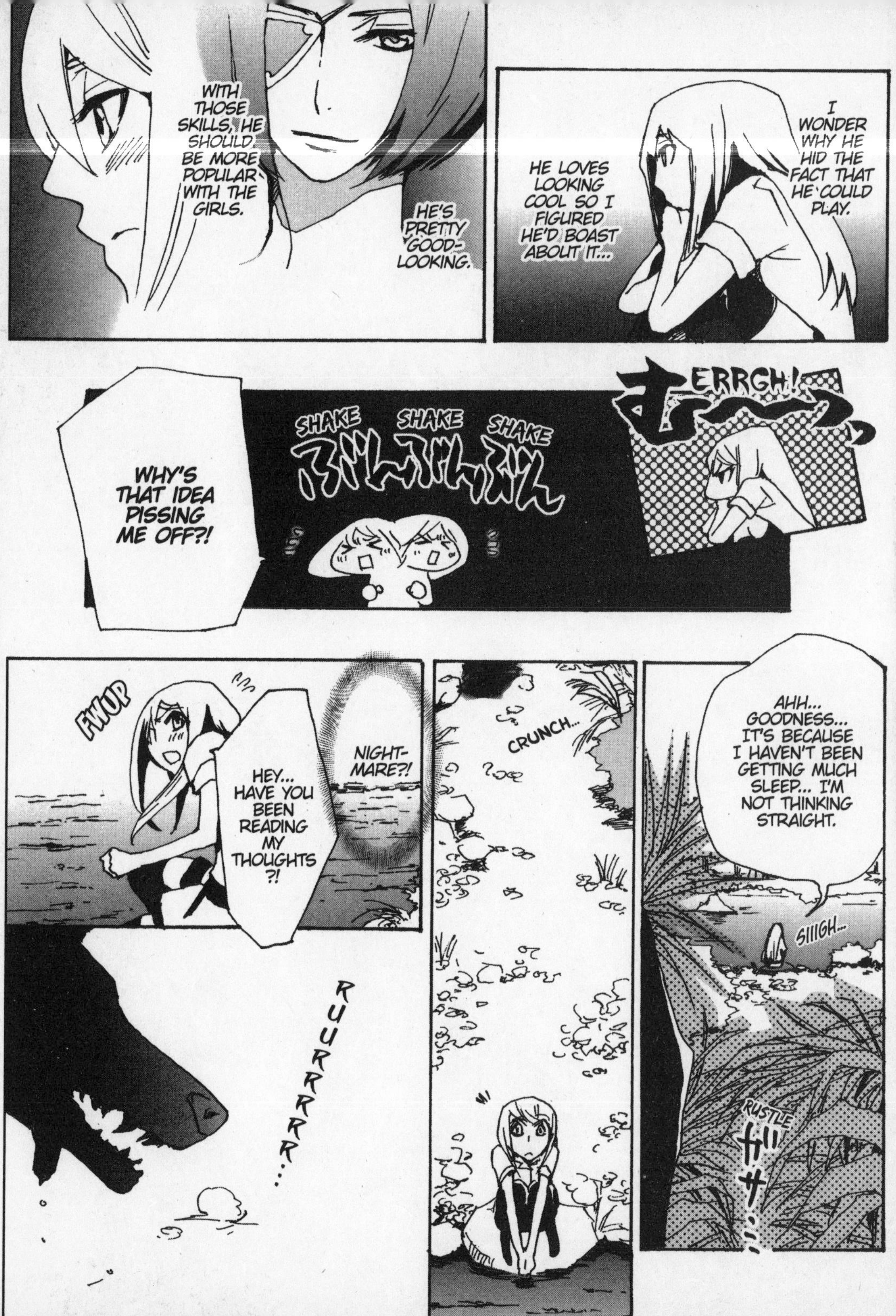
I WONDER WHY HE HID THE FACT THAT HE COULD PLAY.
HE LOVES LOOKING COOL SO I FIGURED HE'D BOAST ABOUT IT...
HE'S PRETTY GOOD-LOOKING.
WITH THOSE SKILLS, HE SHOULD BE MORE POPULAR WITH THE GIRLS.
ERRGH!
SHAKE SHAKE SHAKE
WHY'S THAT IDEA PISSING ME OFF?!
AHH... GOODNESS... IT'S BECAUSE I HAVEN'T BEEN GETTING MUCH SLEEP... I'M NOT THINKING STRAIGHT.
SIIIGH...
RUSTLE
CRUNCH...
FWUP
NIGHT-MARE?!
HEY... HAVE YOU BEEN READING MY THOUGHTS?!
RUURRRRRR...

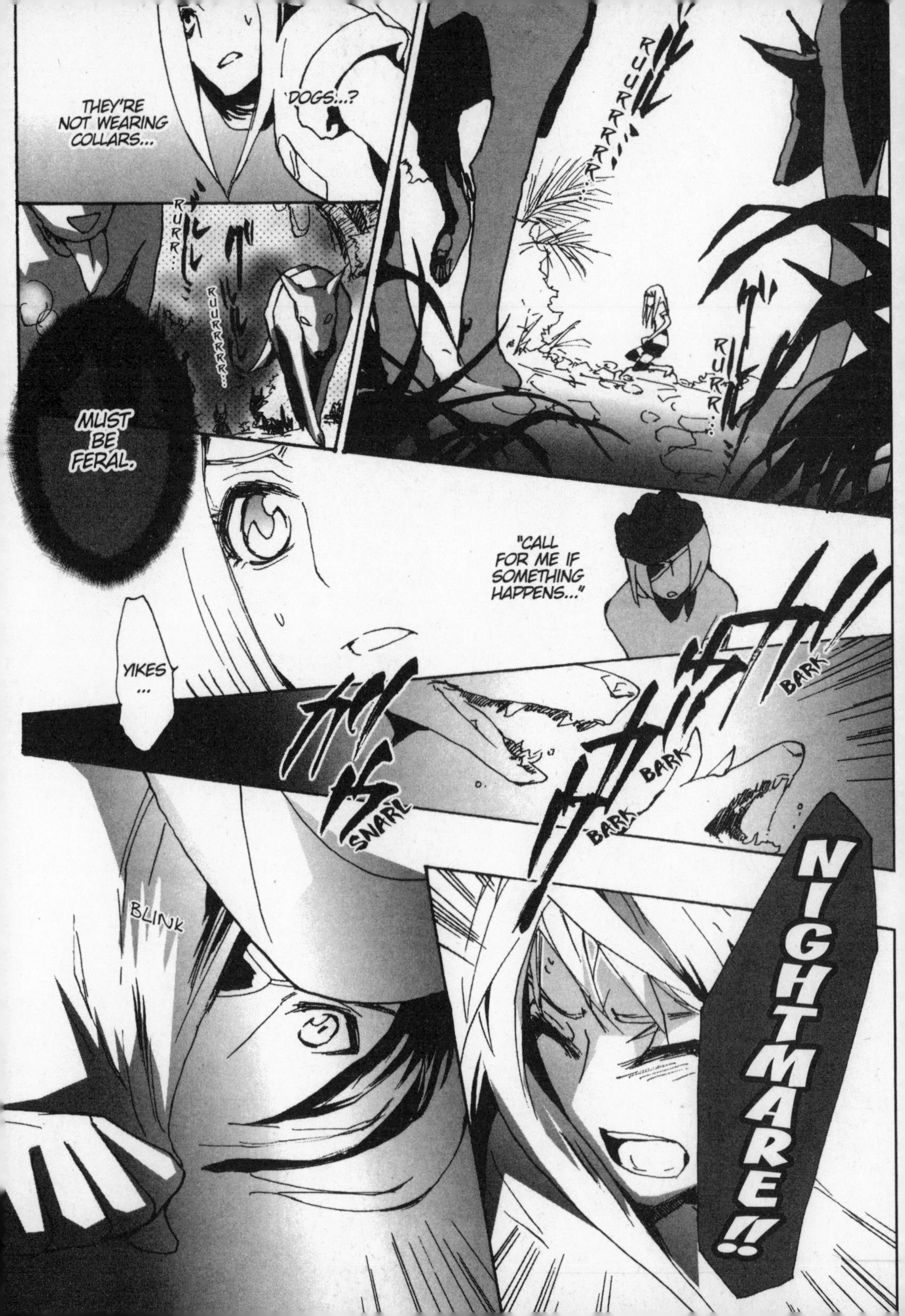
RUURRRRRR...
RURRR...
DOGS...?
THEY'RE NOT WEARING COLLARS...
RURR...
RUURRRRR...
MUST BE FERAL.
"CALL FOR ME IF SOMETHING HAPPENS..."
YIKES...
BARK
BARK
BARK
SNARL
NIGHTMARE!!
BLINK

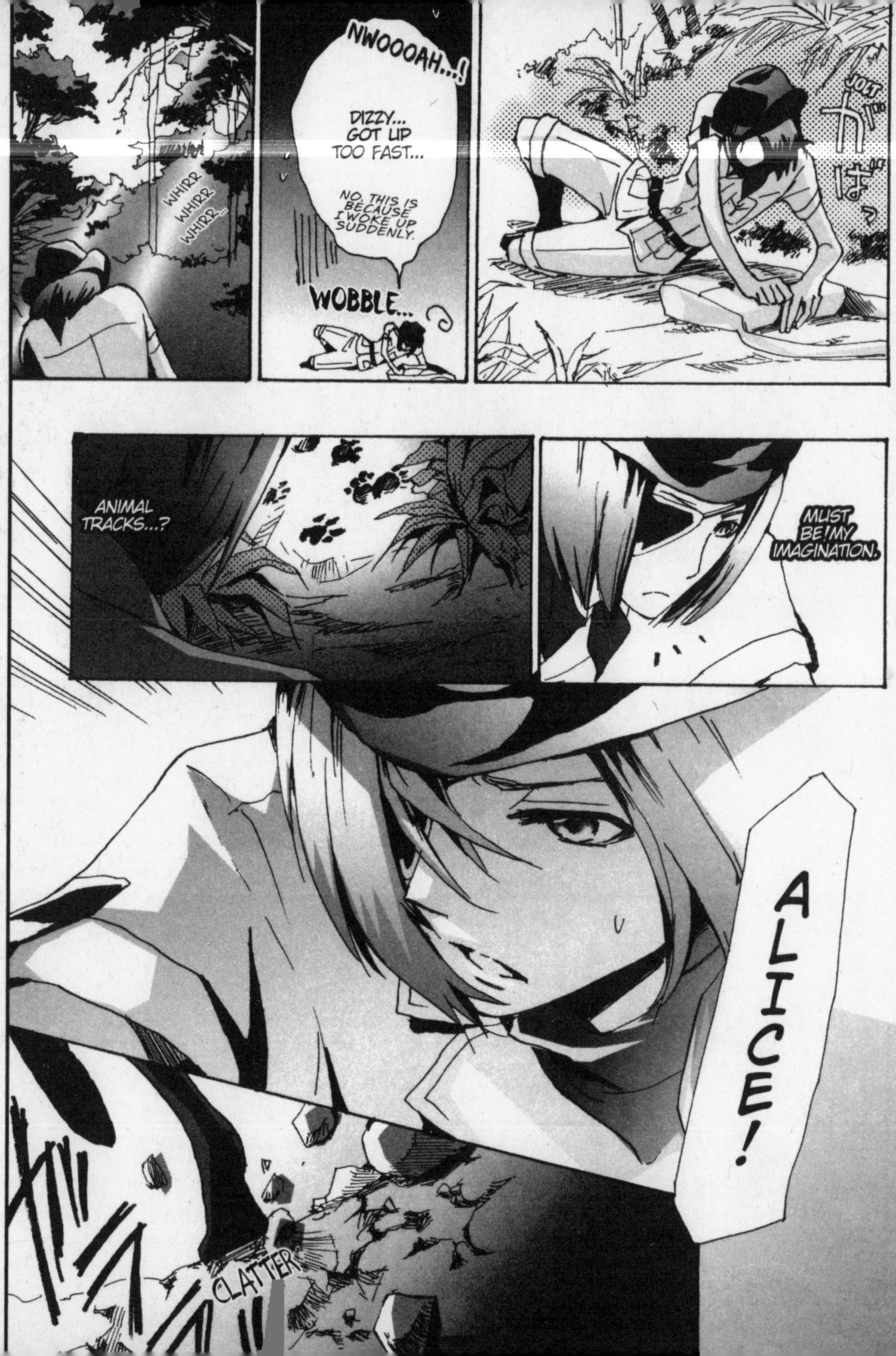
JOLT
NWOOOAH...!
DIZZY... GOT UP TOO FAST...
NO, THIS IS BECAUSE I WOKE UP SUDDENLY.
WOBBLE...
WHIRR WHIRR WHIRR...
MUST BE MY IMAGINATION.
ANIMAL TRACKS...?
ALICE!
CLATTER

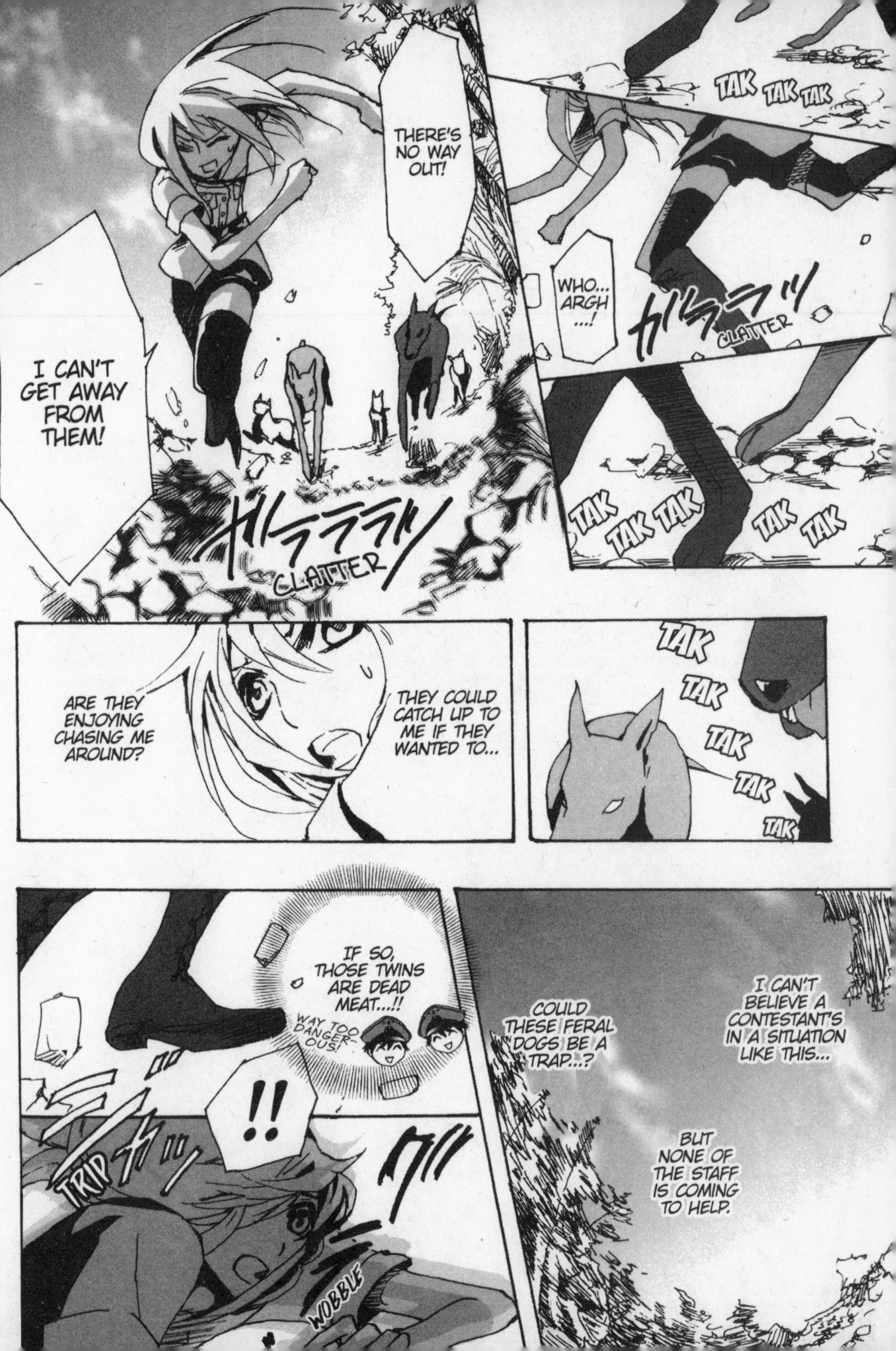
TAK TAK TAK
WHO... ARGH ...!
CLATTER
TAK TAK TAK TAK TAK
THERE'S NO WAY OUT!
I CAN'T GET AWAY FROM THEM!
CLATTER
TAK
TAK
TAK
TAK
TAK
THEY COULD CATCH UP TO ME IF THEY WANTED TO...
ARE THEY ENJOYING CHASING ME AROUND?
I CAN'T BELIEVE A CONTESTANT'S IN A SITUATION LIKE THIS...
COULD THESE FERAL DOGS BE A TRAP...?
BUT NONE OF THE STAFF IS COMING TO HELP.
IF SO, THOSE TWINS ARE DEAD MEAT...!!
WAY TOO DANGER-OUS!
!!
TRIP
WOBBLE

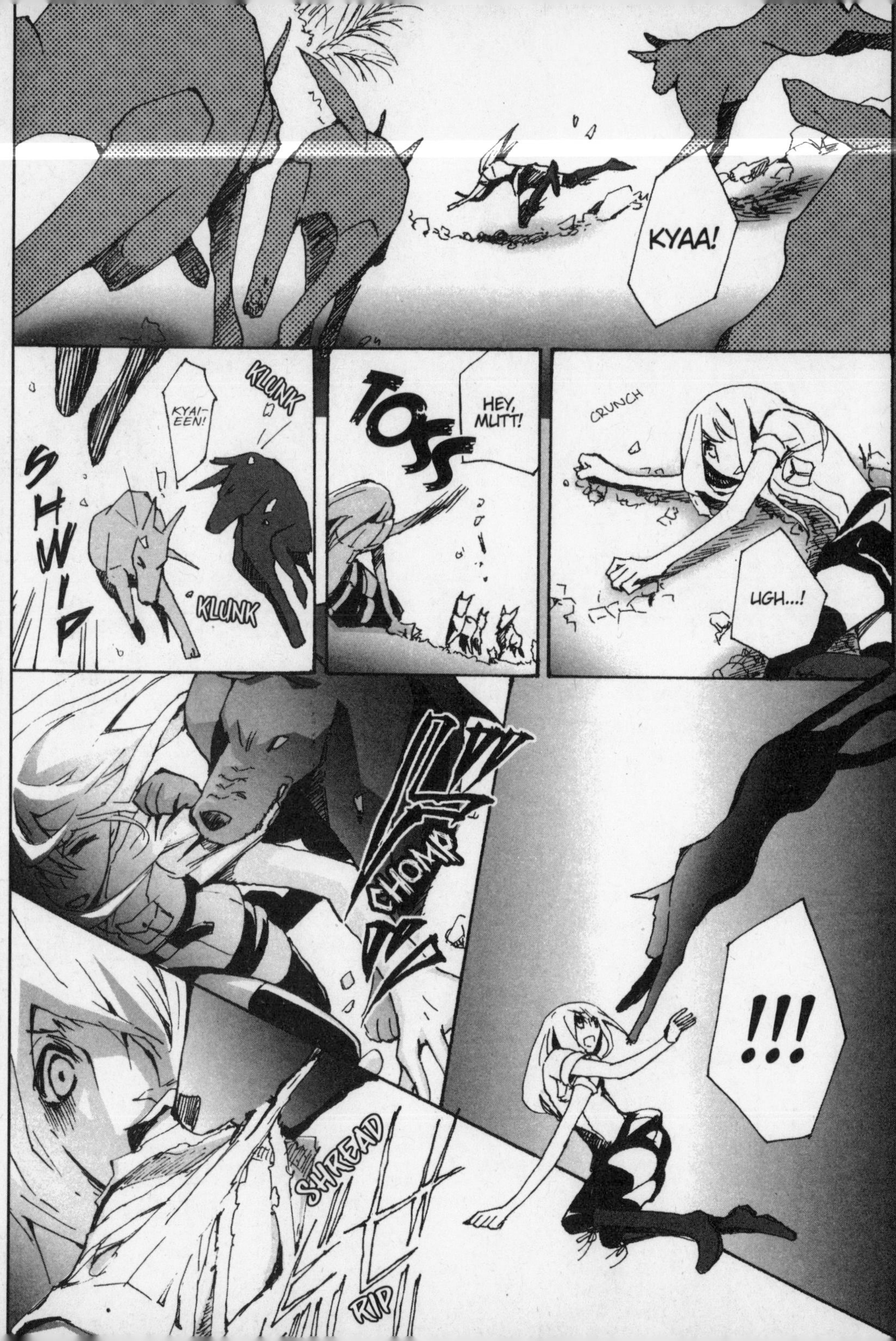
KYAA!
CRUNCH
UGH...!
TOSS
HEY, MUTT!
KLUNK
KYAI-EEN!
SHWIP
KLUNK
!!!
CHOMP
SHREAD
RIP

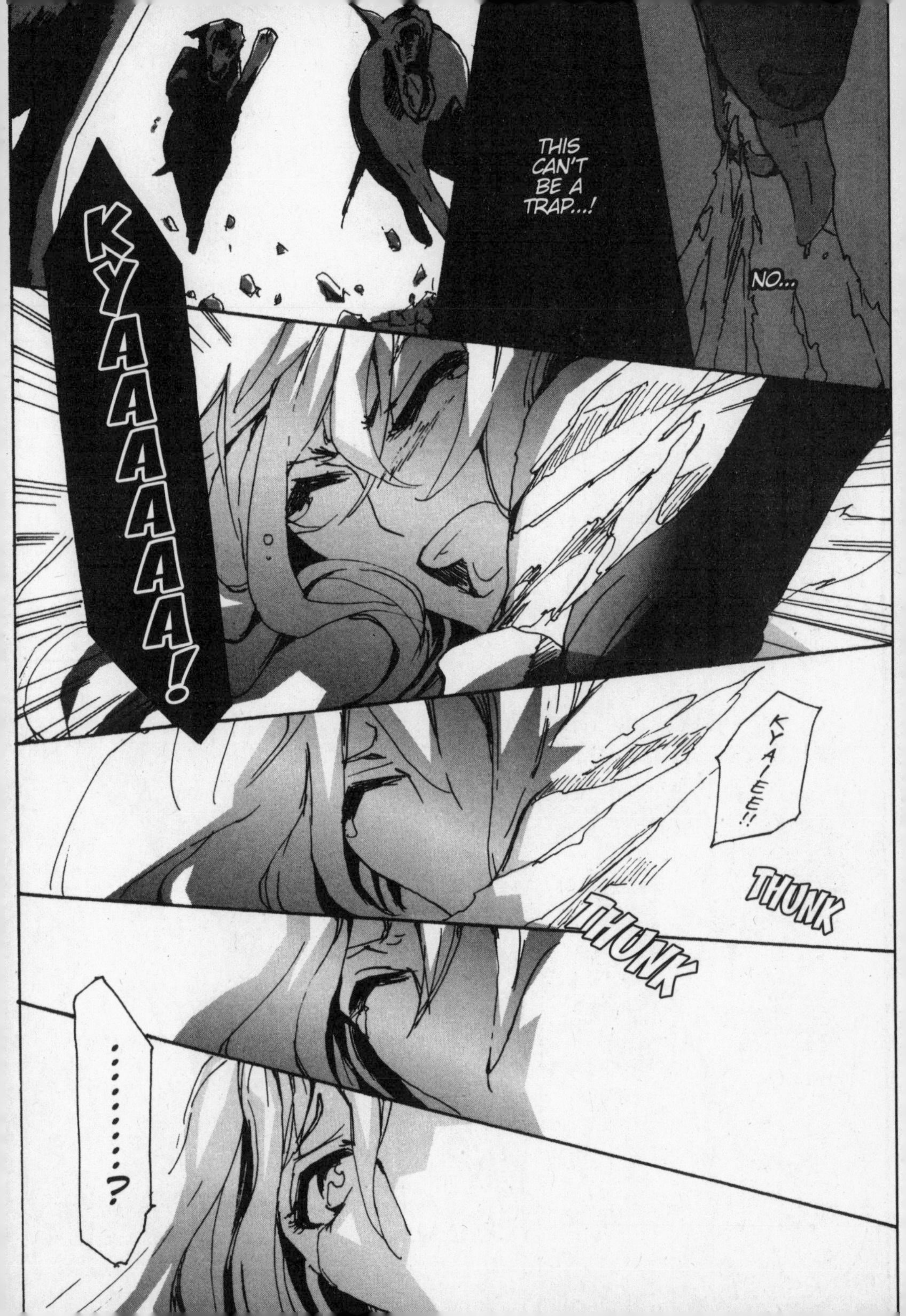
NO...
THIS CAN'T BE A TRAP...!
KYAAAAAAA!
KYAIEE!!
THUNK
THUNK
......?

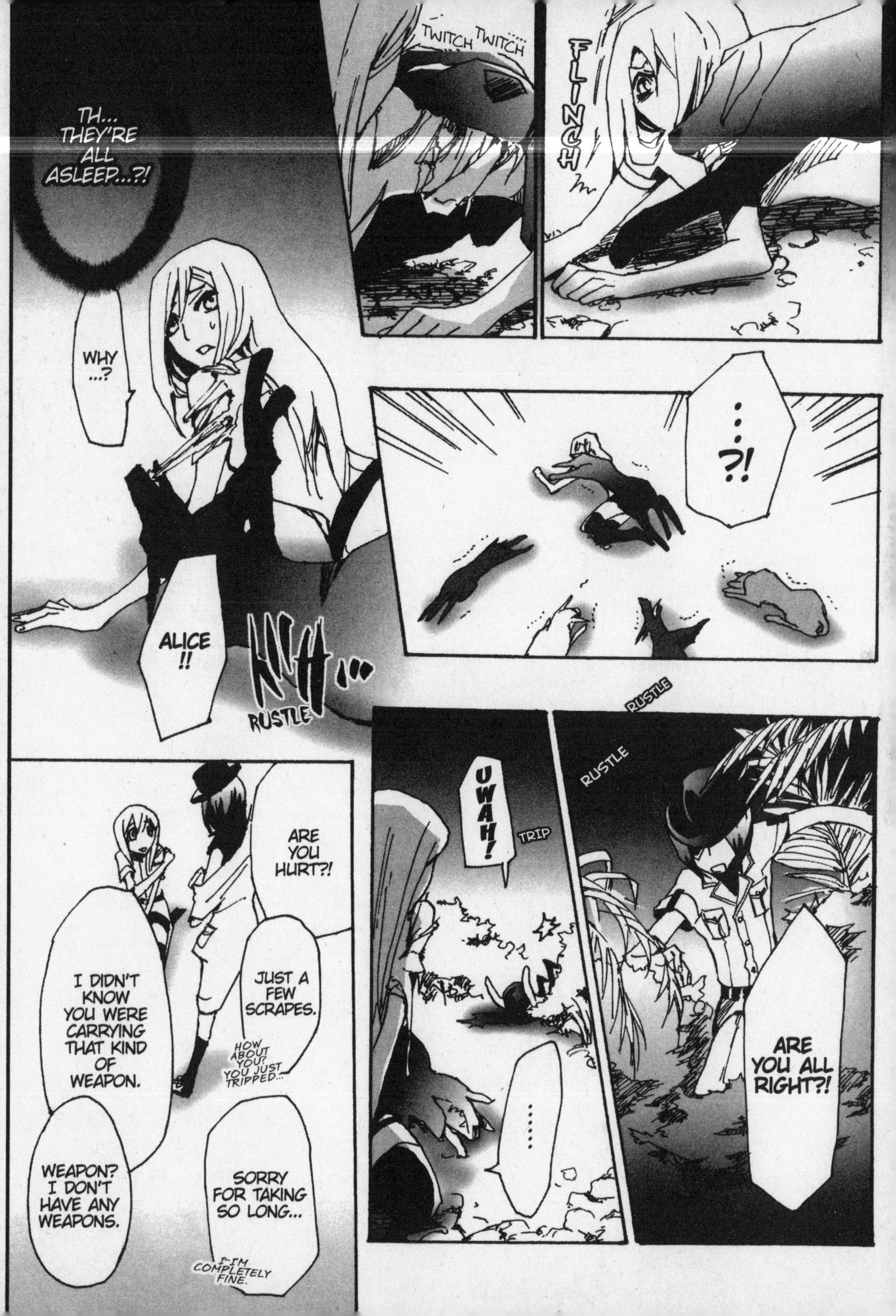
FLINCH
TWITCH TWITCH
......
...?!
TH... THEY'RE ALL ASLEEP...?!
WHY ...?
ALICE !!
RUSTLE
RUSTLE
RUSTLE
ARE YOU ALL RIGHT?!
UWAH!
TRIP
......
ARE YOU HURT?!
JUST A FEW SCRAPES.
HOW ABOUT YOU? YOU JUST TRIPPED...
I DIDN'T KNOW YOU WERE CARRYING THAT KIND OF WEAPON.
SORRY FOR TAKING SO LONG...
I-I'M COMPLETELY FINE.
WEAPON? I DON'T HAVE ANY WEAPONS.

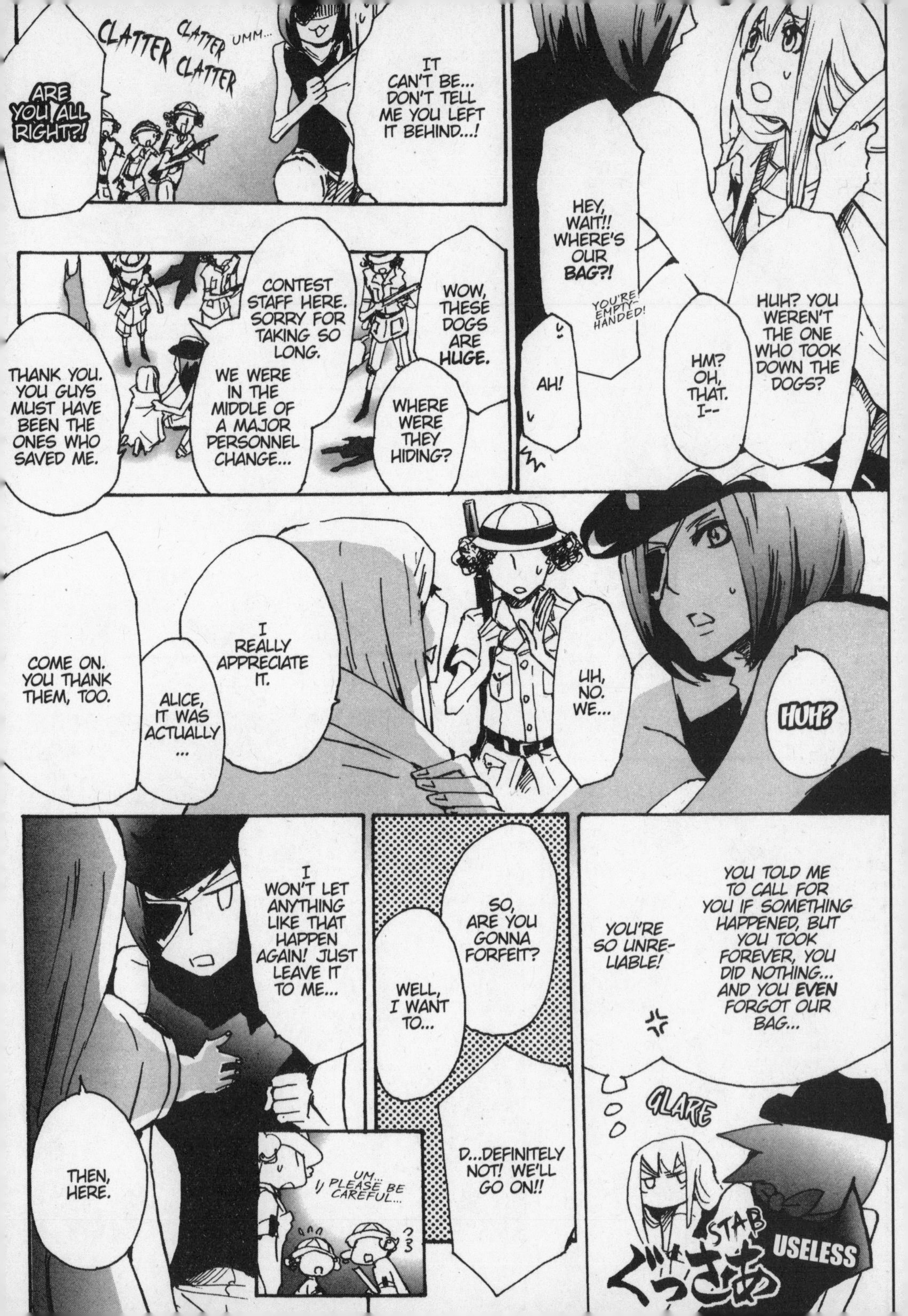
HUH? YOU WEREN'T THE ONE WHO TOOK DOWN THE DOGS?
HM? OH, THAT. I--
AH!
HEY, WAIT!! WHERE'S OUR BAG?!
YOU'RE EMPTY-HANDED!
IT CAN'T BE... DON'T TELL ME YOU LEFT IT BEHIND...!
UMM...
CLATTER CLATTER CLATTER
ARE YOU ALL RIGHT?!
WOW, THESE DOGS ARE HUGE.
WHERE WERE THEY HIDING?
CONTEST STAFF HERE. SORRY FOR TAKING SO LONG.
WE WERE IN THE MIDDLE OF A MAJOR PERSONNEL CHANGE...
THANK YOU. YOU GUYS MUST HAVE BEEN THE ONES WHO SAVED ME.
HUH?
UH, NO. WE...
I REALLY APPRECIATE IT.
ALICE, IT WAS ACTUALLY...
COME ON. YOU THANK THEM, TOO.
YOU TOLD ME TO CALL FOR YOU IF SOMETHING HAPPENED, BUT YOU TOOK FOREVER, YOU DID NOTHING... AND YOU EVEN FORGOT OUR BAG...
YOU'RE SO UNRE-LIABLE!
GLARE
STAB
ぐっさあ
USELESS
SO, ARE YOU GONNA FORFEIT?
WELL, I WANT TO...
D...DEFINITELY NOT! WE'LL GO ON!!
UM... PLEASE BE CAREFUL...
I WON'T LET ANYTHING LIKE THAT HAPPEN AGAIN! JUST LEAVE IT TO ME...
THEN, HERE.

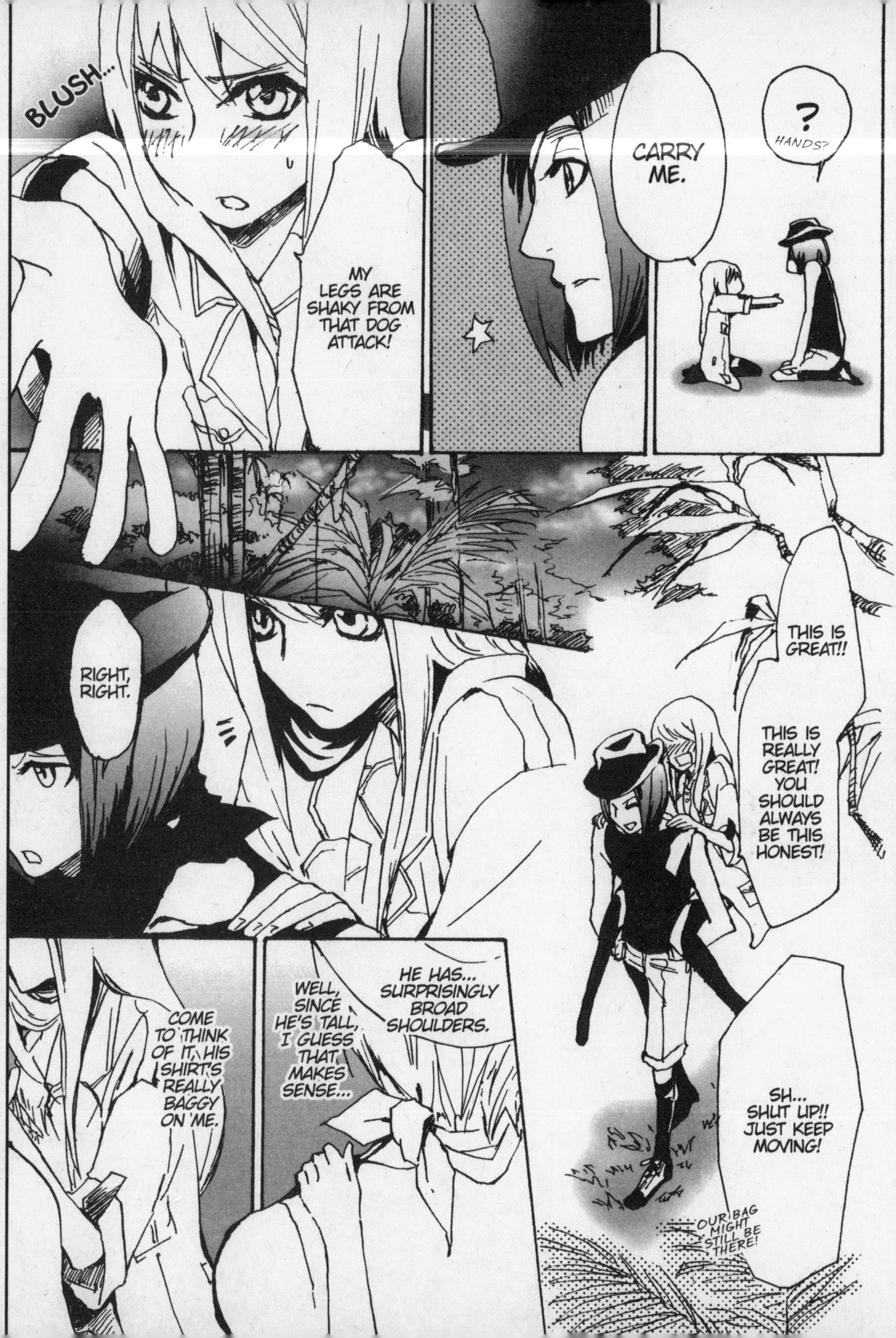
?
HANDS?
CARRY ME.
BLUSH...
MY LEGS ARE SHAKY FROM THAT DOG ATTACK!
THIS IS GREAT!!
THIS IS REALLY GREAT! YOU SHOULD ALWAYS BE THIS HONEST!
SH... SHUT UP!! JUST KEEP MOVING!
OUR BAG MIGHT STILL BE THERE!
RIGHT, RIGHT.
HE HAS... SURPRISINGLY BROAD SHOULDERS.
WELL, SINCE HE'S TALL, I GUESS THAT MAKES SENSE...
COME TO THINK OF IT, HIS SHIRT'S REALLY BAGGY ON ME.

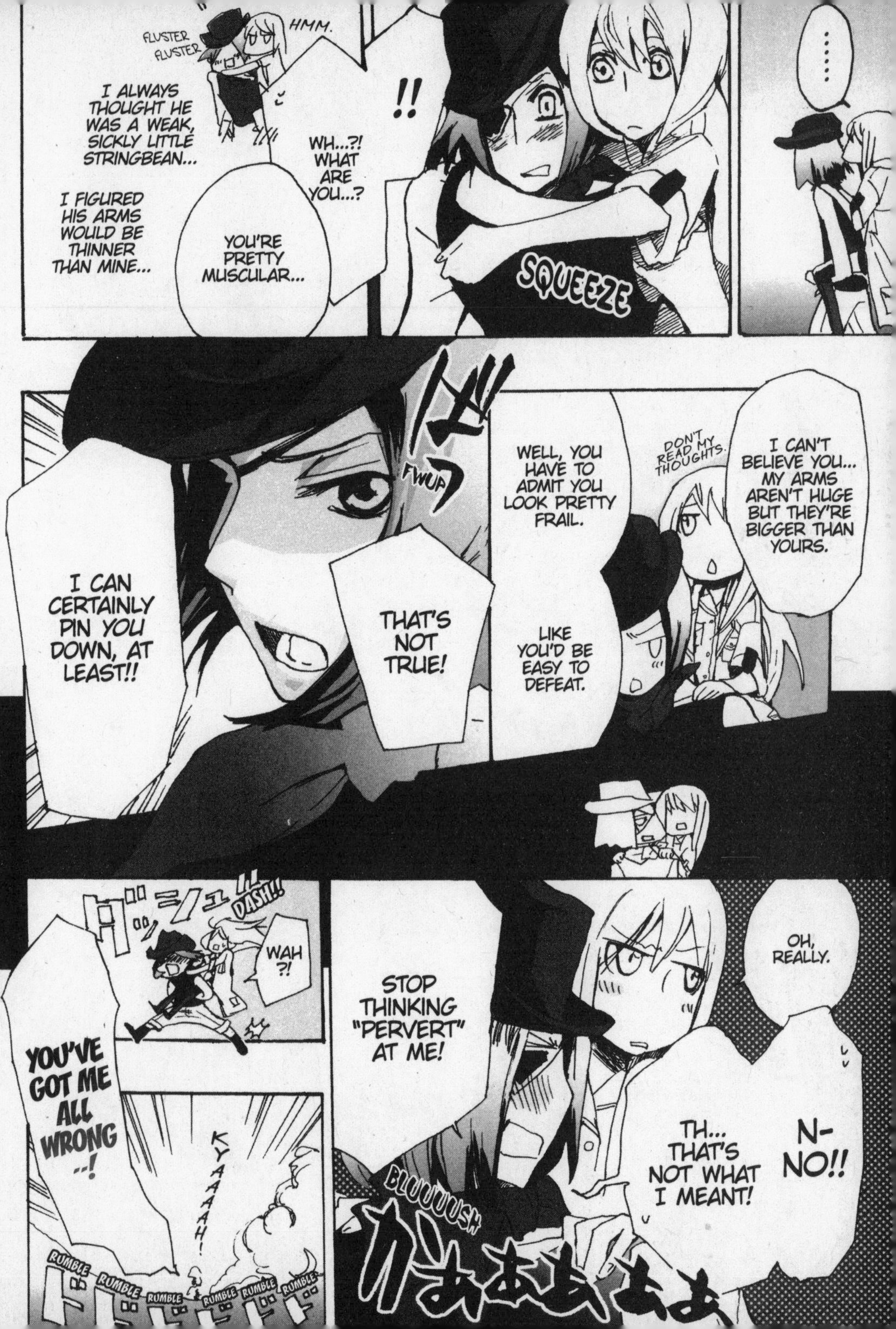
......
!!
WH...?! WHAT ARE YOU...?
SQUEEZE
HMM.
FLUSTER FLUSTER
YOU'RE PRETTY MUSCULAR...
I ALWAYS THOUGHT HE WAS A WEAK, SICKLY LITTLE STRINGBEAN...
I FIGURED HIS ARMS WOULD BE THINNER THAN MINE...
I CAN'T BELIEVE YOU... MY ARMS AREN'T HUGE BUT THEY'RE BIGGER THAN YOURS.
DON'T READ MY THOUGHTS.
WELL, YOU HAVE TO ADMIT YOU LOOK PRETTY FRAIL.
LIKE YOU'D BE EASY TO DEFEAT.
FWUP
THAT'S NOT TRUE!
I CAN CERTAINLY PIN YOU DOWN, AT LEAST!!
OH, REALLY.
N-NO!!
TH... THAT'S NOT WHAT I MEANT!
STOP THINKING "PERVERT" AT ME!
BLUUUUSH
DASH!!
WAH?!
YOU'VE GOT ME ALL WRONG--!
KYAAAAAH!
RUMBLE RUMBLE RUMBLE RUMBLE RUMBLE RUMBLE

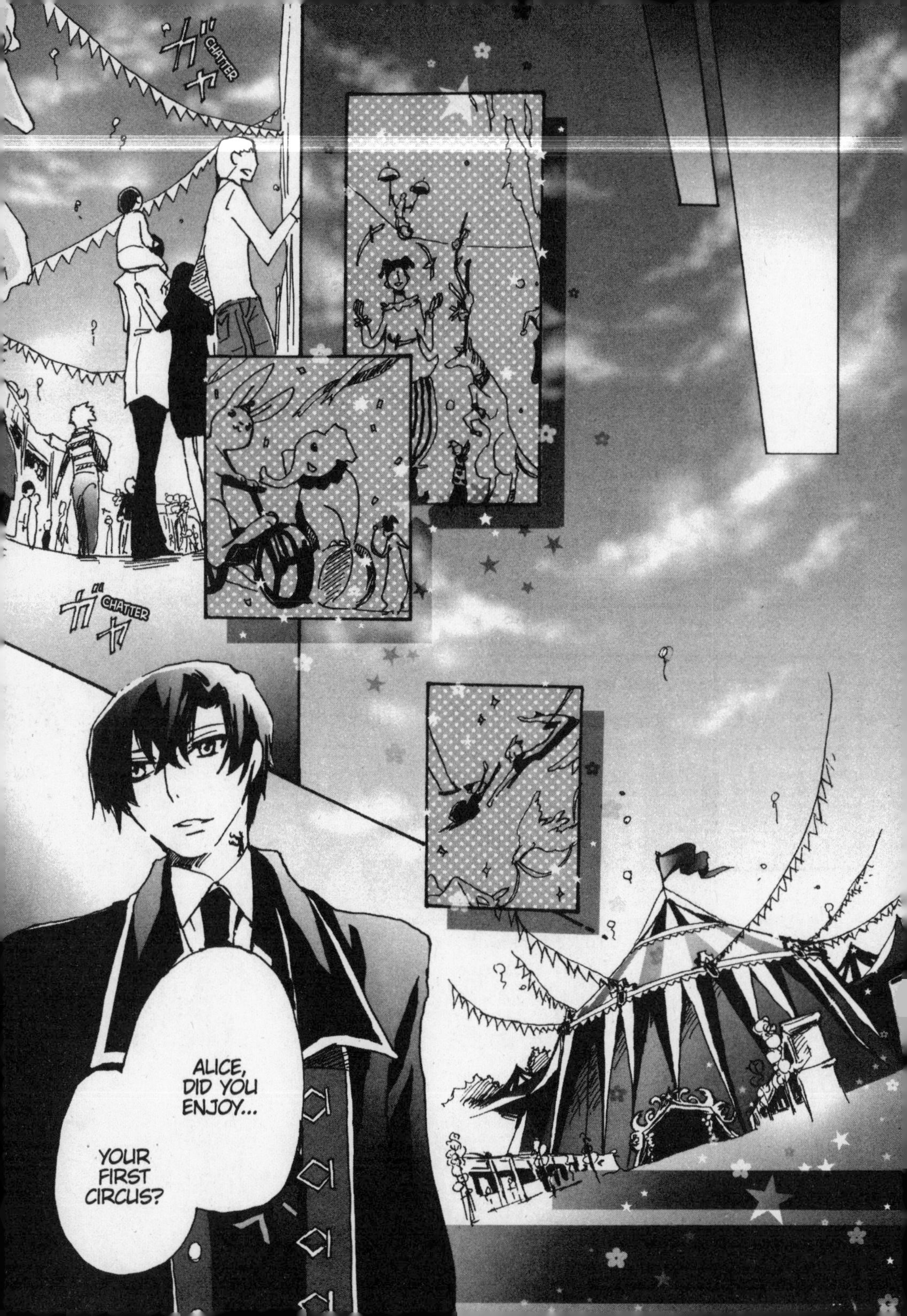
ガヤ CHATTER
ガヤ CHATTER
ALICE, DID YOU ENJOY...
YOUR FIRST CIRCUS?

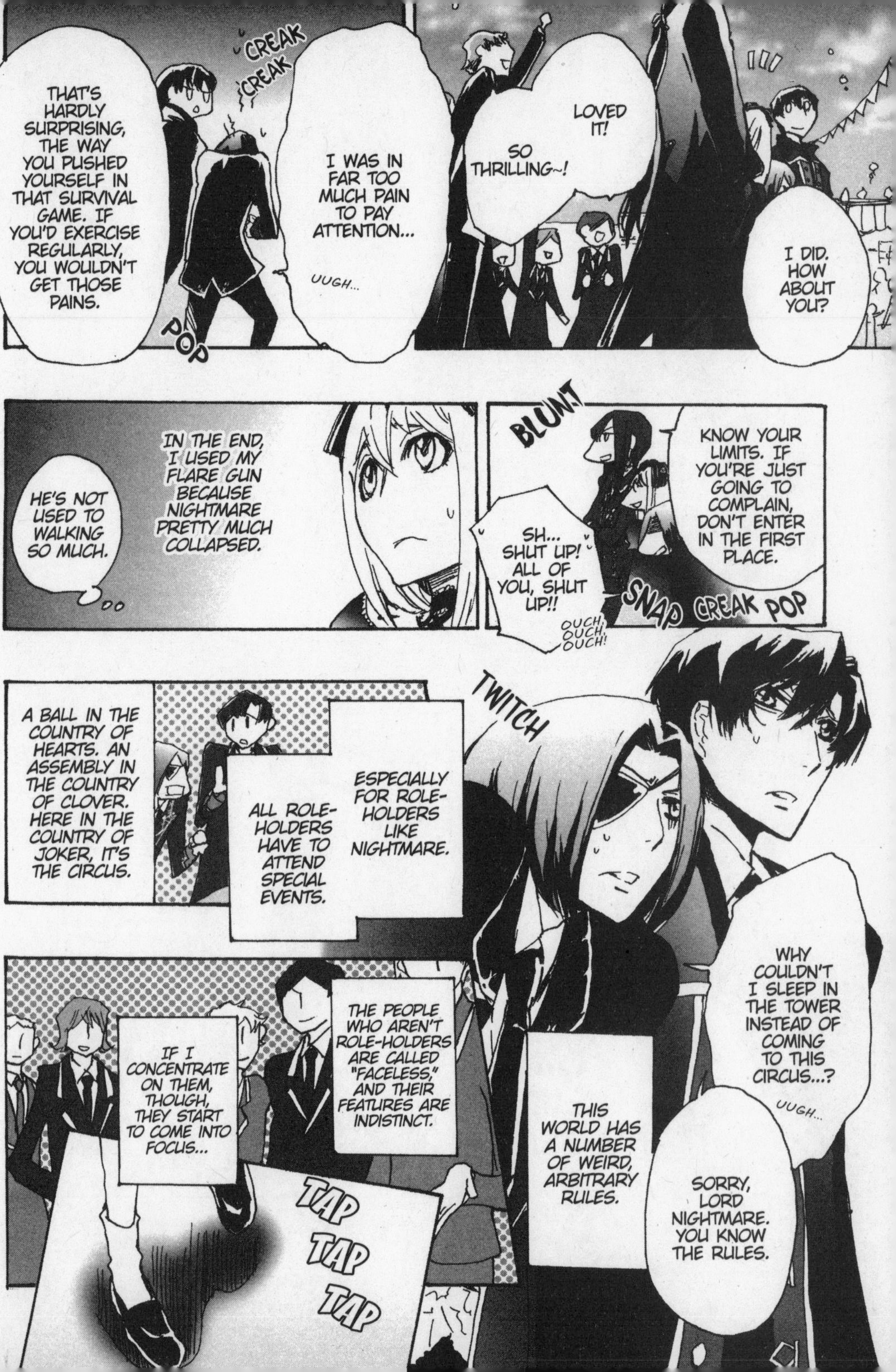
I DID. HOW ABOUT YOU?
LOVED IT!
SO THRILLING~!
I WAS IN FAR TOO MUCH PAIN TO PAY ATTENTION...
UUGH...
CREAK CREAK
THAT'S HARDLY SURPRISING, THE WAY YOU PUSHED YOURSELF IN THAT SURVIVAL GAME. IF YOU'D EXERCISE REGULARLY, YOU WOULDN'T GET THOSE PAINS.
POP
BLUNT
KNOW YOUR LIMITS. IF YOU'RE JUST GOING TO COMPLAIN, DON'T ENTER IN THE FIRST PLACE.
SH... SHUT UP! ALL OF YOU, SHUT UP!!
OUCH, OUCH, OUCH!
SNAP CREAK POP
IN THE END, I USED MY FLARE GUN BECAUSE NIGHTMARE PRETTY MUCH COLLAPSED.
HE'S NOT USED TO WALKING SO MUCH.
TWITCH
WHY COULDN'T I SLEEP IN THE TOWER INSTEAD OF COMING TO THIS CIRCUS...?
UUGH...
SORRY, LORD NIGHTMARE. YOU KNOW THE RULES.
ESPECIALLY FOR ROLE-HOLDERS LIKE NIGHTMARE.
ALL ROLE-HOLDERS HAVE TO ATTEND SPECIAL EVENTS.
A BALL IN THE COUNTRY OF HEARTS. AN ASSEMBLY IN THE COUNTRY OF CLOVER. HERE IN THE COUNTRY OF JOKER, IT'S THE CIRCUS.
THIS WORLD HAS A NUMBER OF WEIRD, ARBITRARY RULES.
THE PEOPLE WHO AREN'T ROLE-HOLDERS ARE CALLED "FACELESS," AND THEIR FEATURES ARE INDISTINCT.
IF I CONCENTRATE ON THEM, THOUGH, THEY START TO COME INTO FOCUS...
TAP
TAP
TAP

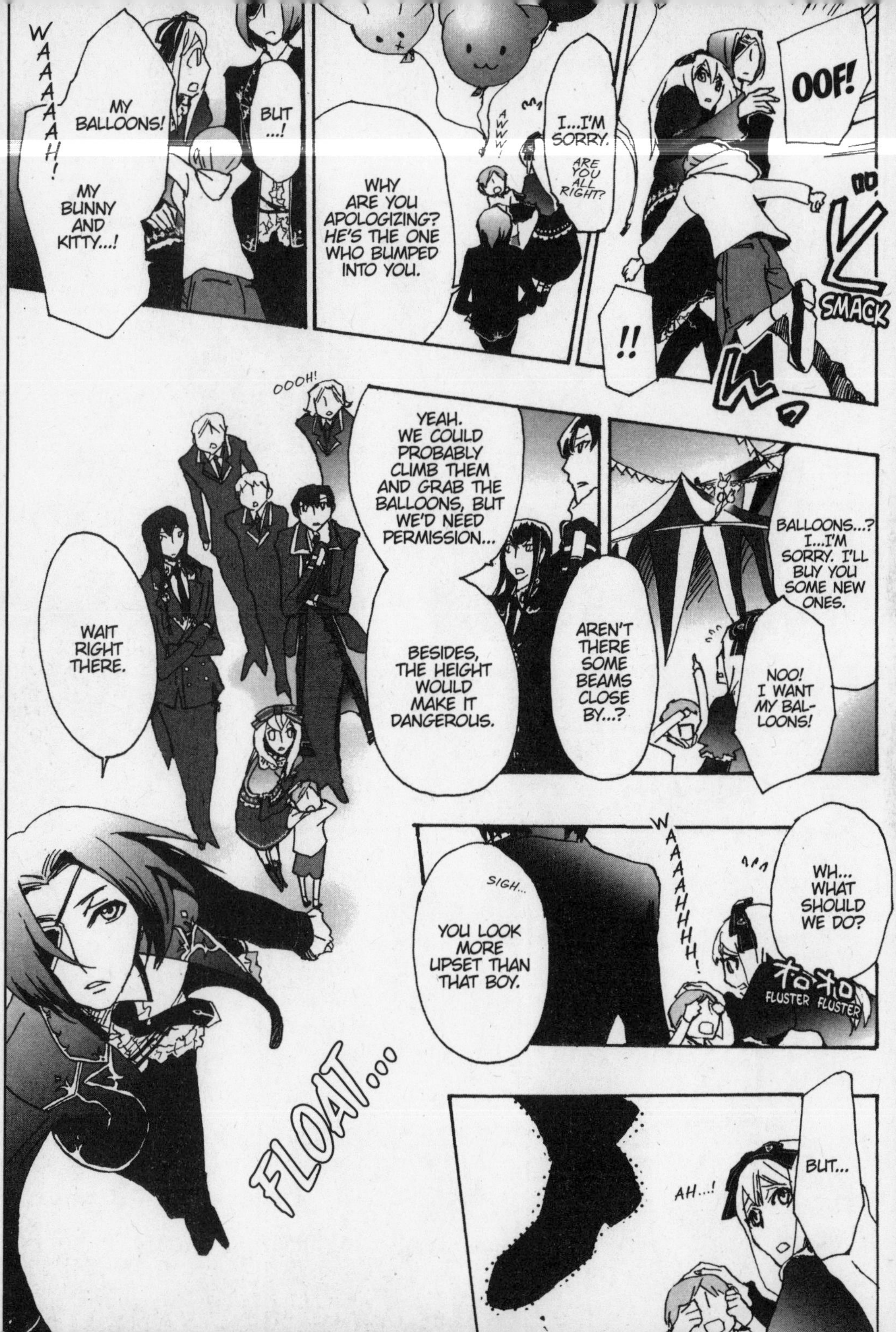
OOF!
SMACK
!!
I...I'M SORRY.
ARE YOU ALL RIGHT?
AWWW!
WHY ARE YOU APOLOGIZING? HE'S THE ONE WHO BUMPED INTO YOU.
WAAAAAAH!
MY BALLOONS!
BUT ...!
MY BUNNY AND KITTY...!
BALLOONS...? I...I'M SORRY. I'LL BUY YOU SOME NEW ONES.
NOO! I WANT MY BAL-LOONS!
AREN'T THERE SOME BEAMS CLOSE BY...?
YEAH. WE COULD PROBABLY CLIMB THEM AND GRAB THE BALLOONS, BUT WE'D NEED PERMISSION...
BESIDES, THE HEIGHT WOULD MAKE IT DANGEROUS.
WH... WHAT SHOULD WE DO?
FLUSTER FLUSTER
WAAAAHHHH!
SIGH...
YOU LOOK MORE UPSET THAN THAT BOY.
BUT...
AH...!
OOOH!
WAIT RIGHT THERE.
FLOAT...

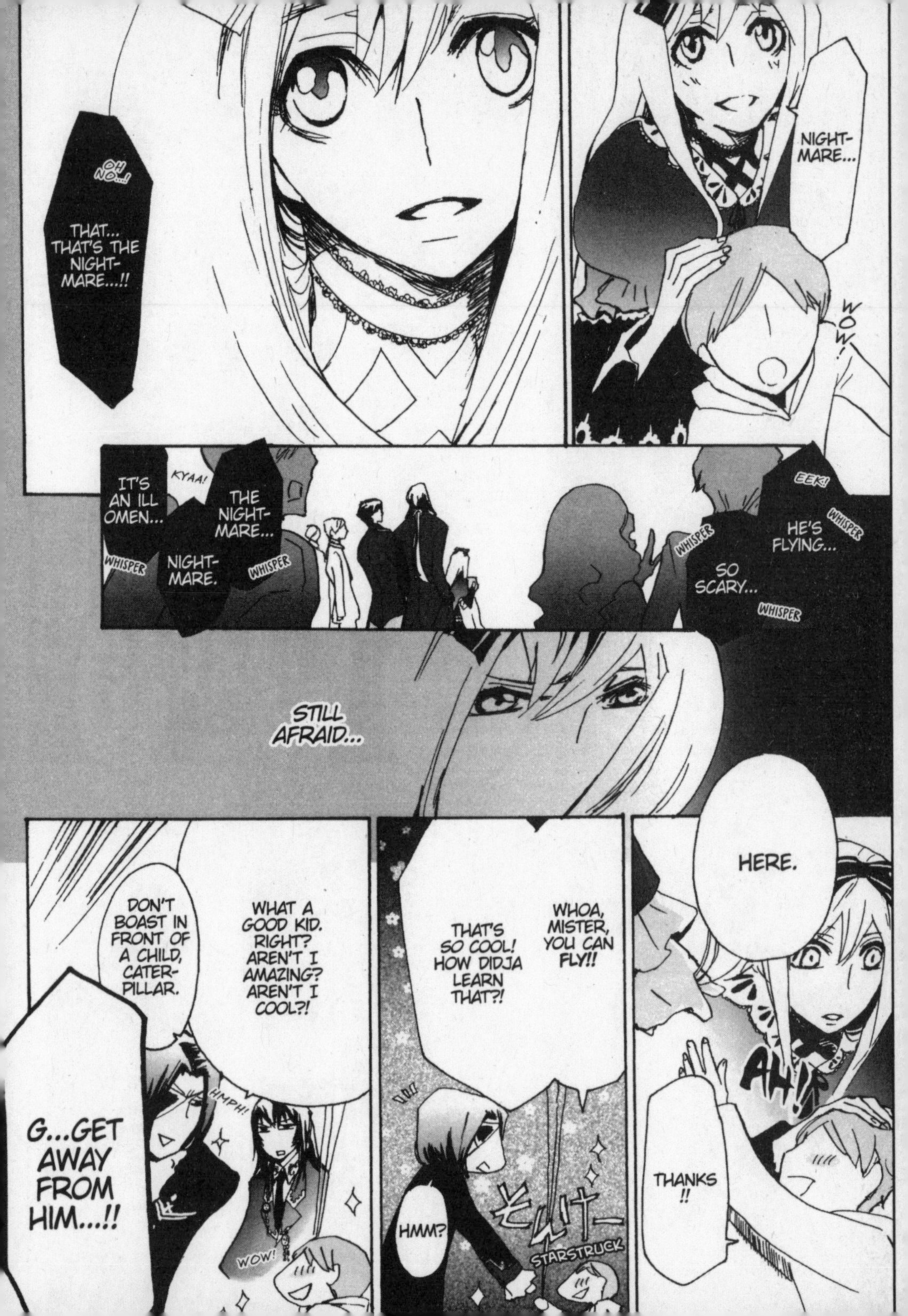
NIGHT-MARE...
WOW!
OH NO...!
THAT... THAT'S THE NIGHT-MARE...!!
EEK!
HE'S FLYING...
WHISPER
WHISPER
SO SCARY...
WHISPER
THE NIGHT-MARE...
KYAA!
IT'S AN ILL OMEN...
NIGHT-MARE.
WHISPER
WHISPER
STILL AFRAID...
HERE.
AH!
THANKS!!
WHOA, MISTER, YOU CAN FLY!!
THAT'S SO COOL! HOW DIDJA LEARN THAT?!
HMM?
そんけー
STARSTRUCK
WHAT A GOOD KID. RIGHT? AREN'T I AMAZING? AREN'T I COOL?!
DON'T BOAST IN FRONT OF A CHILD, CATER-PILLAR.
HMPH!
WOW!
G...GET AWAY FROM HIM...!!

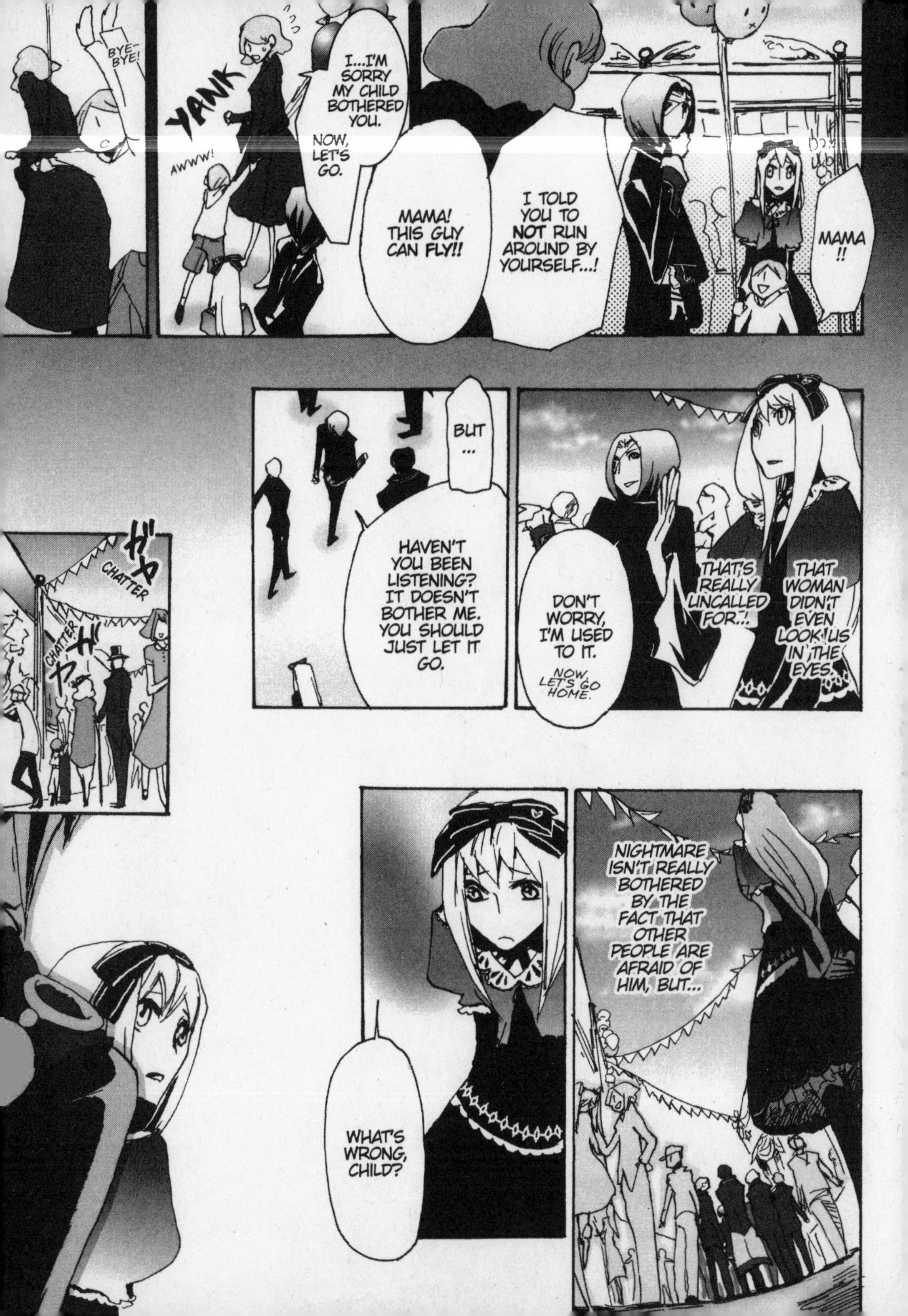
MAMA!!
I TOLD YOU TO NOT RUN AROUND BY YOURSELF...!
MAMA! THIS GUY CAN FLY!!
I...I'M SORRY MY CHILD BOTHERED YOU.
NOW, LET'S GO.
YANK
AWWW!
BYE-BYE!
THAT WOMAN DIDN'T EVEN LOOK US IN THE EYES.
THAT'S REALLY UNCALLED FOR...!
DON'T WORRY, I'M USED TO IT.
NOW, LET'S GO HOME.
BUT ...
HAVEN'T YOU BEEN LISTENING? IT DOESN'T BOTHER ME. YOU SHOULD JUST LET IT GO.
ガヤ
CHATTER
ガヤ
CHATTER
NIGHTMARE ISN'T REALLY BOTHERED BY THE FACT THAT OTHER PEOPLE ARE AFRAID OF HIM, BUT...
WHAT'S WRONG, CHILD?

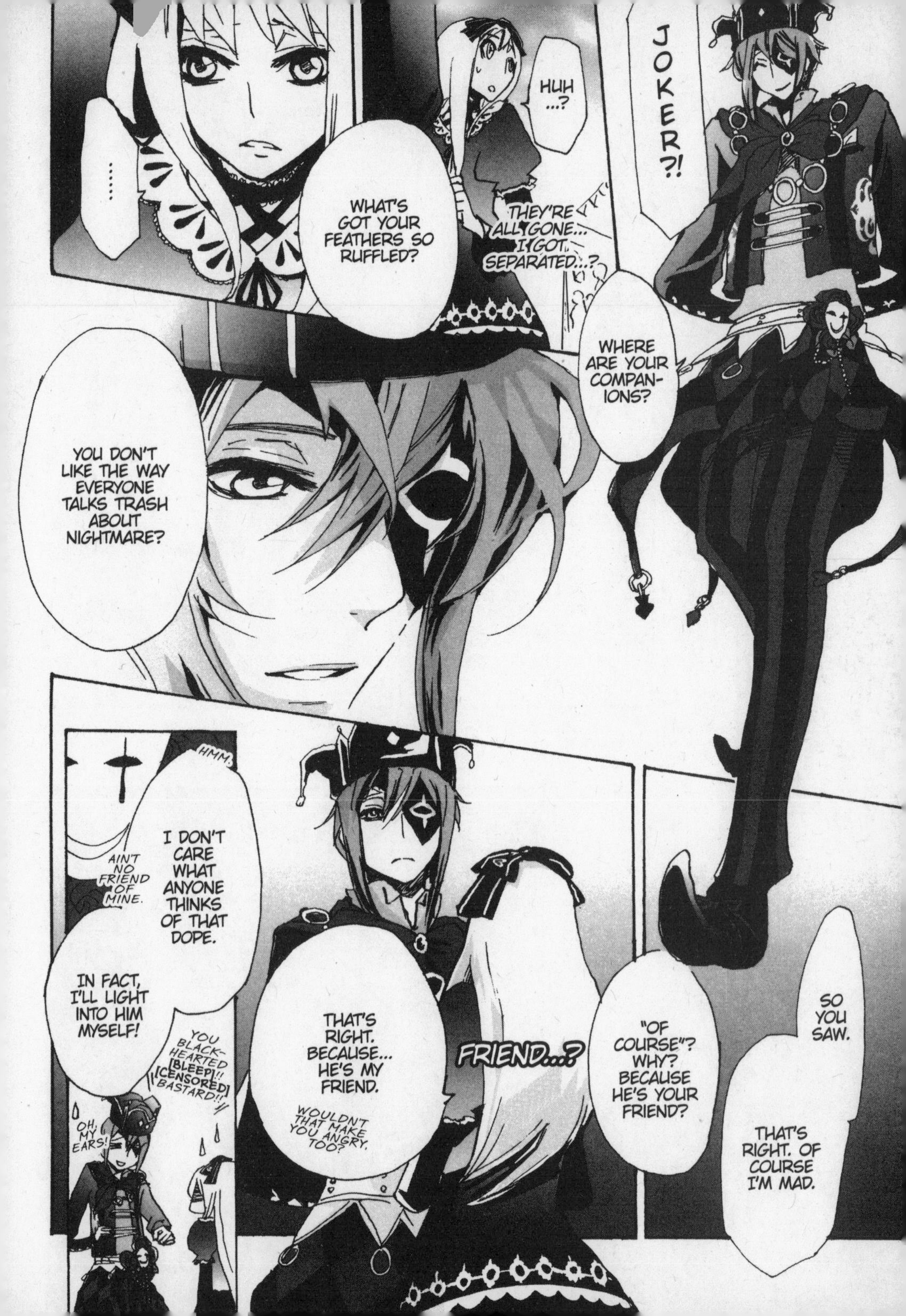
JOKER?!
HUH ...?
THEY'RE ALL GONE... I GOT SEPARATED...?
WHERE ARE YOUR COMPANIONS?
WHAT'S GOT YOUR FEATHERS SO RUFFLED?
......
YOU DON'T LIKE THE WAY EVERYONE TALKS TRASH ABOUT NIGHTMARE?
SO YOU SAW.
THAT'S RIGHT. OF COURSE I'M MAD.
"OF COURSE"? WHY? BECAUSE HE'S YOUR FRIEND?
FRIEND...?
THAT'S RIGHT. BECAUSE... HE'S MY FRIEND.
WOULDN'T THAT MAKE YOU ANGRY, TOO?
HMM.
I DON'T CARE WHAT ANYONE THINKS OF THAT DOPE.
AIN'T NO FRIEND OF MINE.
IN FACT, I'LL LIGHT INTO HIM MYSELF!
YOU BLACK-HEARTED [BLEEP]!! [CENSORED] BASTARD!!
OH, MY EARS!

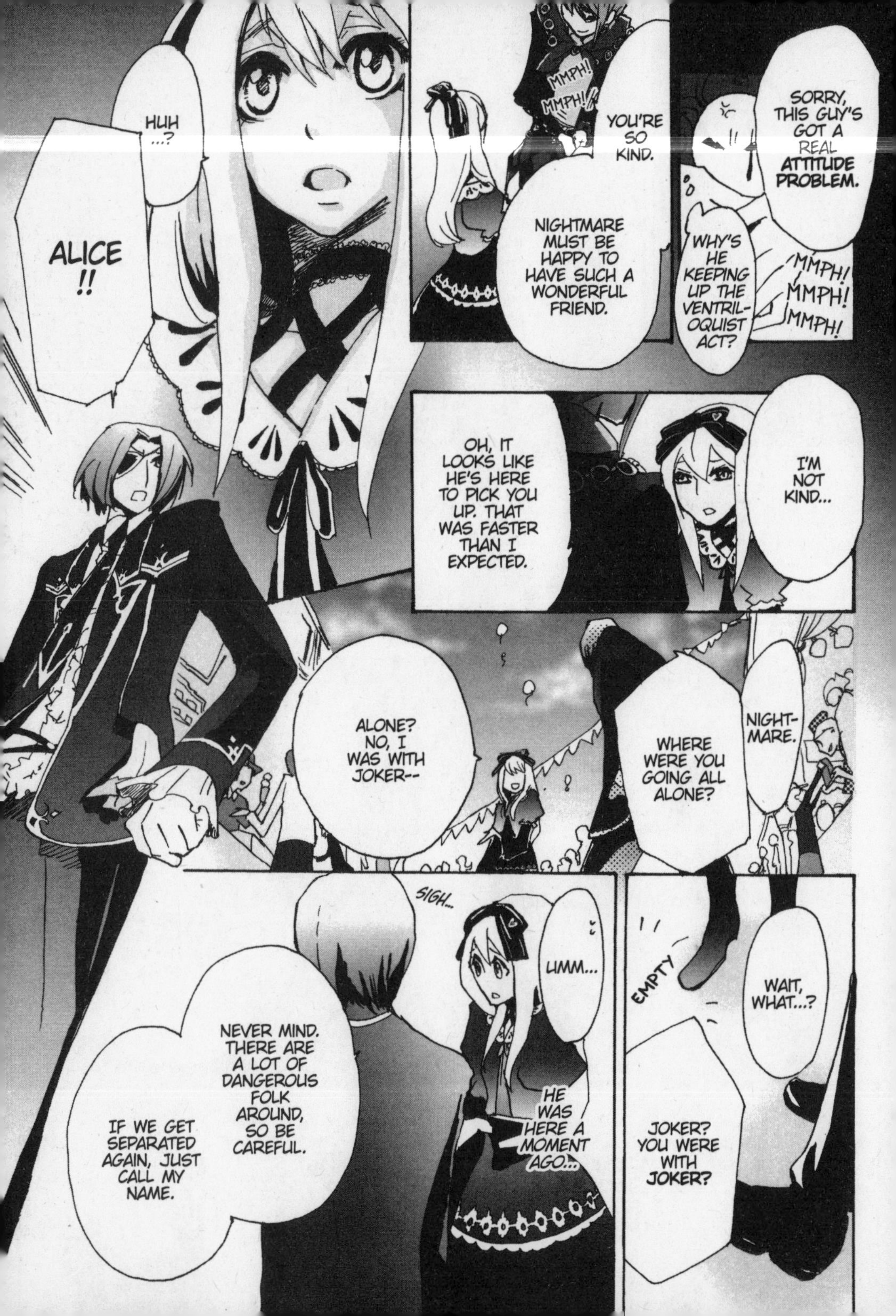
SORRY, THIS GUY'S GOT A REAL ATTITUDE PROBLEM.
WHY'S HE KEEPING UP THE VENTRIL-OQUIST ACT?
MMPH! MMPH! MMPH!
MMPH! MMPH!
YOU'RE SO KIND.
NIGHTMARE MUST BE HAPPY TO HAVE SUCH A WONDERFUL FRIEND.
I'M NOT KIND...
OH, IT LOOKS LIKE HE'S HERE TO PICK YOU UP. THAT WAS FASTER THAN I EXPECTED.
HUH ...?
ALICE !!
NIGHT-MARE.
WHERE WERE YOU GOING ALL ALONE?
ALONE? NO, I WAS WITH JOKER--
WAIT, WHAT...?
EMPTY
JOKER? YOU WERE WITH JOKER?
SIGH...
UMM...
HE WAS HERE A MOMENT AGO...
NEVER MIND. THERE ARE A LOT OF DANGEROUS FOLK AROUND, SO BE CAREFUL.
IF WE GET SEPARATED AGAIN, JUST CALL MY NAME.

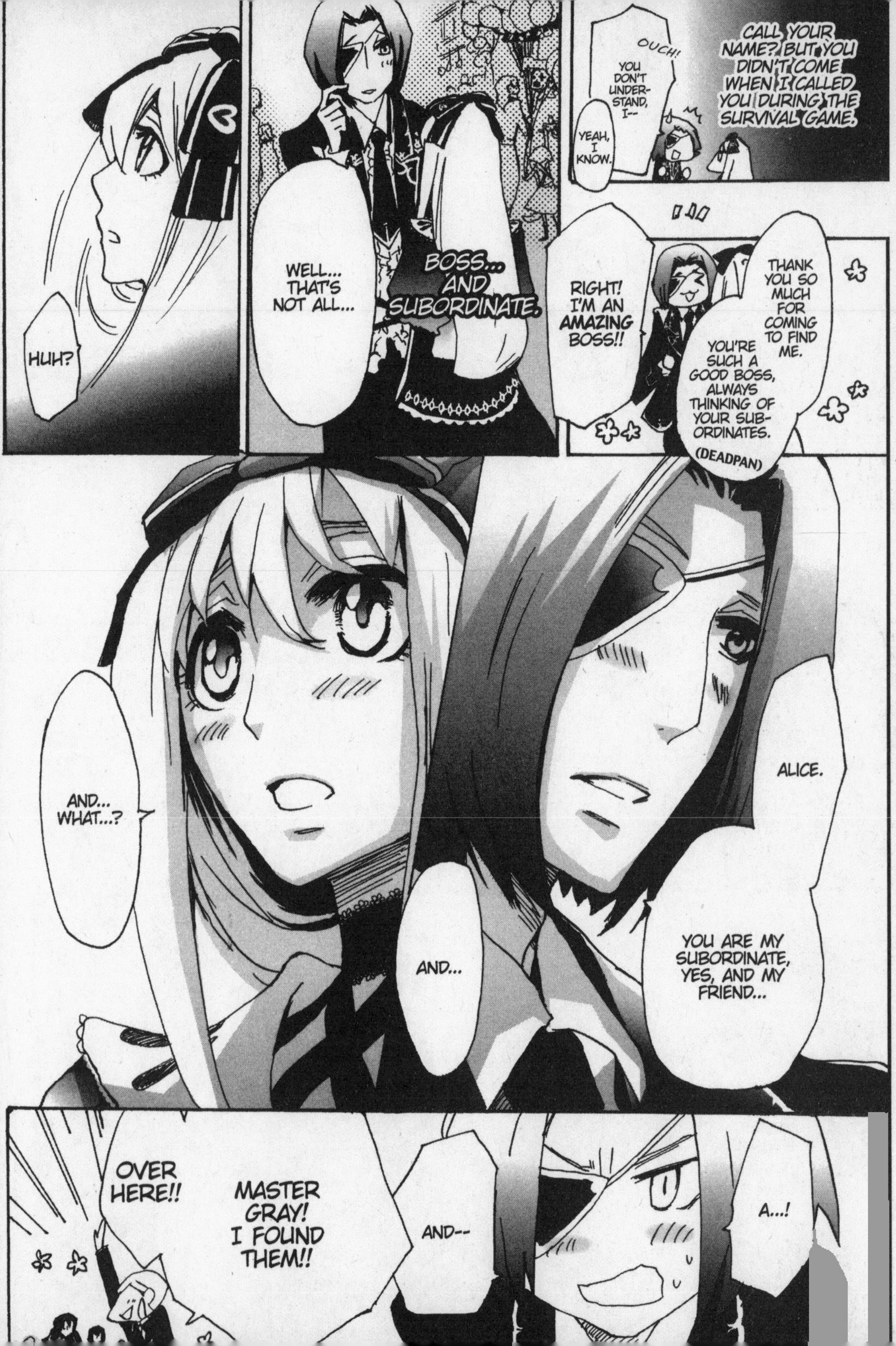
CALL YOUR NAME? BUT YOU DIDN'T COME WHEN I CALLED YOU DURING THE SURVIVAL GAME.
OUCH!
YOU DON'T UNDER-STAND, I--
YEAH, I KNOW.
THANK YOU SO MUCH FOR COMING TO FIND ME.
YOU'RE SUCH A GOOD BOSS, ALWAYS THINKING OF YOUR SUB-ORDINATES.
(DEADPAN)
RIGHT! I'M AN AMAZING BOSS!!
BOSS... AND SUBORDINATE.
WELL... THAT'S NOT ALL...
HUH?
ALICE.
YOU ARE MY SUBORDINATE, YES, AND MY FRIEND...
AND...
AND... WHAT...?
A...!
AND--
MASTER GRAY! I FOUND THEM!!
OVER HERE!!

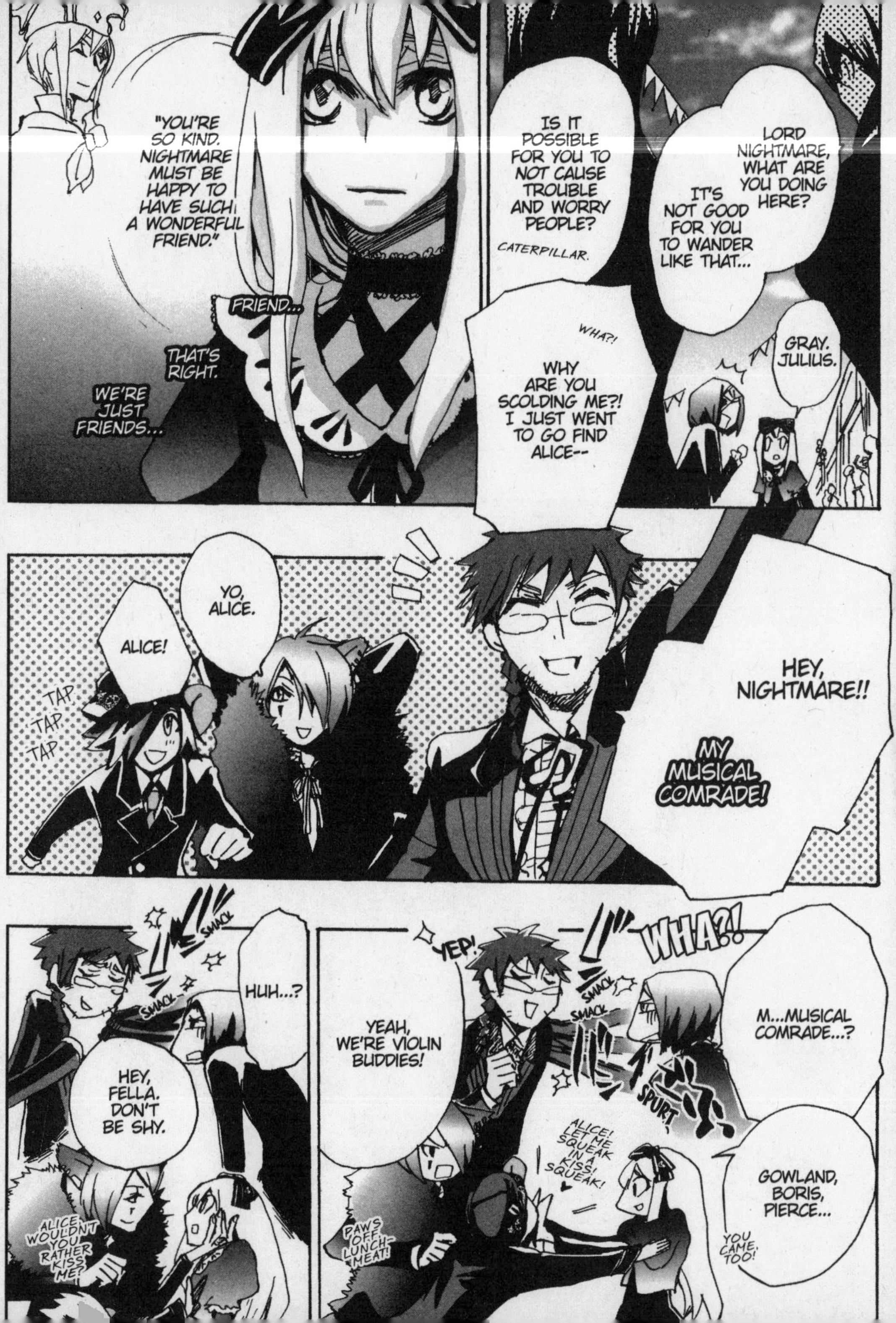
LORD NIGHTMARE, WHAT ARE YOU DOING HERE?
IT'S NOT GOOD FOR YOU TO WANDER LIKE THAT...
IS IT POSSIBLE FOR YOU TO NOT CAUSE TROUBLE AND WORRY PEOPLE?
CATERPILLAR.
GRAY. JULIUS.
WHA?!
WHY ARE YOU SCOLDING ME?! I JUST WENT TO GO FIND ALICE--
"YOU'RE SO KIND. NIGHTMARE MUST BE HAPPY TO HAVE SUCH A WONDERFUL FRIEND."
FRIEND...
THAT'S RIGHT.
WE'RE JUST FRIENDS...
HEY, NIGHTMARE!!
MY MUSICAL COMRADE!
YO, ALICE.
ALICE!
TAP TAP TAP
WHA?!
M...MUSICAL COMRADE...?
SMACK
SMACK
YEP!
YEAH, WE'RE VIOLIN BUDDIES!
SPURT
GOWLAND, BORIS, PIERCE...
YOU CAME, TOO!
ALICE! LET ME SQUEAK IN A KISS! SQUEAK!
PAWS OFF, LUNCH-MEAT!
SMACK
HUH...?
SMACK
HEY, FELLA. DON'T BE SHY.
ALICE WOULDN'T YOU RATHER KISS ME?

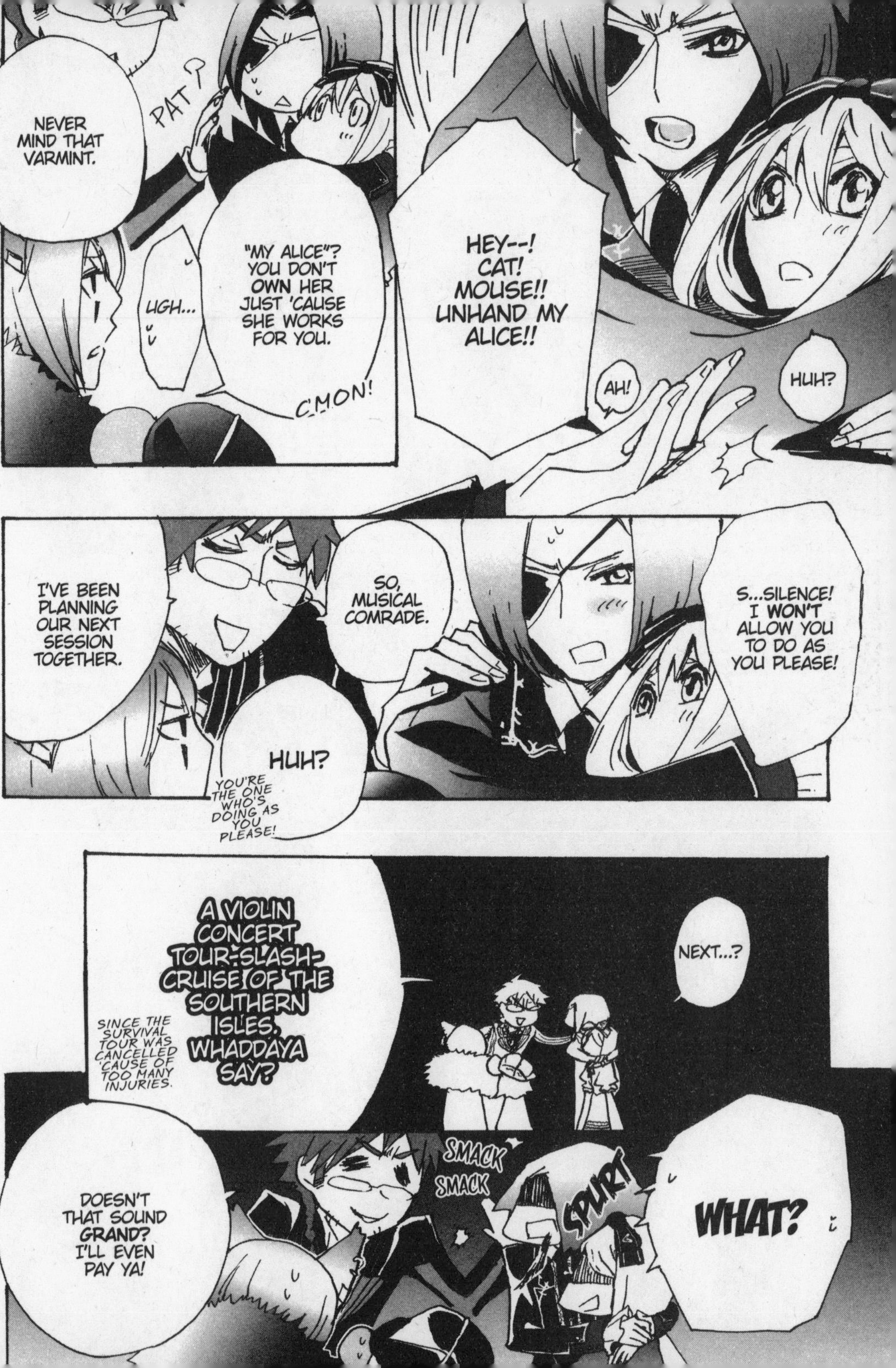
HEY--! CAT! MOUSE!! UNHAND MY ALICE!!
HUH?
AH!
PAT?
"MY ALICE"? YOU DON'T OWN HER JUST 'CAUSE SHE WORKS FOR YOU.
UGH...
C'MON!
NEVER MIND THAT VARMINT.
S...SILENCE! I WON'T ALLOW YOU TO DO AS YOU PLEASE!
SO, MUSICAL COMRADE.
HUH?
YOU'RE THE ONE WHO'S DOING AS YOU PLEASE!
I'VE BEEN PLANNING OUR NEXT SESSION TOGETHER.
NEXT...?
A VIOLIN CONCERT TOUR-SLASH-CRUISE OF THE SOUTHERN ISLES. WHADDAYA SAY?
SINCE THE SURVIVAL TOUR WAS CANCELLED 'CAUSE OF TOO MANY INJURIES.
WHAT?
SPURT
SMACK
SMACK
DOESN'T THAT SOUND GRAND? I'LL EVEN PAY YA!

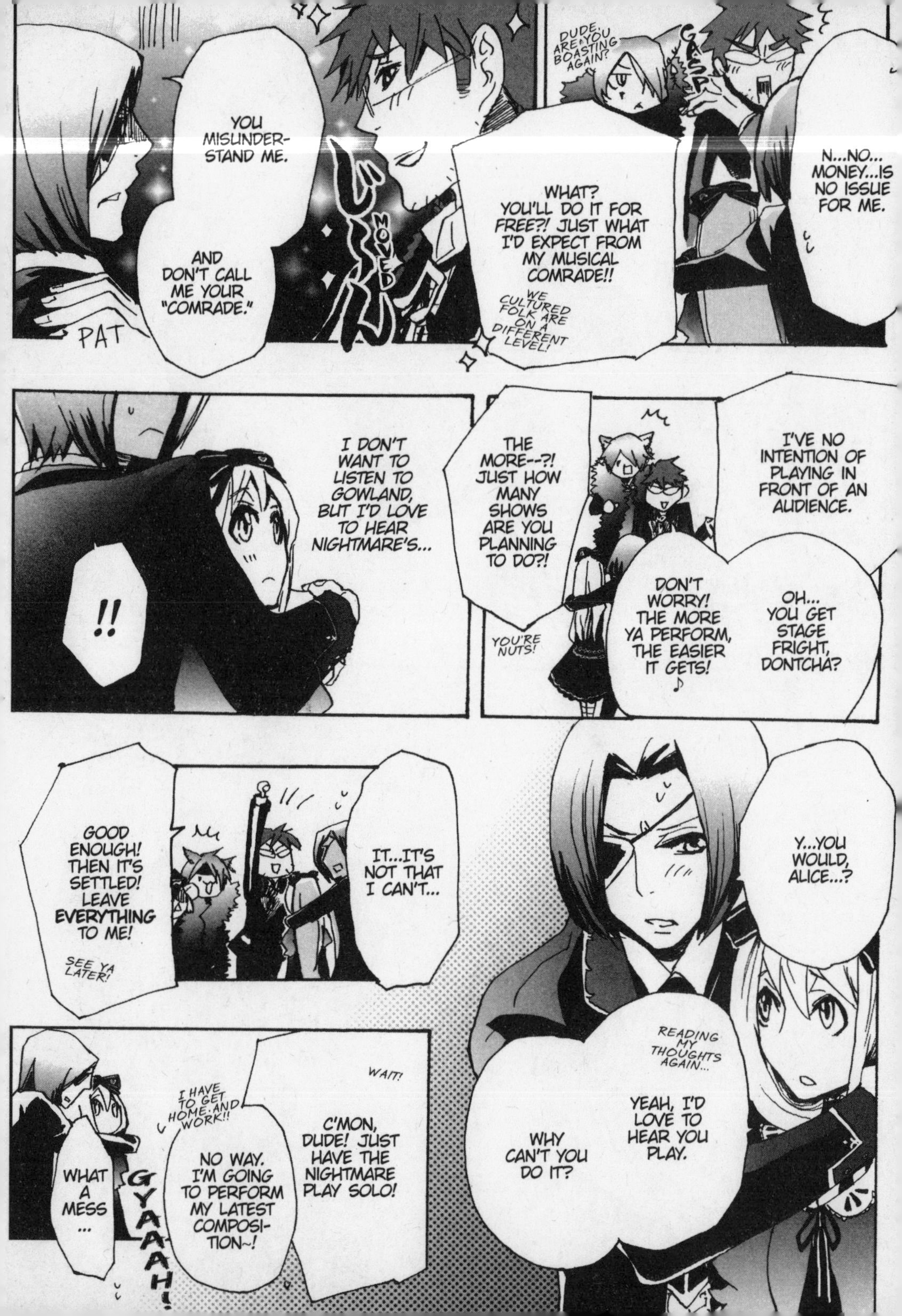
DUDE, ARE YOU BOASTING AGAIN?
GASP
N...NO... MONEY...IS NO ISSUE FOR ME.
WHAT? YOU'LL DO IT FOR FREE?! JUST WHAT I'D EXPECT FROM MY MUSICAL COMRADE!!
WE CULTURED FOLK ARE ON A DIFFERENT LEVEL!
MOVED
YOU MISUNDER-STAND ME.
AND DON'T CALL ME YOUR "COMRADE."
PAT
I'VE NO INTENTION OF PLAYING IN FRONT OF AN AUDIENCE.
OH... YOU GET STAGE FRIGHT, DONTCHA?
DON'T WORRY! THE MORE YA PERFORM, THE EASIER IT GETS! ♪
THE MORE--?! JUST HOW MANY SHOWS ARE YOU PLANNING TO DO?!
YOU'RE NUTS!
I DON'T WANT TO LISTEN TO GOWLAND, BUT I'D LOVE TO HEAR NIGHTMARE'S...
!!
Y...YOU WOULD, ALICE...?
READING MY THOUGHTS AGAIN...
YEAH, I'D LOVE TO HEAR YOU PLAY.
WHY CAN'T YOU DO IT?
IT...IT'S NOT THAT I CAN'T...
GOOD ENOUGH! THEN IT'S SETTLED! LEAVE EVERYTHING TO ME!
SEE YA LATER!
WAIT!
C'MON, DUDE! JUST HAVE THE NIGHTMARE PLAY SOLO!
I HAVE TO GET HOME AND WORK!!
NO WAY. I'M GOING TO PERFORM MY LATEST COMPOSI-TION~!
GYAAAAH!
WHAT A MESS ...

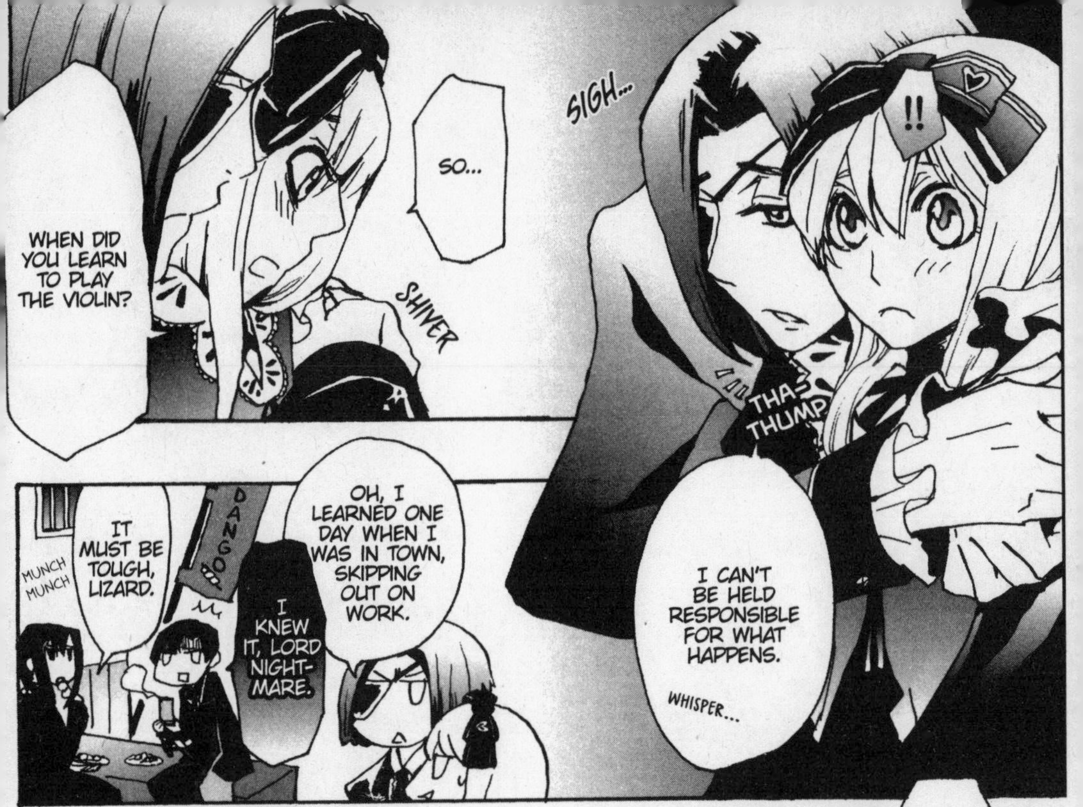
SIGH...
!!
THA-THUMP
I CAN'T BE HELD RESPONSIBLE FOR WHAT HAPPENS.
WHISPER...
SO...
WHEN DID YOU LEARN TO PLAY THE VIOLIN?
SHIVER
OH, I LEARNED ONE DAY WHEN I WAS IN TOWN, SKIPPING OUT ON WORK.
I KNEW IT, LORD NIGHTMARE.
DANGO
IT MUST BE TOUGH, LIZARD.
MUNCH MUNCH

*Dango: Japanese snack made of balls of mochi (glutinous rice).
**Taiyaki: Sweet red bean paste baked into a fish-shaped cake.

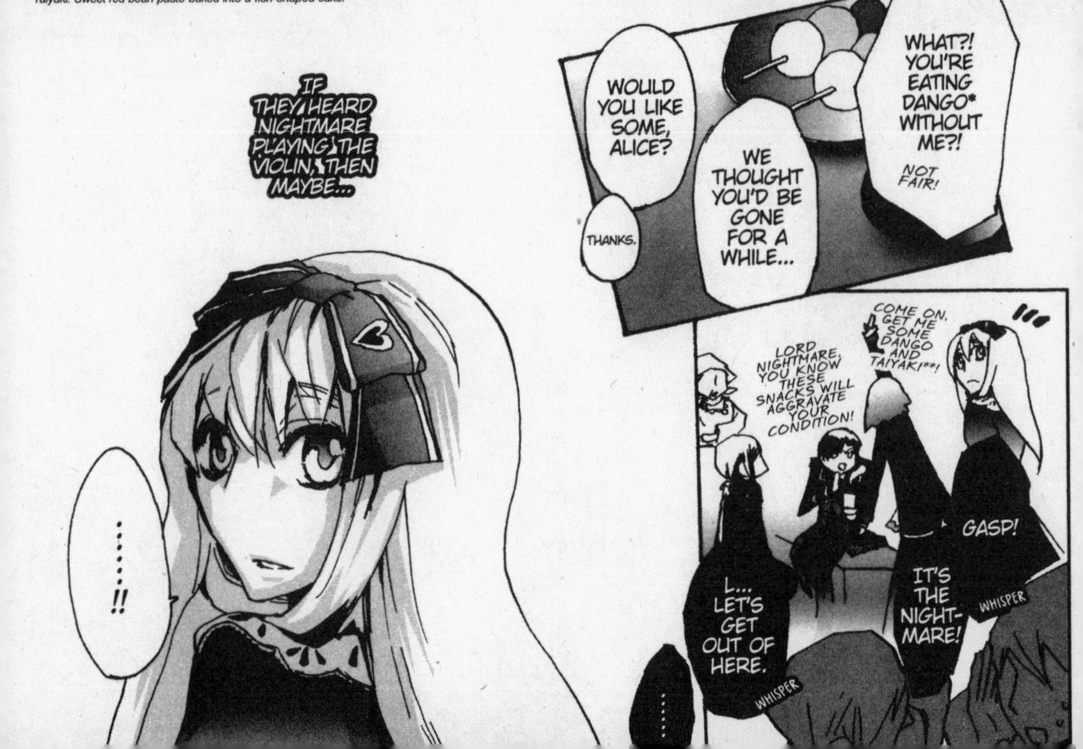
WHAT?! YOU'RE EATING DANGO* WITHOUT ME?!
NOT FAIR!
WOULD YOU LIKE SOME, ALICE?
WE THOUGHT YOU'D BE GONE FOR A WHILE...
THANKS.
COME ON, GET ME SOME DANGO AND TAIYAKI**!
LORD NIGHTMARE, YOU KNOW THESE SNACKS WILL AGGRAVATE YOUR CONDITION!
GASP!
IT'S THE NIGHTMARE!
WHISPER
L... LET'S GET OUT OF HERE.
WHISPER
......
IF THEY HEARD NIGHTMARE PLAYING THE VIOLIN, THEN MAYBE...
......!!

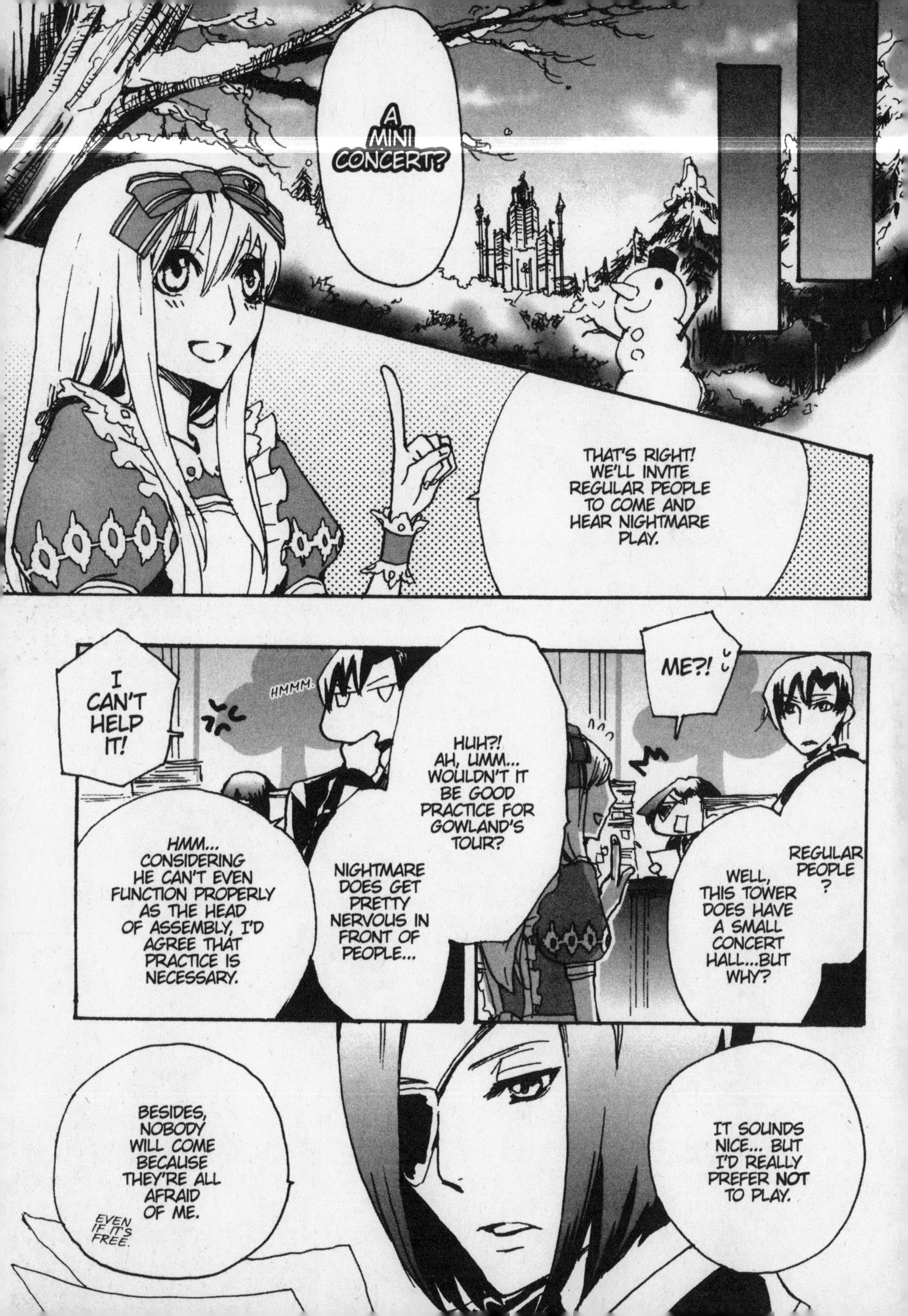
A MINI CONCERT?
THAT'S RIGHT! WE'LL INVITE REGULAR PEOPLE TO COME AND HEAR NIGHTMARE PLAY.
REGULAR PEOPLE?
WELL, THIS TOWER DOES HAVE A SMALL CONCERT HALL...BUT WHY?
HUH?! AH, UMM... WOULDN'T IT BE GOOD PRACTICE FOR GOWLAND'S TOUR?
ME?!
NIGHTMARE DOES GET PRETTY NERVOUS IN FRONT OF PEOPLE...
HMMM.
HMM... CONSIDERING HE CAN'T EVEN FUNCTION PROPERLY AS THE HEAD OF ASSEMBLY, I'D AGREE THAT PRACTICE IS NECESSARY.
I CAN'T HELP IT!
IT SOUNDS NICE... BUT I'D REALLY PREFER NOT TO PLAY.
BESIDES, NOBODY WILL COME BECAUSE THEY'RE ALL AFRAID OF ME.
EVEN IF IT'S FREE.

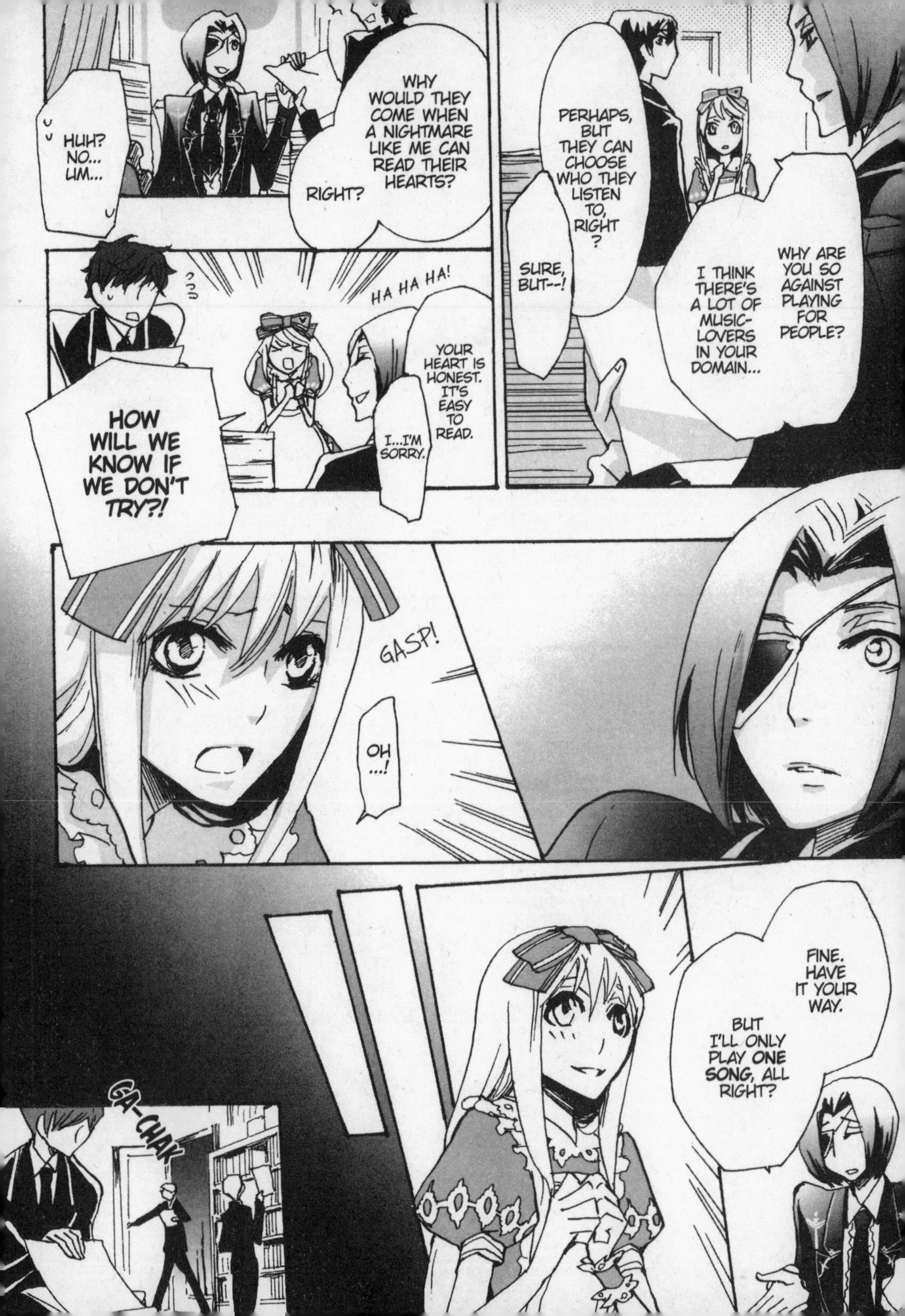
WHY ARE YOU SO AGAINST PLAYING FOR PEOPLE?
I THINK THERE'S A LOT OF MUSIC-LOVERS IN YOUR DOMAIN...
PERHAPS, BUT THEY CAN CHOOSE WHO THEY LISTEN TO, RIGHT?
SURE, BUT--!
WHY WOULD THEY COME WHEN A NIGHTMARE LIKE ME CAN READ THEIR HEARTS?
RIGHT?
HUH? NO... UM...
HA HA HA!
YOUR HEART IS HONEST. IT'S EASY TO READ.
I...I'M SORRY.
HOW WILL WE KNOW IF WE DON'T TRY?!
GASP!
OH ...!
FINE. HAVE IT YOUR WAY.
BUT I'LL ONLY PLAY ONE SONG, ALL RIGHT?
GA-CHAK

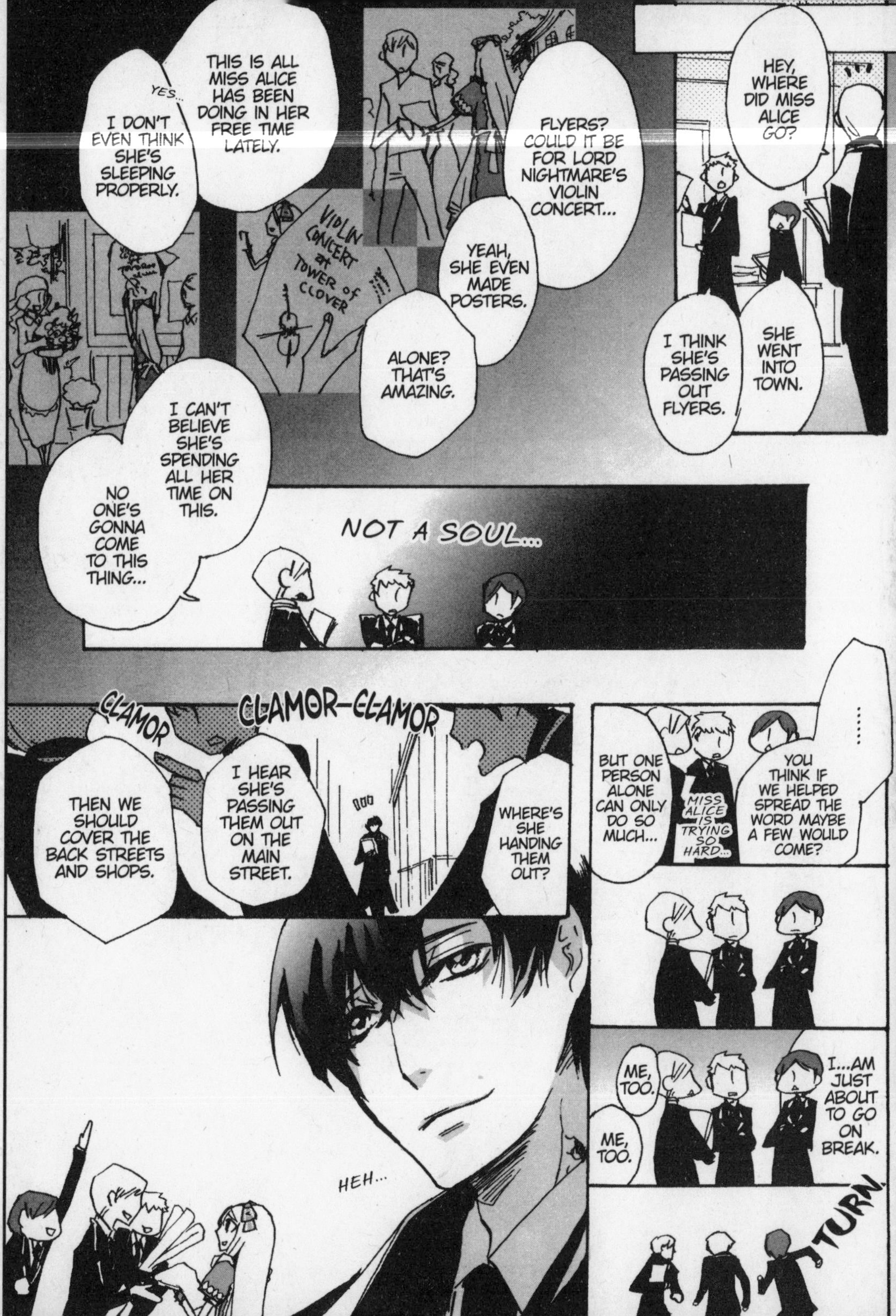
HEY, WHERE DID MISS ALICE GO?
SHE WENT INTO TOWN.
I THINK SHE'S PASSING OUT FLYERS.
FLYERS? COULD IT BE FOR LORD NIGHTMARE'S VIOLIN CONCERT...
YEAH, SHE EVEN MADE POSTERS.
VIOLIN CONCERT at TOWER of CLOVER
ALONE? THAT'S AMAZING.
THIS IS ALL MISS ALICE HAS BEEN DOING IN HER FREE TIME LATELY.
YES...
I DON'T EVEN THINK SHE'S SLEEPING PROPERLY.
I CAN'T BELIEVE SHE'S SPENDING ALL HER TIME ON THIS.
NO ONE'S GONNA COME TO THIS THING...
NOT A SOUL...
......
YOU THINK IF WE HELPED SPREAD THE WORD MAYBE A FEW WOULD COME?
MISS ALICE IS TRYING SO HARD...
BUT ONE PERSON ALONE CAN ONLY DO SO MUCH...
I...AM JUST ABOUT TO GO ON BREAK.
ME, TOO.
ME, TOO.
TURN.
CLAMOR-CLAMOR
WHERE'S SHE HANDING THEM OUT?
I HEAR SHE'S PASSING THEM OUT ON THE MAIN STREET.
THEN WE SHOULD COVER THE BACK STREETS AND SHOPS.
CLAMOR
HEH...

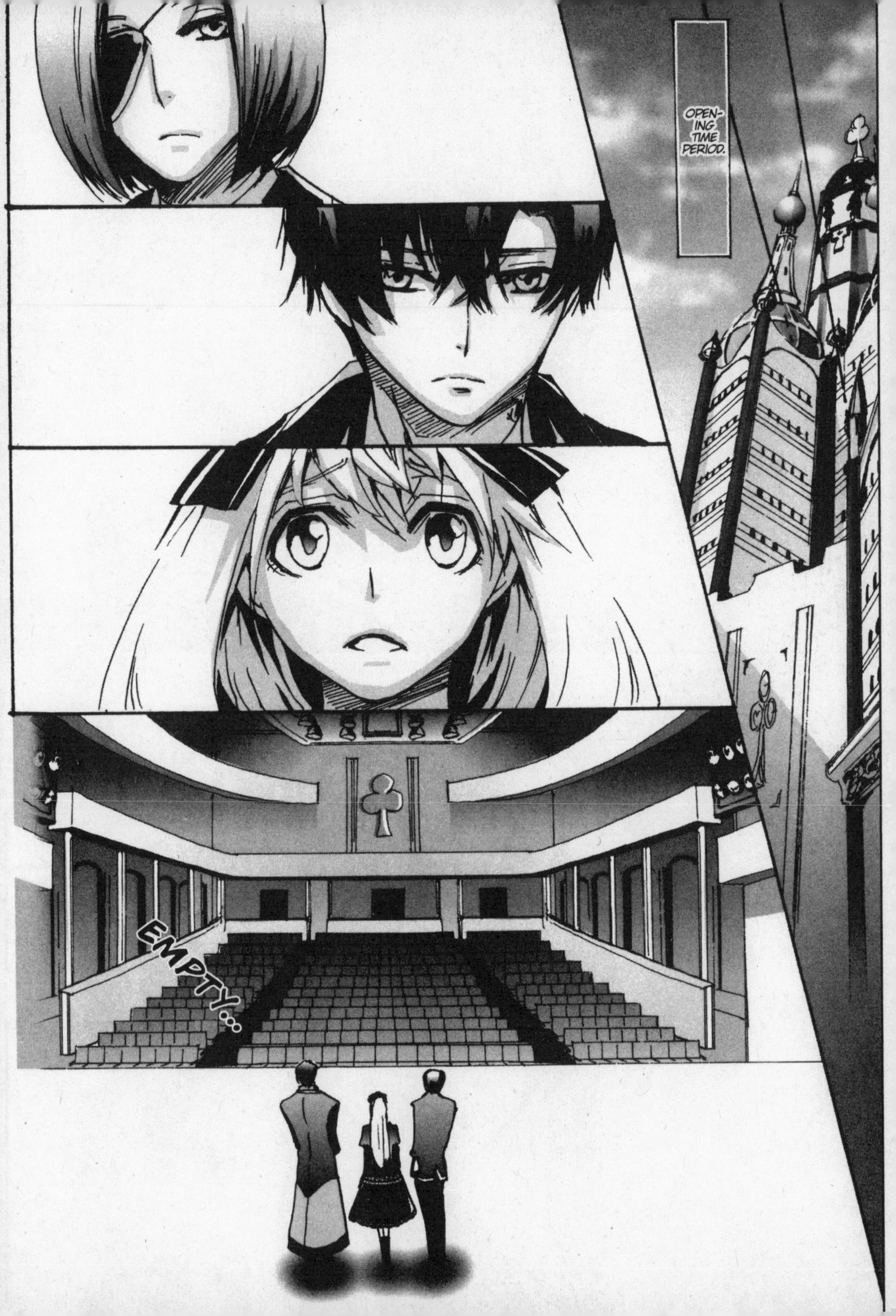
OPEN-ING TIME PERIOD.
EMPTY...

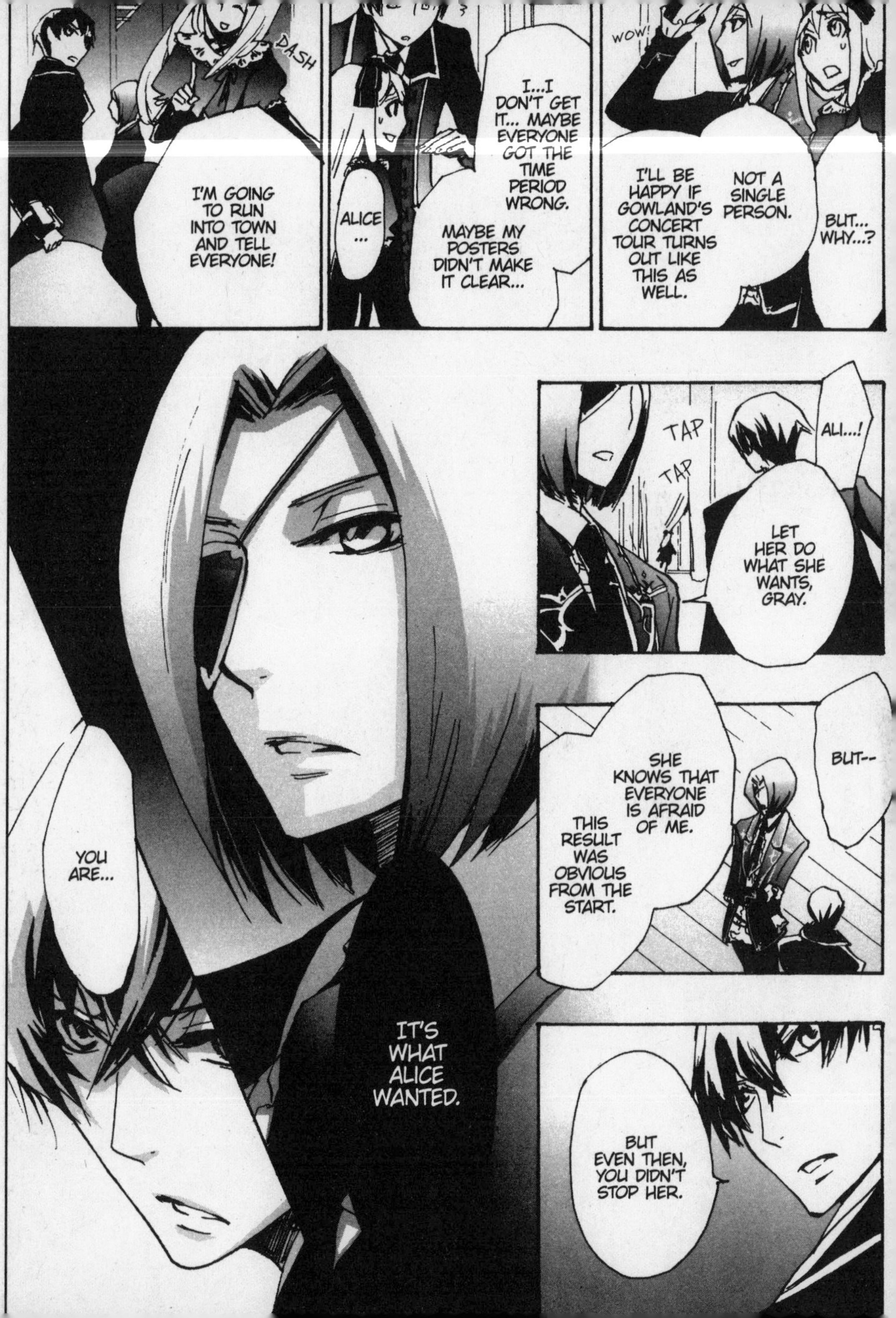
WOW!
NOT A SINGLE PERSON.
BUT... WHY...?
I'LL BE HAPPY IF GOWLAND'S CONCERT TOUR TURNS OUT LIKE THIS AS WELL.
I...I DON'T GET IT... MAYBE EVERYONE GOT THE TIME PERIOD WRONG.
MAYBE MY POSTERS DIDN'T MAKE IT CLEAR...
ALICE ...
DASH
I'M GOING TO RUN INTO TOWN AND TELL EVERYONE!
ALI...!
TAP
TAP
LET HER DO WHAT SHE WANTS, GRAY.
BUT--
SHE KNOWS THAT EVERYONE IS AFRAID OF ME.
THIS RESULT WAS OBVIOUS FROM THE START.
BUT EVEN THEN, YOU DIDN'T STOP HER.
YOU ARE...
IT'S WHAT ALICE WANTED.

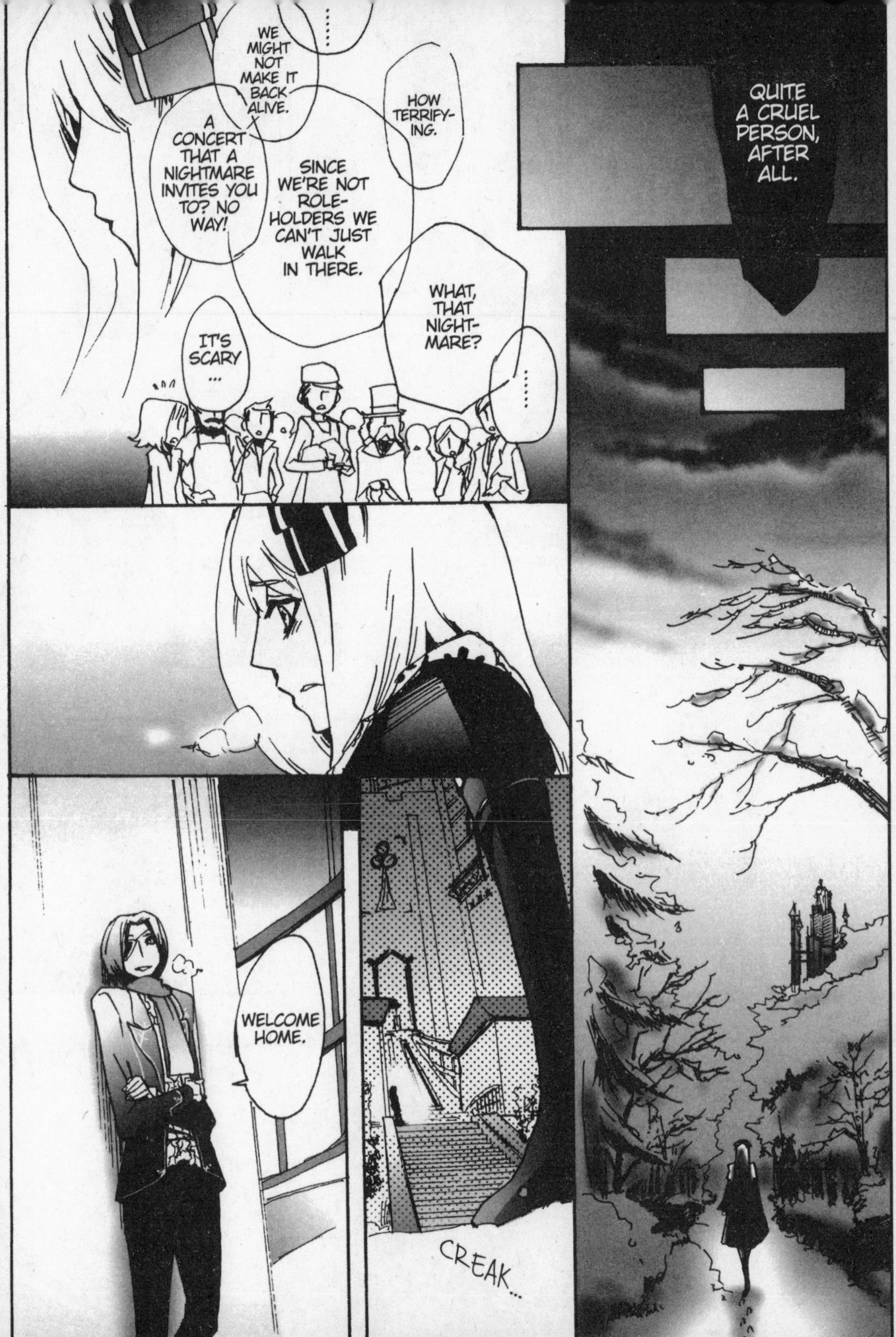
QUITE A CRUEL PERSON, AFTER ALL.
......
WE MIGHT NOT MAKE IT BACK ALIVE.
HOW TERRIFYING.
A CONCERT THAT A NIGHTMARE INVITES YOU TO? NO WAY!
SINCE WE'RE NOT ROLE-HOLDERS WE CAN'T JUST WALK IN THERE.
WHAT, THAT NIGHTMARE?
......
IT'S SCARY ...
CREAK...
WELCOME HOME.

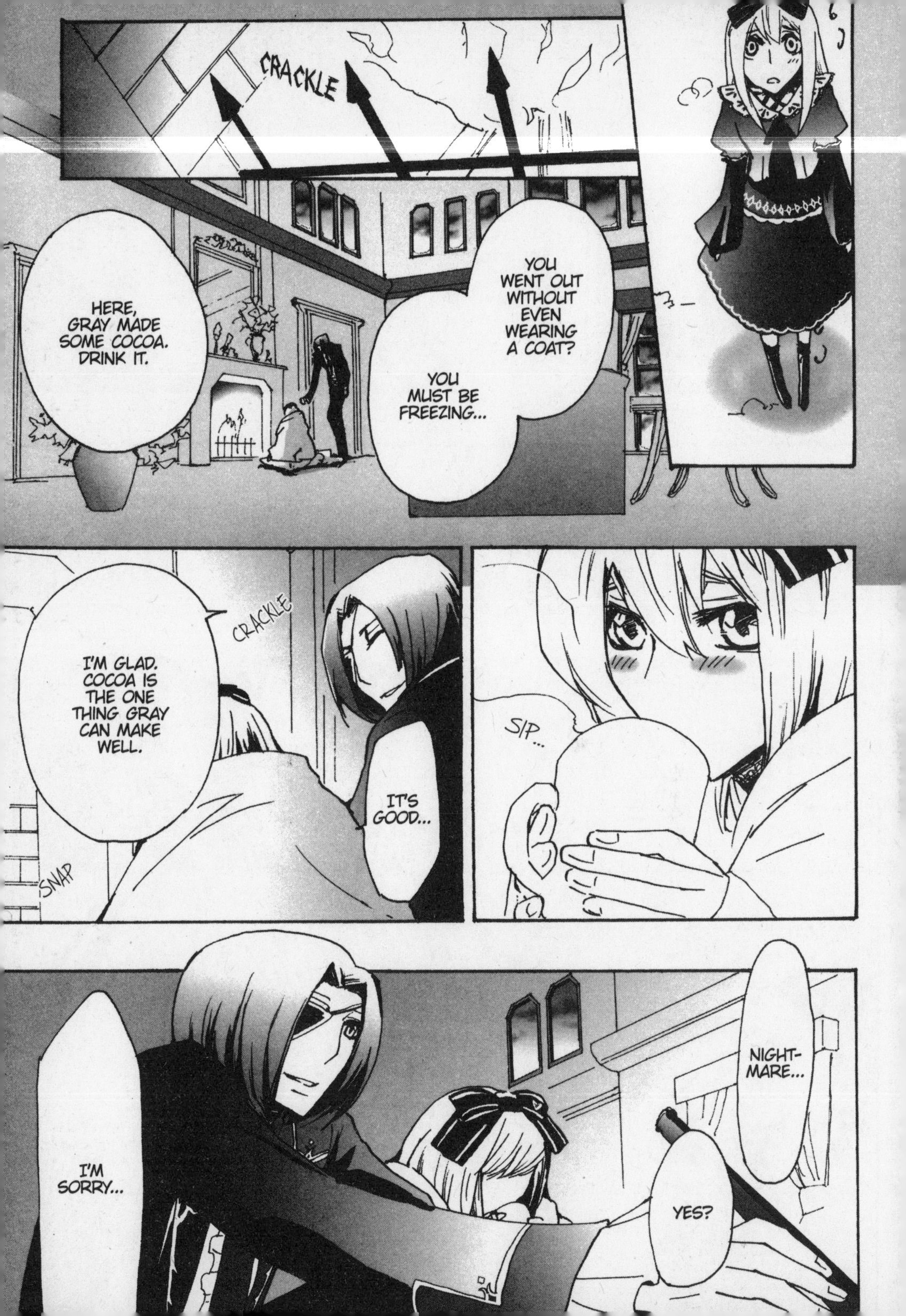
CRACKLE
YOU WENT OUT WITHOUT EVEN WEARING A COAT?
YOU MUST BE FREEZING...
HERE, GRAY MADE SOME COCOA. DRINK IT.
SIP...
CRACKLE
IT'S GOOD...
I'M GLAD. COCOA IS THE ONE THING GRAY CAN MAKE WELL.
SNAP
NIGHT-MARE...
YES?
I'M SORRY...

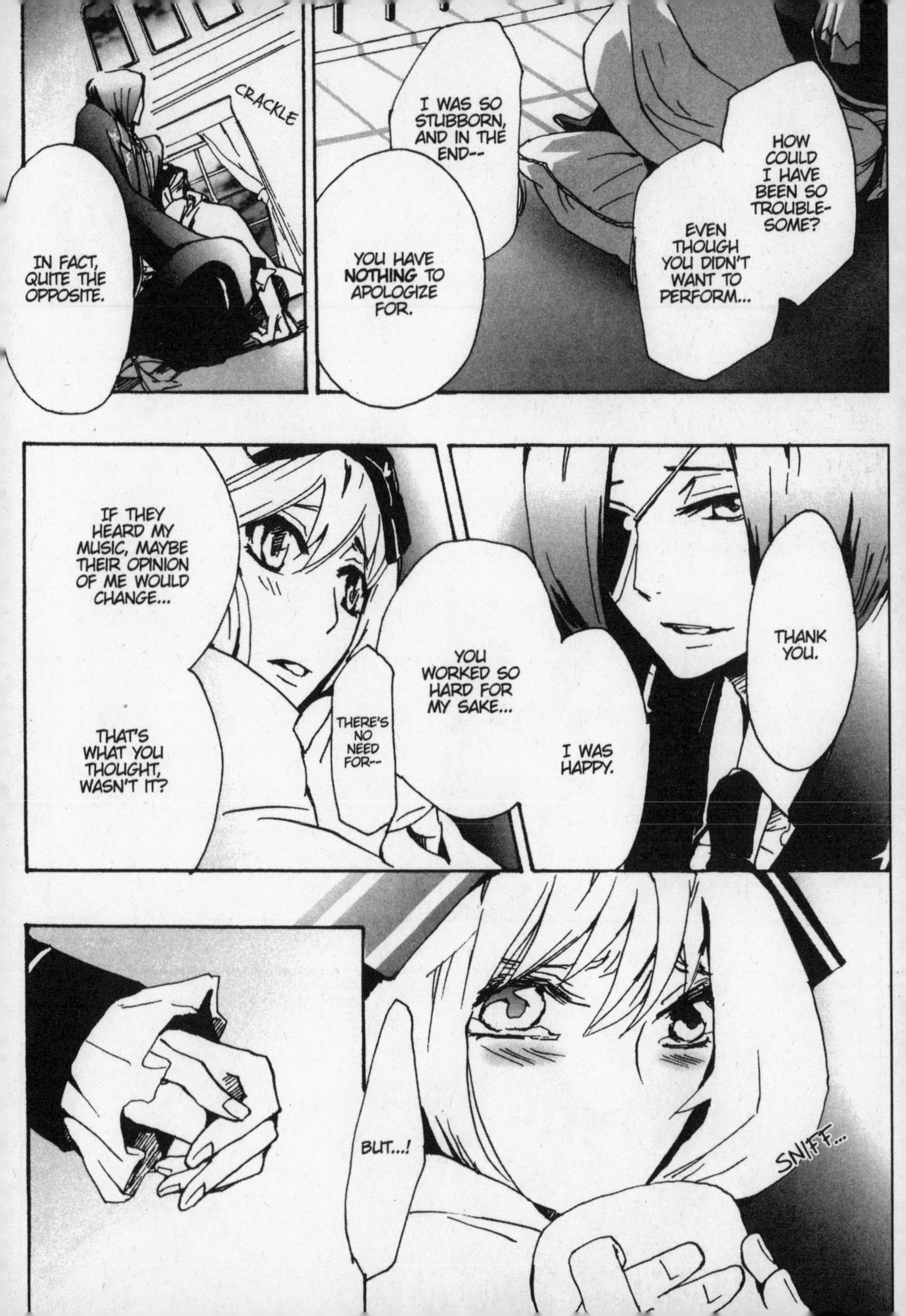
HOW COULD I HAVE BEEN SO TROUBLE-SOME?
EVEN THOUGH YOU DIDN'T WANT TO PERFORM...
I WAS SO STUBBORN, AND IN THE END--
YOU HAVE **NOTHING** TO APOLOGIZE FOR.
CRACKLE
IN FACT, QUITE THE OPPOSITE.
THANK YOU.
YOU WORKED SO HARD FOR MY SAKE...
I WAS HAPPY.
THERE'S NO NEED FOR--
IF THEY HEARD MY MUSIC, MAYBE THEIR OPINION OF ME WOULD CHANGE...
THAT'S WHAT YOU THOUGHT, WASN'T IT?
SNIFF...
BUT...!

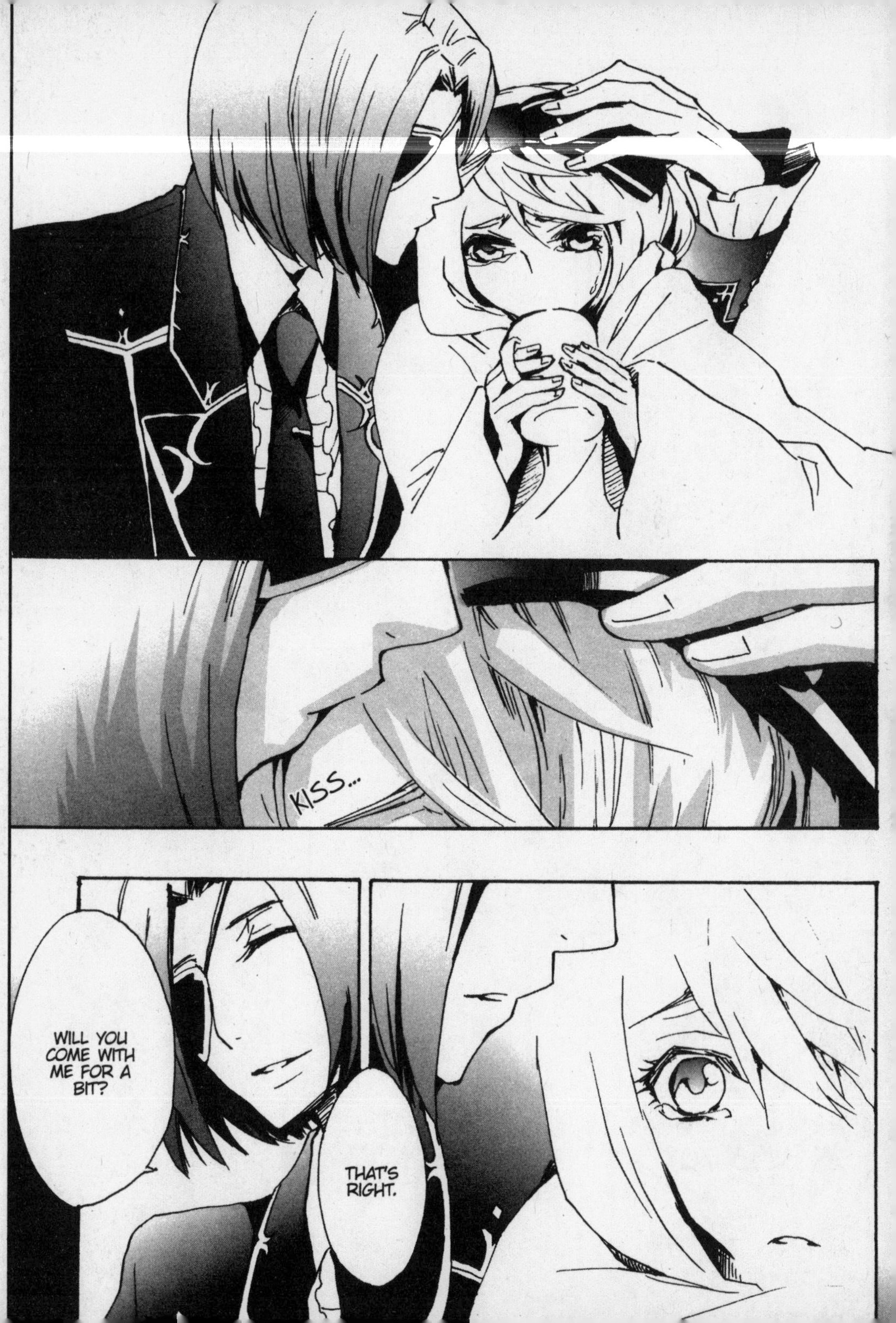
KISS...
WILL YOU COME WITH ME FOR A BIT?
THAT'S RIGHT.

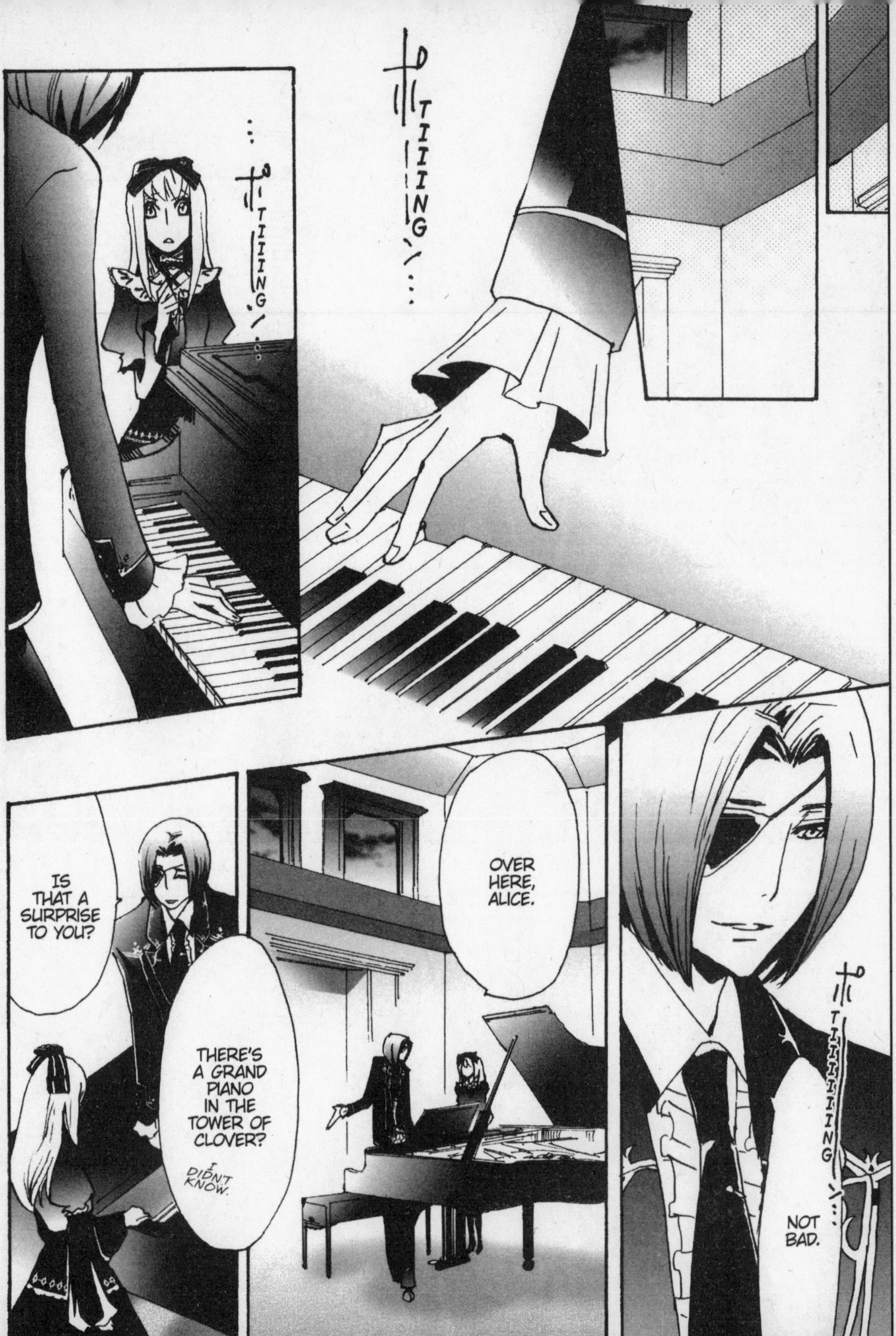
TIIIING...
...TIIIING...
TIIIIIIIIING...
NOT BAD.
OVER HERE, ALICE.
THERE'S A GRAND PIANO IN THE TOWER OF CLOVER?
I DIDN'T KNOW.
IS THAT A SURPRISE TO YOU?

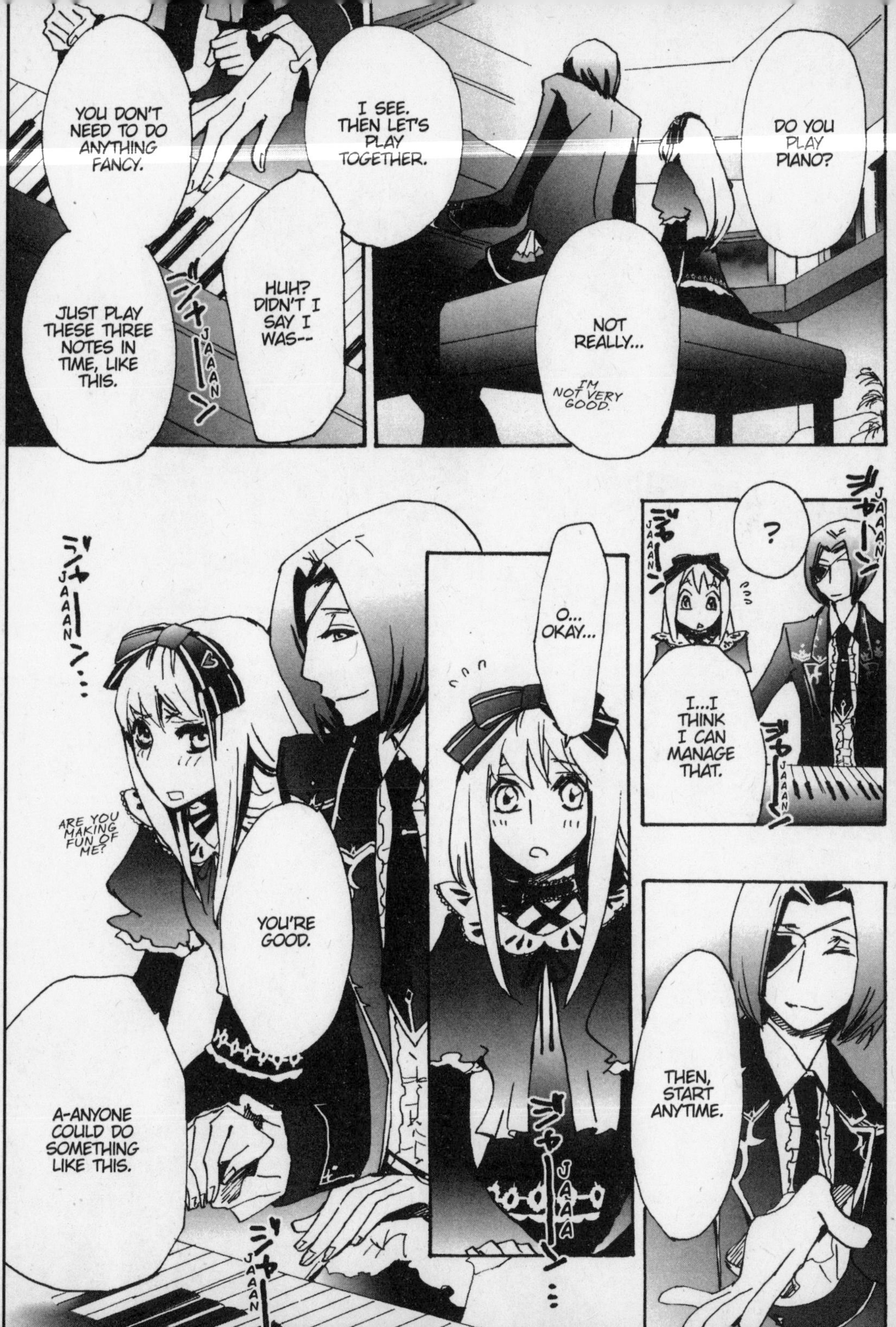
DO YOU PLAY PIANO?
NOT REALLY...
I'M NOT VERY GOOD.
I SEE. THEN LET'S PLAY TOGETHER.
HUH? DIDN'T I SAY I WAS--
YOU DON'T NEED TO DO ANYTHING FANCY.
JAAAN
JUST PLAY THESE THREE NOTES IN TIME, LIKE THIS.
JAAAN
?
JAAAN
I...I THINK I CAN MANAGE THAT.
JAAAN
THEN, START ANYTIME.
O... OKAY...
JAAA...
JAAAN...
YOU'RE GOOD.
ARE YOU MAKING FUN OF ME?
A-ANYONE COULD DO SOMETHING LIKE THIS.
JAAAN

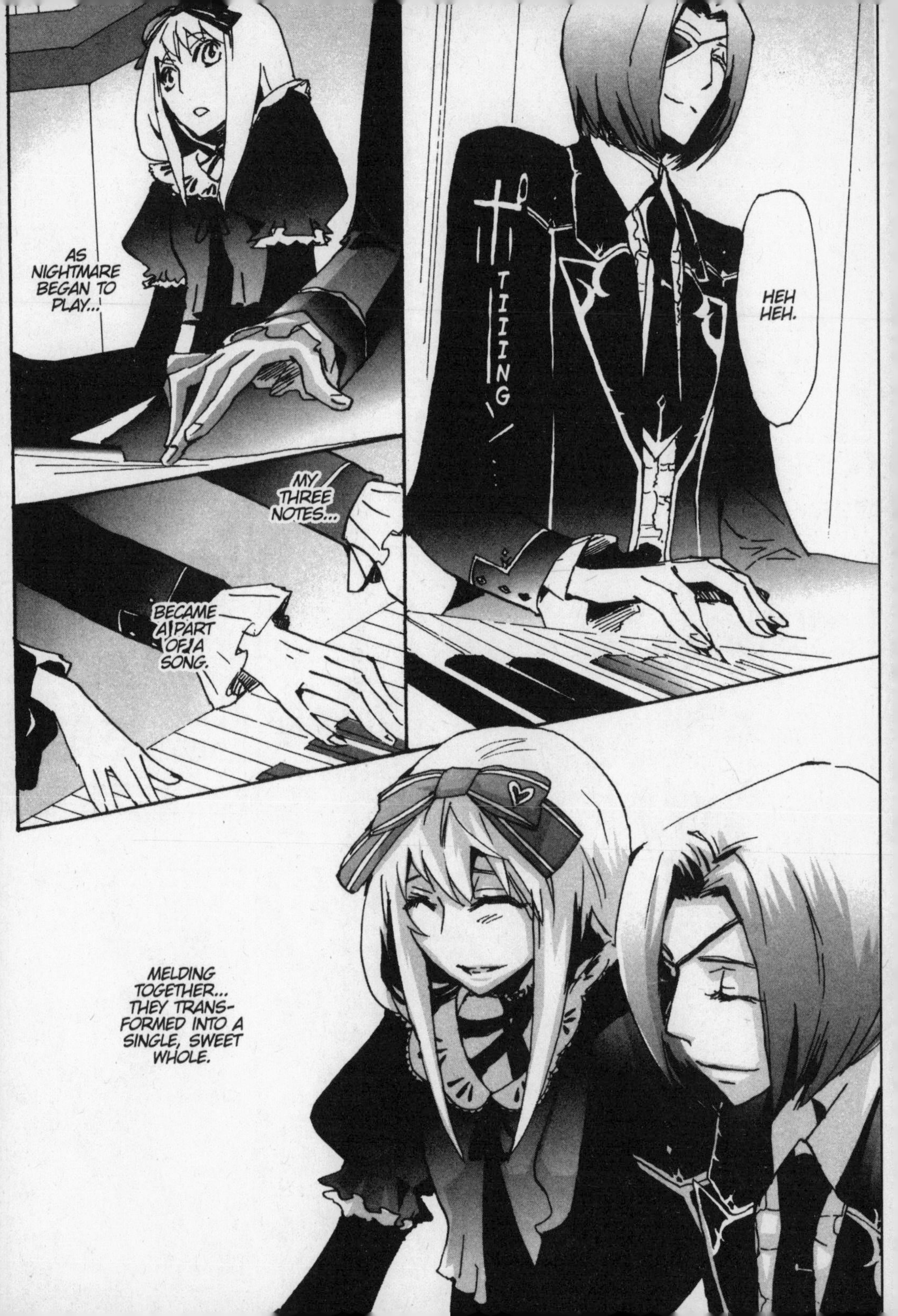
HEH HEH.
TIIIING
AS NIGHTMARE BEGAN TO PLAY...
MY THREE NOTES...
BECAME A PART OF A SONG.
MELDING TOGETHER... THEY TRANS-FORMED INTO A SINGLE, SWEET WHOLE.

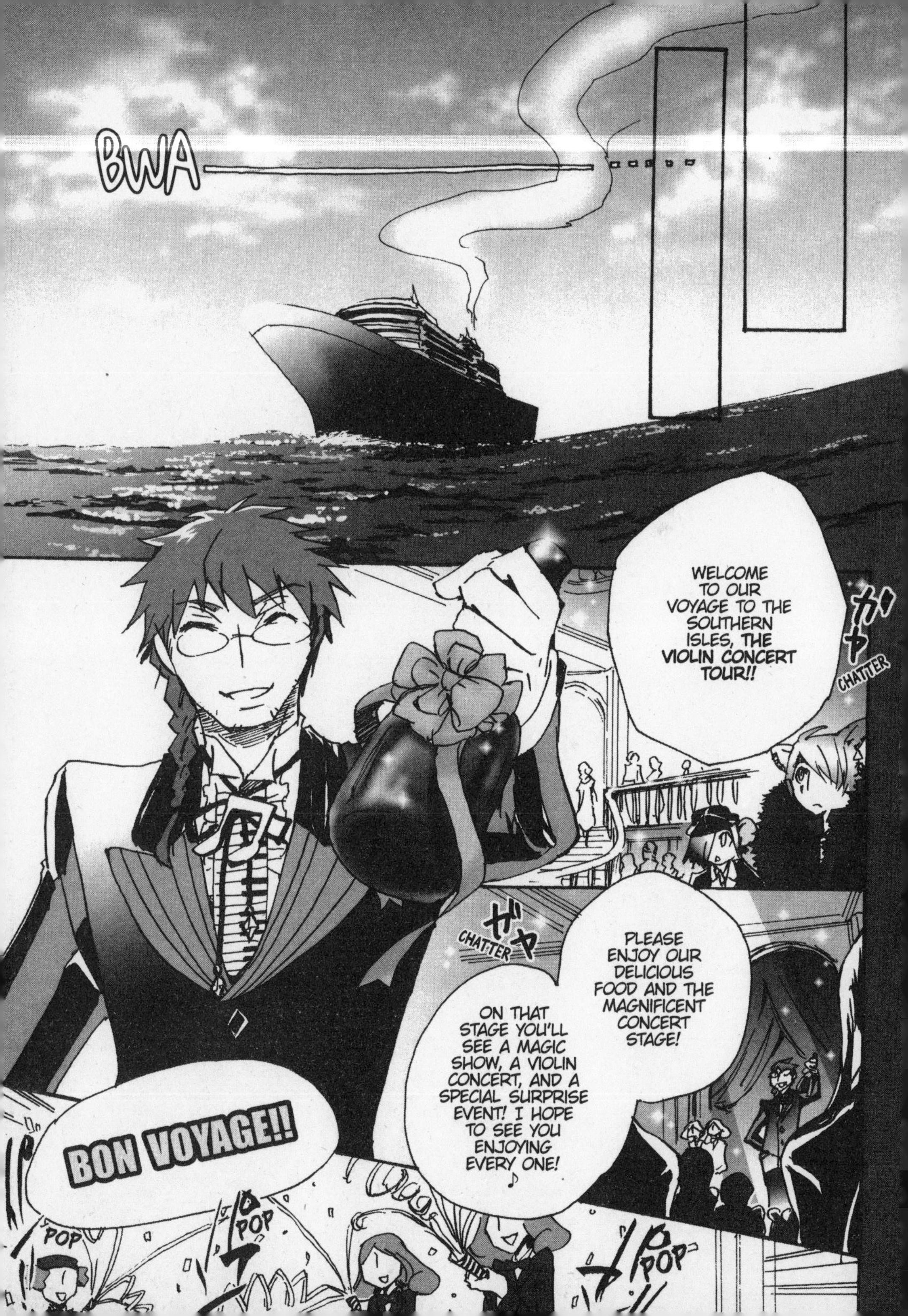
BWA
WELCOME TO OUR VOYAGE TO THE SOUTHERN ISLES, THE VIOLIN CONCERT TOUR!!
CHATTER
CHATTER
PLEASE ENJOY OUR DELICIOUS FOOD AND THE MAGNIFICENT CONCERT STAGE!
ON THAT STAGE YOU'LL SEE A MAGIC SHOW, A VIOLIN CONCERT, AND A SPECIAL SURPRISE EVENT! I HOPE TO SEE YOU ENJOYING EVERY ONE! ♪
BON VOYAGE!!
POP
POP
POP
POP

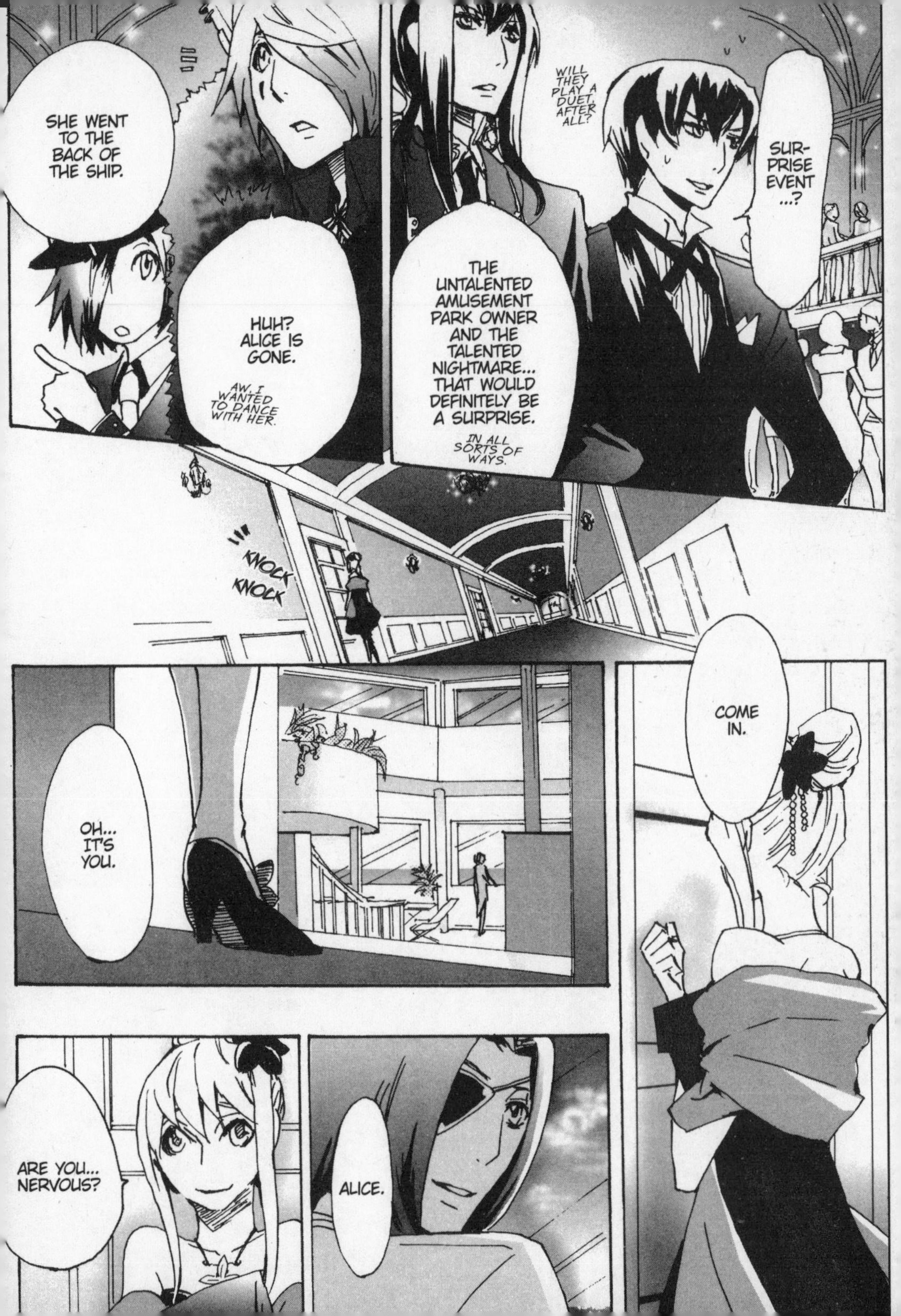
SUR-PRISE EVENT ...?
WILL THEY PLAY A DUET, AFTER ALL?
THE UNTALENTED AMUSEMENT PARK OWNER AND THE TALENTED NIGHTMARE... THAT WOULD DEFINITELY BE A SURPRISE.
IN ALL SORTS OF WAYS.
HUH? ALICE IS GONE.
AW, I WANTED TO DANCE WITH HER.
SHE WENT TO THE BACK OF THE SHIP.
KNOCK KNOCK
COME IN.
OH... IT'S YOU.
ALICE.
ARE YOU... NERVOUS?

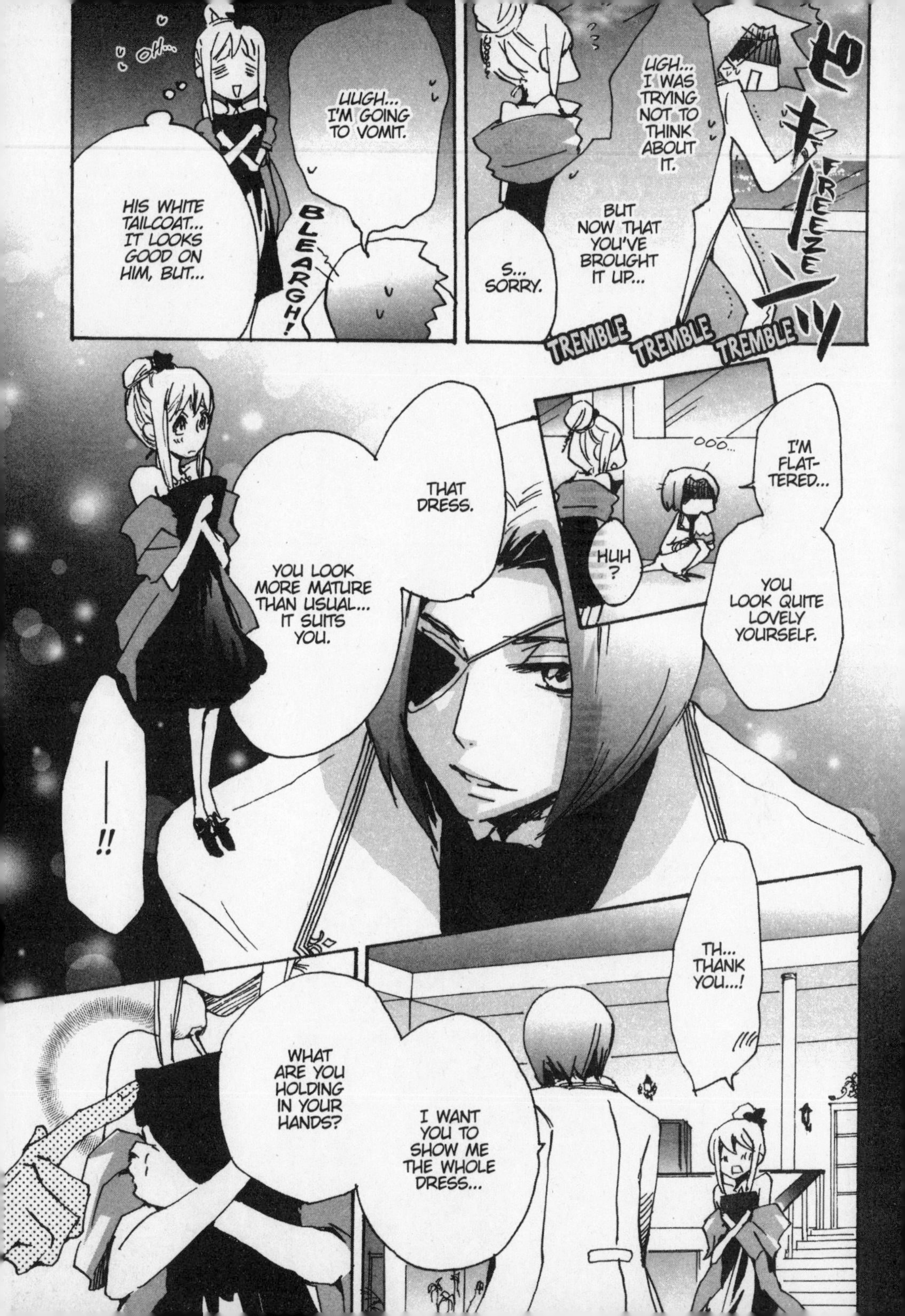
UGH... I WAS TRYING NOT TO THINK ABOUT IT.
BUT NOW THAT YOU'VE BROUGHT IT UP...
S... SORRY.
FREEZE
TREMBLE TREMBLE TREMBLE
UUGH... I'M GOING TO VOMIT.
OH...
HIS WHITE TAILCOAT... IT LOOKS GOOD ON HIM, BUT...
BLEARGH!
I'M FLATTERED...
OOO...
YOU LOOK QUITE LOVELY YOURSELF.
HUH?
THAT DRESS.
YOU LOOK MORE MATURE THAN USUAL... IT SUITS YOU.
—!!
TH... THANK YOU...!
I WANT YOU TO SHOW ME THE WHOLE DRESS...
WHAT ARE YOU HOLDING IN YOUR HANDS?

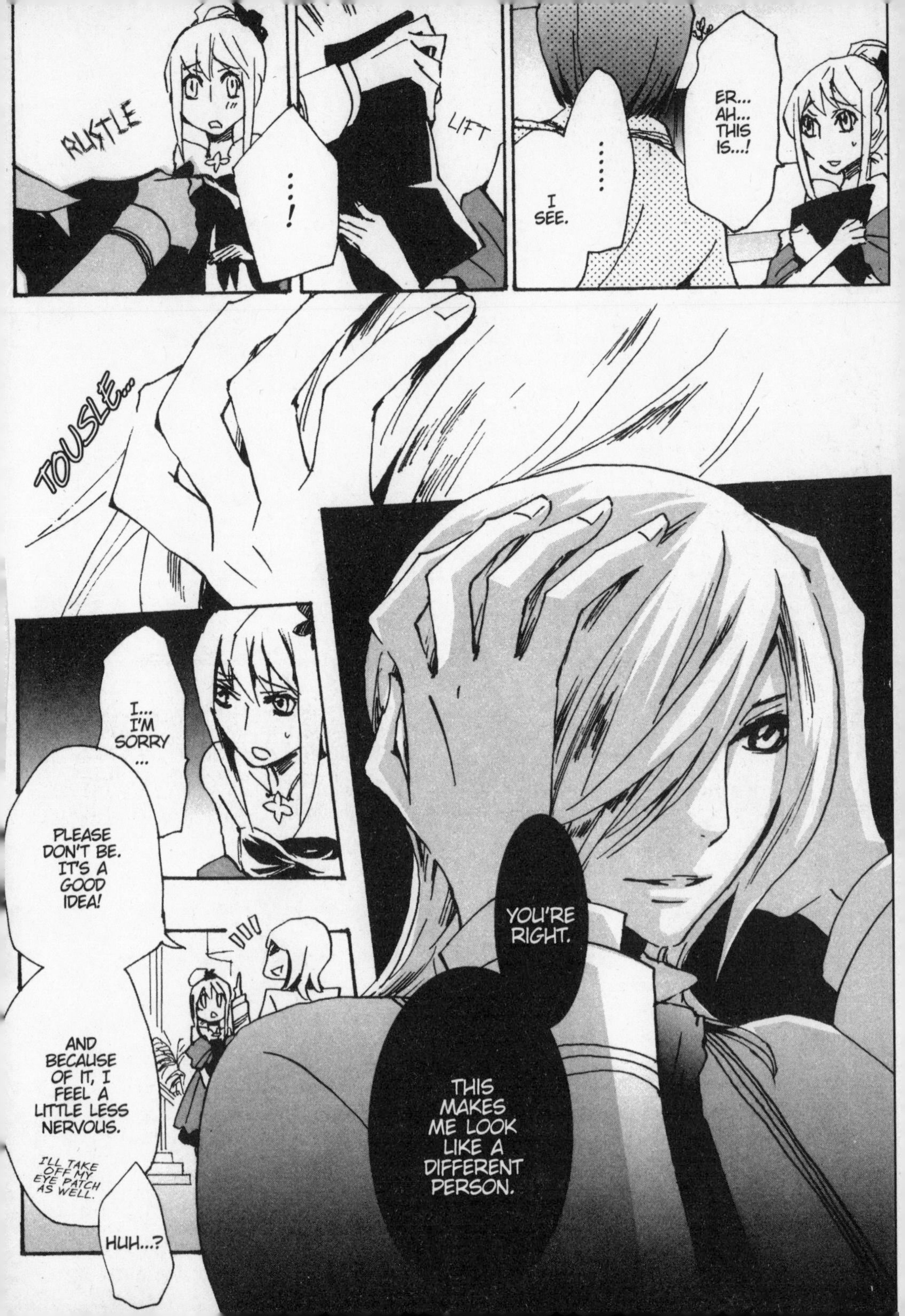
ER... AH... THIS IS...!
......
I SEE.
LIFT
...!
RUSTLE
TOUSLE...
YOU'RE RIGHT.
THIS MAKES ME LOOK LIKE A DIFFERENT PERSON.
I... I'M SORRY ...
PLEASE DON'T BE. IT'S A GOOD IDEA!
AND BECAUSE OF IT, I FEEL A LITTLE LESS NERVOUS.
!!!
I'LL TAKE OFF MY EYE PATCH AS WELL.
HUH...?

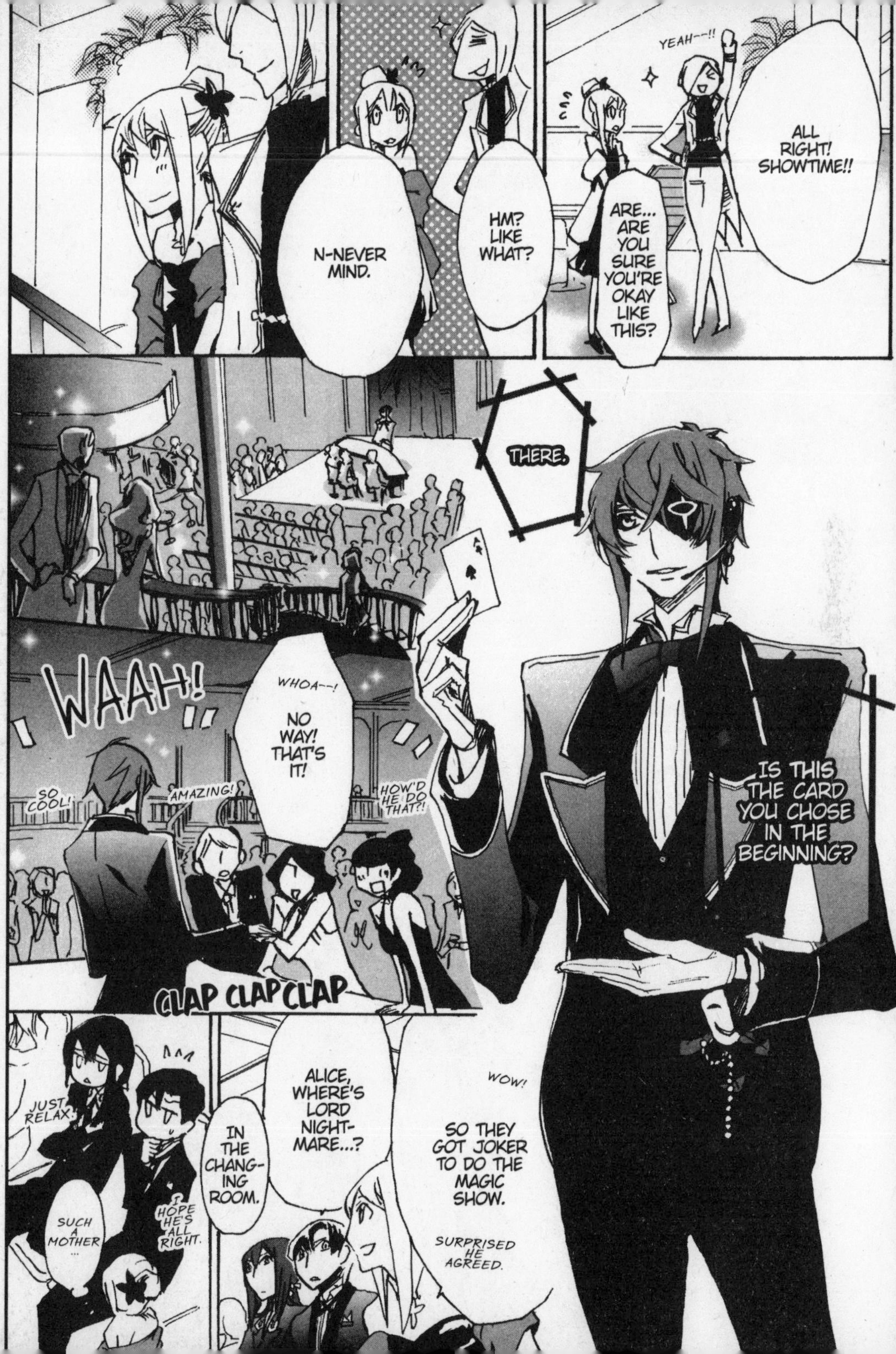
YEAH--!!
ALL RIGHT! SHOWTIME!!
ARE... ARE YOU SURE YOU'RE OKAY LIKE THIS?
HM? LIKE WHAT?
N-NEVER MIND.
THERE.
IS THIS THE CARD YOU CHOSE IN THE BEGINNING?
WHOA--!
NO WAY! THAT'S IT!
HOW'D HE DO THAT?!
AMAZING!
SO COOL!
WAAH!
CLAP CLAP CLAP
WOW!
SO THEY GOT JOKER TO DO THE MAGIC SHOW.
SURPRISED HE AGREED.
ALICE, WHERE'S LORD NIGHTMARE...?
IN THE CHANGING ROOM.
JUST RELAX.
I HOPE HE'S ALL RIGHT.
SUCH A MOTHER...

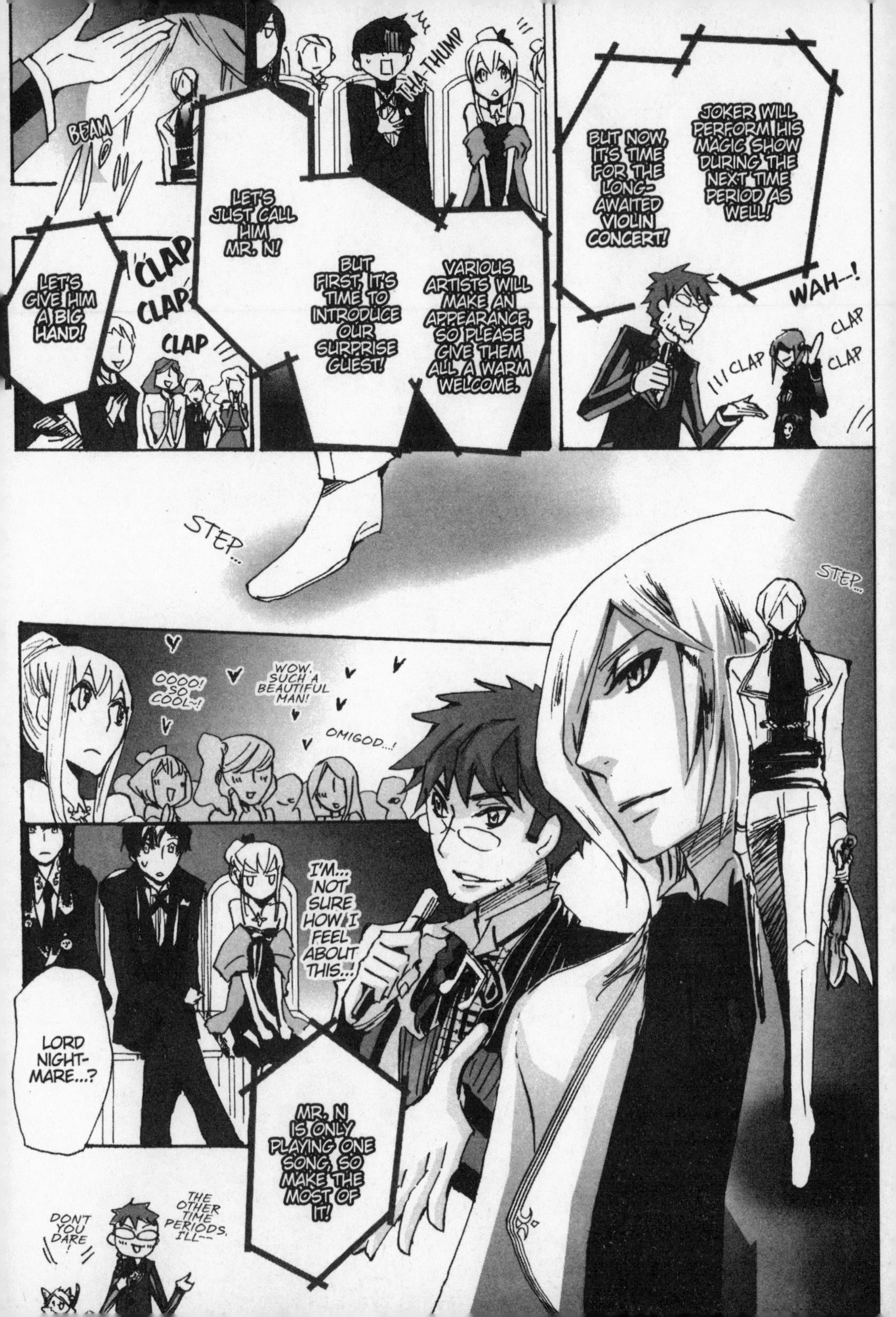
JOKER WILL PERFORM HIS MAGIC SHOW DURING THE NEXT TIME PERIOD AS WELL!
BUT NOW, IT'S TIME FOR THE LONG-AWAITED VIOLIN CONCERT!
WAH--!
CLAP CLAP
CLAP
VARIOUS ARTISTS WILL MAKE AN APPEARANCE, SO PLEASE GIVE THEM ALL A WARM WELCOME.
BUT FIRST, IT'S TIME TO INTRODUCE OUR SURPRISE GUEST!
THA-THUMP
LET'S JUST CALL HIM MR. N!
BEAM
CLAP
CLAP
CLAP
LET'S GIVE HIM A BIG HAND!
STEP...
STEP...
MR. N IS ONLY PLAYING ONE SONG, SO MAKE THE MOST OF IT!
THE OTHER TIME PERIODS, I'LL--
DON'T YOU DARE!
WOW, SUCH A BEAUTIFUL MAN!
OOOO! SO COOL~!
OMIGOD...!
I'M... NOT SURE HOW I FEEL ABOUT THIS...
LORD NIGHT-MARE...?

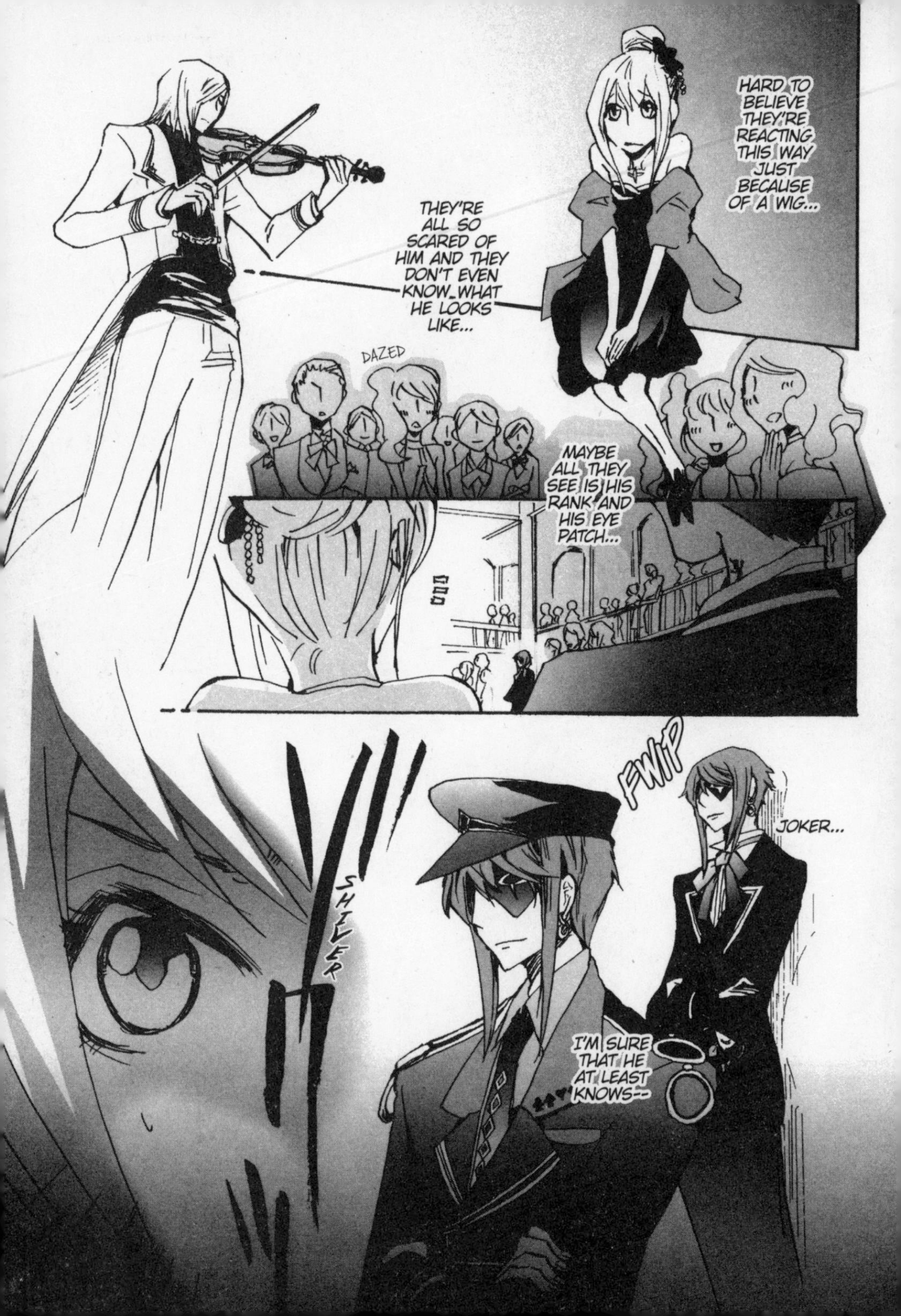
HARD TO BELIEVE THEY'RE REACTING THIS WAY JUST BECAUSE OF A WIG...
THEY'RE ALL SO SCARED OF HIM AND THEY DON'T EVEN KNOW WHAT HE LOOKS LIKE...
DAZED
MAYBE ALL THEY SEE IS HIS RANK AND HIS EYE PATCH...
FWIP
JOKER...
SHIVER
I'M SURE THAT HE AT LEAST KNOWS--

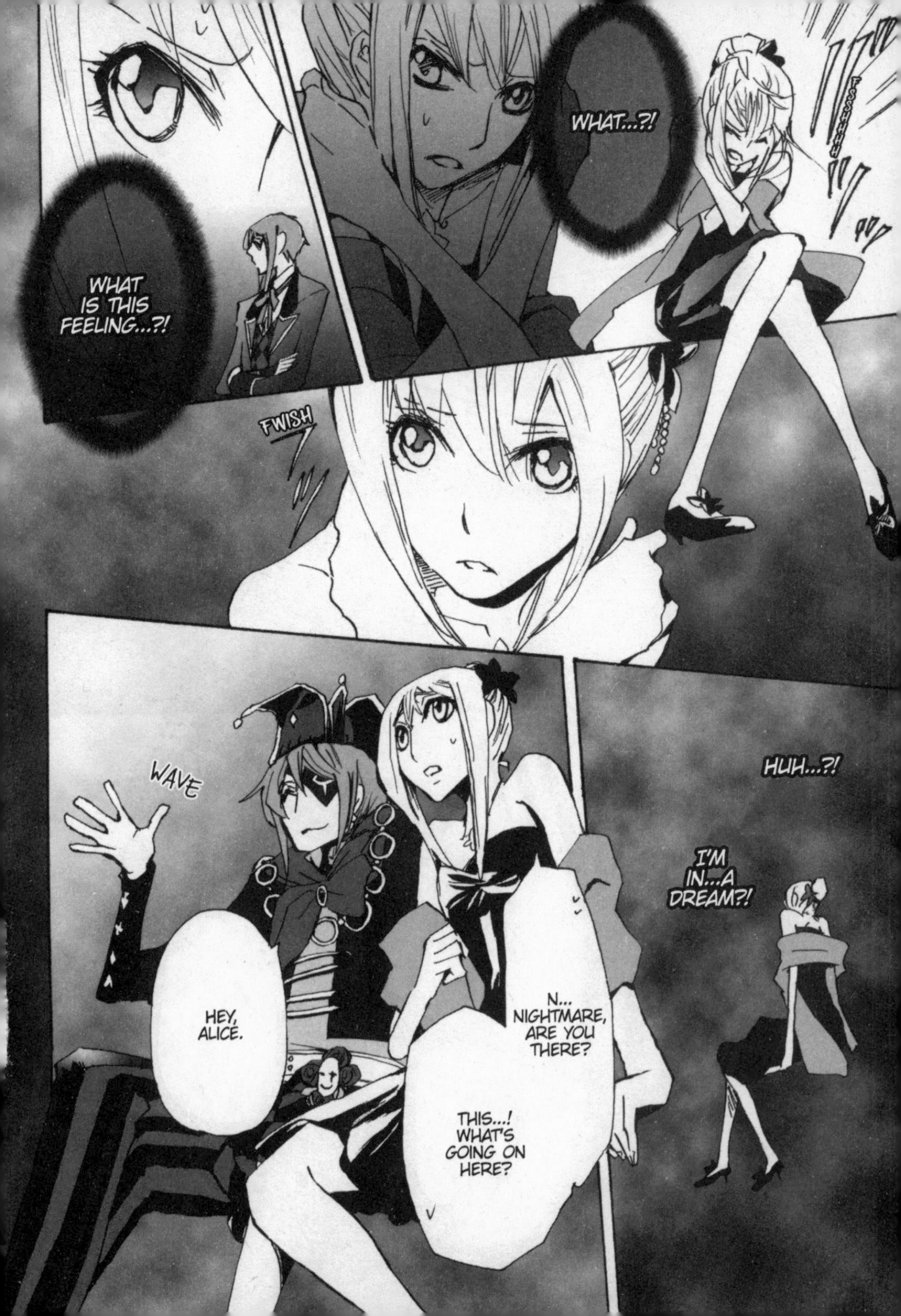
FSSHHHH
WHAT...?!
WHAT IS THIS FEELING...?!
FWISH
HUH...?!
I'M IN...A DREAM?!
N... NIGHTMARE, ARE YOU THERE?
WAVE
HEY, ALICE.
THIS...! WHAT'S GOING ON HERE?

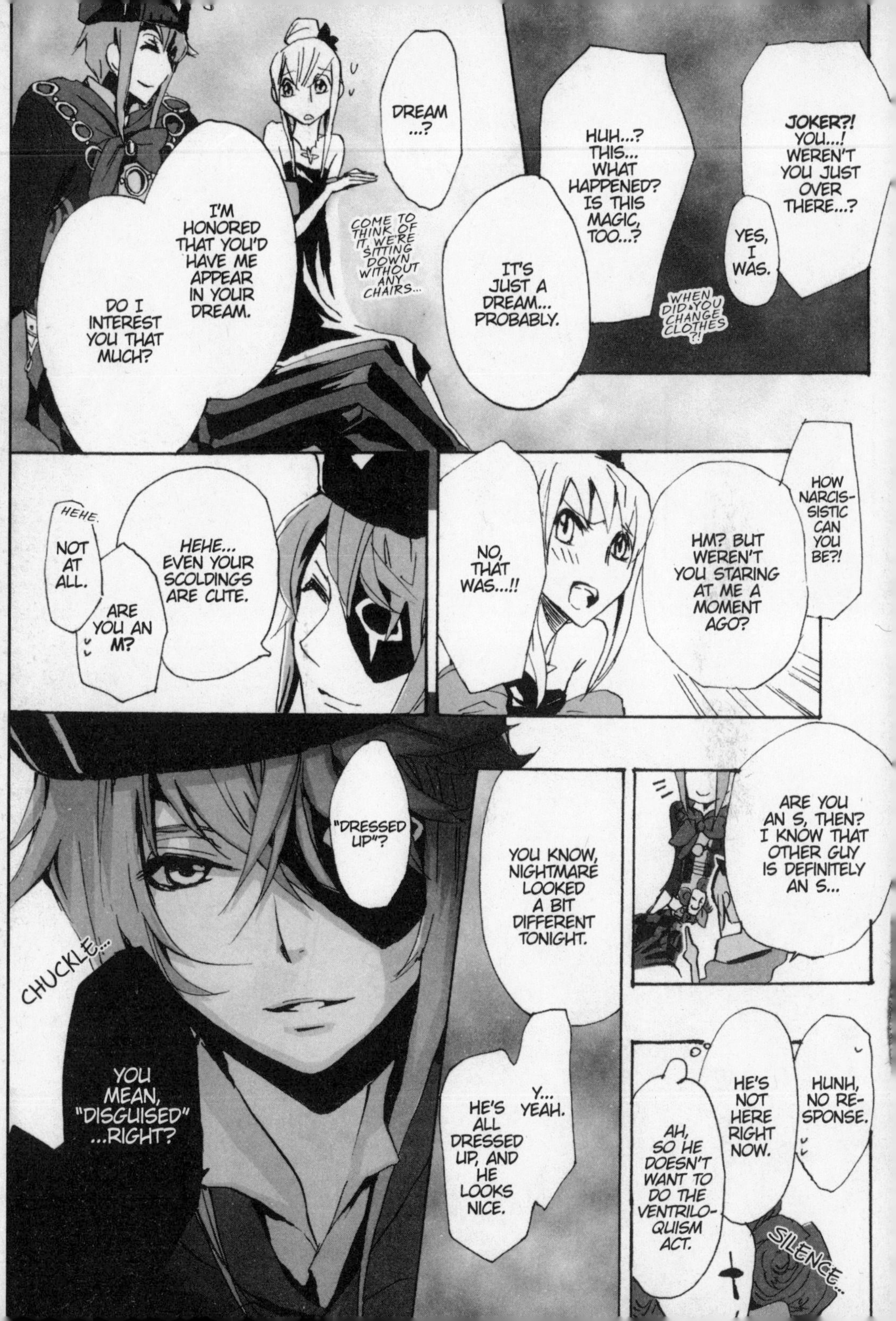
JOKER?! YOU...! WEREN'T YOU JUST OVER THERE...?
YES, I WAS.
WHEN DID YOU CHANGE CLOTHES?!
HUH...? THIS... WHAT HAPPENED? IS THIS MAGIC, TOO...?
IT'S JUST A DREAM... PROBABLY.
DREAM...?
COME TO THINK OF IT, WE'RE SITTING DOWN WITHOUT ANY CHAIRS...
I'M HONORED THAT YOU'D HAVE ME APPEAR IN YOUR DREAM.
DO I INTEREST YOU THAT MUCH?
HOW NARCISSISTIC CAN YOU BE?!
HM? BUT WEREN'T YOU STARING AT ME A MOMENT AGO?
NO, THAT WAS...!!
HEHE... EVEN YOUR SCOLDINGS ARE CUTE.
HEHE.
NOT AT ALL.
ARE YOU AN M?
ARE YOU AN S, THEN? I KNOW THAT OTHER GUY IS DEFINITELY AN S...
HUNH, NO RESPONSE.
HE'S NOT HERE RIGHT NOW.
AH, SO HE DOESN'T WANT TO DO THE VENTRILOQUISM ACT.
SILENCE...
YOU KNOW, NIGHTMARE LOOKED A BIT DIFFERENT TONIGHT.
Y... YEAH.
HE'S ALL DRESSED UP, AND HE LOOKS NICE.
"DRESSED UP"?
CHUCKLE...
YOU MEAN, "DISGUISED" ...RIGHT?

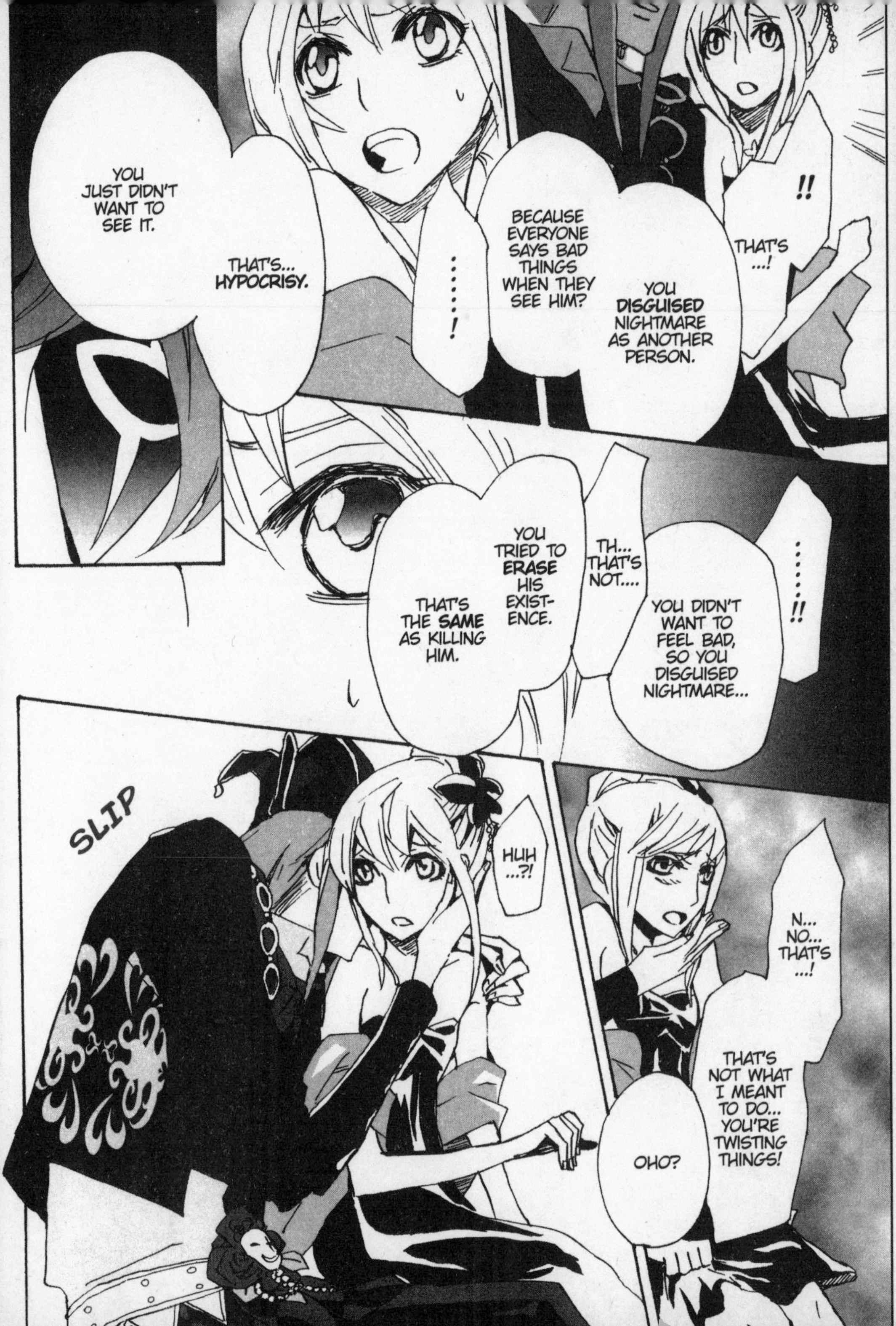
!!
THAT'S ...!
YOU DISGUISED NIGHTMARE AS ANOTHER PERSON.
BECAUSE EVERYONE SAYS BAD THINGS WHEN THEY SEE HIM?
......!
THAT'S... HYPOCRISY.
YOU JUST DIDN'T WANT TO SEE IT.
......!!
YOU DIDN'T WANT TO FEEL BAD, SO YOU DISGUISED NIGHTMARE...
TH... THAT'S NOT....
YOU TRIED TO ERASE HIS EXISTENCE.
THAT'S THE SAME AS KILLING HIM.
N... NO... THAT'S ...!
THAT'S NOT WHAT I MEANT TO DO... YOU'RE TWISTING THINGS!
OHO?
HUH ...?!
SLIP

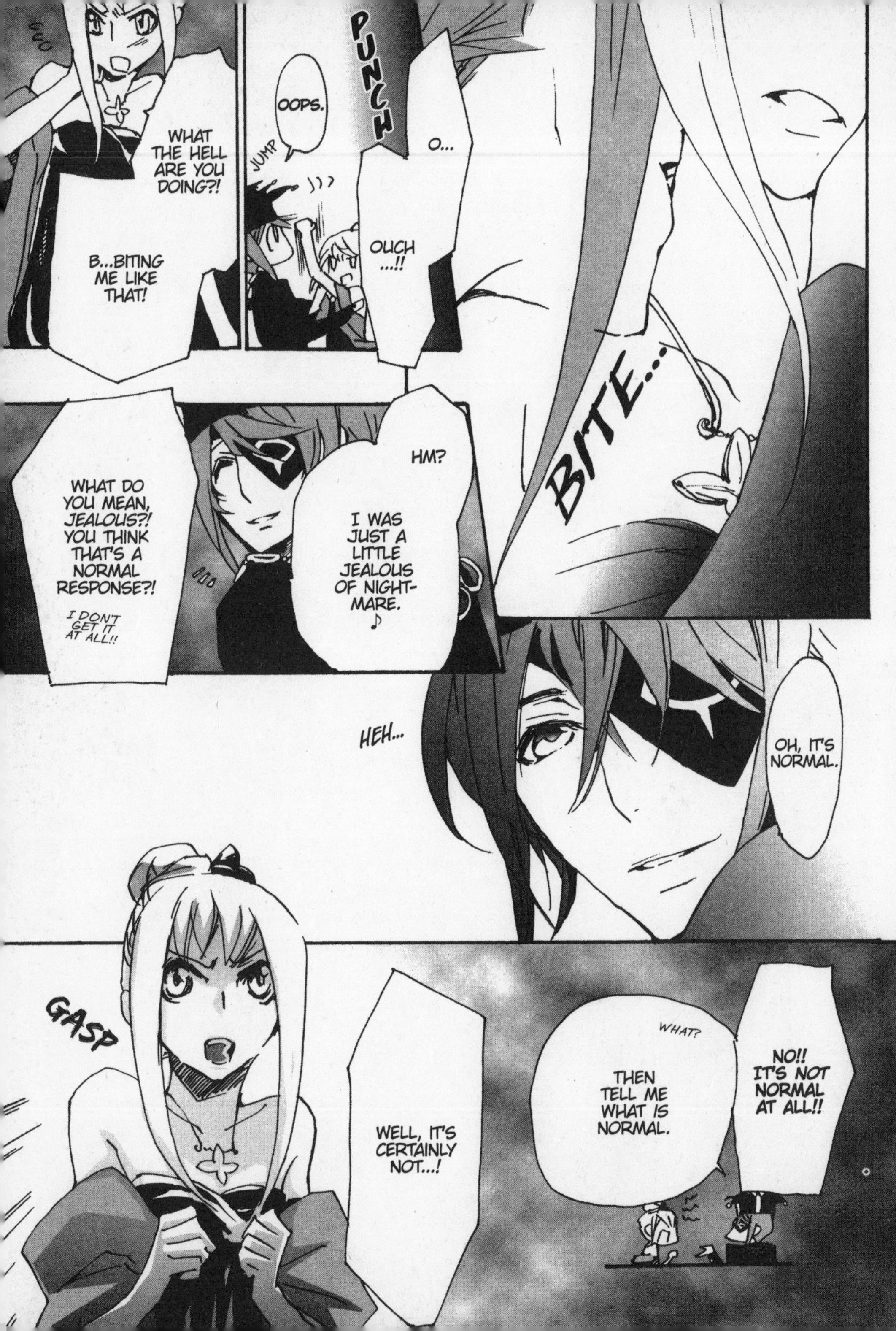
BITE...
PUNCH
O...
OOPS.
JUMP
OUCH ...!!
WHAT THE HELL ARE YOU DOING?!
B...BITING ME LIKE THAT!
HM?
I WAS JUST A LITTLE JEALOUS OF NIGHT-MARE. ♪
WHAT DO YOU MEAN, JEALOUS?! YOU THINK THAT'S A NORMAL RESPONSE?!
I DON'T GET IT AT ALL!!
OH, IT'S NORMAL.
HEH...
NO!! IT'S NOT NORMAL AT ALL!!
WHAT?
THEN TELL ME WHAT IS NORMAL.
WELL, IT'S CERTAINLY NOT...!
GASP

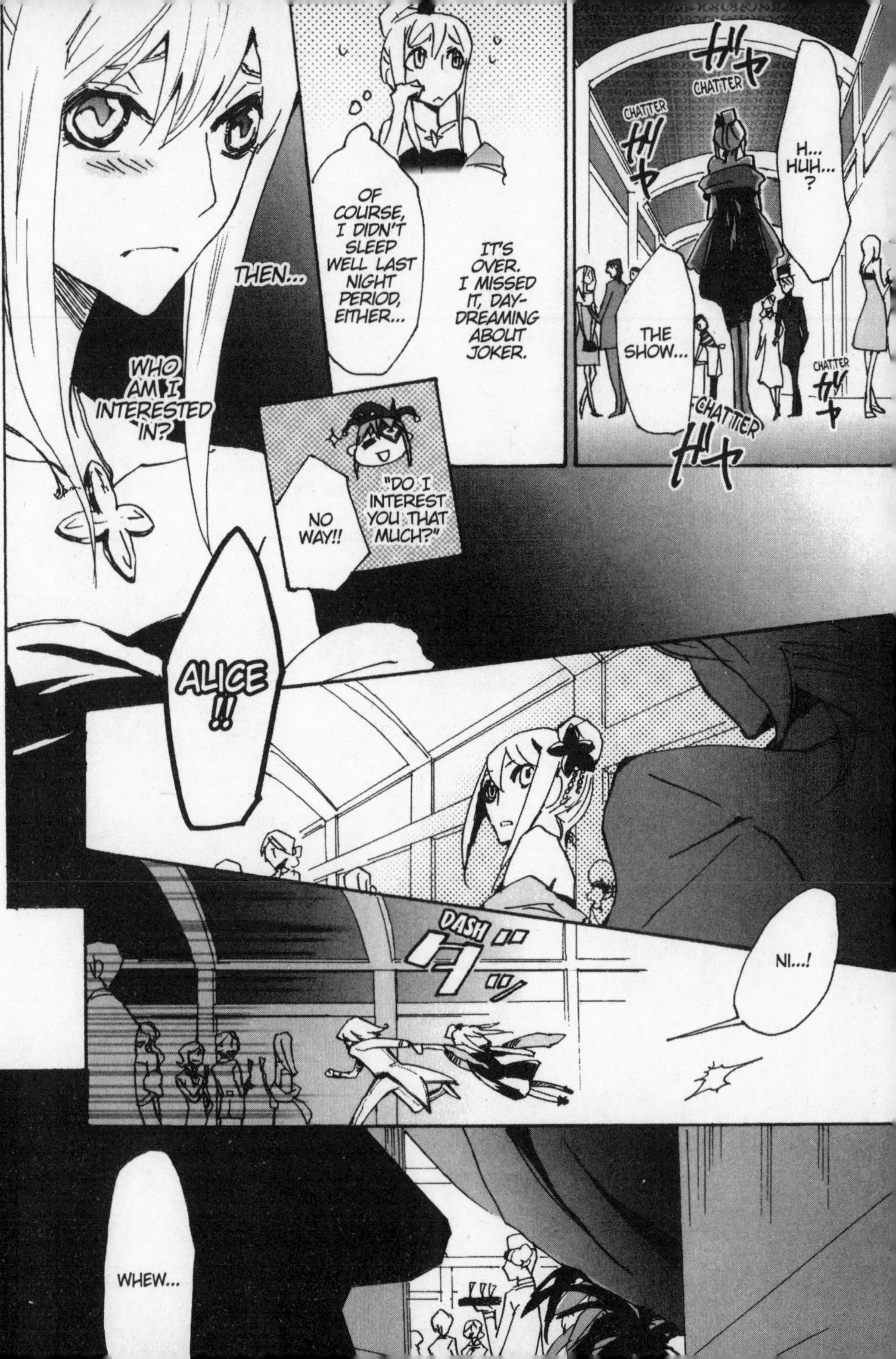

CHATTER
ガヤ
H... HUH...?
CHATTER
ガヤ
THE SHOW...
CHATTER
ガヤ
CHATTER
ガヤ
IT'S OVER. I MISSED IT, DAY-DREAMING ABOUT JOKER.
OF COURSE, I DIDN'T SLEEP WELL LAST NIGHT PERIOD, EITHER...
THEN...
WHO AM I INTERESTED IN?
"DO I INTEREST YOU THAT MUCH?"
NO WAY!!
ALICE!!
DASH
NI...!
WHEW...

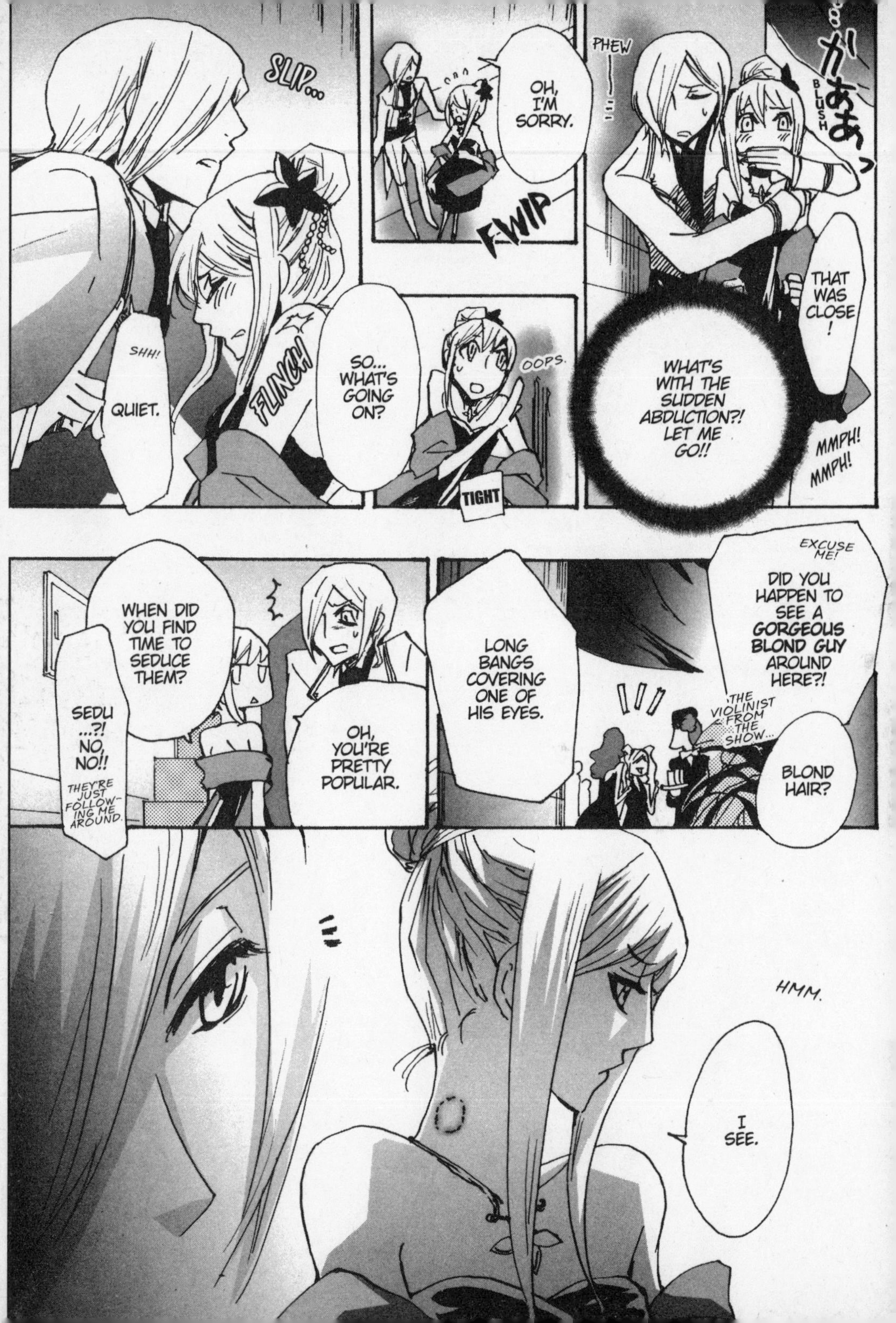
BLUSH
THAT WAS CLOSE!
WHAT'S WITH THE SUDDEN ABDUCTION?! LET ME GO!!
MMPH! MMPH!
PHEW
OH, I'M SORRY.
FWIP
OOPS.
SO... WHAT'S GOING ON?
TIGHT
SLIP...
FLINCH
SHH!
QUIET.
EXCUSE ME!
DID YOU HAPPEN TO SEE A GORGEOUS BLOND GUY AROUND HERE?!
THE VIOLINIST FROM THE SHOW...
BLOND HAIR?
LONG BANGS COVERING ONE OF HIS EYES.
WHEN DID YOU FIND TIME TO SEDUCE THEM?
OH, YOU'RE PRETTY POPULAR.
SEDU...?! NO, NO!!
THEY'RE JUST FOLLOWING ME AROUND.
HMM.
I SEE.

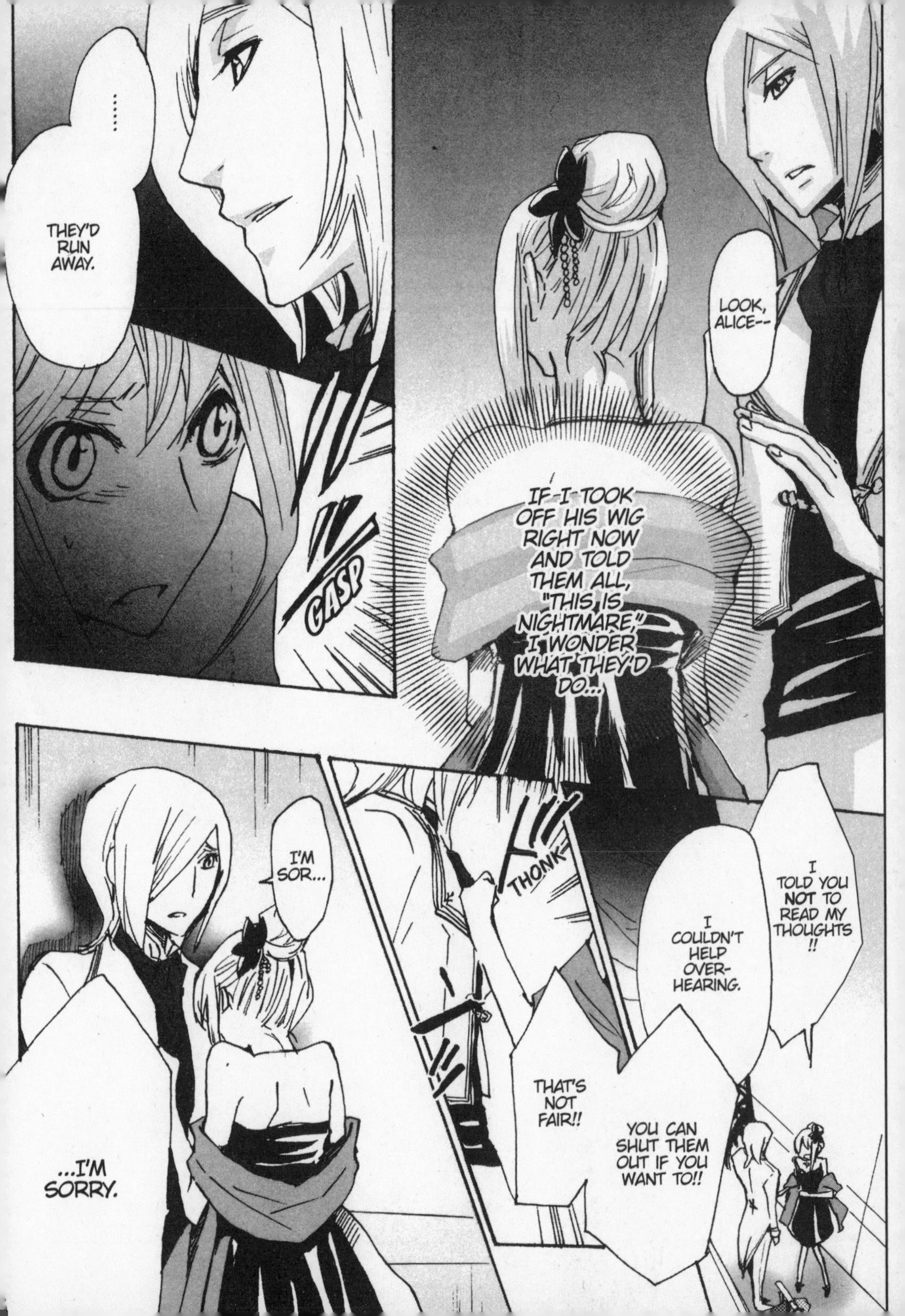

LOOK, ALICE--
IF I TOOK OFF HIS WIG RIGHT NOW AND TOLD THEM ALL, "THIS IS NIGHTMARE," I WONDER WHAT THEY'D DO...
......
THEY'D RUN AWAY.
GASP
I TOLD YOU NOT TO READ MY THOUGHTS!!
I COULDN'T HELP OVER-HEARING.
THAT'S NOT FAIR!!
YOU CAN SHUT THEM OUT IF YOU WANT TO!!
THONK
!!
I'M SOR...
...I'M SORRY.

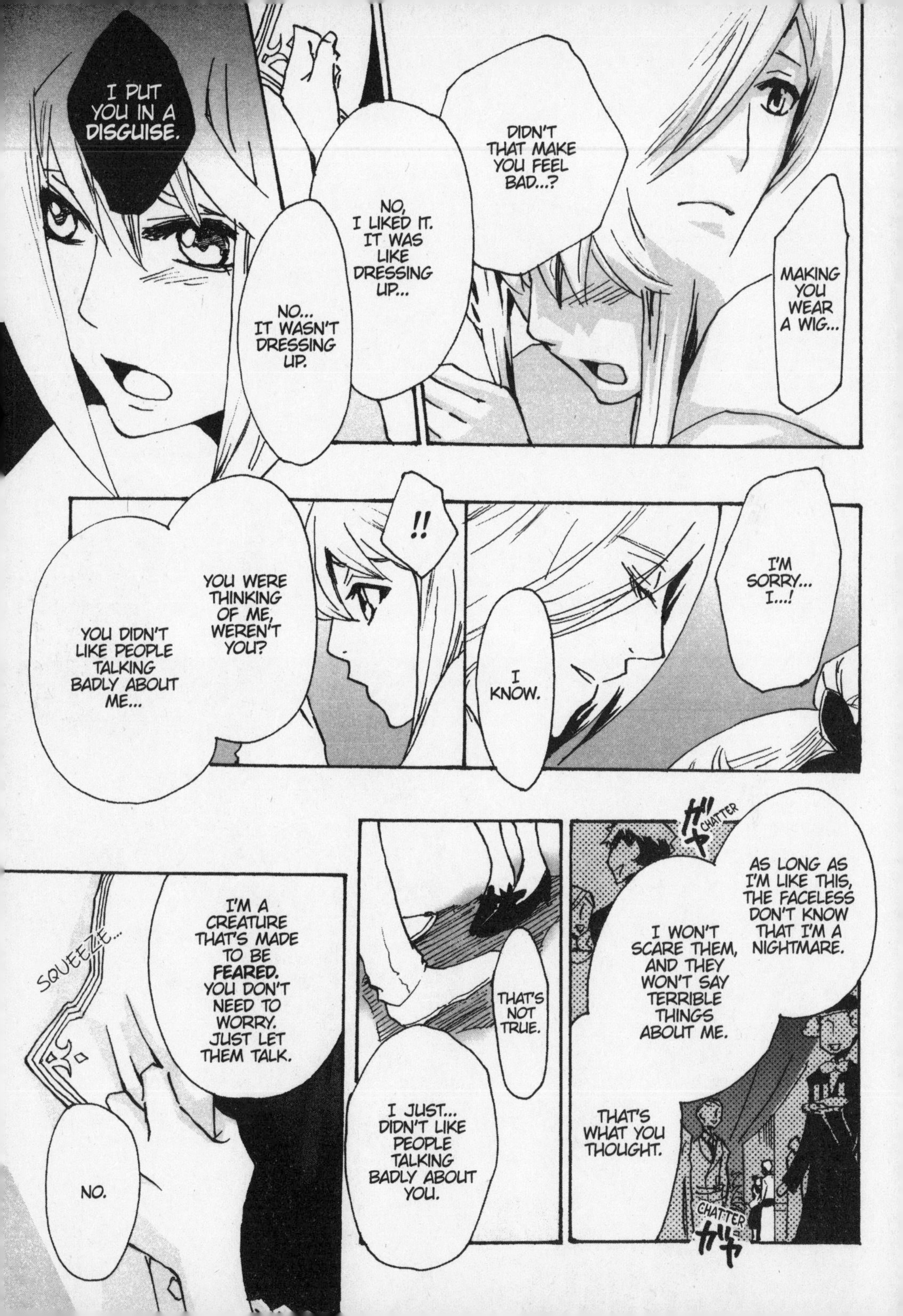
MAKING YOU WEAR A WIG...
DIDN'T THAT MAKE YOU FEEL BAD...?
NO, I LIKED IT. IT WAS LIKE DRESSING UP...
I PUT YOU IN A DISGUISE.
NO... IT WASN'T DRESSING UP.
I'M SORRY... I...!
I KNOW.
!!
YOU WERE THINKING OF ME, WEREN'T YOU?
YOU DIDN'T LIKE PEOPLE TALKING BADLY ABOUT ME...
ガヤ CHATTER
AS LONG AS I'M LIKE THIS, THE FACELESS DON'T KNOW THAT I'M A NIGHTMARE.
I WON'T SCARE THEM, AND THEY WON'T SAY TERRIBLE THINGS ABOUT ME.
THAT'S WHAT YOU THOUGHT.
CHATTER ガヤ
THAT'S NOT TRUE.
I JUST... DIDN'T LIKE PEOPLE TALKING BADLY ABOUT YOU.
I'M A CREATURE THAT'S MADE TO BE FEARED. YOU DON'T NEED TO WORRY. JUST LET THEM TALK.
SQUEEZE...
NO.

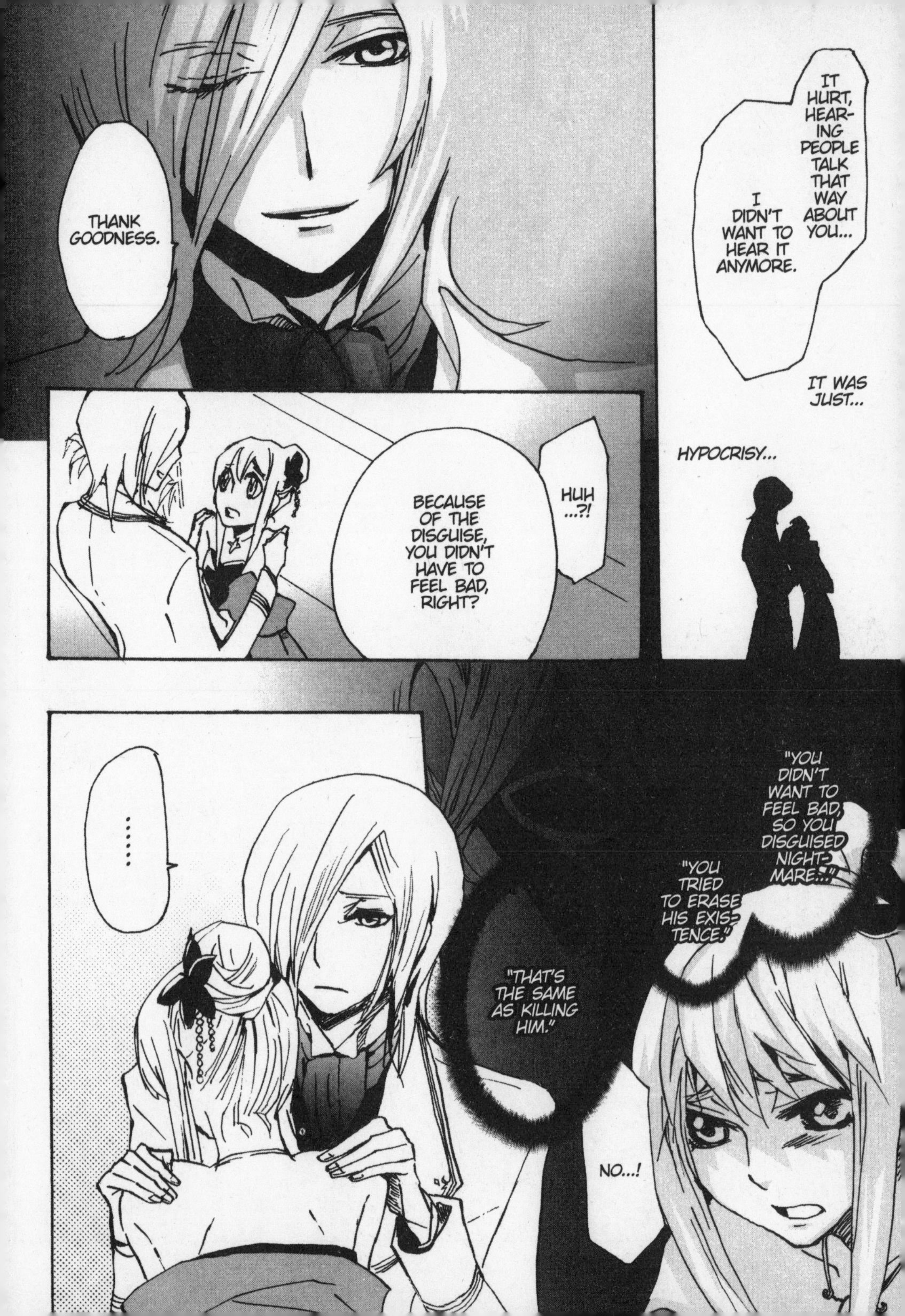
IT HURT, HEARING PEOPLE TALK THAT WAY ABOUT YOU...
I DIDN'T WANT TO HEAR IT ANYMORE.
THANK GOODNESS.
HUH ...?!
BECAUSE OF THE DISGUISE, YOU DIDN'T HAVE TO FEEL BAD, RIGHT?
IT WAS JUST...
HYPOCRISY...
"YOU DIDN'T WANT TO FEEL BAD, SO YOU DISGUISED NIGHTMARE..."
"YOU TRIED TO ERASE HIS EXISTENCE."
"THAT'S THE SAME AS KILLING HIM."
NO...!
......

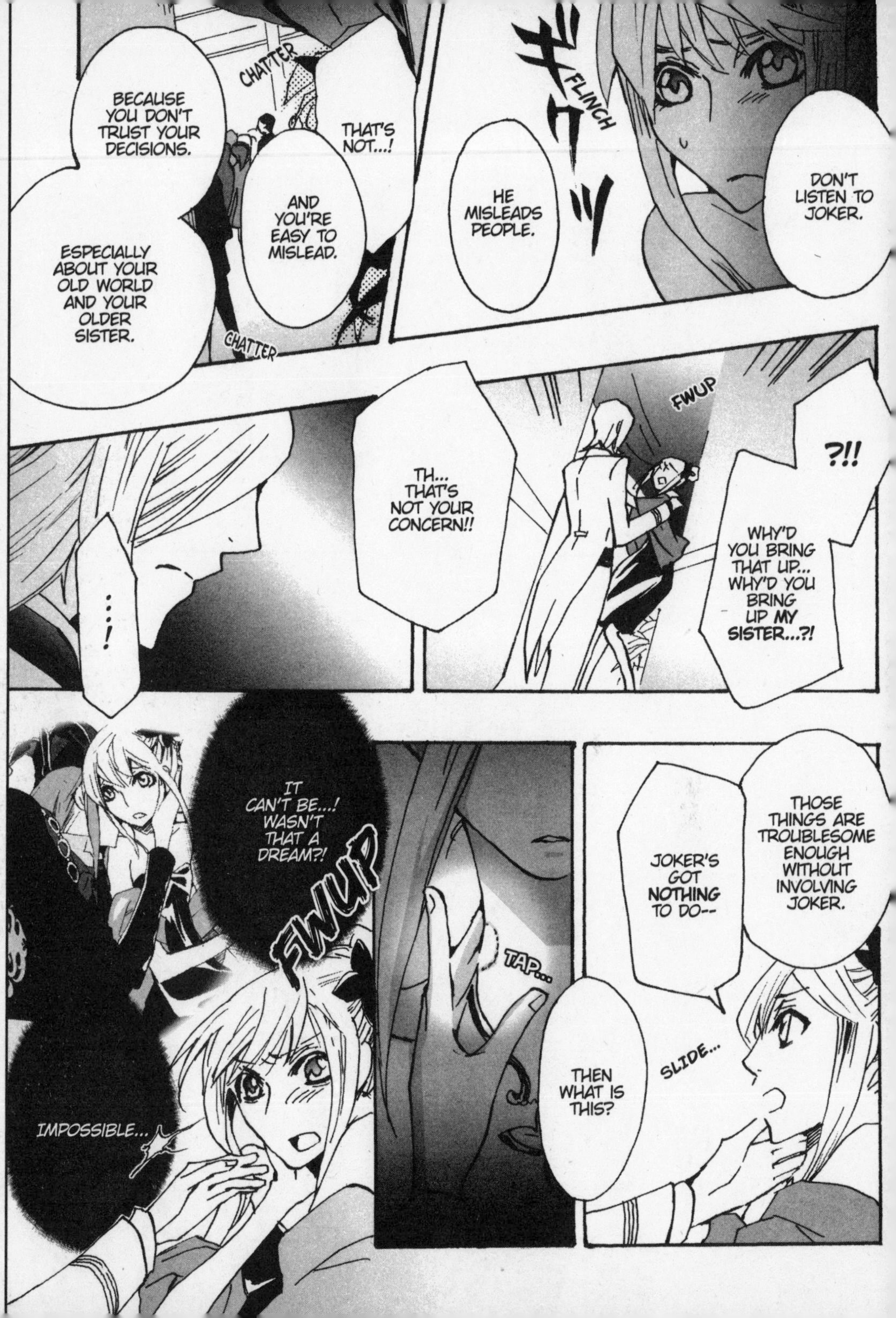
DON'T LISTEN TO JOKER.
ギクッ
FLINCH
HE MISLEADS PEOPLE.
CHATTER
THAT'S NOT...!
BECAUSE YOU DON'T TRUST YOUR DECISIONS.
AND YOU'RE EASY TO MISLEAD.
ESPECIALLY ABOUT YOUR OLD WORLD AND YOUR OLDER SISTER.
CHATTER
?!!
FWUP
WHY'D YOU BRING THAT UP... WHY'D YOU BRING UP MY SISTER...?!
TH... THAT'S NOT YOUR CONCERN!!
...!
THOSE THINGS ARE TROUBLESOME ENOUGH WITHOUT INVOLVING JOKER.
JOKER'S GOT NOTHING TO DO--
SLIDE...
THEN WHAT IS THIS?
TAP...
IT CAN'T BE...! WASN'T THAT A DREAM?!
FWUP
IMPOSSIBLE...

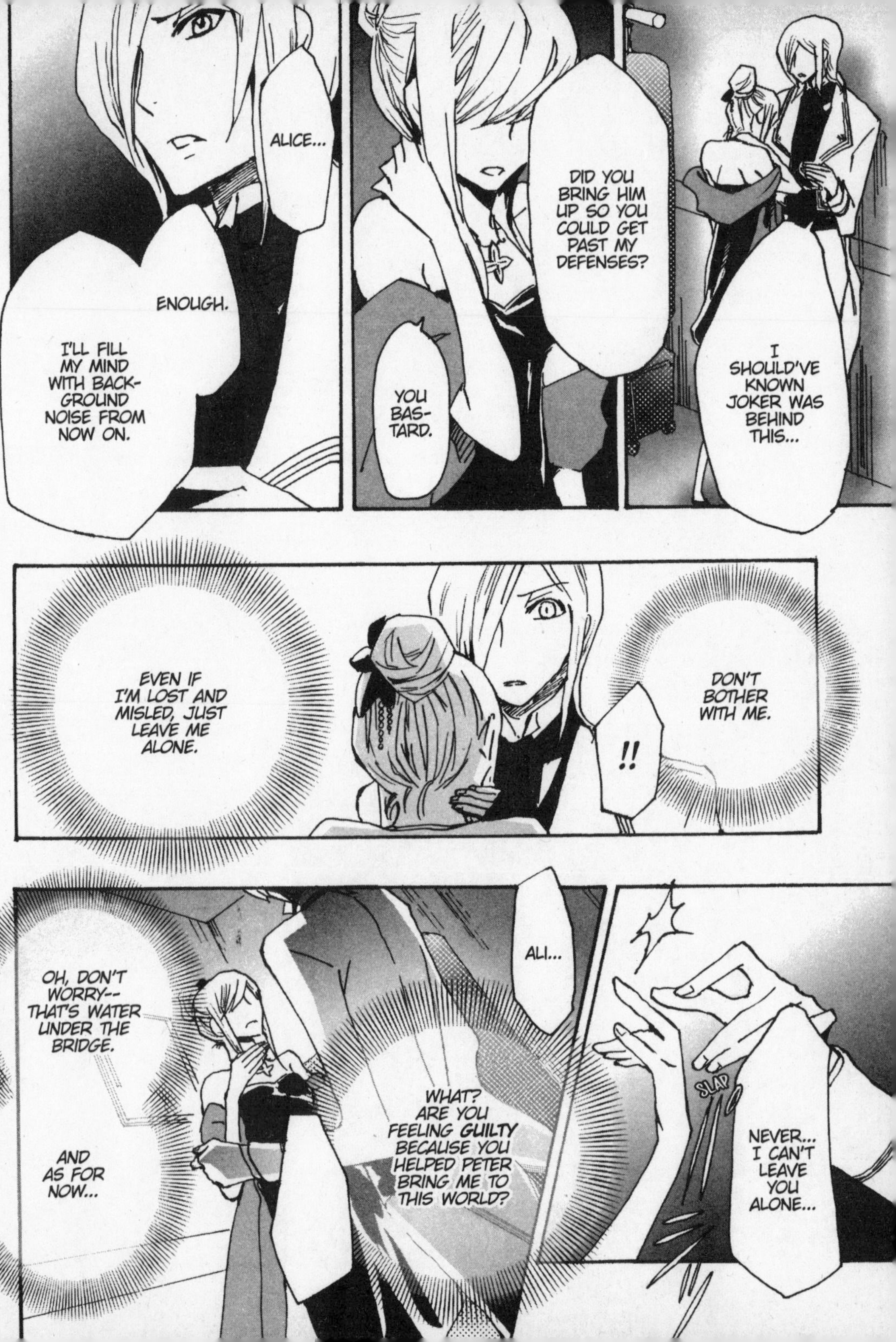
I SHOULD'VE KNOWN JOKER WAS BEHIND THIS...
DID YOU BRING HIM UP SO YOU COULD GET PAST MY DEFENSES?
YOU BASTARD.
ALICE...
ENOUGH.
I'LL FILL MY MIND WITH BACK-GROUND NOISE FROM NOW ON.
DON'T BOTHER WITH ME.
!!
EVEN IF I'M LOST AND MISLED, JUST LEAVE ME ALONE.
NEVER... I CAN'T LEAVE YOU ALONE...
SLAP
ALI...
WHAT? ARE YOU FEELING GUILTY BECAUSE YOU HELPED PETER BRING ME TO THIS WORLD?
OH, DON'T WORRY--THAT'S WATER UNDER THE BRIDGE.
AND AS FOR NOW...

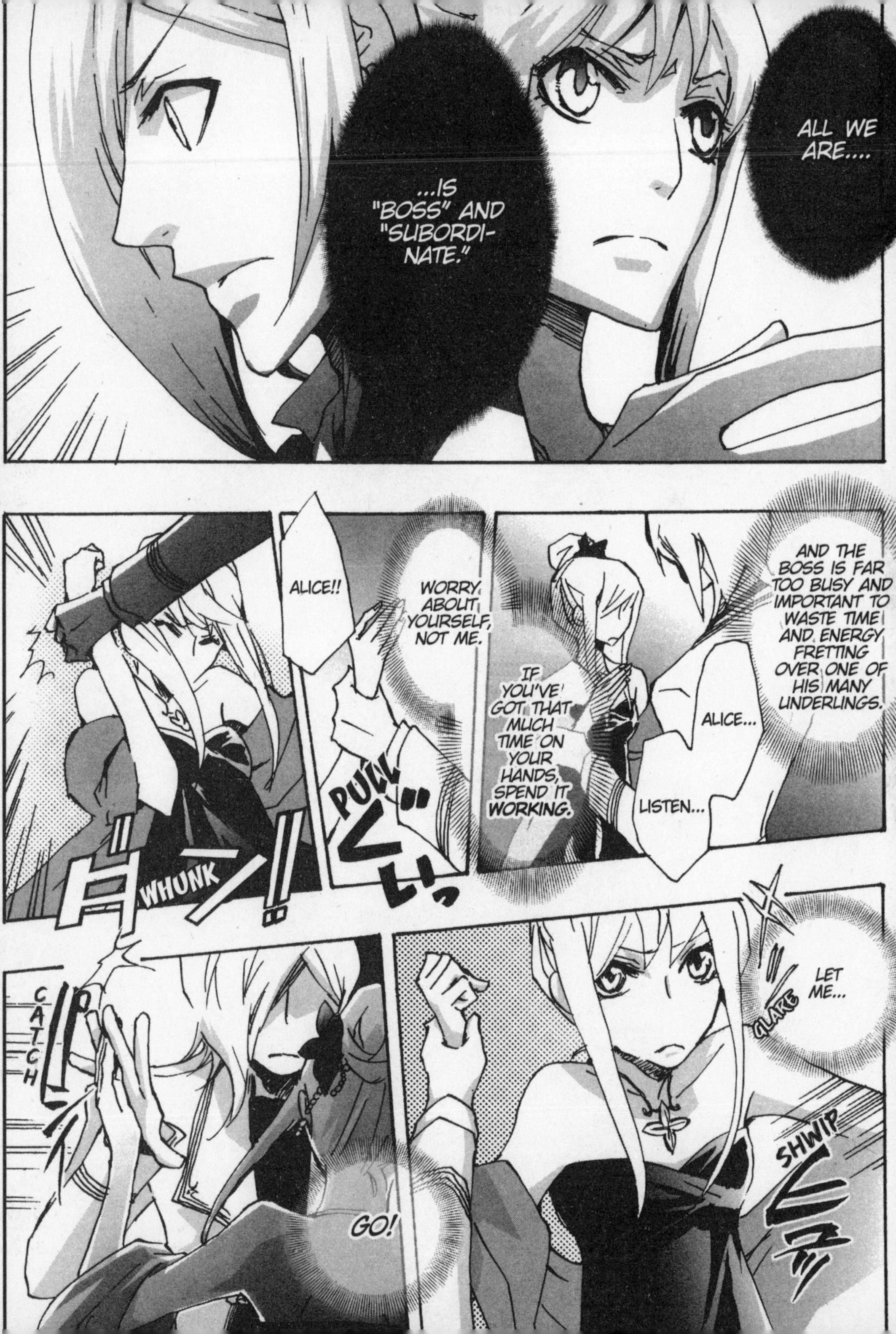
ALL WE ARE....
...IS "BOSS" AND "SUBORDI-NATE."
AND THE BOSS IS FAR TOO BUSY AND IMPORTANT TO WASTE TIME AND ENERGY FRETTING OVER ONE OF HIS MANY UNDERLINGS.
ALICE...
IF YOU'VE GOT THAT MUCH TIME ON YOUR HANDS, SPEND IT WORKING.
LISTEN...
WORRY ABOUT YOURSELF, NOT ME.
PULL
ALICE!!
WHUNK
LET ME...
GLARE
SHWIP
GO!
CATCH

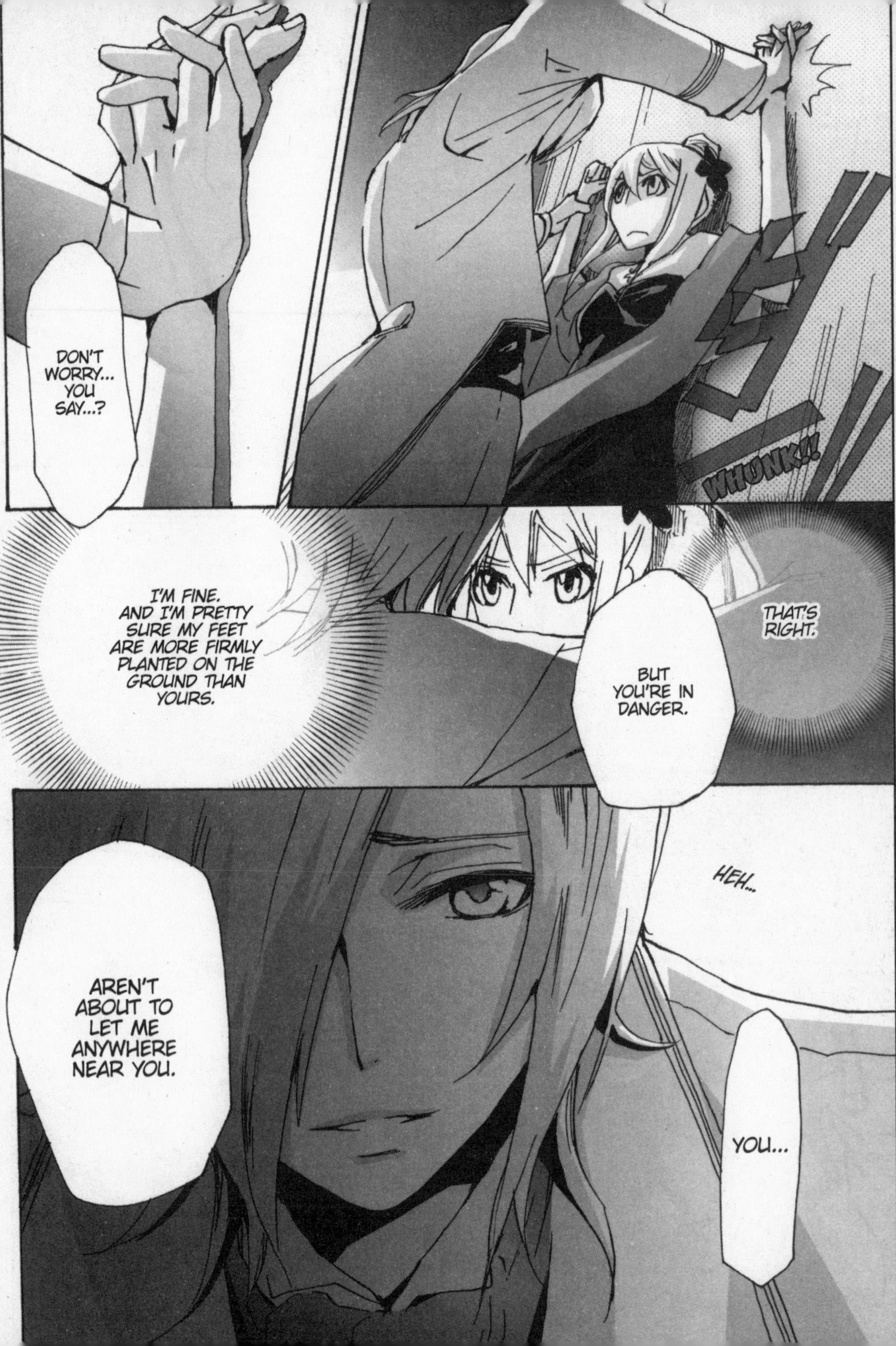
WHONK!!
DON'T WORRY... YOU SAY...?
THAT'S RIGHT.
BUT YOU'RE IN DANGER.
I'M FINE. AND I'M PRETTY SURE MY FEET ARE MORE FIRMLY PLANTED ON THE GROUND THAN YOURS.
HEH...
YOU...
AREN'T ABOUT TO LET ME ANYWHERE NEAR YOU.

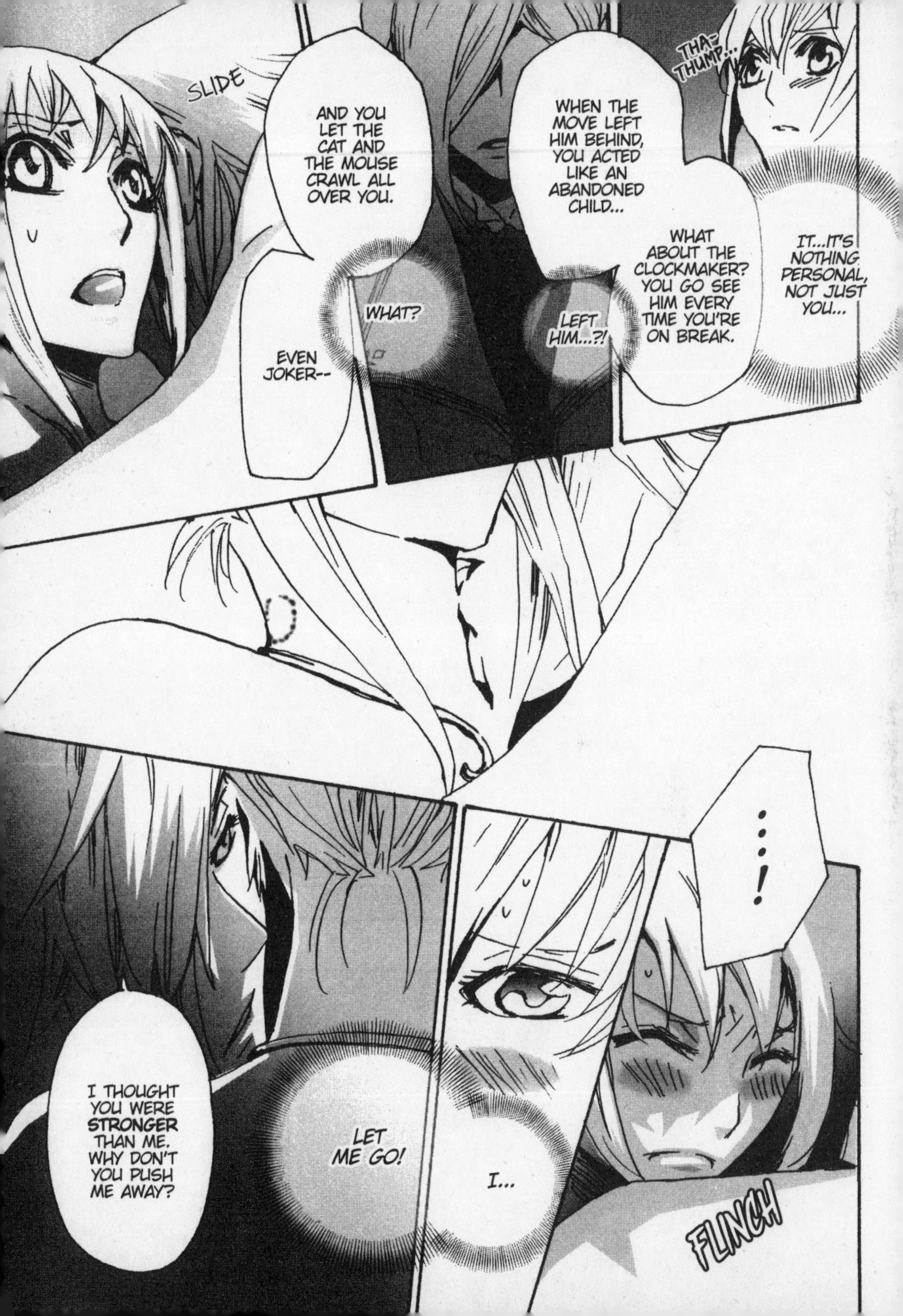
THA-THUMP...
IT...IT'S NOTHING PERSONAL, NOT JUST YOU...
WHAT ABOUT THE CLOCKMAKER? YOU GO SEE HIM EVERY TIME YOU'RE ON BREAK.
WHEN THE MOVE LEFT HIM BEHIND, YOU ACTED LIKE AN ABANDONED CHILD...
LEFT HIM...?!
AND YOU LET THE CAT AND THE MOUSE CRAWL ALL OVER YOU.
WHAT?
EVEN JOKER--
SLIDE
...!
I...
FLINCH
I THOUGHT YOU WERE **STRONGER** THAN ME. WHY DON'T YOU PUSH ME AWAY?
LET ME GO!

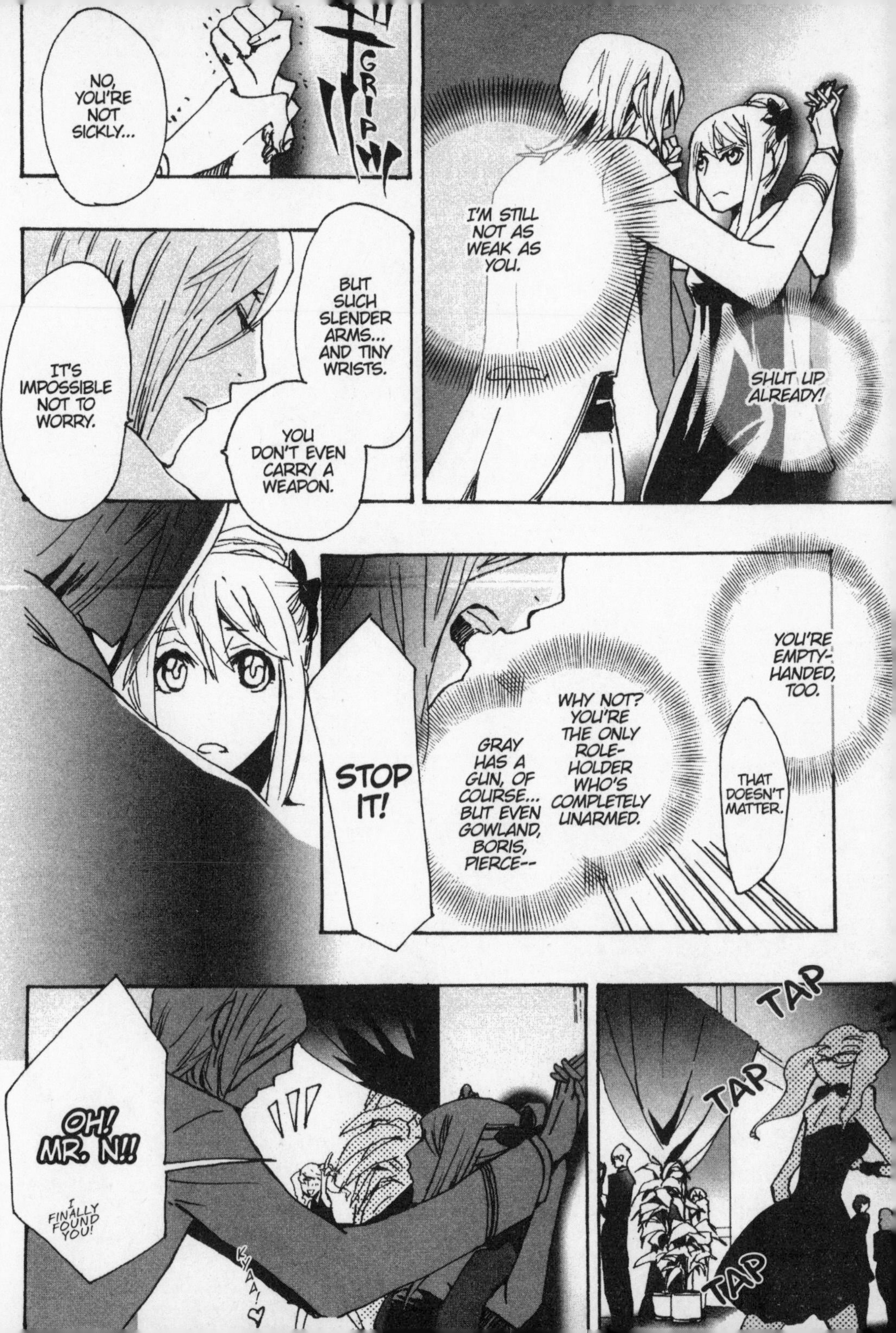
I'M STILL NOT AS WEAK AS YOU.
SHUT UP ALREADY!
GRIP
NO, YOU'RE NOT SICKLY...
BUT SUCH SLENDER ARMS... AND TINY WRISTS.
YOU DON'T EVEN CARRY A WEAPON.
IT'S IMPOSSIBLE NOT TO WORRY.
YOU'RE EMPTY-HANDED, TOO.
THAT DOESN'T MATTER.
WHY NOT? YOU'RE THE ONLY ROLE-HOLDER WHO'S COMPLETELY UNARMED.
GRAY HAS A GUN, OF COURSE... BUT EVEN GOWLAND, BORIS, PIERCE--
STOP IT!
TAP
TAP
TAP
TAP
OH! MR. N!!
I FINALLY FOUND YOU!
KYAA!

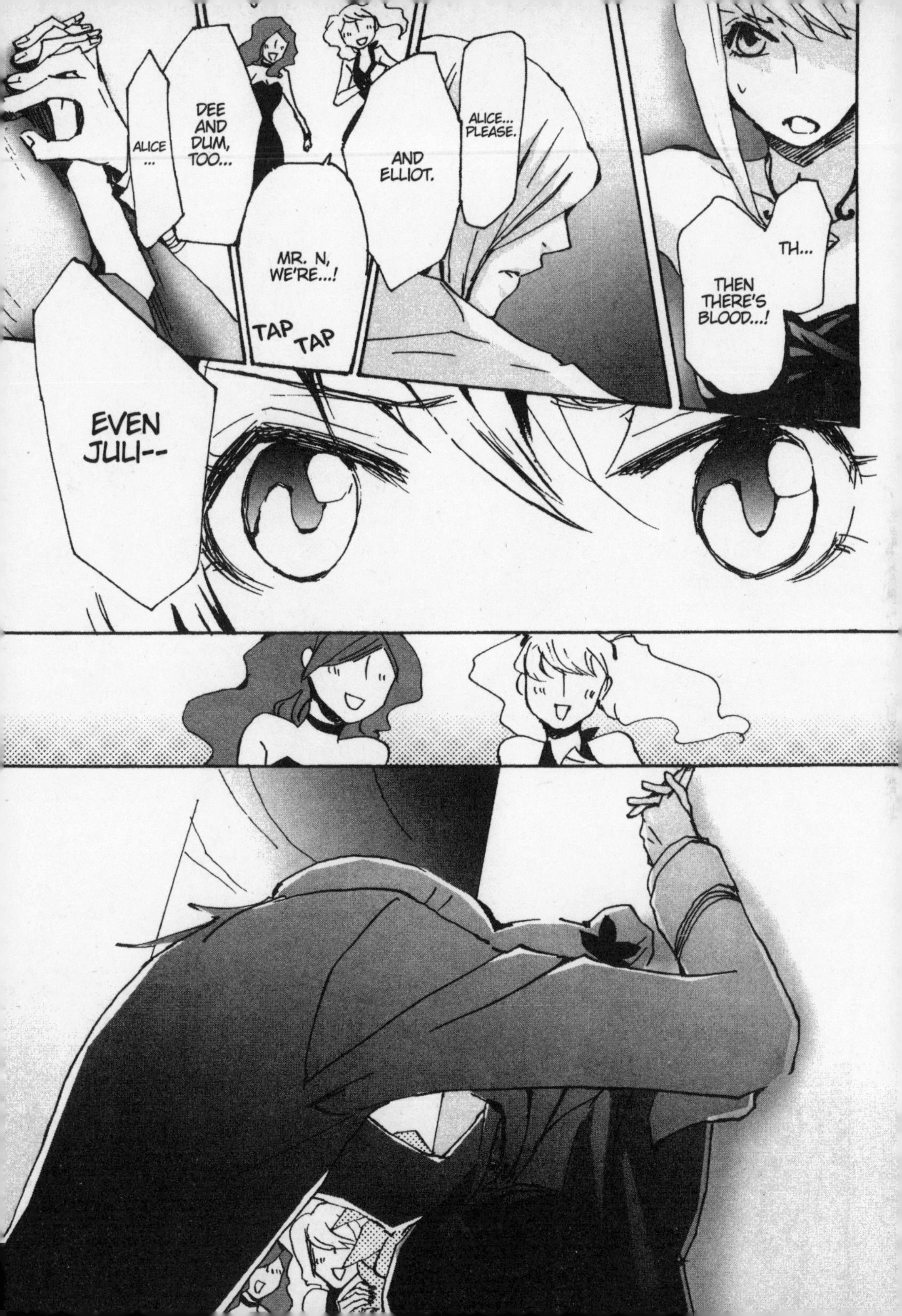
TH...
THEN THERE'S BLOOD...!
ALICE... PLEASE.
AND ELLIOT.
DEE AND DUM, TOO...
ALICE ...
MR. N, WE'RE...!
TAP TAP
EVEN JULI--

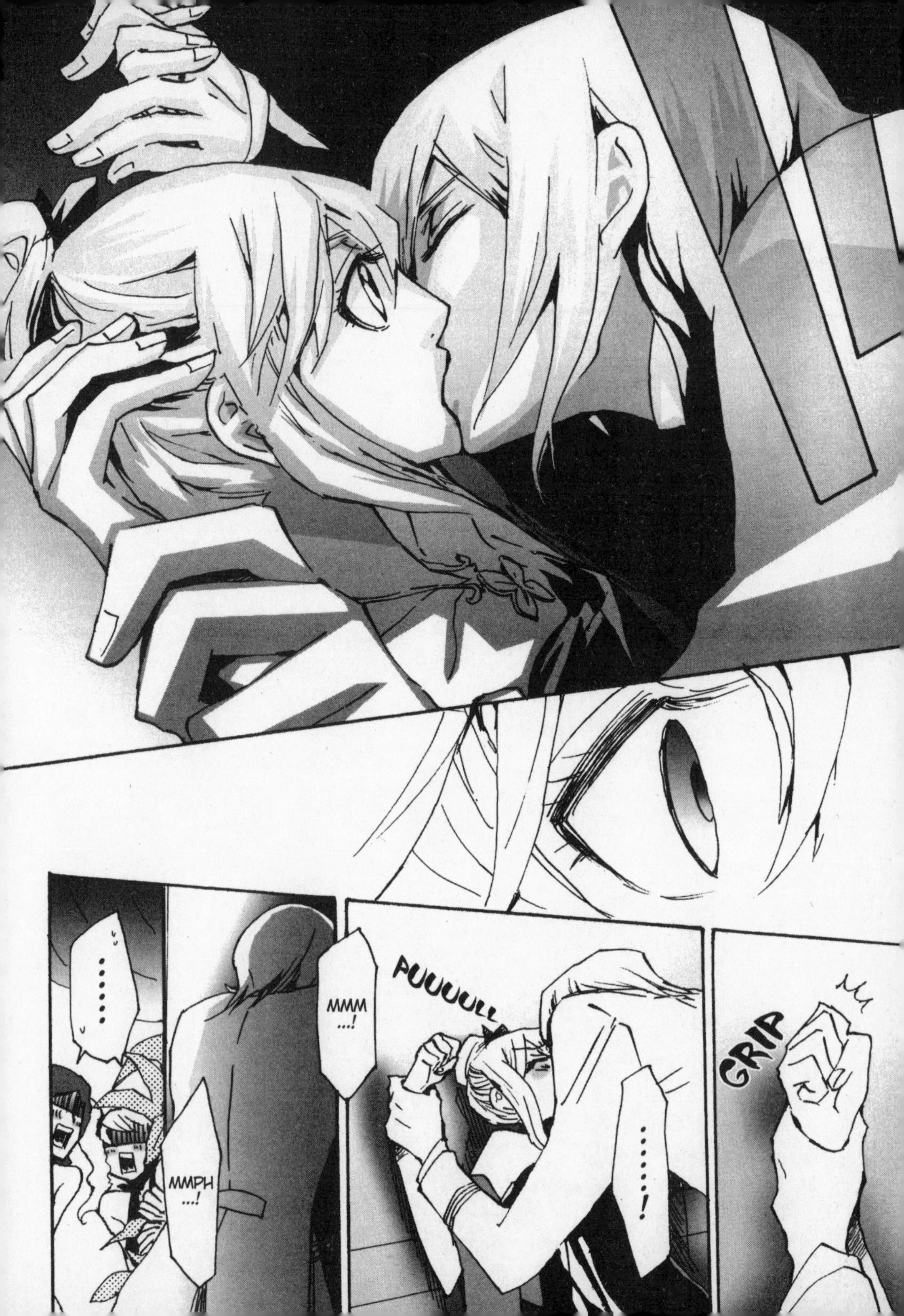
GRIP
PUUUULL
MMM ...!
.......!
......
MMPH ...!

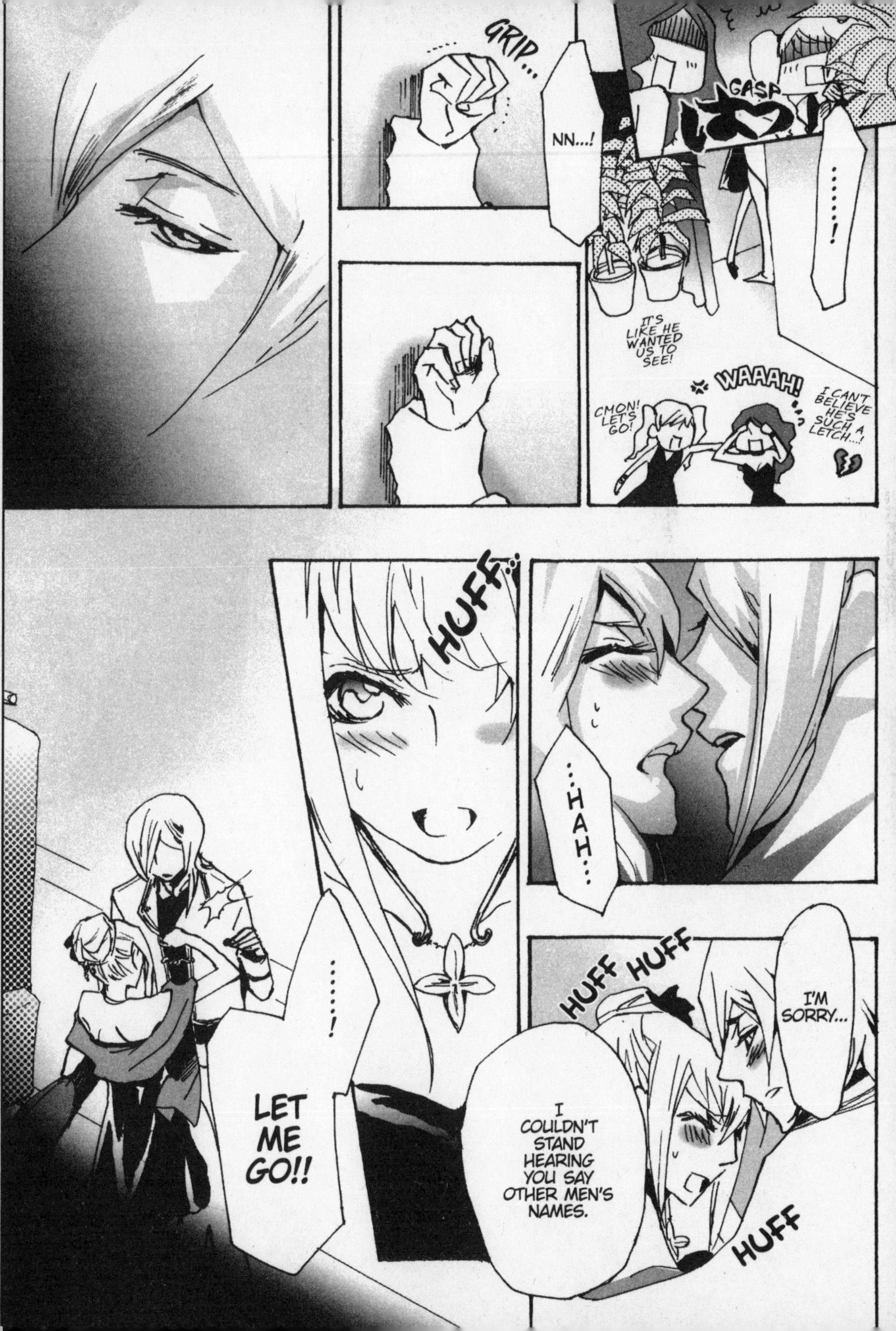
GASP
......!
IT'S LIKE HE WANTED US TO SEE!
WAAAH!
I CAN'T BELIEVE HE'S SUCH A LETCH...!
CMON! LET'S GO!
GRIP...
.....
NN...!
...HAH...
I'M SORRY...
HUFF HUFF
I COULDN'T STAND HEARING YOU SAY OTHER MEN'S NAMES.
HUFF
HUFF...
......!
LET ME GO!!

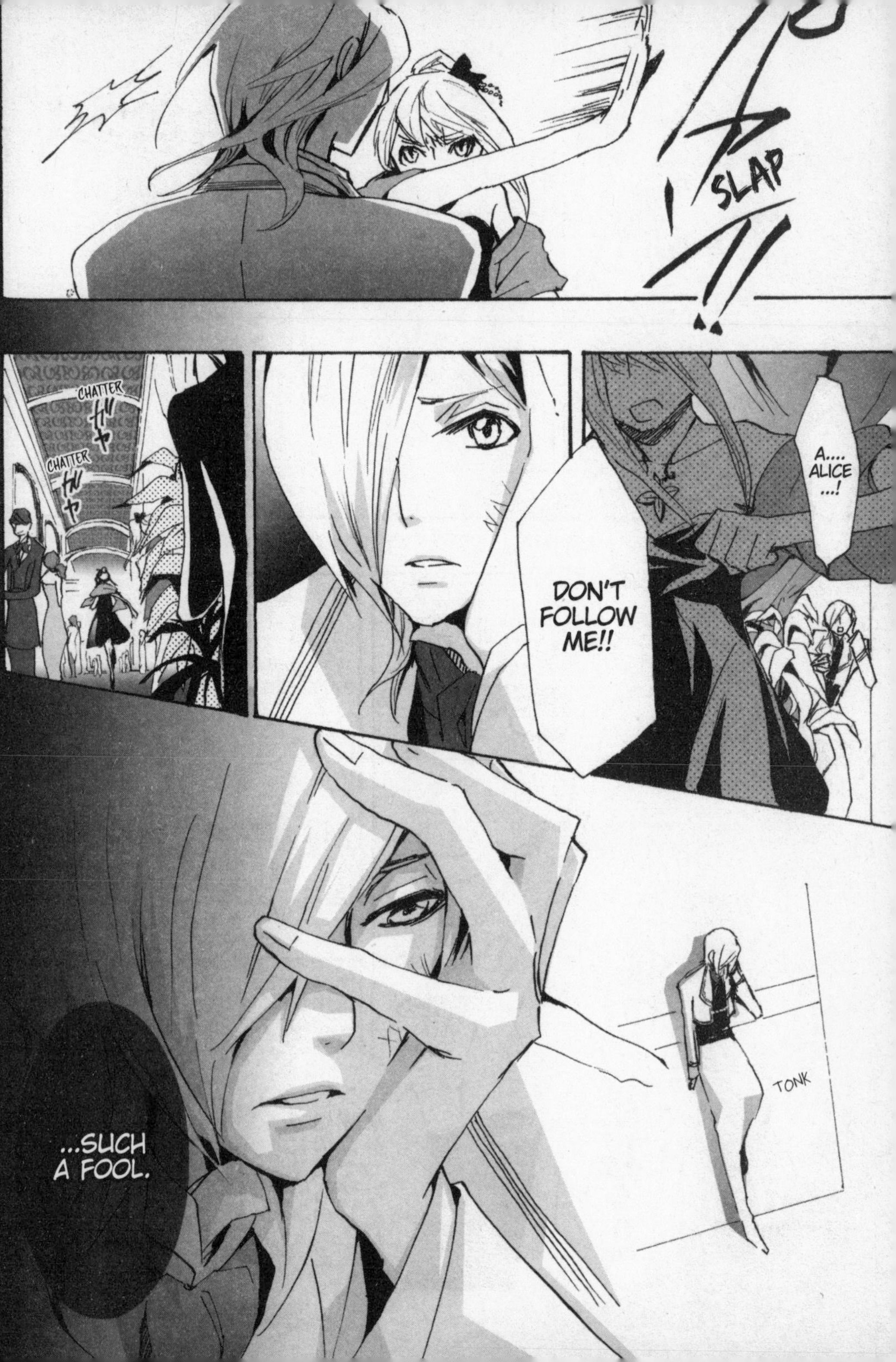
SLAP
A.... ALICE ...!
DON'T FOLLOW ME!!
CHATTER
CHATTER
TONK
...SUCH A FOOL.

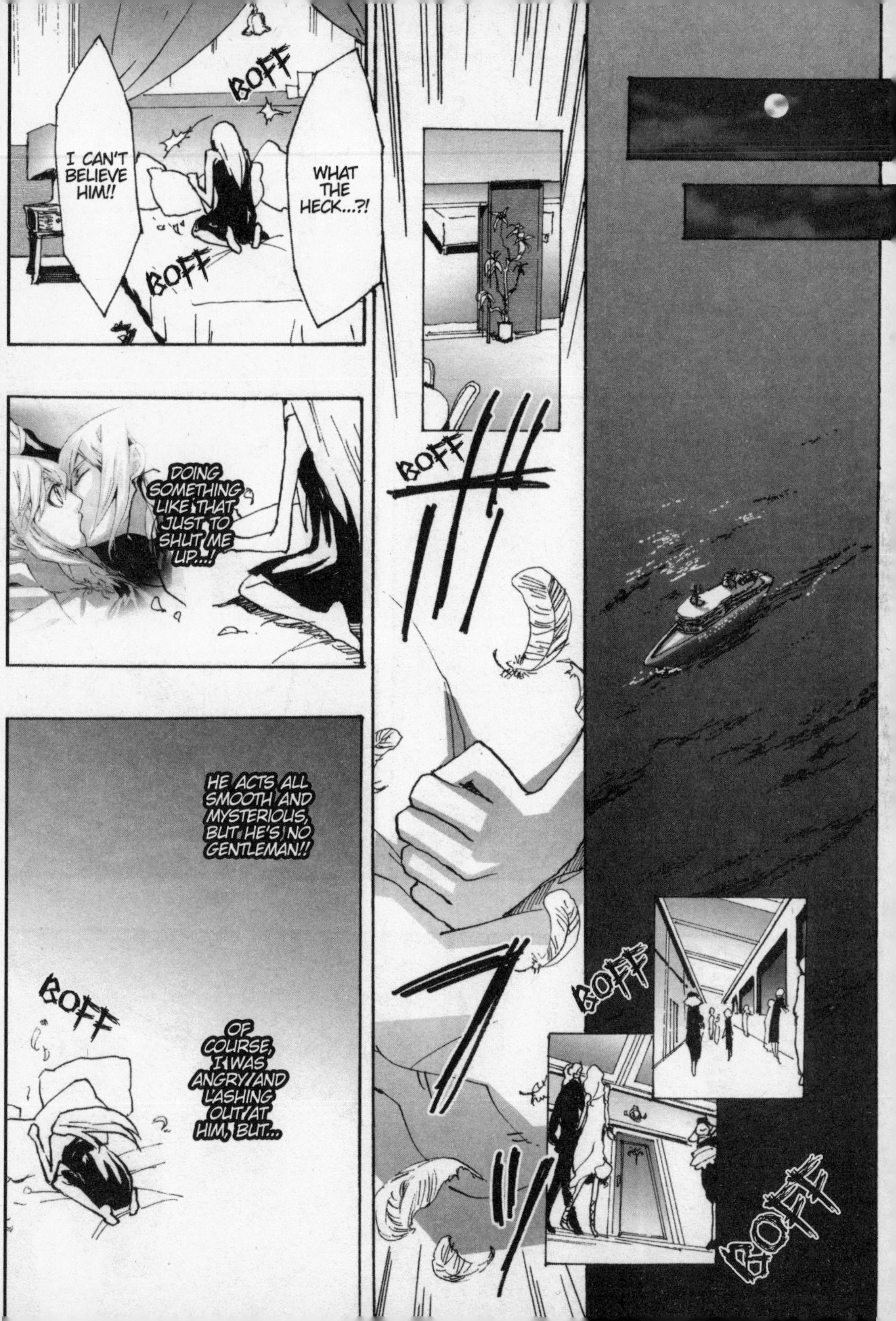
BOFF
BOFF
BOFF
WHAT THE HECK...?!
BOFF
I CAN'T BELIEVE HIM!!
BOFF
DOING SOMETHING LIKE THAT JUST TO SHUT ME UP...!
HE ACTS ALL SMOOTH AND MYSTERIOUS, BUT HE'S NO GENTLEMAN!!
BOFF
OF COURSE, I WAS ANGRY AND LASHING OUT AT HIM, BUT...

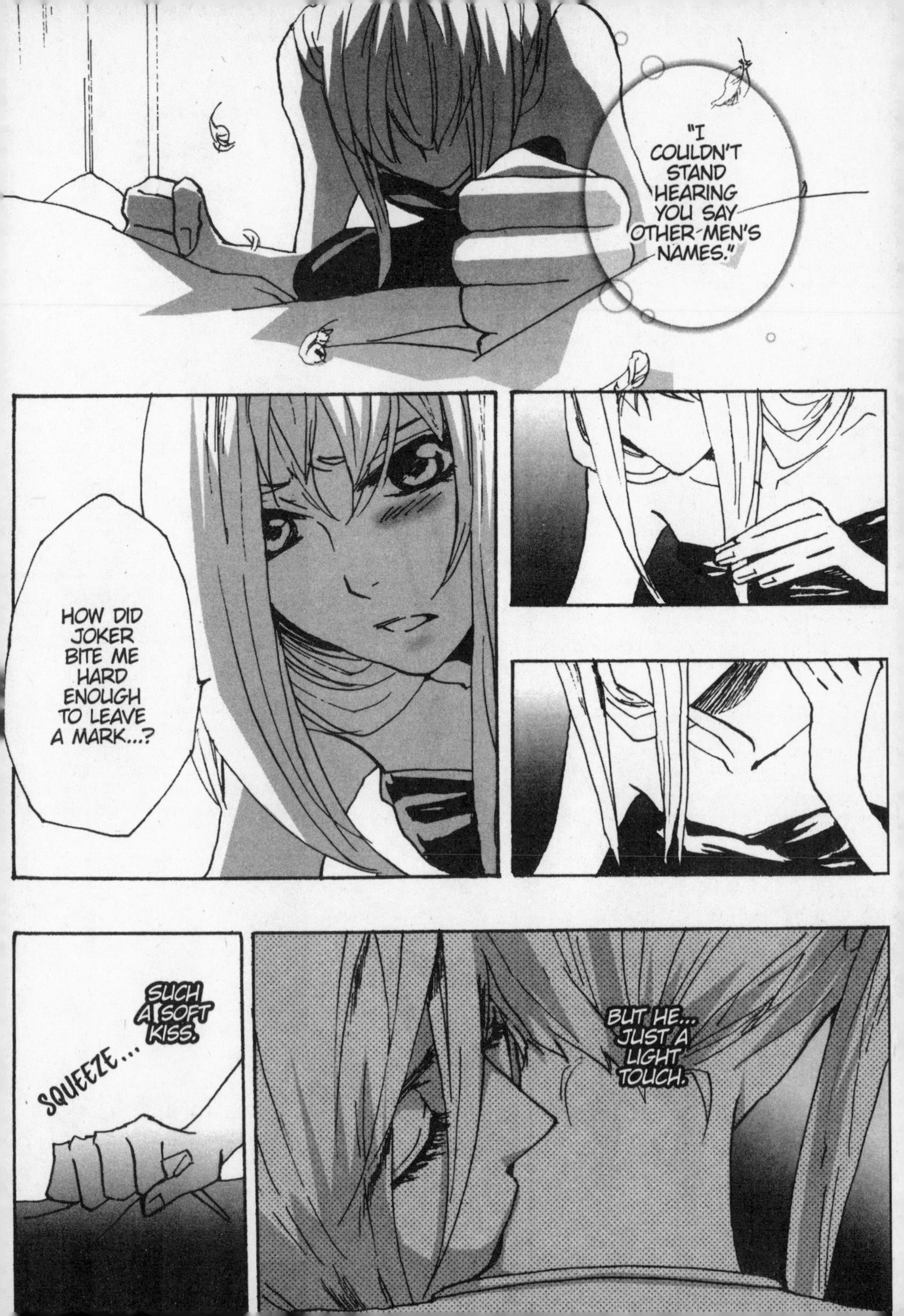
"I COULDN'T STAND HEARING YOU SAY OTHER-MEN'S NAMES."
HOW DID JOKER BITE ME HARD ENOUGH TO LEAVE A MARK...?
BUT HE... JUST A LIGHT TOUCH.
SUCH A SOFT KISS.
SQUEEZE...

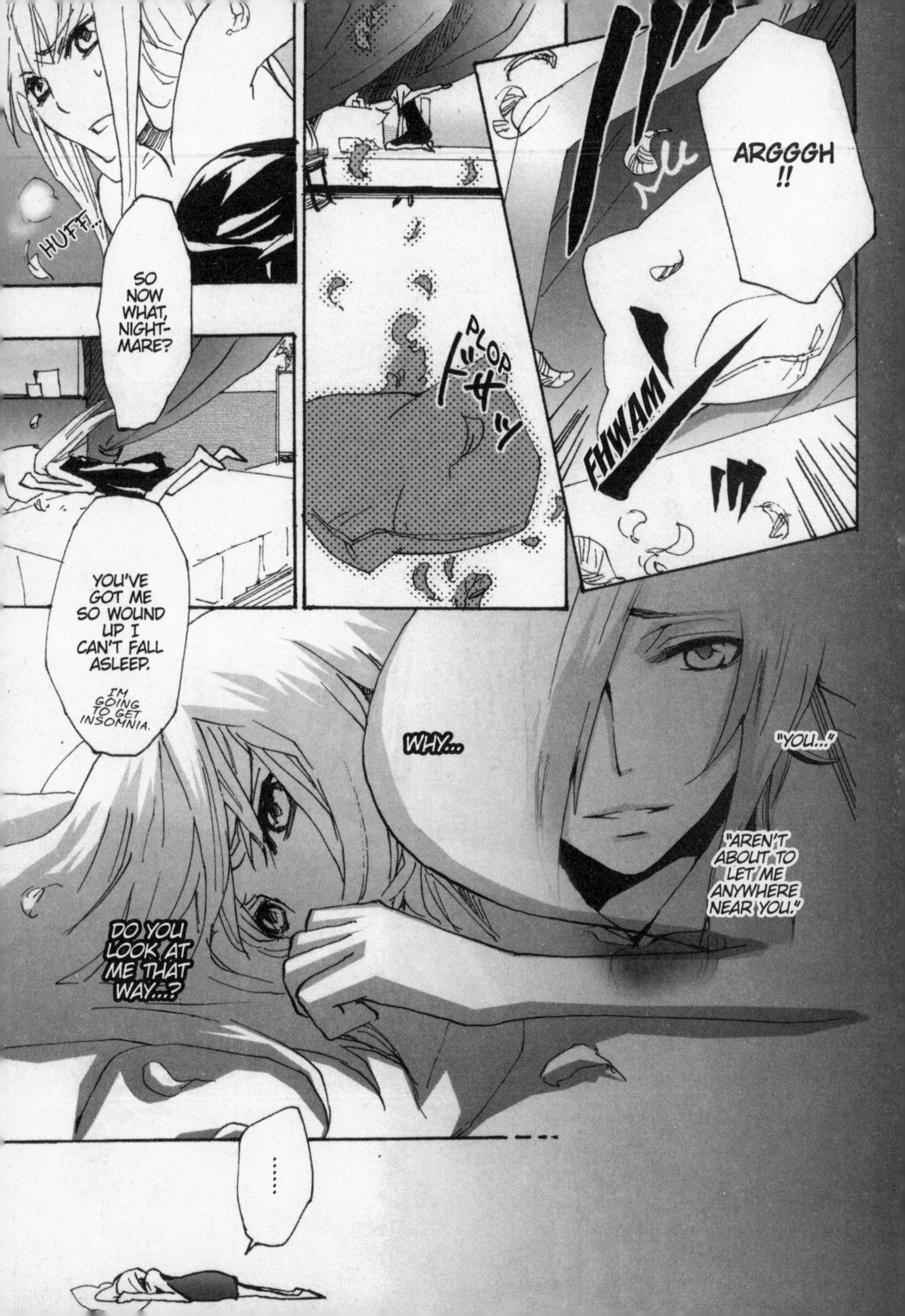
ARGGGH!!
FHWAM
PLOP
ドサッ
HUFF...
SO NOW WHAT, NIGHT-MARE?
YOU'VE GOT ME SO WOUND UP I CAN'T FALL ASLEEP.
I'M GOING TO GET INSOMNIA.
"YOU..."
"AREN'T ABOUT TO LET ME ANYWHERE NEAR YOU."
WHY...
DO YOU LOOK AT ME THAT WAY...?
......

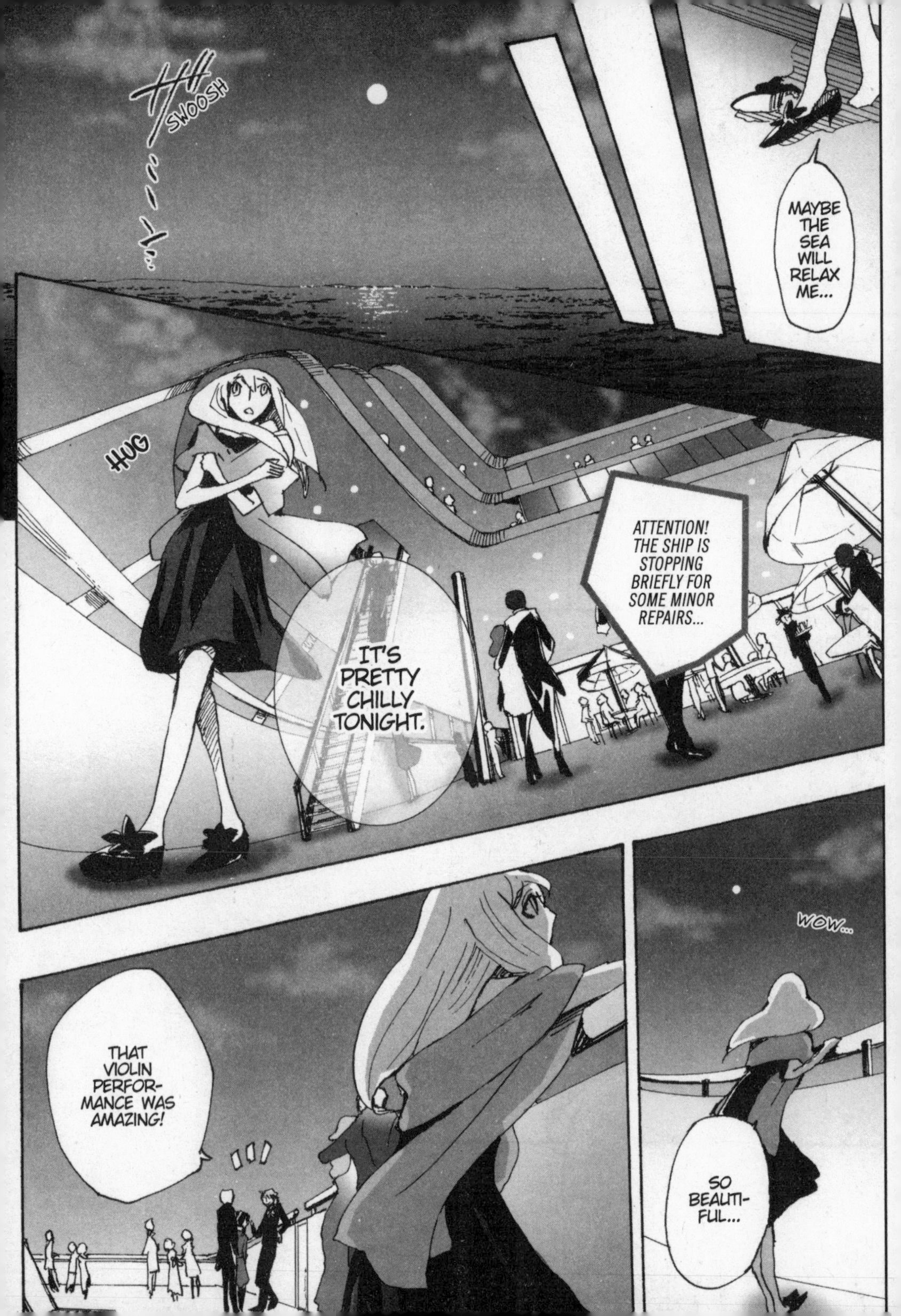
MAYBE THE SEA WILL RELAX ME...
SWOOSH
ATTENTION! THE SHIP IS STOPPING BRIEFLY FOR SOME MINOR REPAIRS...
HUG
IT'S PRETTY CHILLY TONIGHT.
WOW...
SO BEAUTI-FUL...
THAT VIOLIN PERFOR-MANCE WAS AMAZING!
!!!

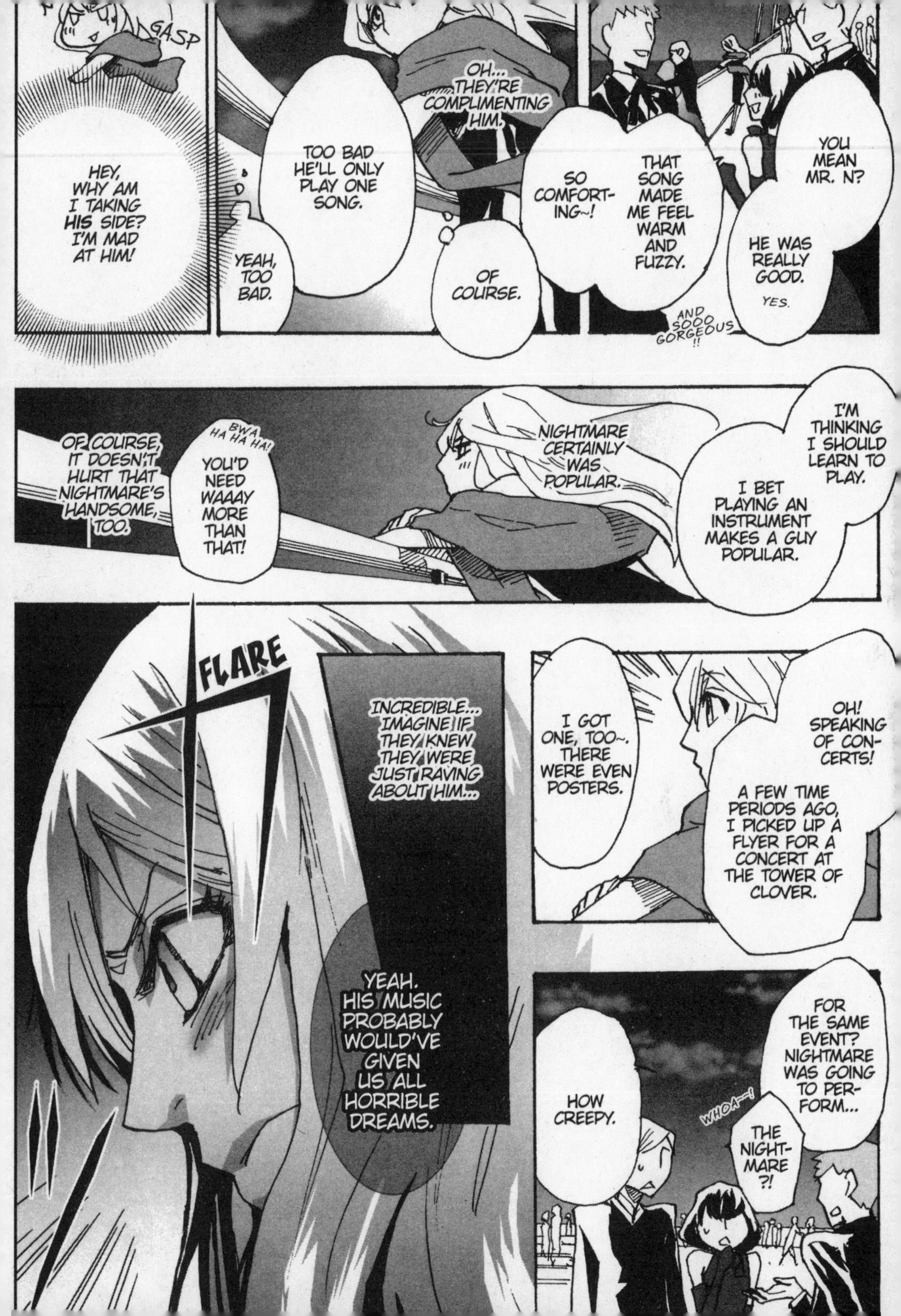
YOU MEAN MR. N?
HE WAS REALLY GOOD.
YES.
AND SOOO GORGEOUS!!
THAT SONG MADE ME FEEL WARM AND FUZZY.
SO COMFORT-ING~!
OF COURSE.
OH... THEY'RE COMPLIMENTING HIM.
TOO BAD HE'LL ONLY PLAY ONE SONG.
YEAH, TOO BAD.
GASP
HEY, WHY AM I TAKING HIS SIDE? I'M MAD AT HIM!
I'M THINKING I SHOULD LEARN TO PLAY.
I BET PLAYING AN INSTRUMENT MAKES A GUY POPULAR.
NIGHTMARE CERTAINLY WAS POPULAR.
BWA HA HA HA!
YOU'D NEED WAAAY MORE THAN THAT!
OF COURSE, IT DOESN'T HURT THAT NIGHTMARE'S HANDSOME, TOO.
OH! SPEAKING OF CON-CERTS!
A FEW TIME PERIODS AGO, I PICKED UP A FLYER FOR A CONCERT AT THE TOWER OF CLOVER.
I GOT ONE, TOO~. THERE WERE EVEN POSTERS.
FOR THE SAME EVENT? NIGHTMARE WAS GOING TO PER-FORM...
WHOA~!
THE NIGHT-MARE?!
HOW CREEPY.
FLARE
INCREDIBLE... IMAGINE IF THEY KNEW THEY WERE JUST RAVING ABOUT HIM...
YEAH. HIS MUSIC PROBABLY WOULD'VE GIVEN US ALL HORRIBLE DREAMS.

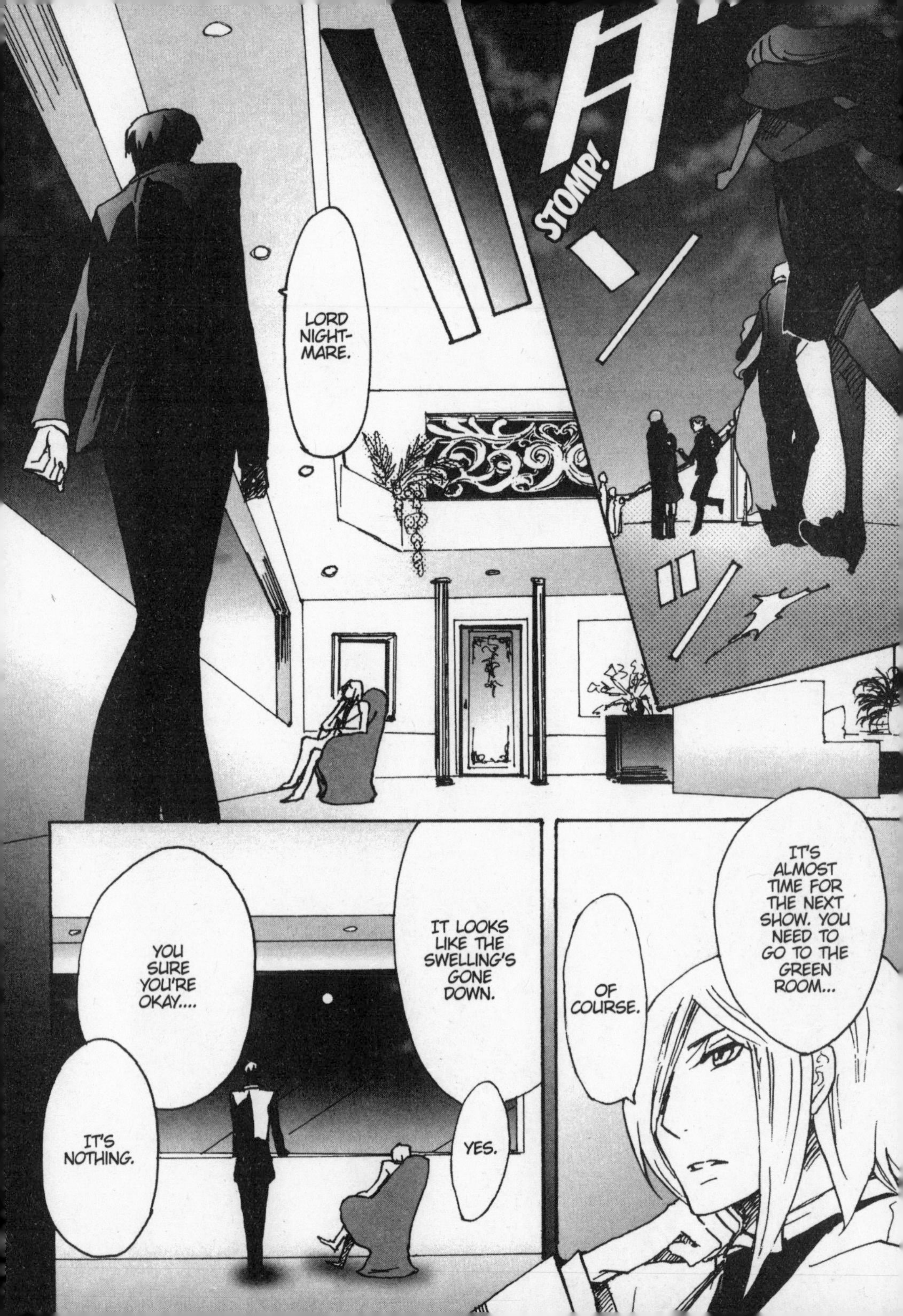
STOMP!
LORD NIGHT-MARE.
IT'S ALMOST TIME FOR THE NEXT SHOW. YOU NEED TO GO TO THE GREEN ROOM...
OF COURSE.
IT LOOKS LIKE THE SWELLING'S GONE DOWN.
YES.
YOU SURE YOU'RE OKAY....
IT'S NOTHING.

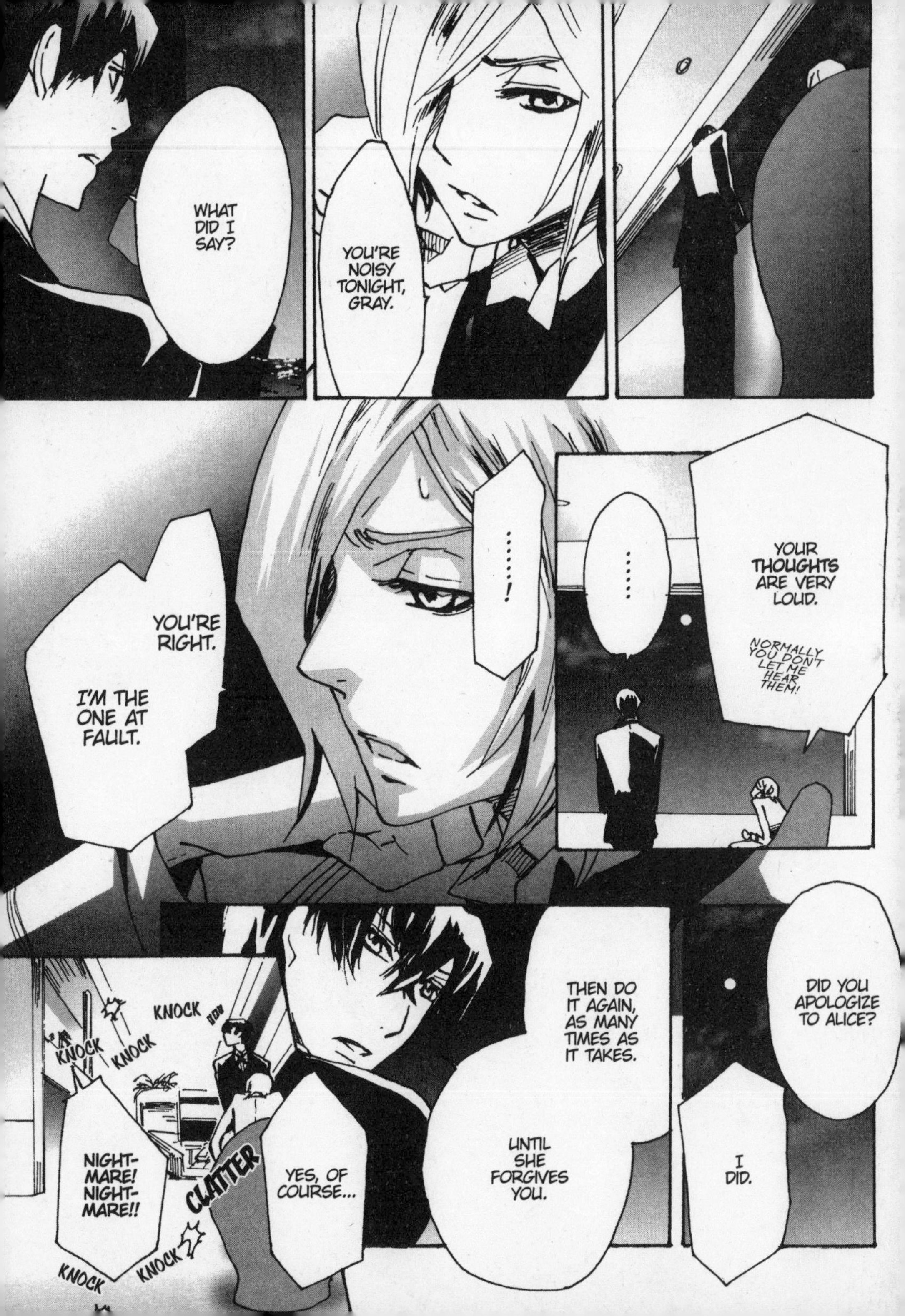
YOU'RE NOISY TONIGHT, GRAY.
WHAT DID I SAY?
YOUR THOUGHTS ARE VERY LOUD.
NORMALLY YOU DON'T LET ME HEAR THEM!
......
......!
YOU'RE RIGHT.
I'M THE ONE AT FAULT.
DID YOU APOLOGIZE TO ALICE?
I DID.
THEN DO IT AGAIN, AS MANY TIMES AS IT TAKES.
UNTIL SHE FORGIVES YOU.
YES, OF COURSE...
KNOCK
KNOCK
KNOCK
NIGHT-MARE! NIGHT-MARE!!
CLATTER
KNOCK
KNOCK

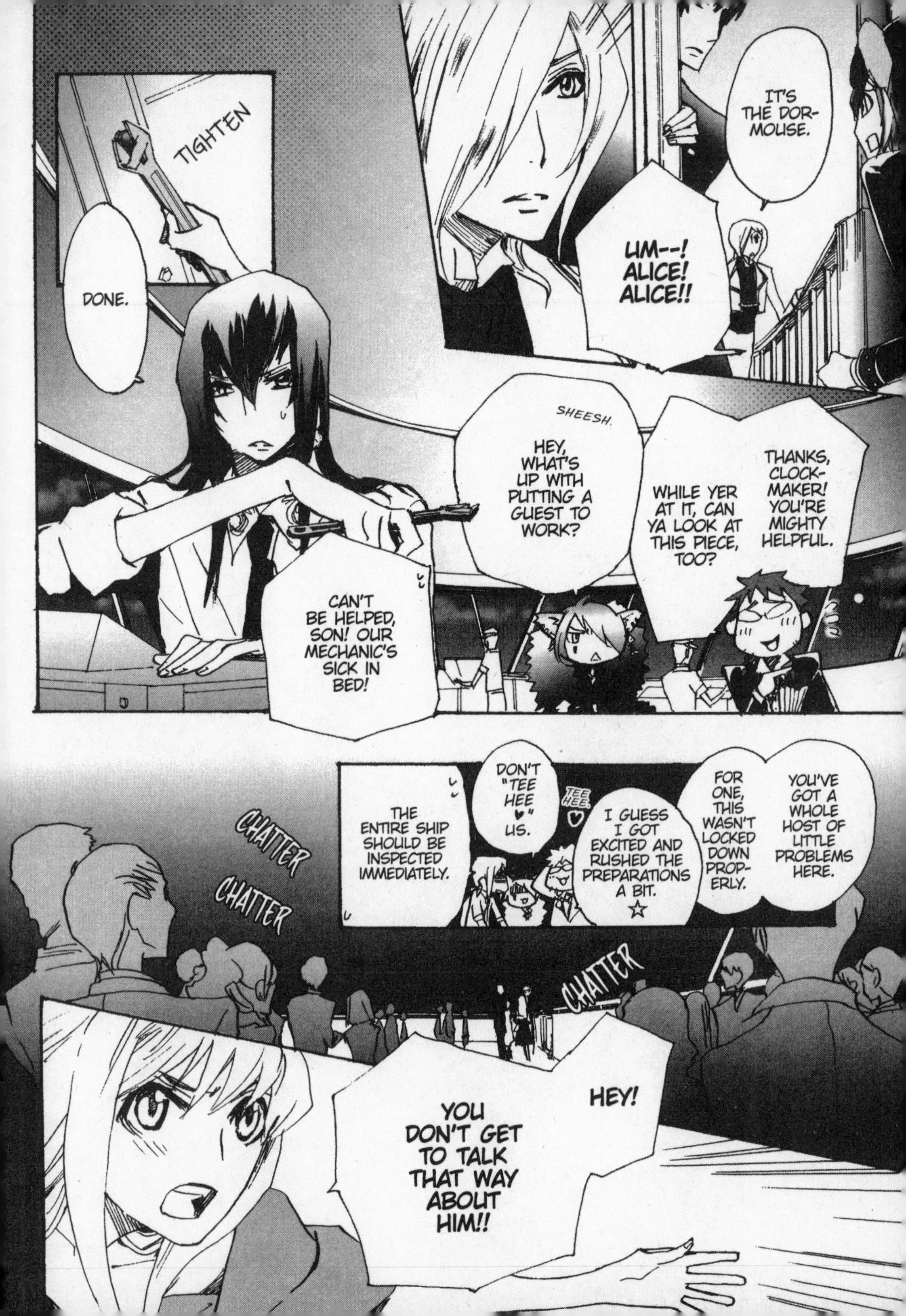
IT'S THE DOR-MOUSE.
UM--! ALICE! ALICE!!
TIGHTEN
DONE.
THANKS, CLOCK-MAKER! YOU'RE MIGHTY HELPFUL.
WHILE YER AT IT, CAN YA LOOK AT THIS PIECE, TOO?
SHEESH.
HEY, WHAT'S UP WITH PUTTING A GUEST TO WORK?
CAN'T BE HELPED, SON! OUR MECHANIC'S SICK IN BED!
YOU'VE GOT A WHOLE HOST OF LITTLE PROBLEMS HERE.
FOR ONE, THIS WASN'T LOCKED DOWN PROP-ERLY.
I GUESS I GOT EXCITED AND RUSHED THE PREPARATIONS A BIT. ☆
TEE HEE.
DON'T "TEE HEE ♥" US.
THE ENTIRE SHIP SHOULD BE INSPECTED IMMEDIATELY.
CHATTER
CHATTER
CHATTER
HEY!
YOU DON'T GET TO TALK THAT WAY ABOUT HIM!!

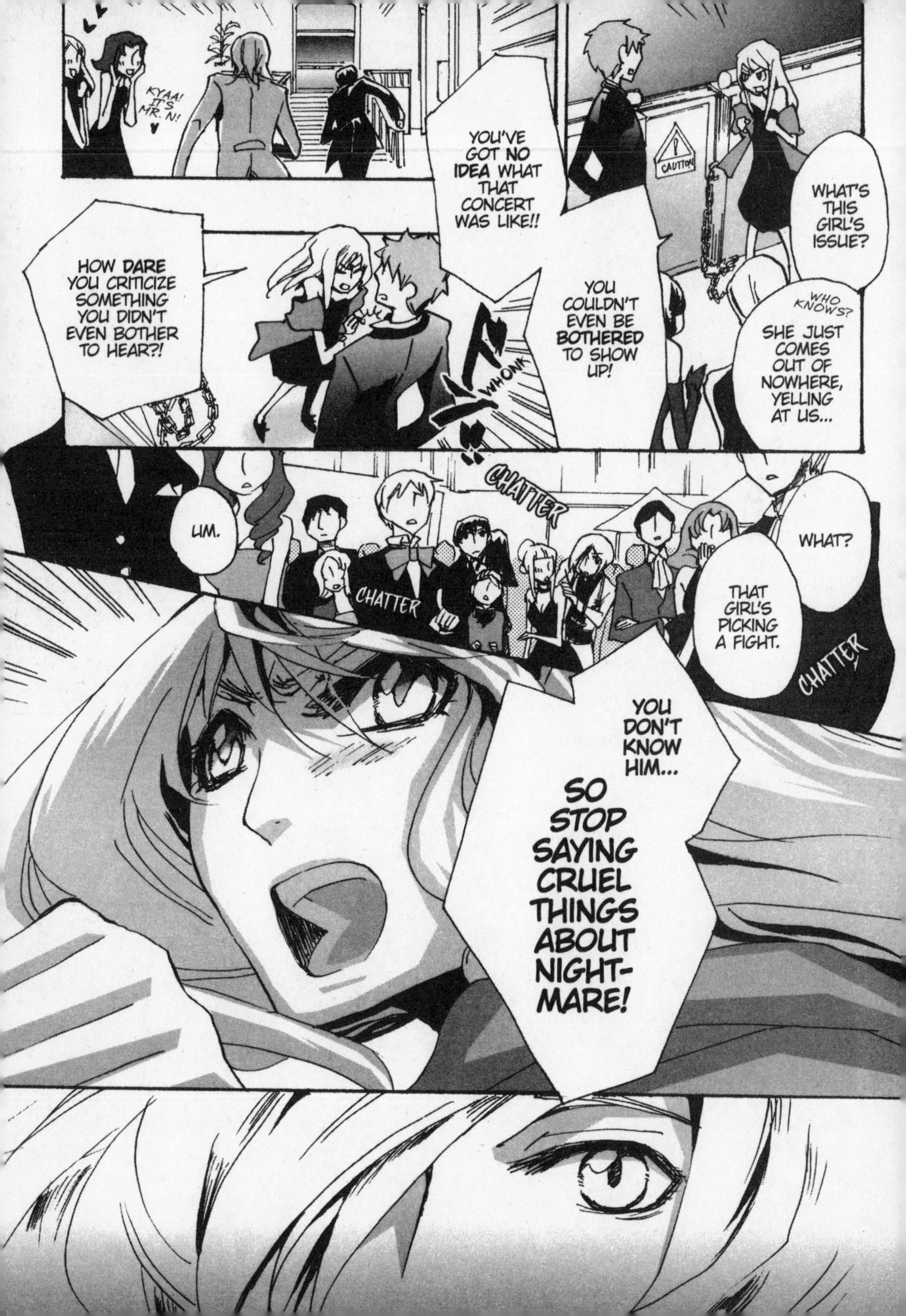
WHAT'S THIS GIRL'S ISSUE?
WHO KNOWS?
SHE JUST COMES OUT OF NOWHERE, YELLING AT US...
KYAA! IT'S MR. N!
YOU'VE GOT NO IDEA WHAT THAT CONCERT WAS LIKE!!
YOU COULDN'T EVEN BE BOTHERED TO SHOW UP!
WHONK
HOW DARE YOU CRITICIZE SOMETHING YOU DIDN'T EVEN BOTHER TO HEAR?!
CHATTER
WHAT?
THAT GIRL'S PICKING A FIGHT.
CHATTER
UM.
CHATTER
YOU DON'T KNOW HIM...
SO STOP SAYING CRUEL THINGS ABOUT NIGHT-MARE!

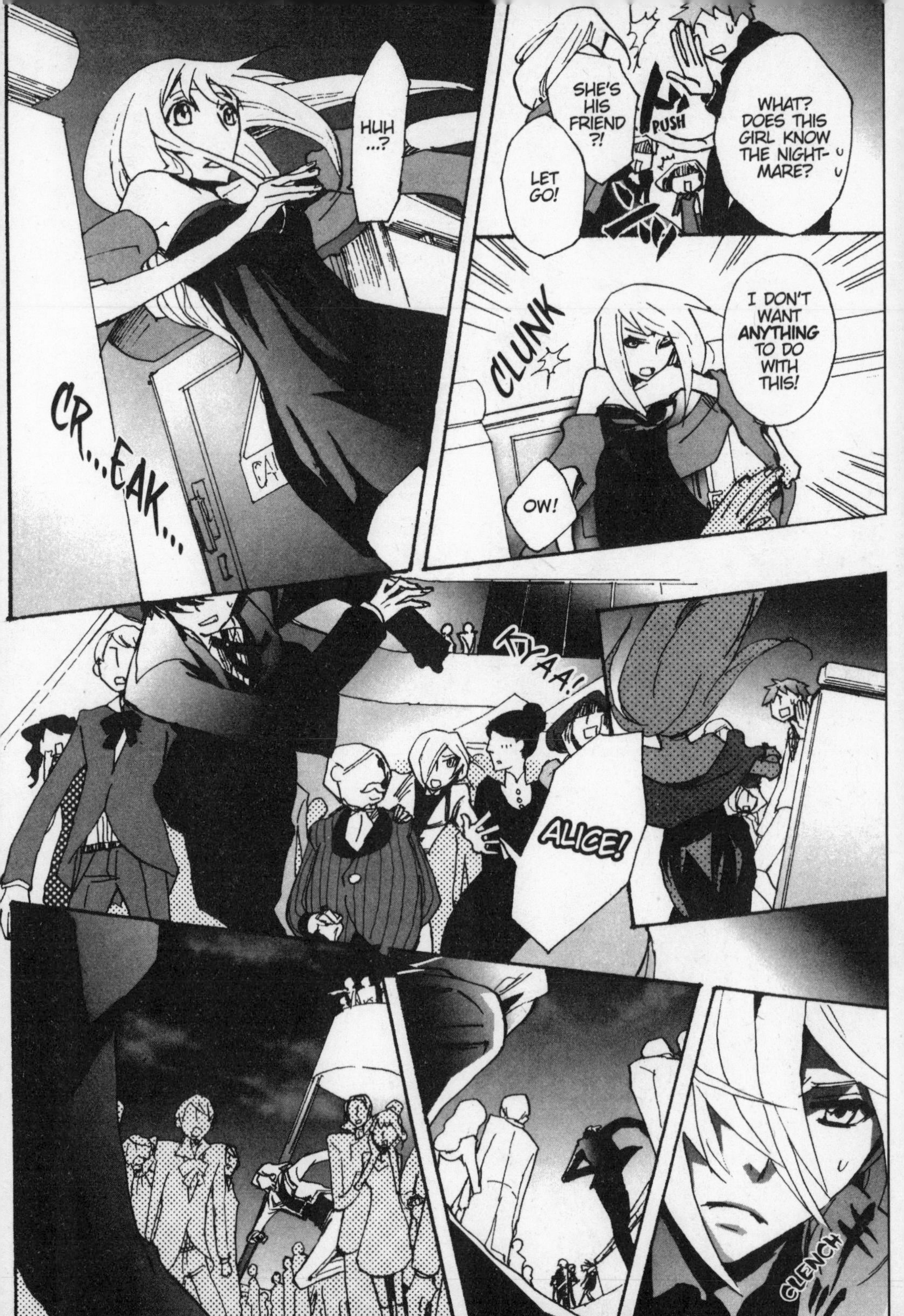
WHAT? DOES THIS GIRL KNOW THE NIGHT-MARE?
PUSH
SHE'S HIS FRIEND ?!
LET GO!
I DON'T WANT ANYTHING TO DO WITH THIS!
CLUNK
OW!
HUH ...?
CR...EAK...
KYAA!
ALICE!
CLENCH

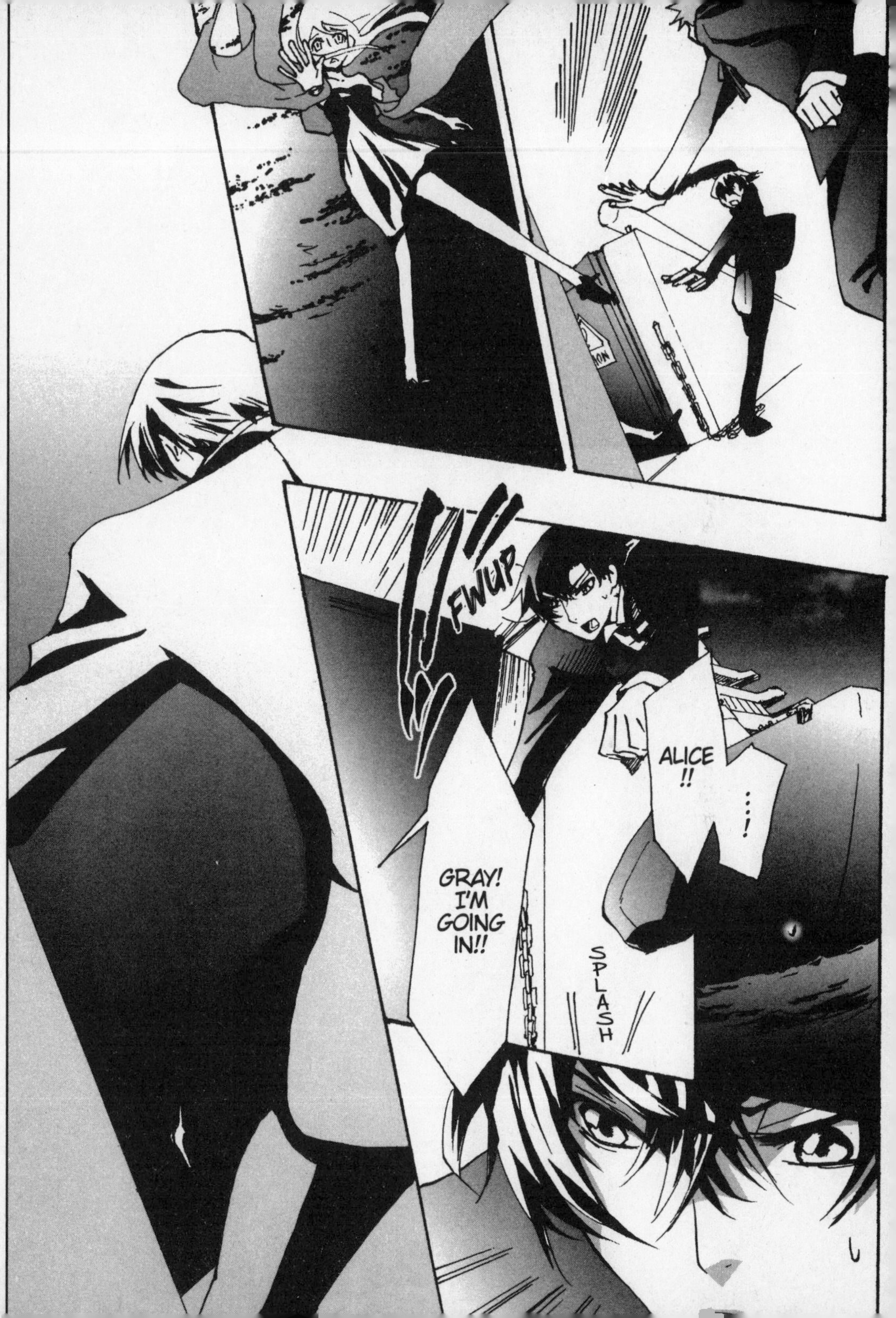
FWUP
ALICE!!
...!
SPLASH
GRAY! I'M GOING IN!!

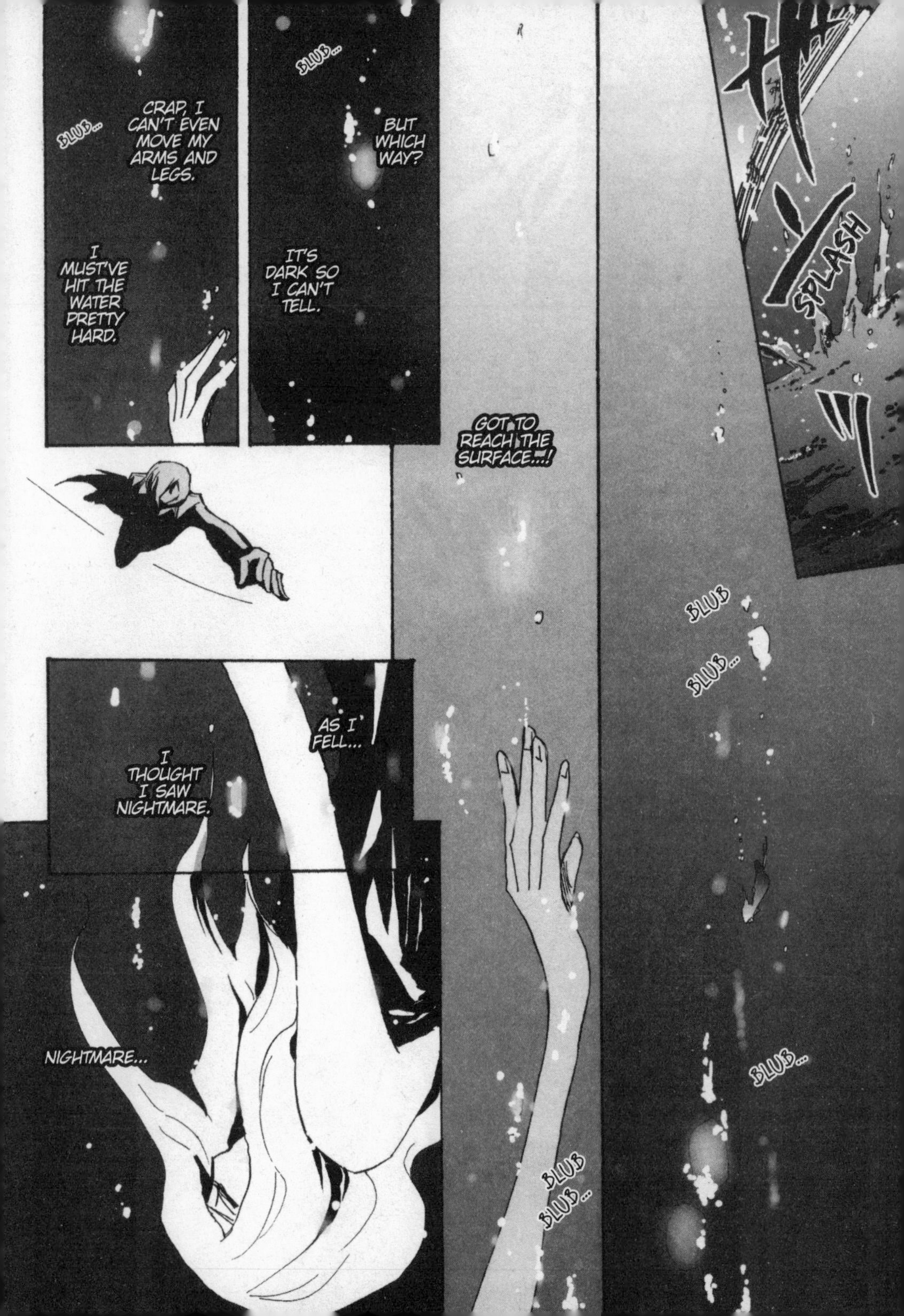
SPLASH
BLUB
BLUB...
BLUB...
GOT TO REACH THE SURFACE...!
BLUB
BLUB...
BLUB...
BUT WHICH WAY?
IT'S DARK SO I CAN'T TELL.
BLUB...
CRAP, I CAN'T EVEN MOVE MY ARMS AND LEGS.
I MUST'VE HIT THE WATER PRETTY HARD.
AS I FELL...
I THOUGHT I SAW NIGHTMARE.
NIGHTMARE...

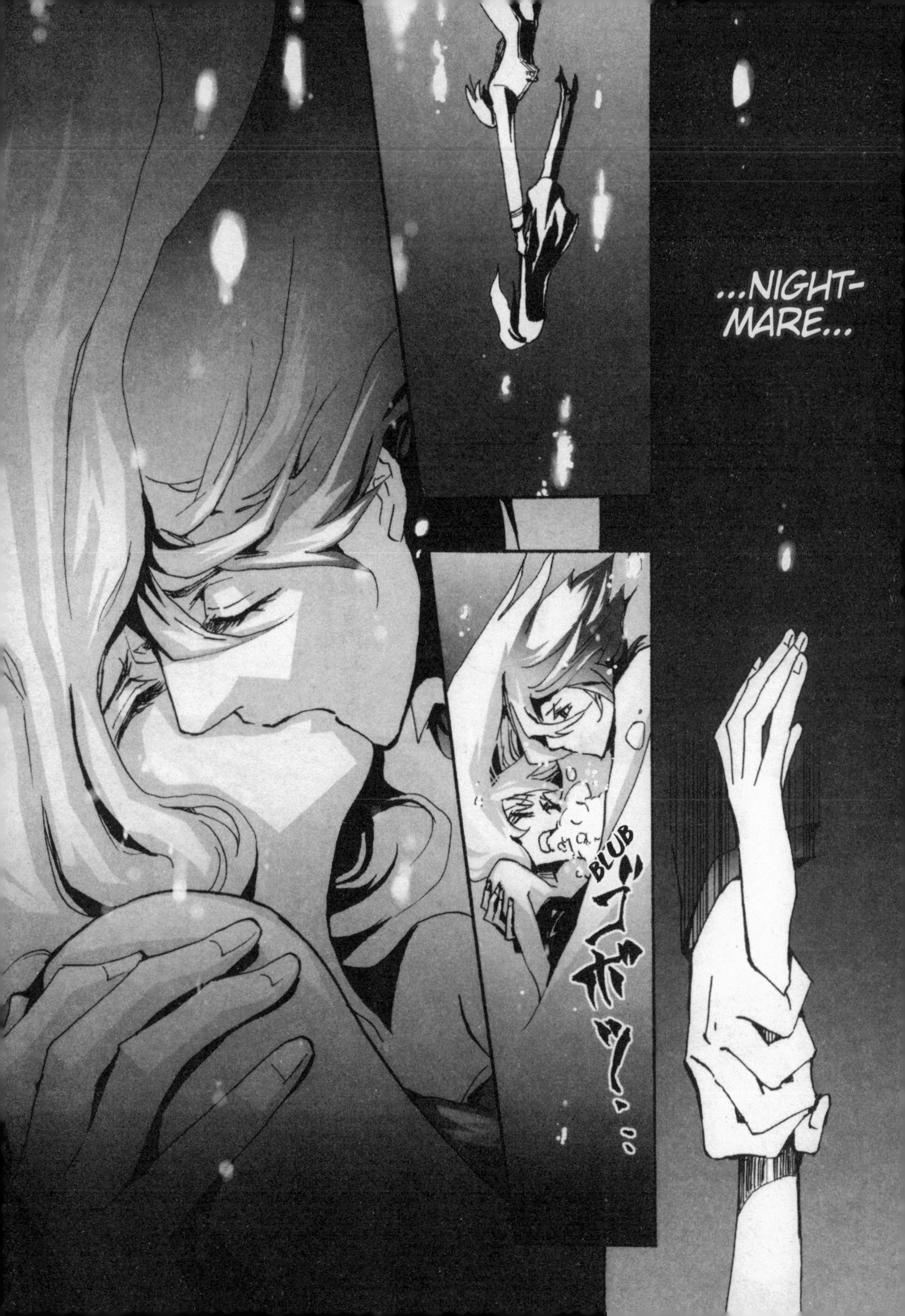
...NIGHT-
MARE...
BLUB

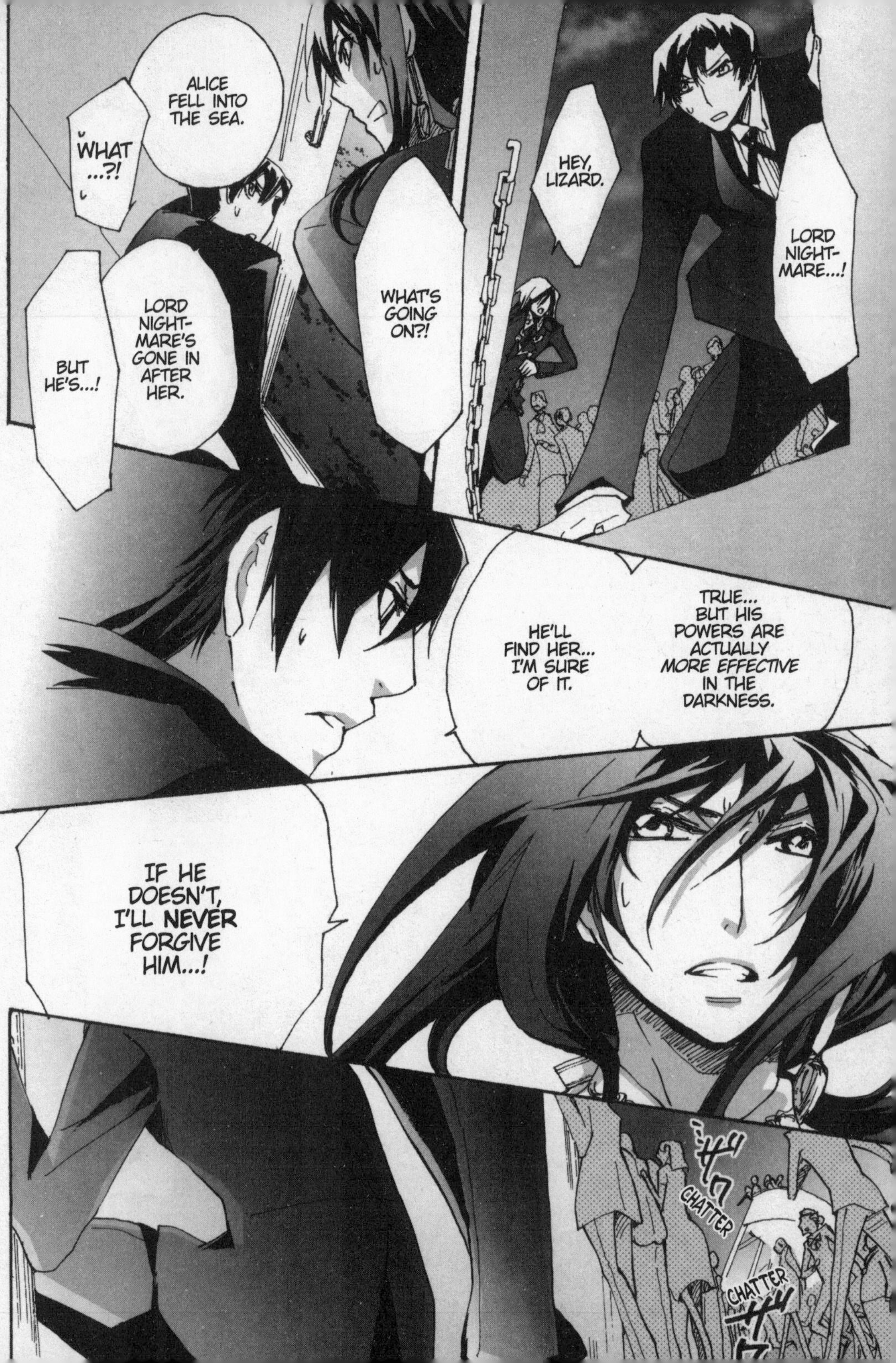
HEY, LIZARD.
LORD NIGHT-MARE...!
WHAT'S GOING ON?!
ALICE FELL INTO THE SEA.
WHAT ...?!
LORD NIGHT-MARE'S GONE IN AFTER HER.
BUT HE'S...!
TRUE... BUT HIS POWERS ARE ACTUALLY MORE EFFECTIVE IN THE DARKNESS.
HE'LL FIND HER... I'M SURE OF IT.
IF HE DOESN'T, I'LL NEVER FORGIVE HIM...!
CHATTER
CHATTER

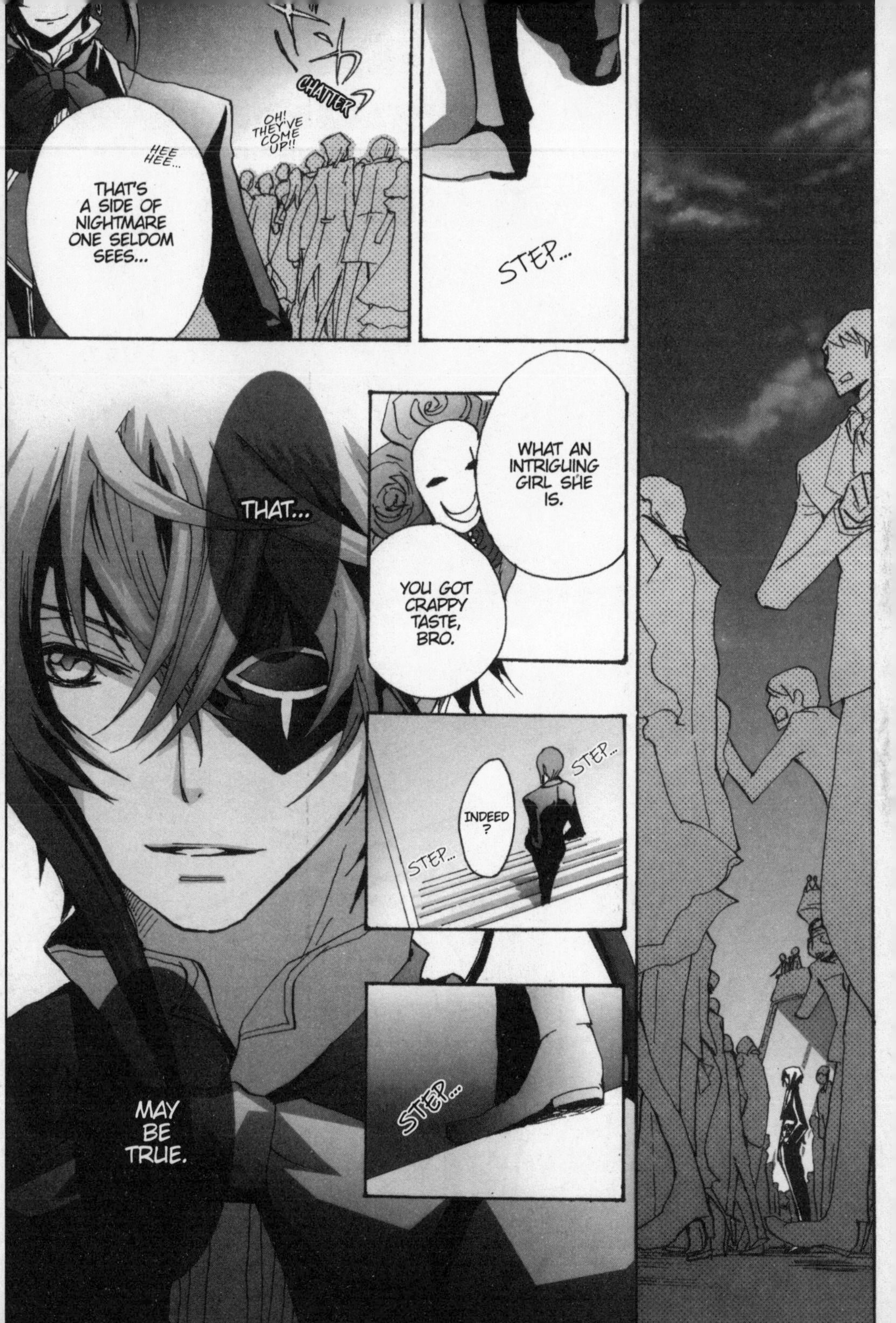
STEP...
CHATTER
OH! THEY'VE COME UP!!
HEE HEE...
THAT'S A SIDE OF NIGHTMARE ONE SELDOM SEES...
WHAT AN INTRIGUING GIRL SHE IS.
YOU GOT CRAPPY TASTE, BRO.
STEP...
INDEED?
STEP...
STEP...
THAT...
MAY BE TRUE.

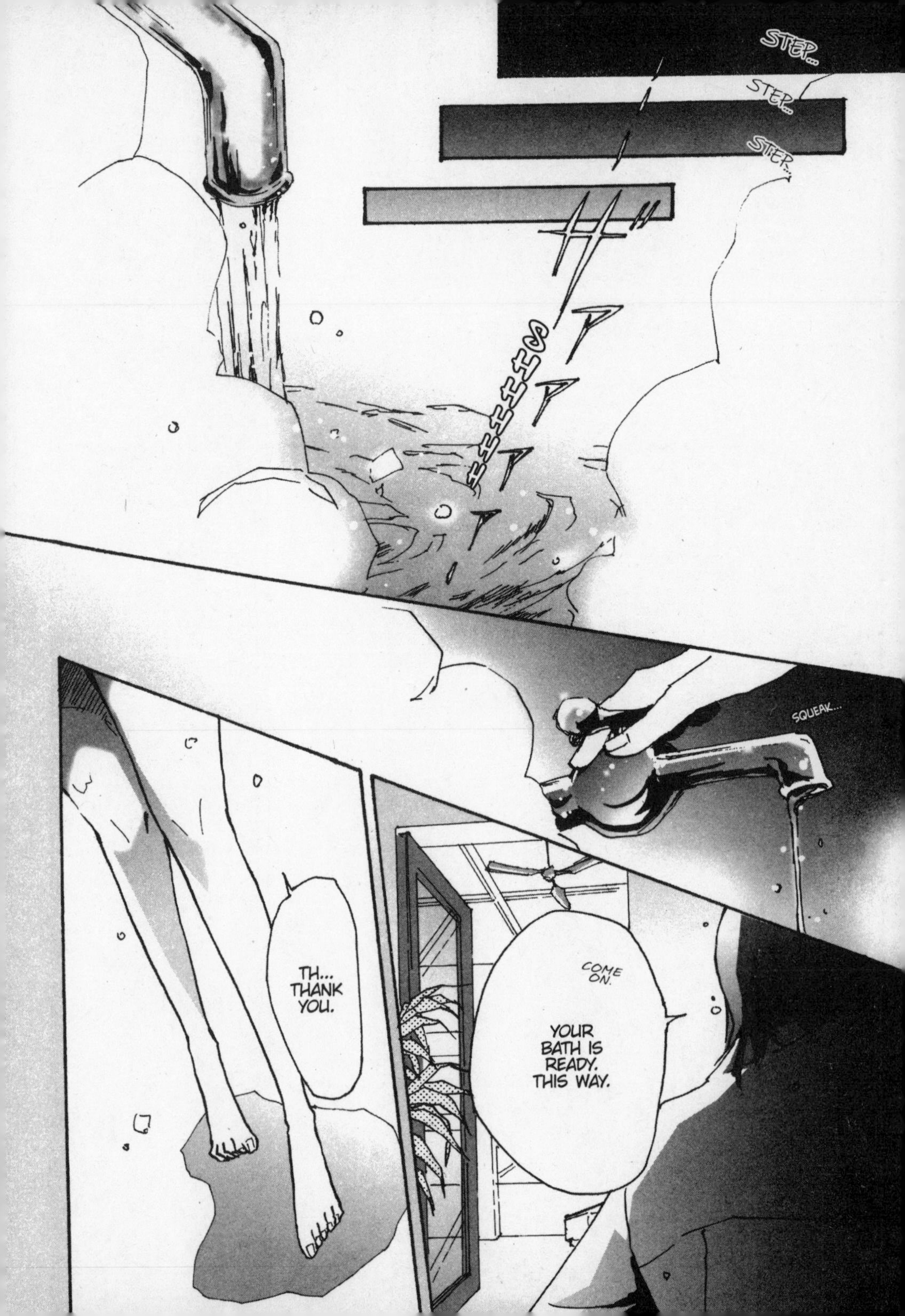
STEP...
STEP...
STEP...
SHHHHH
SQUEAK...
COME ON.
YOUR BATH IS READY. THIS WAY.
TH... THANK YOU.

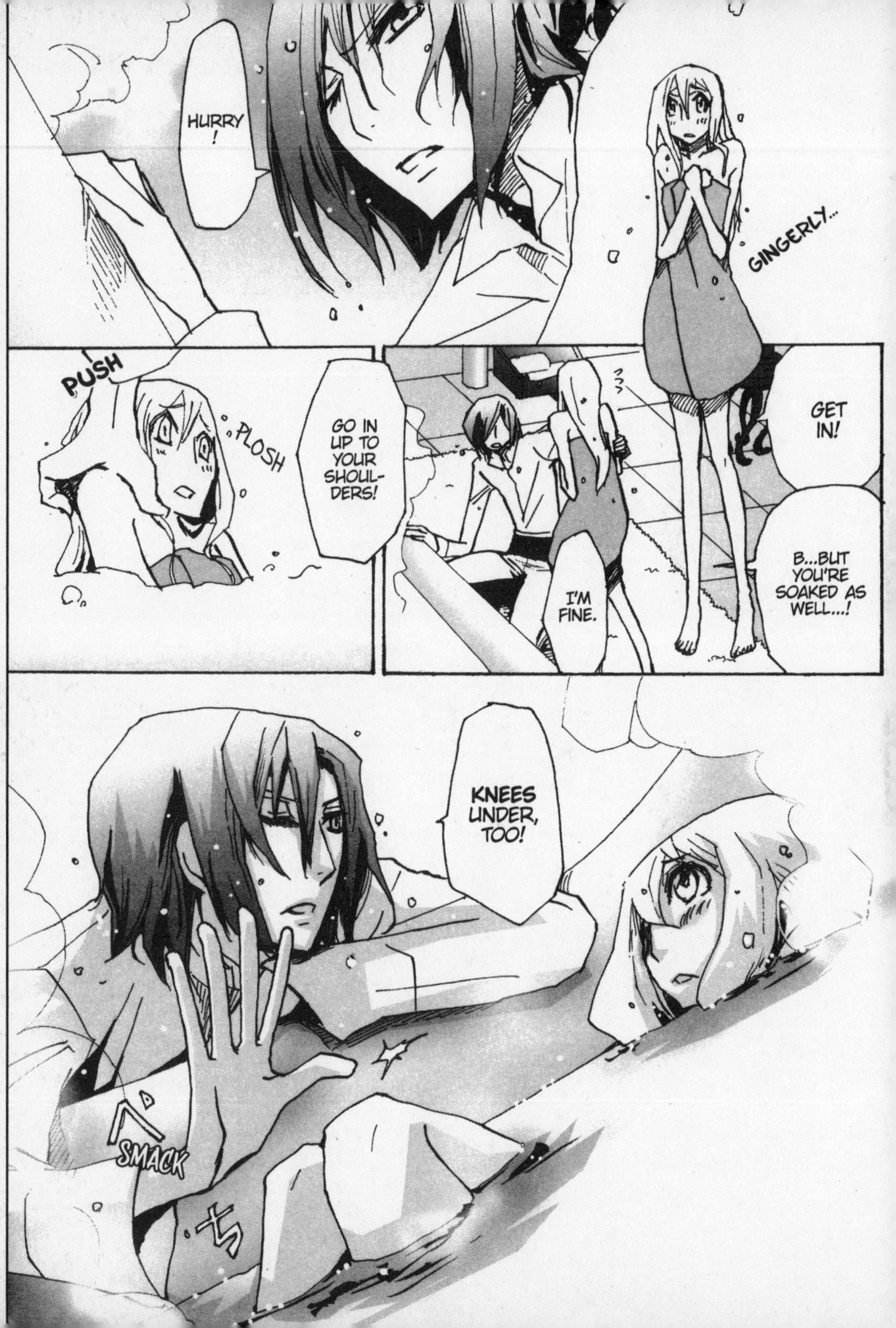
HURRY!
GINGERLY...
GET IN!
B...BUT YOU'RE SOAKED AS WELL...!
I'M FINE.
GO IN UP TO YOUR SHOUL-DERS!
PUSH
PLOSH
KNEES UNDER, TOO!
SMACK

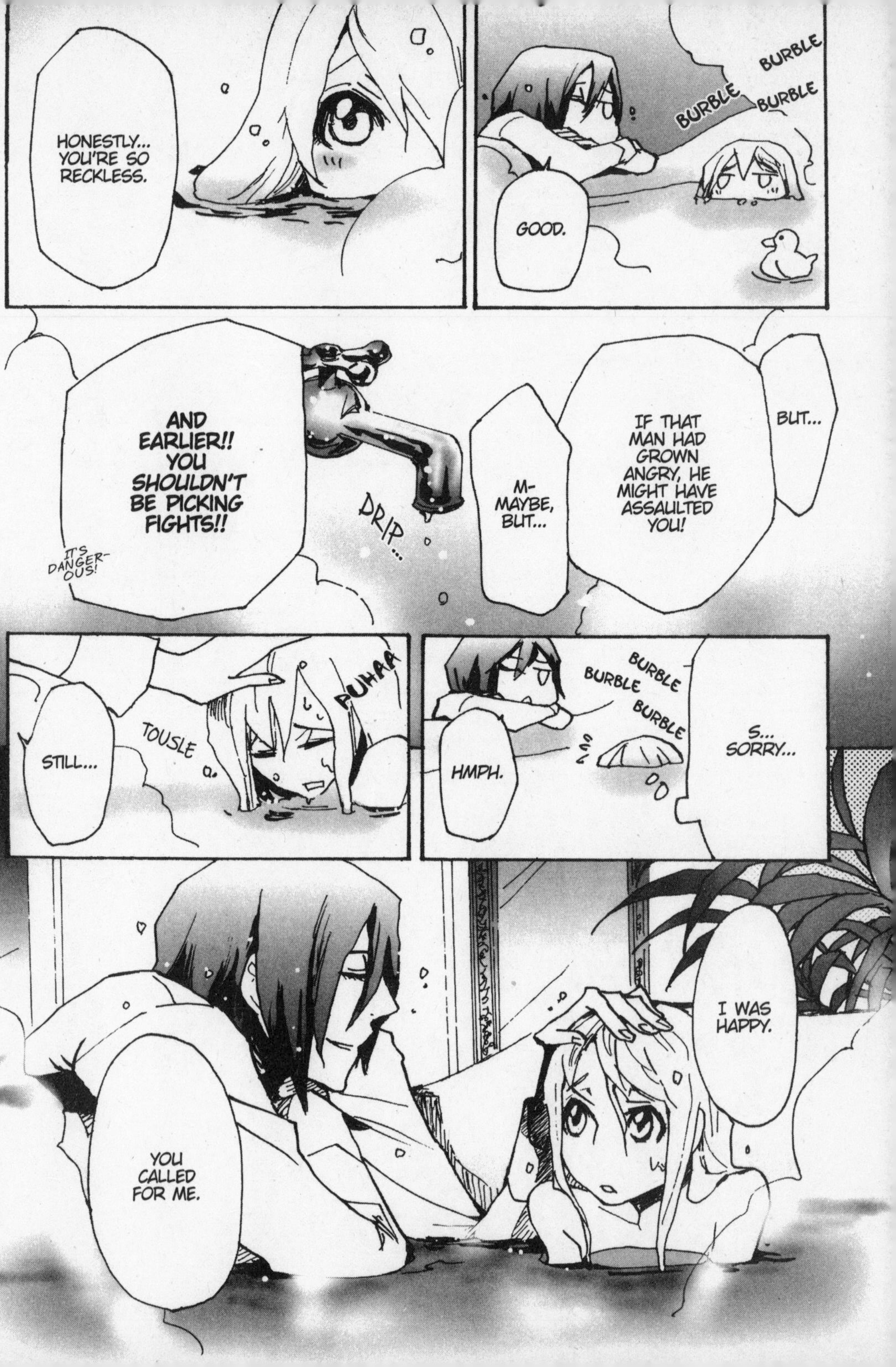
BURBLE
BURBLE
BURBLE
GOOD.
HONESTLY... YOU'RE SO RECKLESS.
BUT...
IF THAT MAN HAD GROWN ANGRY, HE MIGHT HAVE ASSAULTED YOU!
M-MAYBE, BUT...
DRIP...
AND EARLIER!! YOU SHOULDN'T BE PICKING FIGHTS!!
IT'S DANGER-OUS!
S... SORRY...
BURBLE
BURBLE
BURBLE
HMPH.
PUHAA
TOUSLE
STILL...
I WAS HAPPY.
YOU CALLED FOR ME.

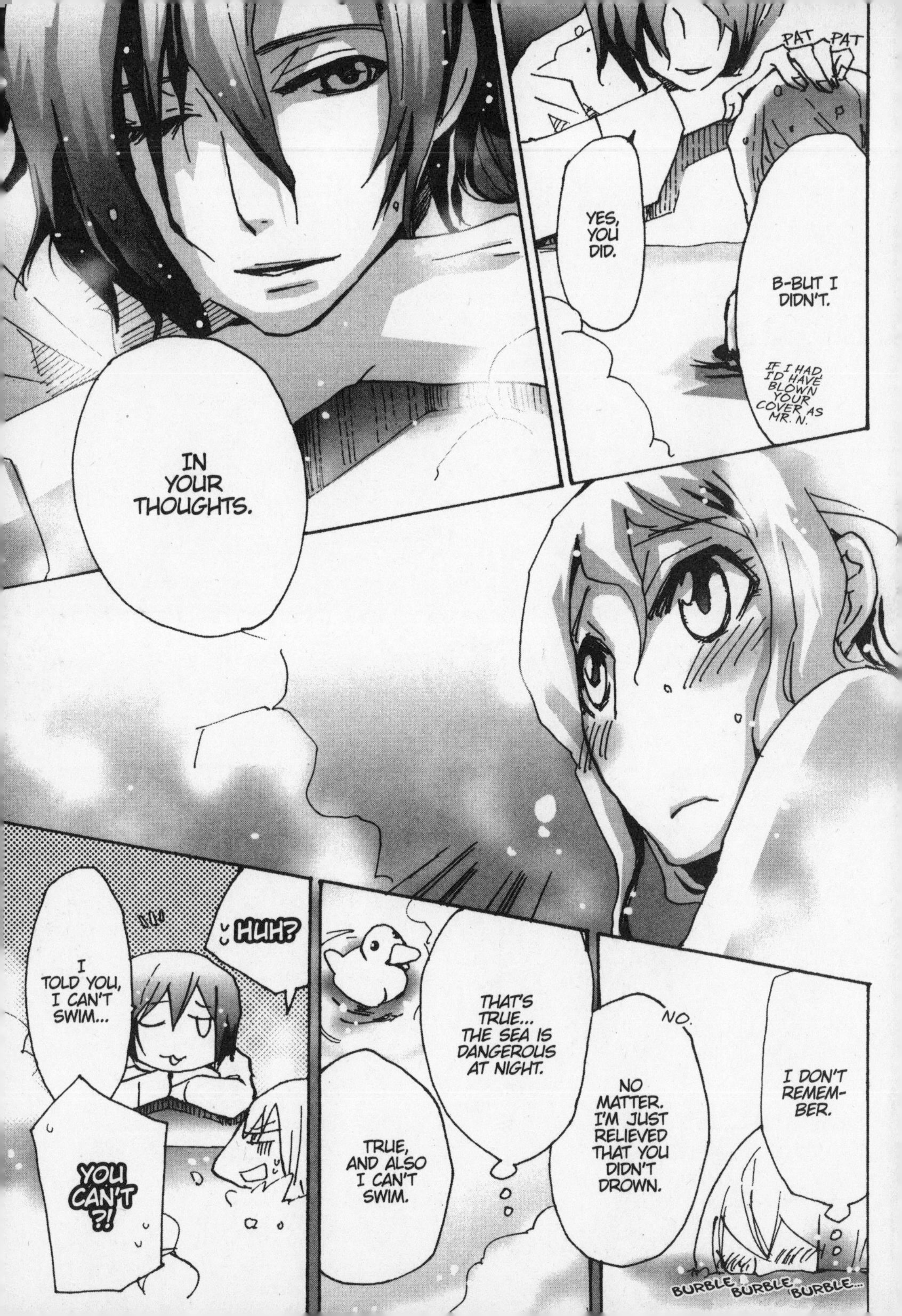
PAT PAT
B-BUT I DIDN'T.
IF I HAD I'D HAVE BLOWN YOUR COVER AS MR. N.
YES, YOU DID.
IN YOUR THOUGHTS.
I DON'T REMEM-BER.
NO.
NO MATTER. I'M JUST RELIEVED THAT YOU DIDN'T DROWN.
BURBLE BURBLE BURBLE...
THAT'S TRUE... THE SEA IS DANGEROUS AT NIGHT.
TRUE, AND ALSO I CAN'T SWIM.
HUH?
I TOLD YOU, I CAN'T SWIM...
YOU CAN'T?!

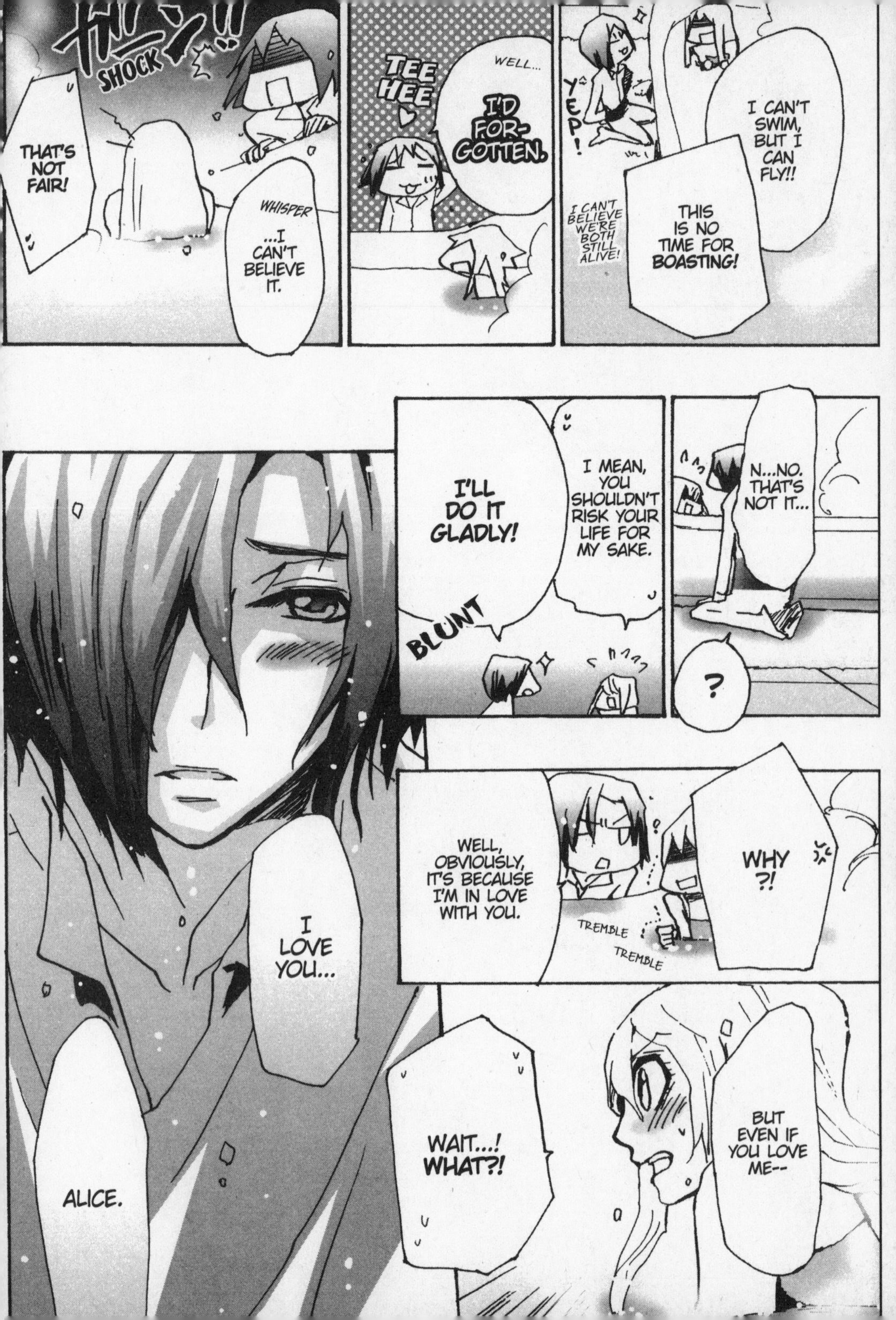

I CAN'T SWIM, BUT I CAN FLY!!
THIS IS NO TIME FOR BOASTING!
YEP!
I CAN'T BELIEVE WE'RE BOTH STILL ALIVE!
WELL...
I'D FOR-GOTTEN.
TEE HEE
SHOCK
WHISPER
...I CAN'T BELIEVE IT.
THAT'S NOT FAIR!
N...NO. THAT'S NOT IT...
?
I MEAN, YOU SHOULDN'T RISK YOUR LIFE FOR MY SAKE.
I'LL DO IT GLADLY!
BLUNT
WHY?!
WELL, OBVIOUSLY, IT'S BECAUSE I'M IN LOVE WITH YOU.
TREMBLE
TREMBLE
BUT EVEN IF YOU LOVE ME--
WAIT...! WHAT?!
I LOVE YOU...
ALICE.

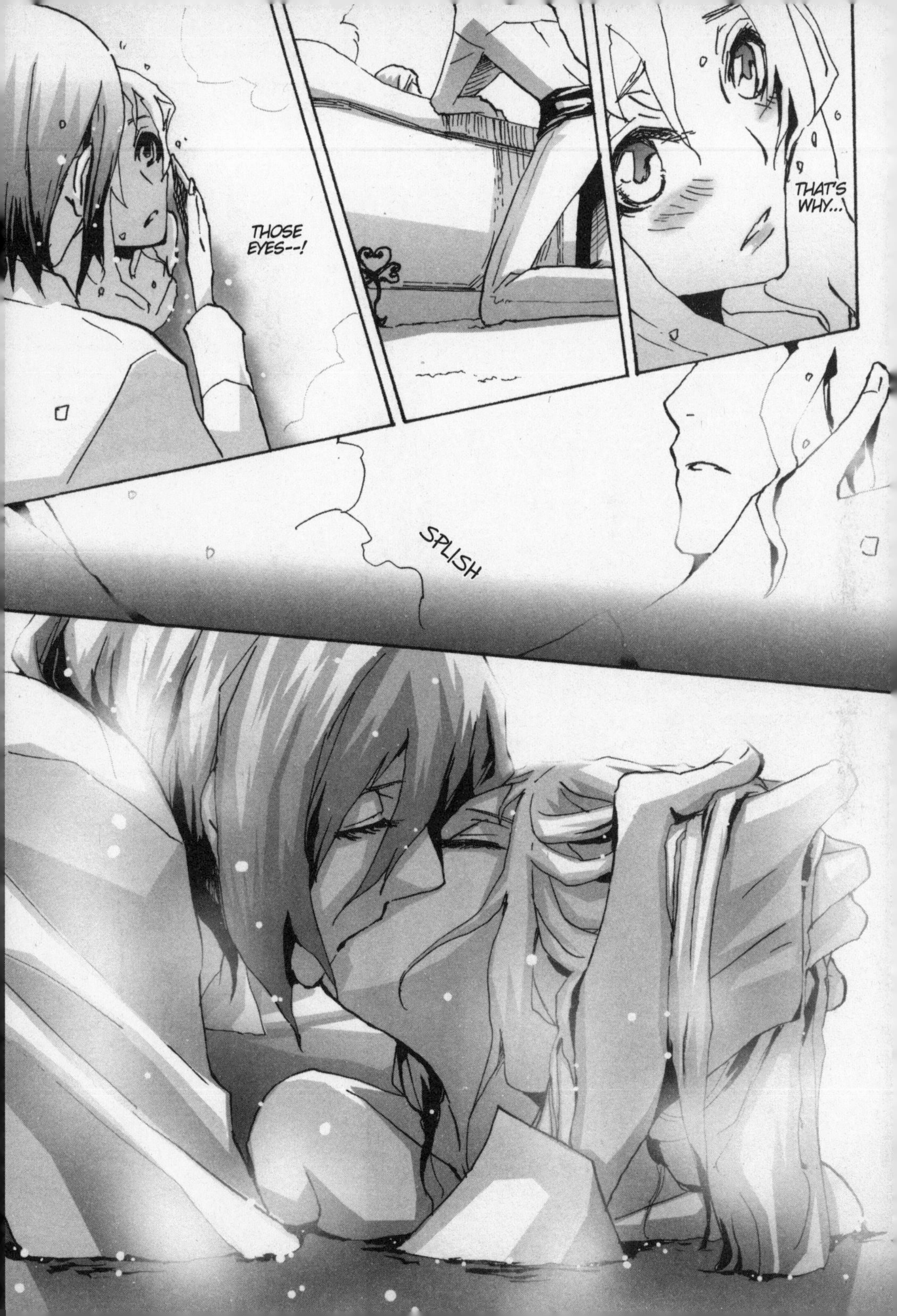
THAT'S WHY...
THOSE EYES--!
SPLISH

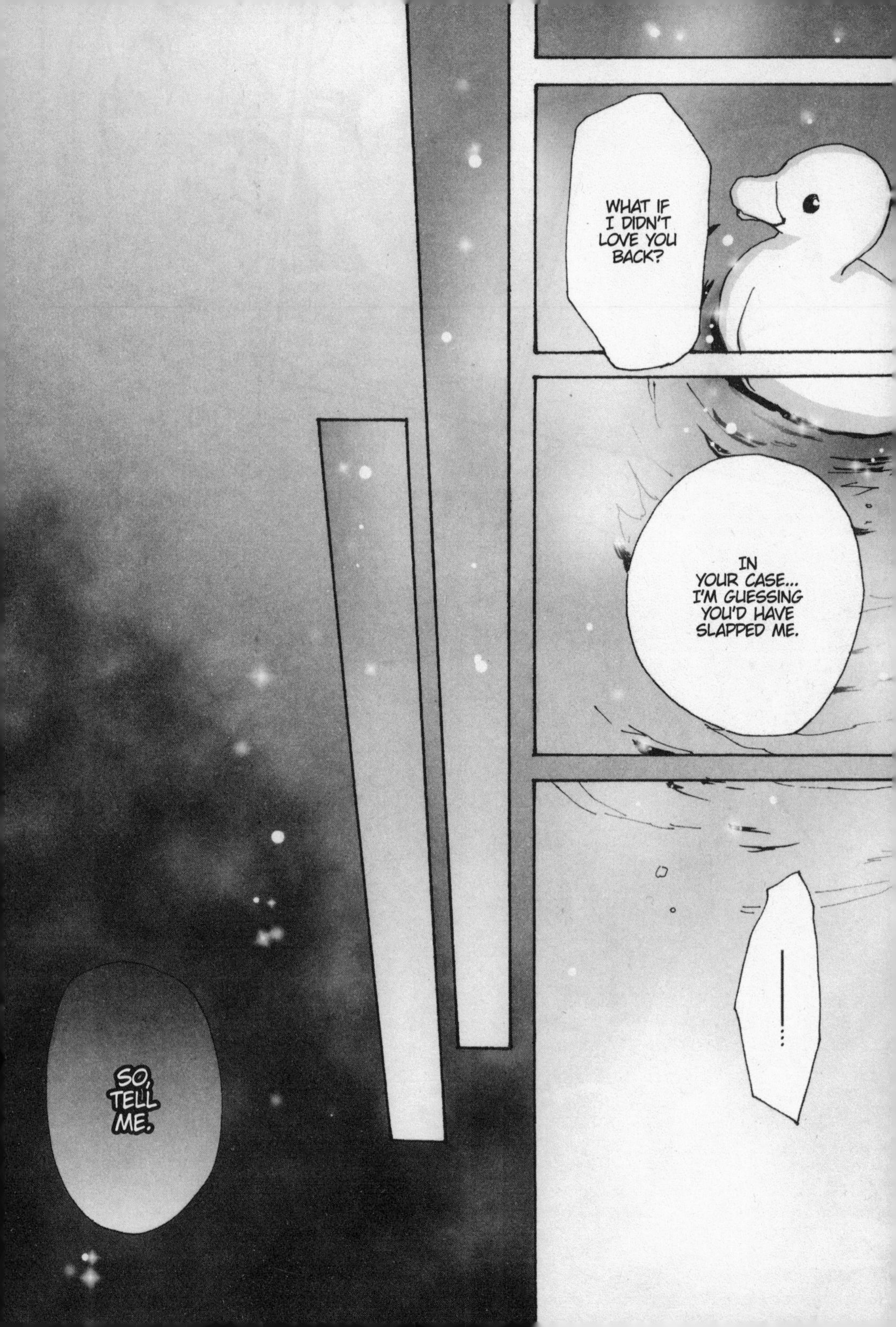
WHAT IF I DIDN'T LOVE YOU BACK?
IN YOUR CASE... I'M GUESSING YOU'D HAVE SLAPPED ME.
SO, TELL ME.

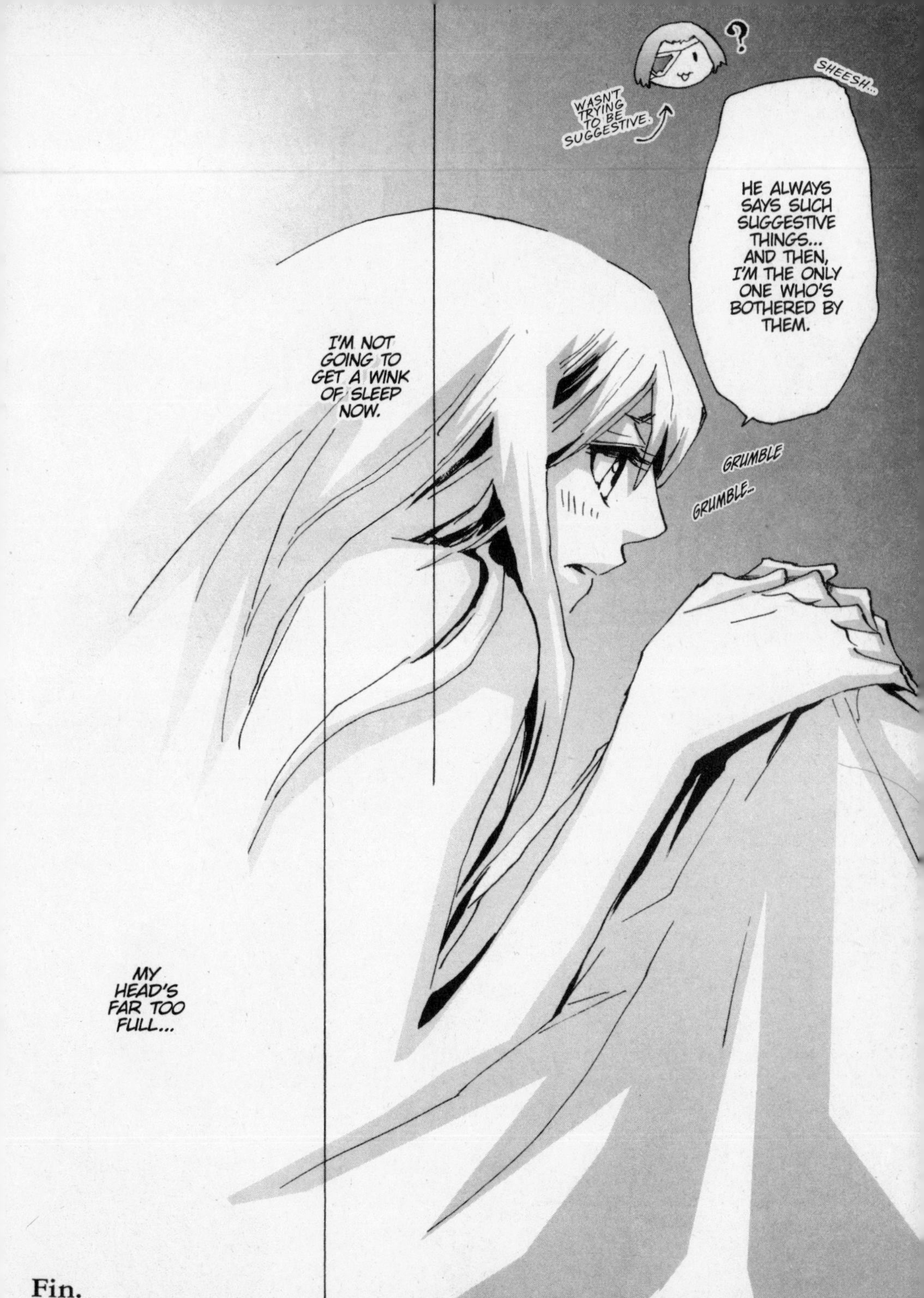
SHEESH...
HE ALWAYS SAYS SUCH SUGGESTIVE THINGS... AND THEN, I'M THE ONLY ONE WHO'S BOTHERED BY THEM.
WASN'T TRYING TO BE SUGGESTIVE.
GRUMBLE
GRUMBLE...
I'M NOT GOING TO GET A WINK OF SLEEP NOW.
MY HEAD'S FAR TOO FULL...

Fin.

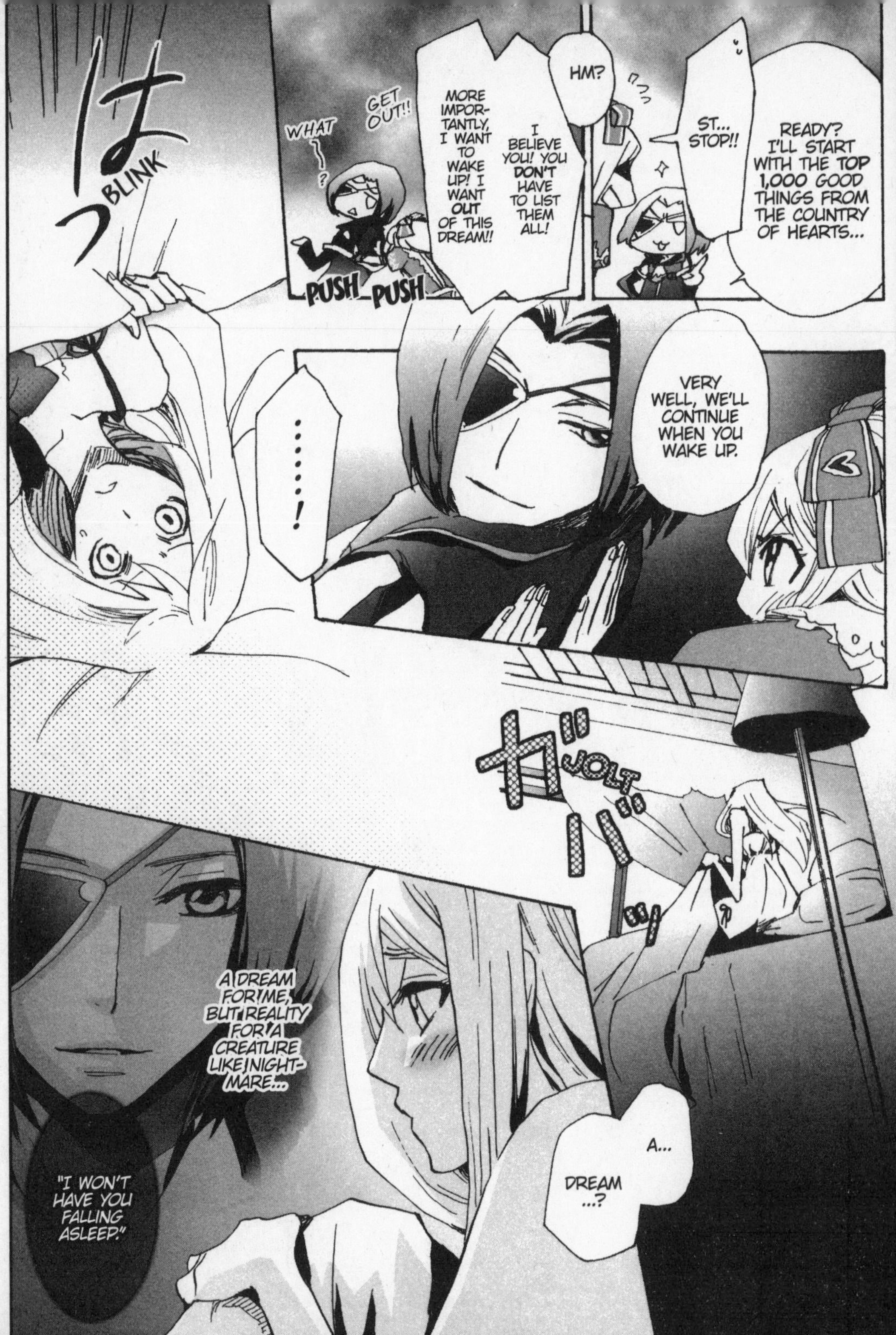
READY? I'LL START WITH THE TOP 1,000 GOOD THINGS FROM THE COUNTRY OF HEARTS...
ST... STOP!!
HM?
I BELIEVE YOU! YOU DON'T HAVE TO LIST THEM ALL!
MORE IMPORTANTLY, I WANT TO WAKE UP! I WANT OUT OF THIS DREAM!!
GET OUT!!
WHAT ~?
PUSH PUSH
はっ
BLINK
VERY WELL, WE'LL CONTINUE WHEN YOU WAKE UP.
......!
ガバッ
JOLT
A... DREAM...?
A DREAM FOR ME, BUT REALITY FOR A CREATURE LIKE NIGHTMARE...
"I WON'T HAVE YOU FALLING ASLEEP."

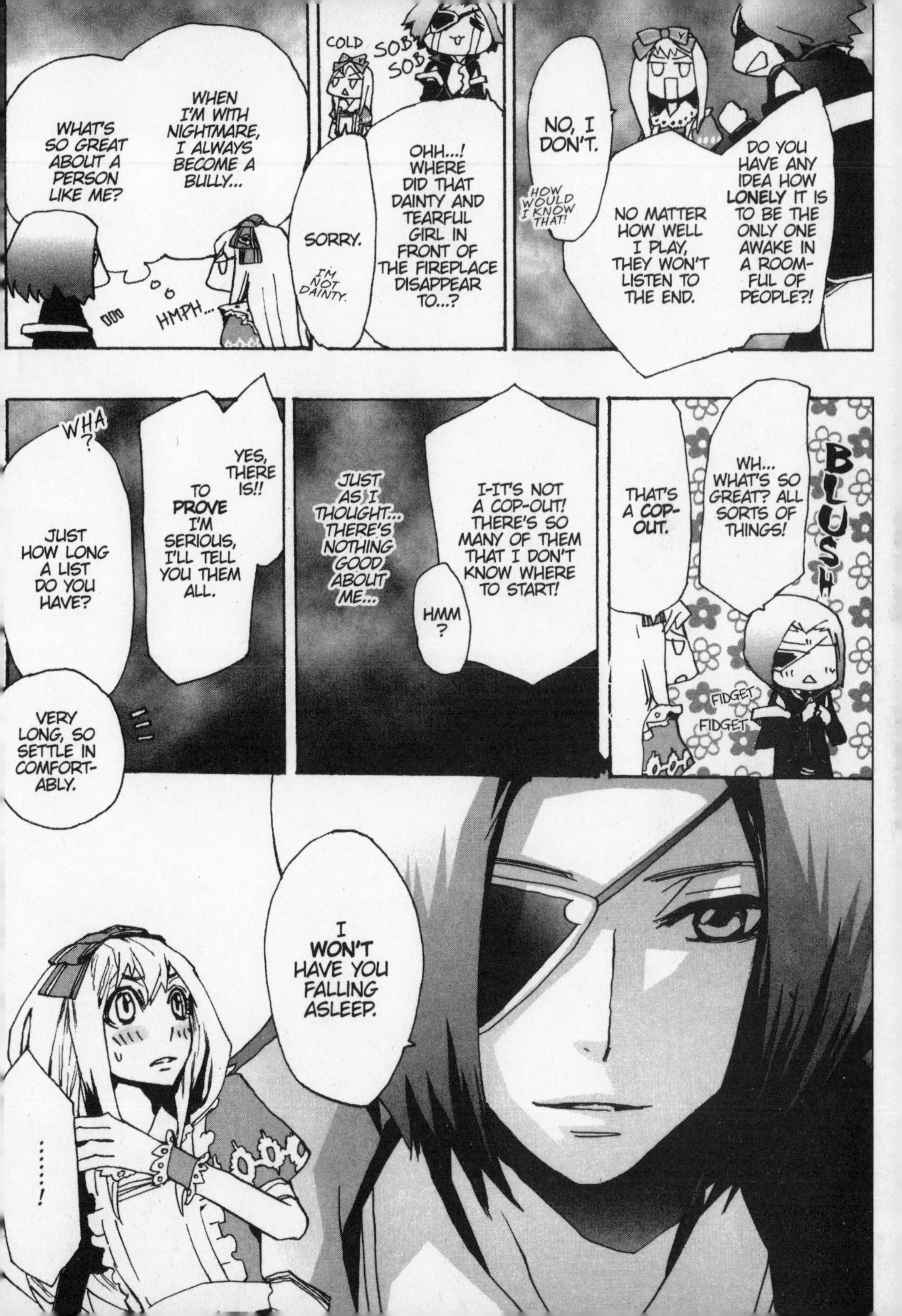

DO YOU HAVE ANY IDEA HOW LONELY IT IS TO BE THE ONLY ONE AWAKE IN A ROOMFUL OF PEOPLE?!
NO MATTER HOW WELL I PLAY, THEY WON'T LISTEN TO THE END.
NO, I DON'T.
HOW WOULD I KNOW THAT!
COLD
SOB SOB
OHH...! WHERE DID THAT DAINTY AND TEARFUL GIRL IN FRONT OF THE FIREPLACE DISAPPEAR TO...?
SORRY.
I'M NOT DAINTY.
WHEN I'M WITH NIGHTMARE, I ALWAYS BECOME A BULLY...
WHAT'S SO GREAT ABOUT A PERSON LIKE ME?
HMPH...
BLUSH
WH... WHAT'S SO GREAT? ALL SORTS OF THINGS!
THAT'S A COP-OUT.
FIDGET
FIDGET
I-IT'S NOT A COP-OUT! THERE'S SO MANY OF THEM THAT I DON'T KNOW WHERE TO START!
JUST AS I THOUGHT... THERE'S NOTHING GOOD ABOUT ME...
HMM?
YES, THERE IS!!
TO PROVE I'M SERIOUS, I'LL TELL YOU THEM ALL.
WHA?
JUST HOW LONG A LIST DO YOU HAVE?
VERY LONG, SO SETTLE IN COMFORTABLY.
I WON'T HAVE YOU FALLING ASLEEP.
......!

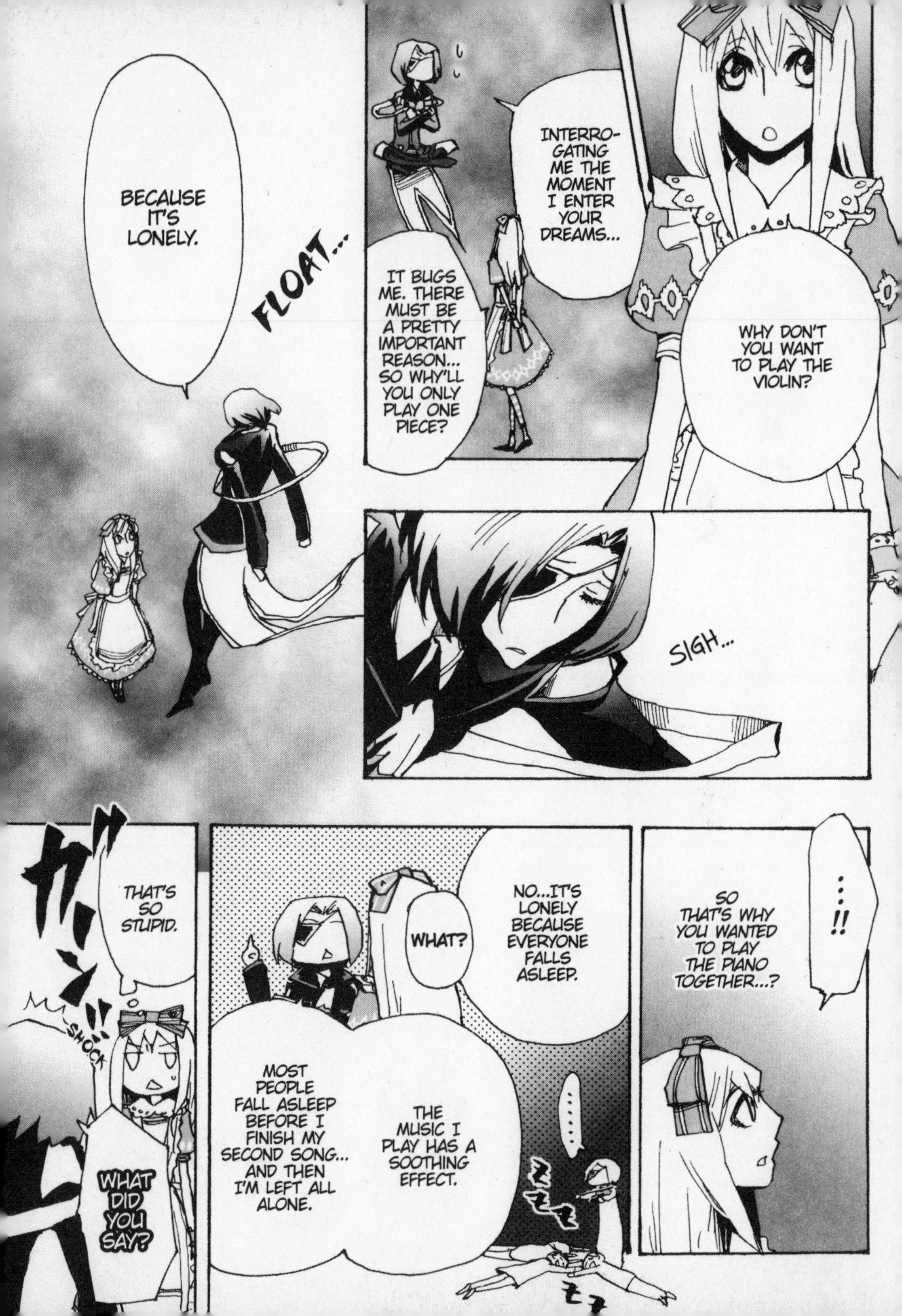
WHY DON'T YOU WANT TO PLAY THE VIOLIN?
INTERROGATING ME THE MOMENT I ENTER YOUR DREAMS...
IT BUGS ME. THERE MUST BE A PRETTY IMPORTANT REASON... SO WHY'LL YOU ONLY PLAY ONE PIECE?
SIGH...
FLOAT...
BECAUSE IT'S LONELY.
...!!
SO THAT'S WHY YOU WANTED TO PLAY THE PIANO TOGETHER...?
NO...IT'S LONELY BECAUSE EVERYONE FALLS ASLEEP.
WHAT?
THE MUSIC I PLAY HAS A SOOTHING EFFECT.
MOST PEOPLE FALL ASLEEP BEFORE I FINISH MY SECOND SONG... AND THEN I'M LEFT ALL ALONE.
......
THAT'S SO STUPID.
SHOCK
WHAT DID YOU SAY?

Alice in the Country of Hearts

ハートの国の

アリス

~ Wonderful Wonder World ~

- STORY -

This is a love adventure game. It is based on *Alice in Wonderland*, but evolves into a completely different story.

The main character is far from a romantic. In fact, she's especially sick of love relationships.

She's pulled (against her will) into the dangerous Country of Hearts, which is not as peaceful as the name makes it sound. The Hatters are a mafia family, and even the employees of the Amusement Park carry weapons.

The leaders of the three domains are constantly trying to kill each other. Many of the skirmishes are the result of territory grabs by three major powers trying to control more land: the Hatter, the Queen of Hearts, and Gowland.

After drinking some strange medicine (again, against her will), the main character is unable to return to her world. She quickly decides that she's trapped in a dream and allows herself to enjoy(?) the extraordinary experience she's been thrown into.

What territory will she stay with and who will she interact with to get herself home?
And will this girl, so jaded about love, fall into a relationship she doesn't expect?

Alice in Country of Hearts
Character Information

Elliot March
VA: Tsuguo Mogami

The No. 2 of the Hatter Family and Blood's right-hand man, Elliot is an ex-criminal and an escaped convict. Very short-tempered, he used to be a "very bad guy" who shot before asking questions. After partnering up with Blood, he rounded out and changed to a "slightly bad guy" who thinks for about three seconds before shooting. In his mind, this is a vast improvement.

Blood Dupre
VA: Katsuyuki Konishi

The dangerous leader of the crime syndicate known as the Hatter Family. Since he enjoys plotting more than working directly, he controls everything from the shadows. He's incredibly smart, but due to his temperamental moods and his desire to keep things "interesting," he often digs his own grave in his secret plans.

Alice Liddell
VA: Rie Kugimiya

She grew up to be a responsible young woman after losing her mother early, but Alice still carries a complex toward her older sister. She respects her older sister very much, but is frustrated about always being compared to her. Since her first love fell for her older sister, she has no confidence in herself when it comes to romance.

Vivaldi
VA: Yuuko Kaida

Ruthless and cruel, the Queen of Hearts is an arrogant beauty with a wild temper. She's enemies with the Hatter and Gowland. Impatient at heart, Vivaldi takes her fury out on everyone around her, including her subordinates, whom she considers pawns. Anyone **not** working for her doesn't even register as existing.

Tweedle Dum
VA: Jun Fukuyama

The second "Bloody Twin" and a dead ringer for his brother—in both appearance and personality. As they often change places, it's uncertain which one is the older twin.

Tweedle Dee
VA: Jun Fukuyama

Gatekeeper of the Hatter territory, and one of the dark, sneaky twins. They sometimes show an innocent side, but they usually have a malicious agenda. Also known as the "Bloody Twins" due to their unsavory activities.

Ace
VA: Daisuke Hirakawa

The knight of Hearts and the ex-subordinate of Vivaldi. He's left the castle and is currently wandering. He's a very unlucky and unfortunate man, yet he remains strangely positive, thus he tends to plow forward and make mistakes that only worsen his situation. He's one of the few friends of the clockmaker, Julius.

Julius Monrey
VA: Takehito Koyasu

The clockmaker, a gloomy machine expert who easily falls into depression. He lives in the Clock Tower and doesn't get out much. He always thinks of everything in the most negative way and tends to distrust people, but he gets along with Ace. He had some part in the imprisonment of the March Hare, Elliot, and is thus the target of Elliot's hatred.

Peter White
VA: Kouki Miyata

Don't be fooled by the cute ears—Peter is the dangerous guide who dragged Alice to Wonderland in the first place. He claims to always be worried about the time, despite having a strange grasp on it. Rumors say his heart is as black as his hair is white.

Nightmare
VA: Tomokazu Sugita

A sickly nightmare. He appears in Alice's dream, sometimes to guide her—and other times, to **misguide** her.

Mary Gowland
VA: Kenyuu Horiuchi

The owner of the Amusement Park. He hides his hated first name, Mary, but pretty much everyone already knows it. His full name is a play on words that sounds like "Merry Go Round" when said quickly. If his musical talent was given a numerical value, it would be closer to negatives than zero.

Boris Airay
VA: Noriaki Sugiyama

A riddle-loving cat with a signature smirk. He sometimes gives hints to his riddles, but the hints usually just cause more confusion. He also has a tendency to pose questions and never answer them.

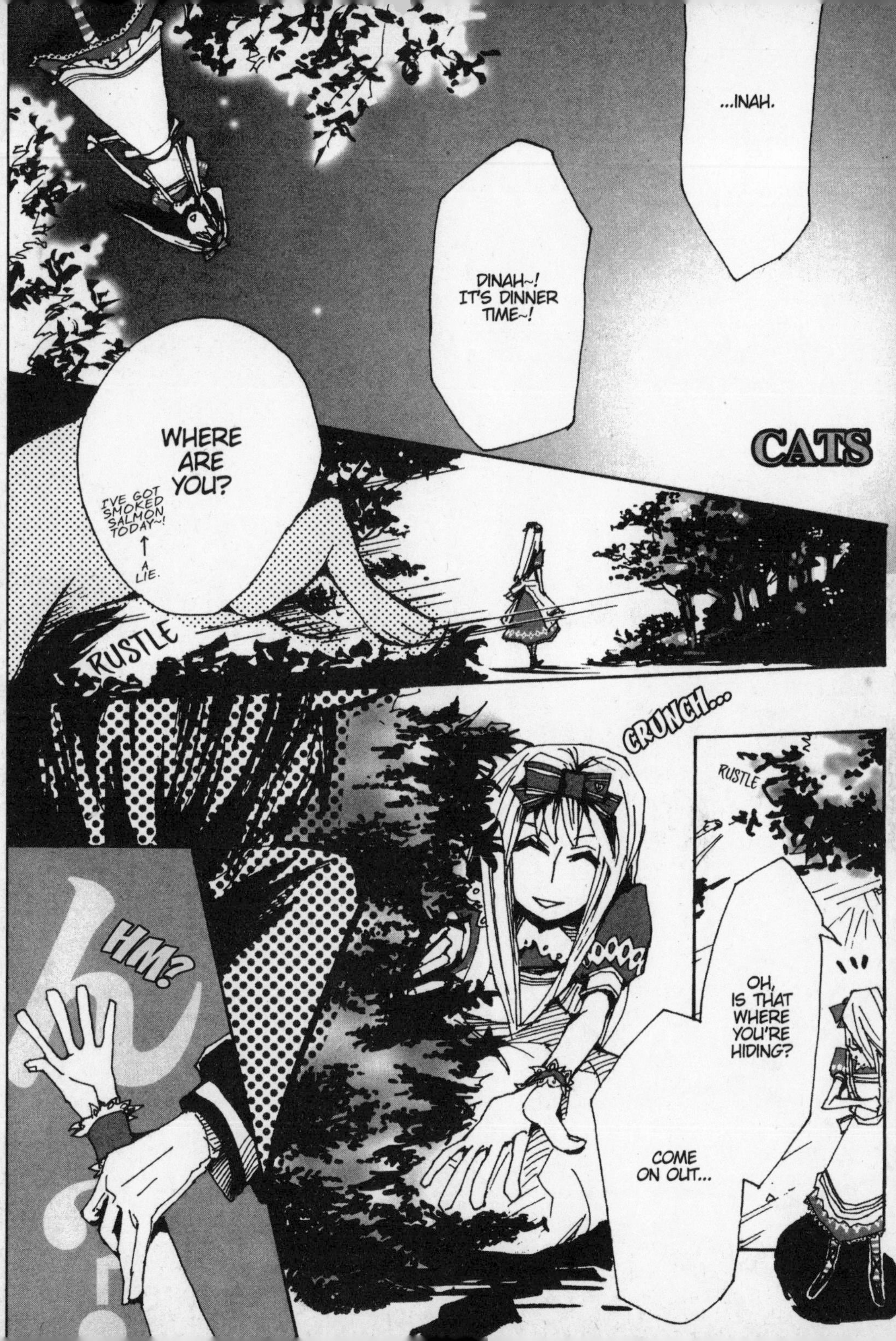
...INAH.
DINAH~! IT'S DINNER TIME~!
CATS
WHERE ARE YOU?
I'VE GOT SMOKED SALMON TODAY~!
↑ A LIE.
RUSTLE
CRUNCH...
RUSTLE
...
OH, IS THAT WHERE YOU'RE HIDING?
COME ON OUT...
HM?

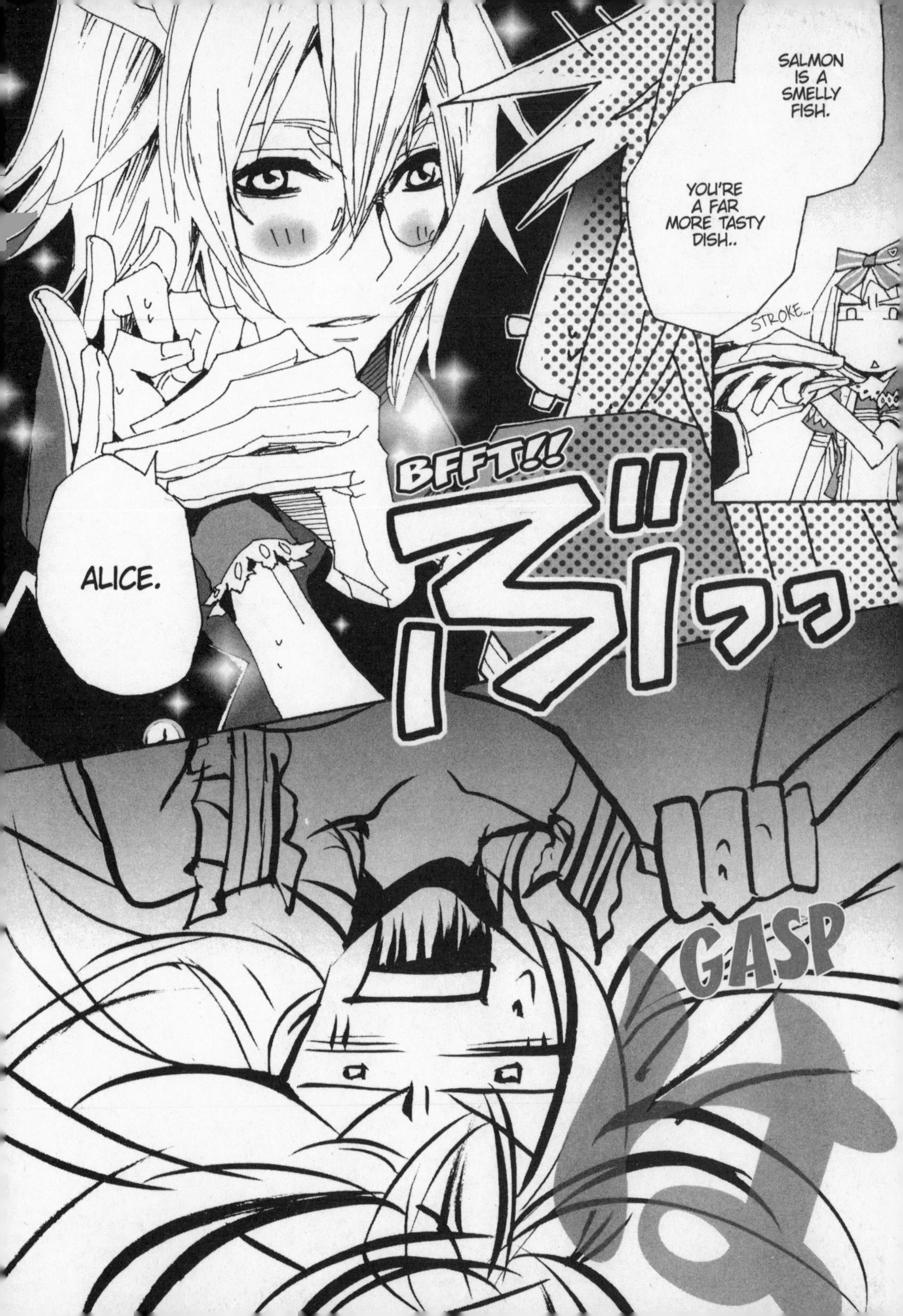
SALMON IS A SMELLY FISH.
YOU'RE A FAR MORE TASTY DISH..
STROKE...
ALICE.
BFFT!!
GASP

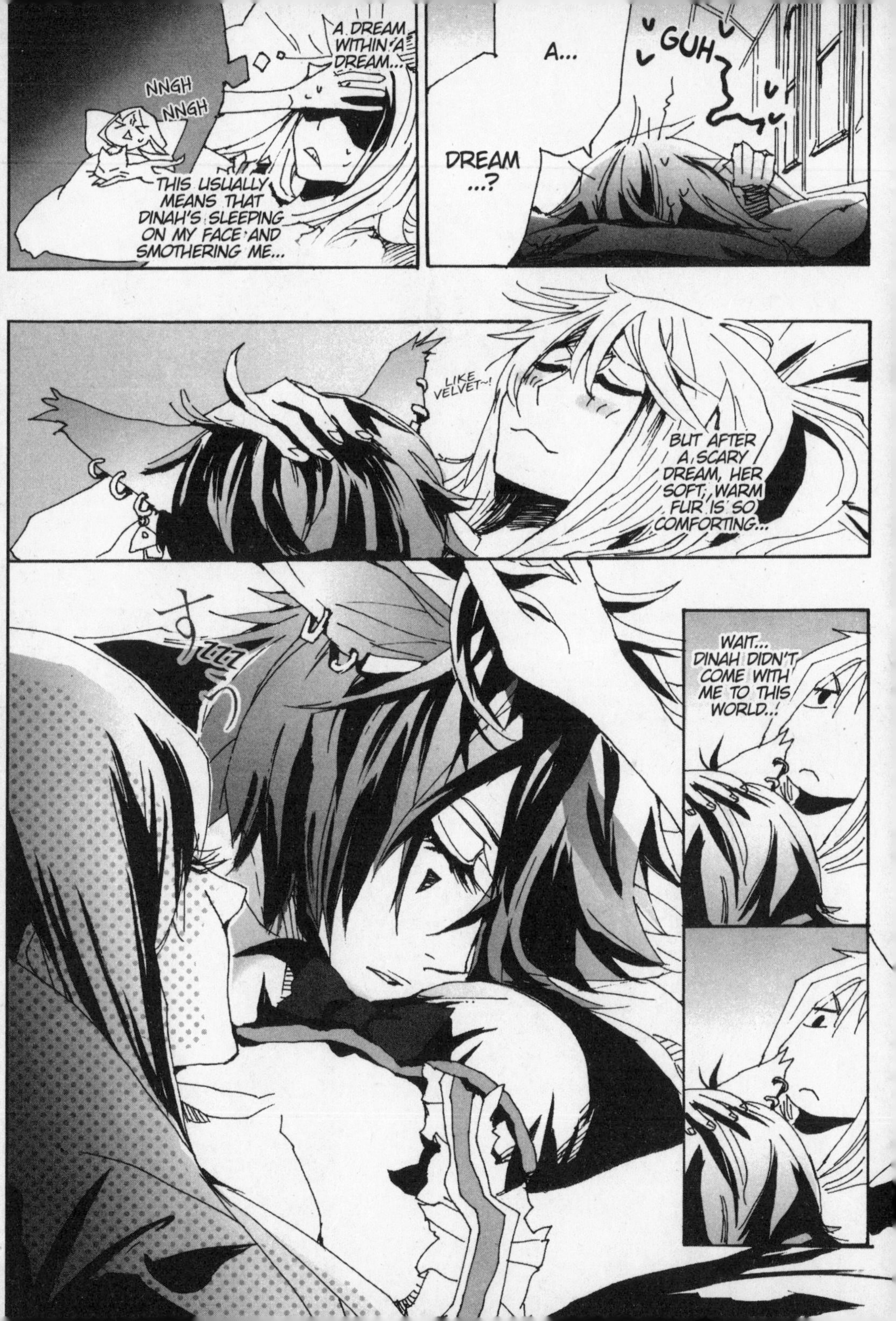
A...
DREAM ...?
GUH
A DREAM WITHIN A DREAM...
NNGH NNGH
THIS USUALLY MEANS THAT DINAH'S SLEEPING ON MY FACE AND SMOTHERING ME...
BUT AFTER A SCARY DREAM, HER SOFT, WARM FUR IS SO COMFORTING...
LIKE VELVET~!
WAIT... DINAH DIDN'T COME WITH ME TO THIS WORLD...

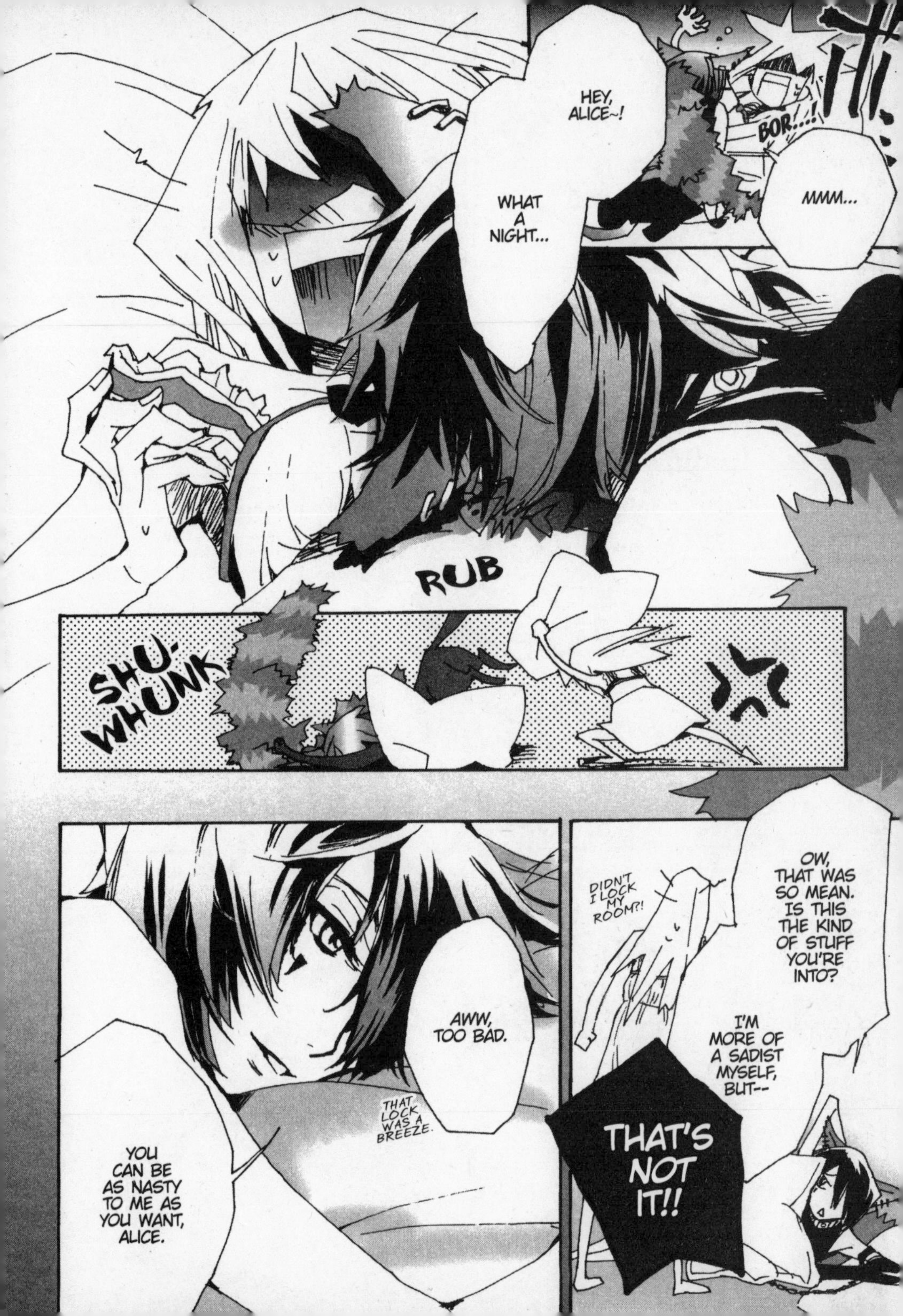
BOR...!
MMM...
HEY, ALICE~!
WHAT A NIGHT...
RUB
SHU-WHUNK
OW, THAT WAS SO MEAN. IS THIS THE KIND OF STUFF YOU'RE INTO?
I'M MORE OF A SADIST MYSELF, BUT--
DIDN'T I LOCK MY ROOM?!
THAT'S NOT IT!!
AWW, TOO BAD.
THAT LOCK WAS A BREEZE.
YOU CAN BE AS NASTY TO ME AS YOU WANT, ALICE.

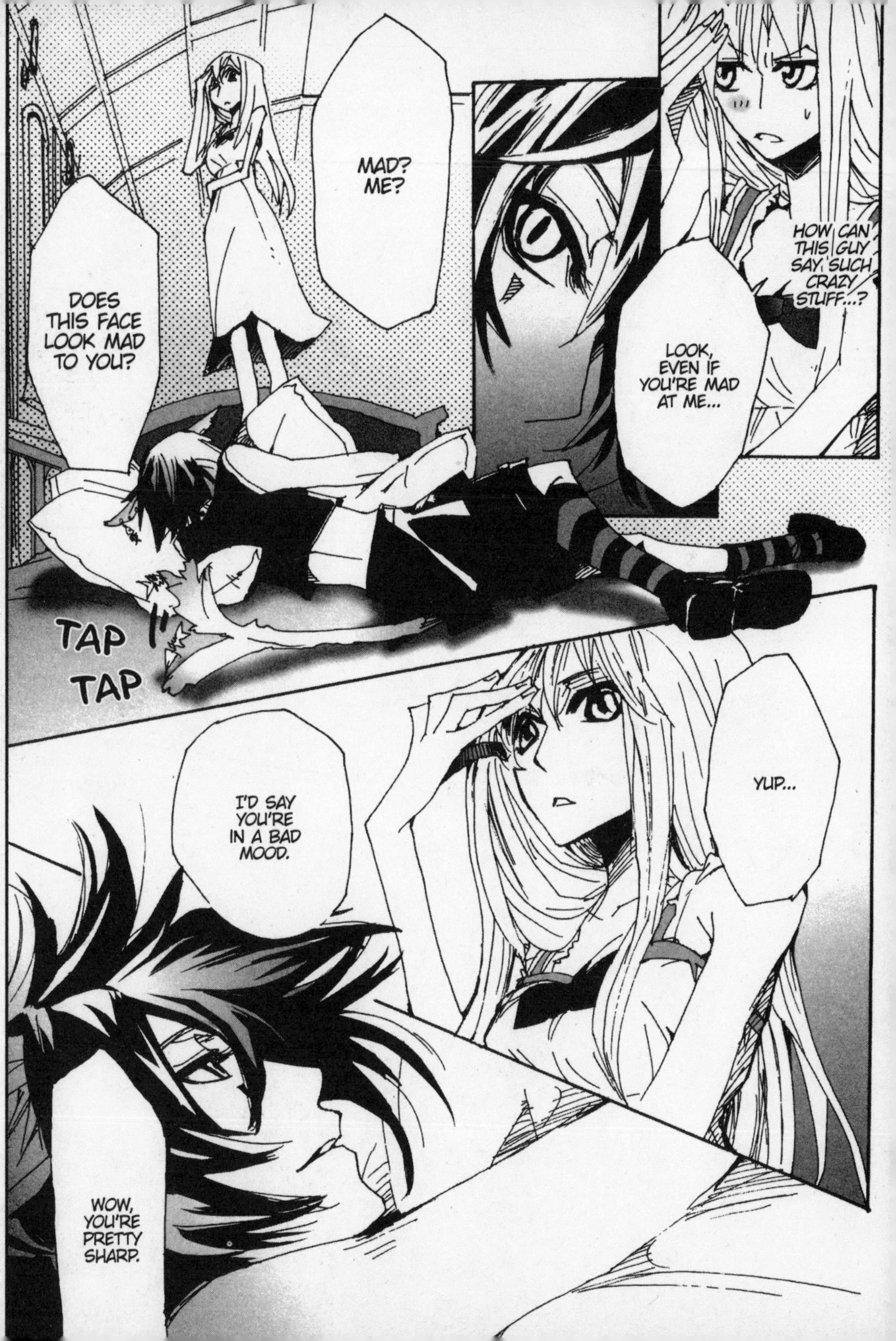
HOW CAN THIS GUY SAY SUCH CRAZY STUFF...?
LOOK, EVEN IF YOU'RE MAD AT ME...
MAD? ME?
DOES THIS FACE LOOK MAD TO YOU?
TAP TAP
YUP...
I'D SAY YOU'RE IN A BAD MOOD.
WOW, YOU'RE PRETTY SHARP.

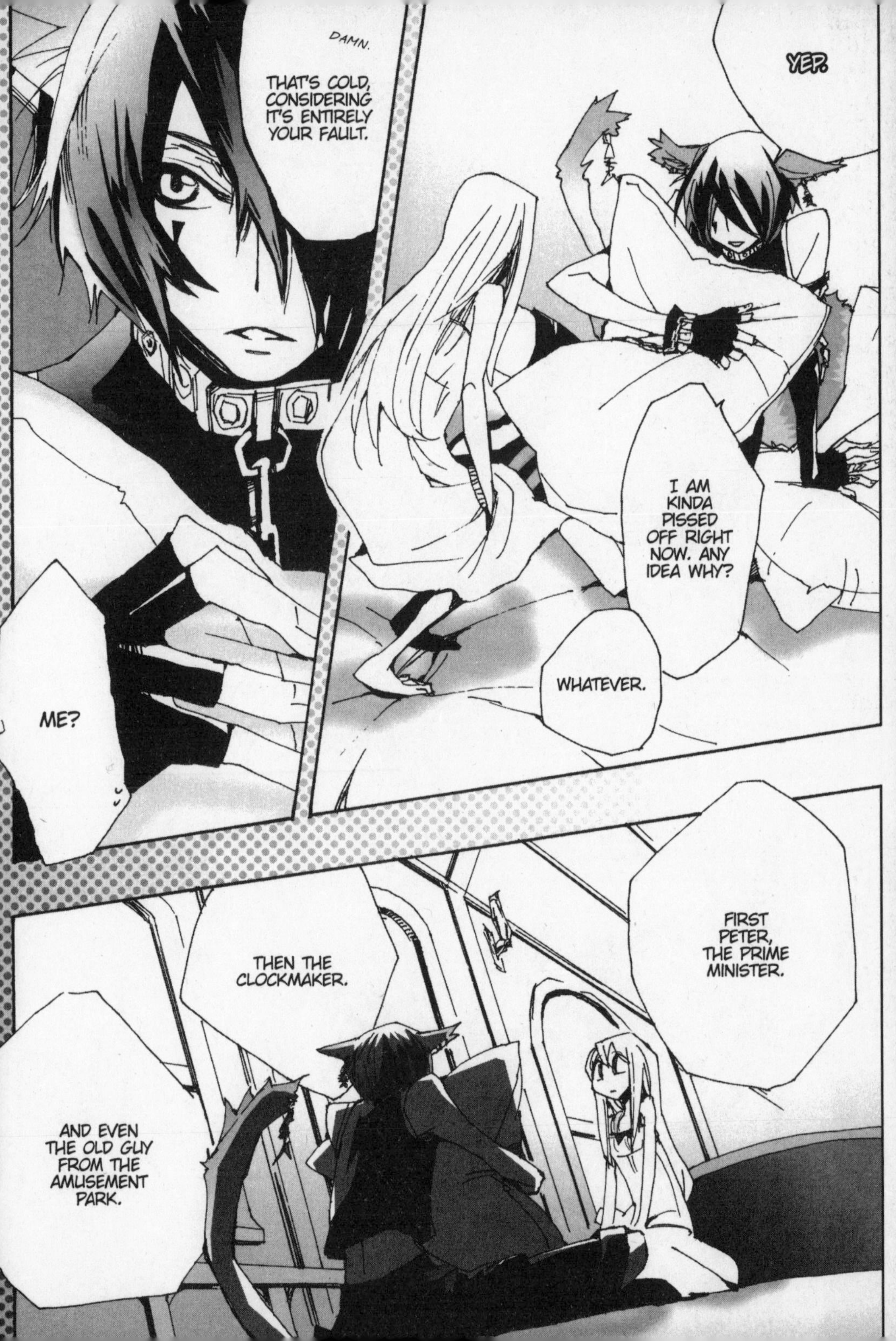
YEP.
I AM KINDA PISSED OFF RIGHT NOW. ANY IDEA WHY?
WHATEVER.
DAMN.
THAT'S COLD, CONSIDERING IT'S ENTIRELY YOUR FAULT.
ME?
FIRST PETER, THE PRIME MINISTER.
THEN THE CLOCKMAKER.
AND EVEN THE OLD GUY FROM THE AMUSEMENT PARK.

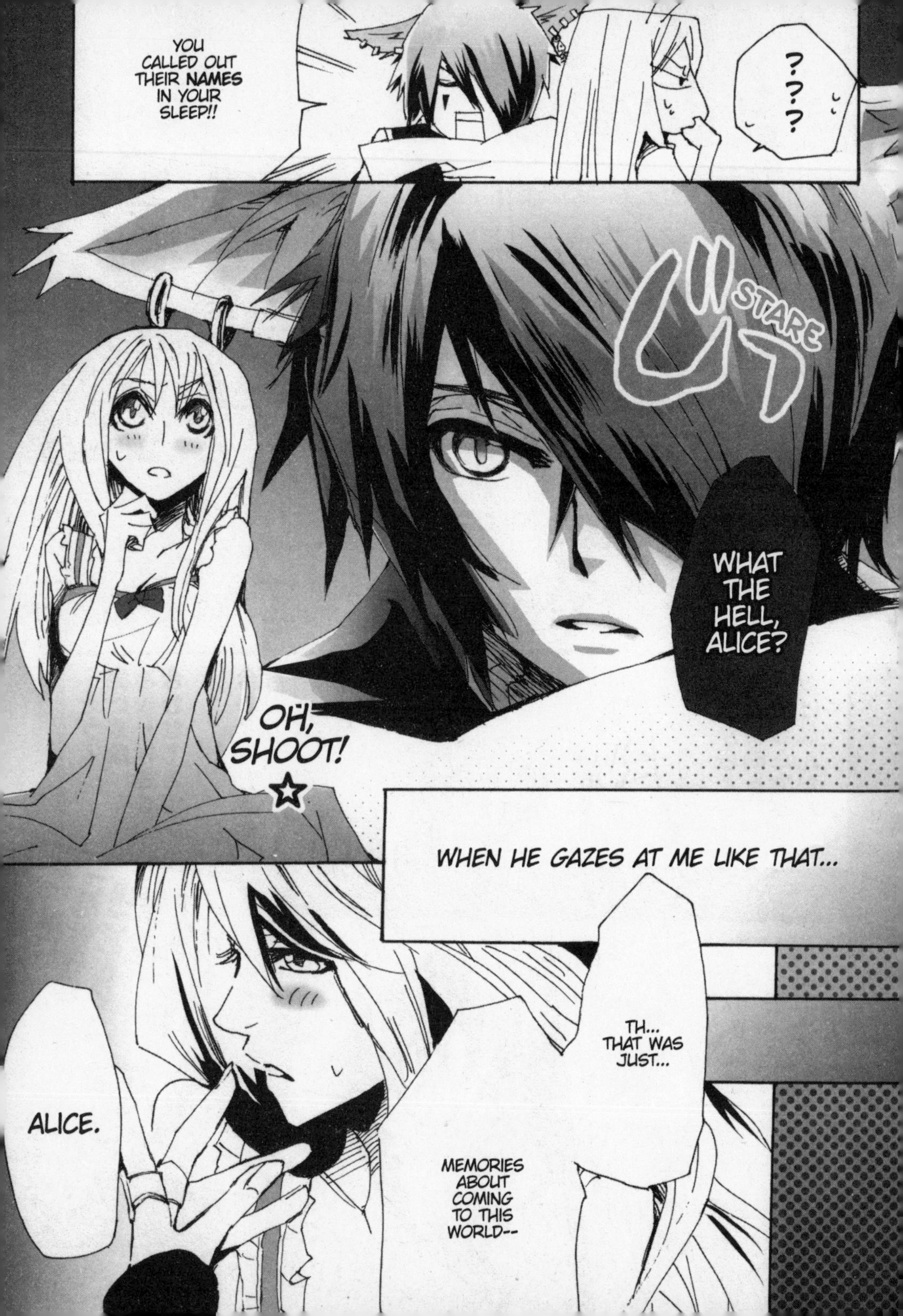
???
YOU CALLED OUT THEIR NAMES IN YOUR SLEEP!!
STARE
WHAT THE HELL, ALICE?
OH, SHOOT! ☆
WHEN HE GAZES AT ME LIKE THAT...
TH... THAT WAS JUST...
MEMORIES ABOUT COMING TO THIS WORLD--
ALICE.

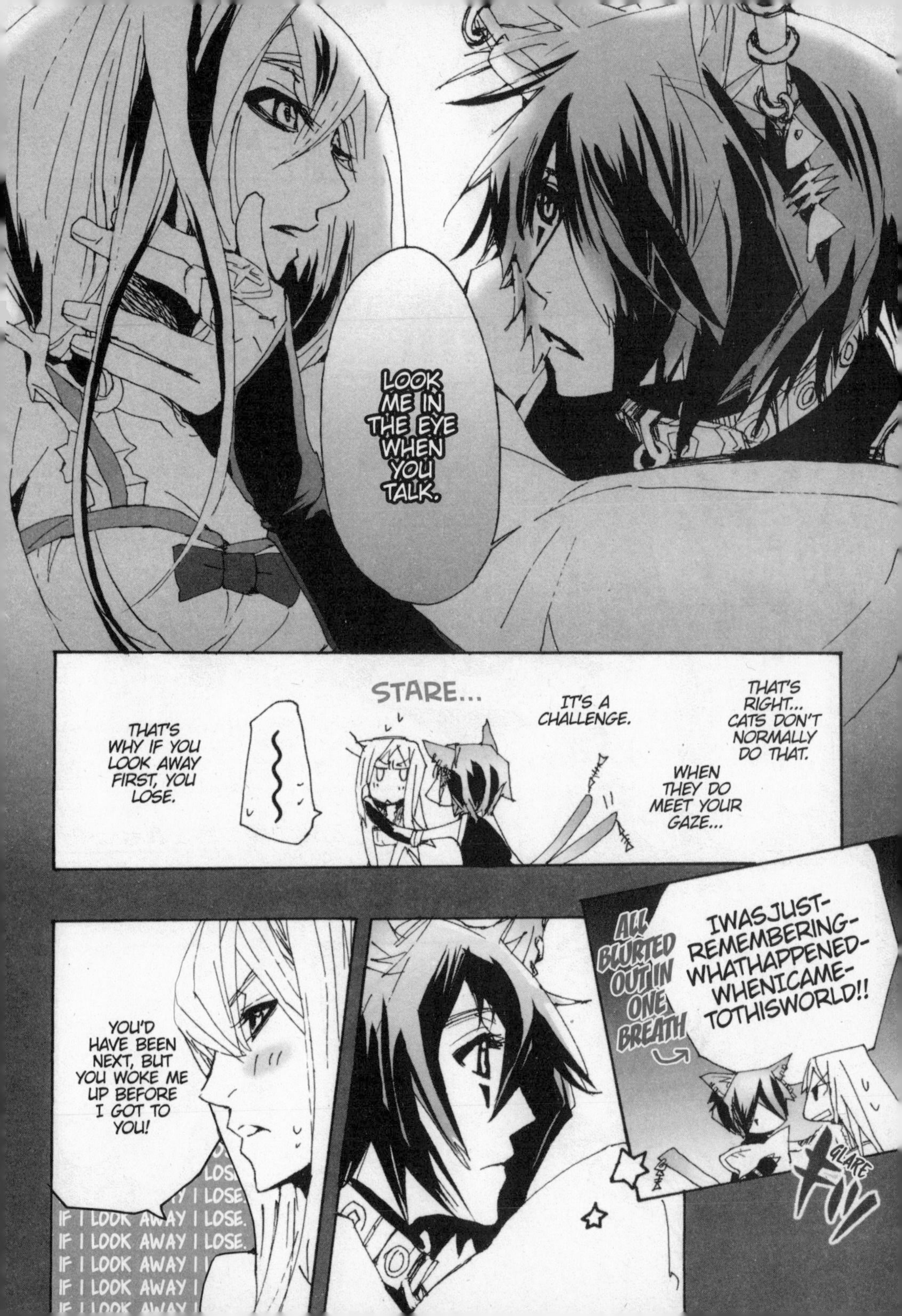
LOOK ME IN THE EYE WHEN YOU TALK.
THAT'S RIGHT... CATS DON'T NORMALLY DO THAT.
WHEN THEY DO MEET YOUR GAZE...
IT'S A CHALLENGE.
STARE...
THAT'S WHY IF YOU LOOK AWAY FIRST, YOU LOSE.
IWASJUST-REMEMBERING-WHATHAPPENED-WHENICAME-TOTHISWORLD!!
ALL BLURTED OUT IN ONE BREATH
GLARE
YOU'D HAVE BEEN NEXT, BUT YOU WOKE ME UP BEFORE I GOT TO YOU!
IF I LOOK AWAY I LOSE.
IF I LOOK AWAY I LOSE.

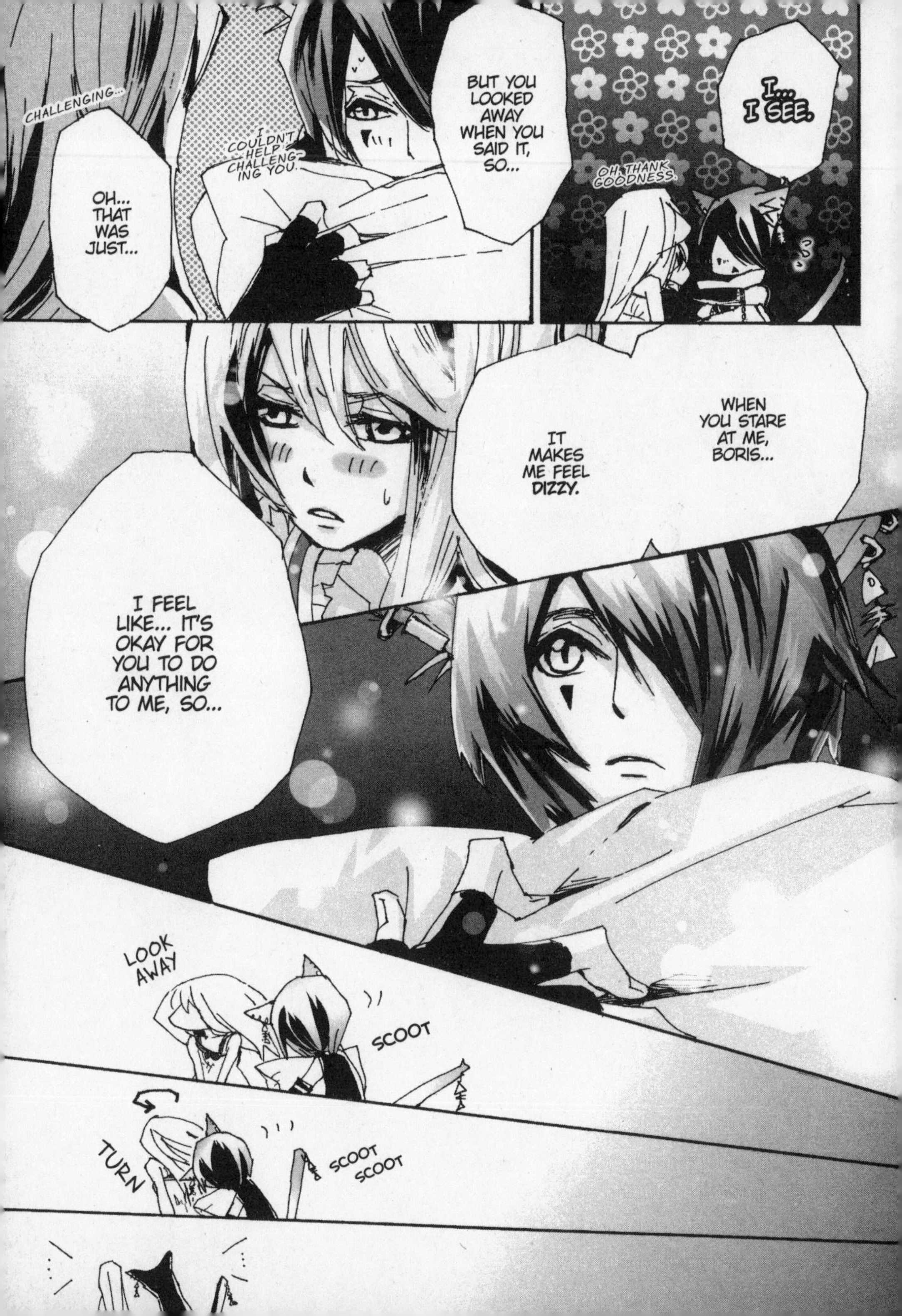
I... I SEE.
OH, THANK GOODNESS.
BUT YOU LOOKED AWAY WHEN YOU SAID IT, SO...
CHALLENGING...
I COULDN'T HELP CHALLENG-ING YOU.
OH... THAT WAS JUST...
WHEN YOU STARE AT ME, BORIS...
IT MAKES ME FEEL DIZZY.
I FEEL LIKE... IT'S OKAY FOR YOU TO DO ANYTHING TO ME, SO...
LOOK AWAY
SCOOT
TURN
SCOOT SCOOT

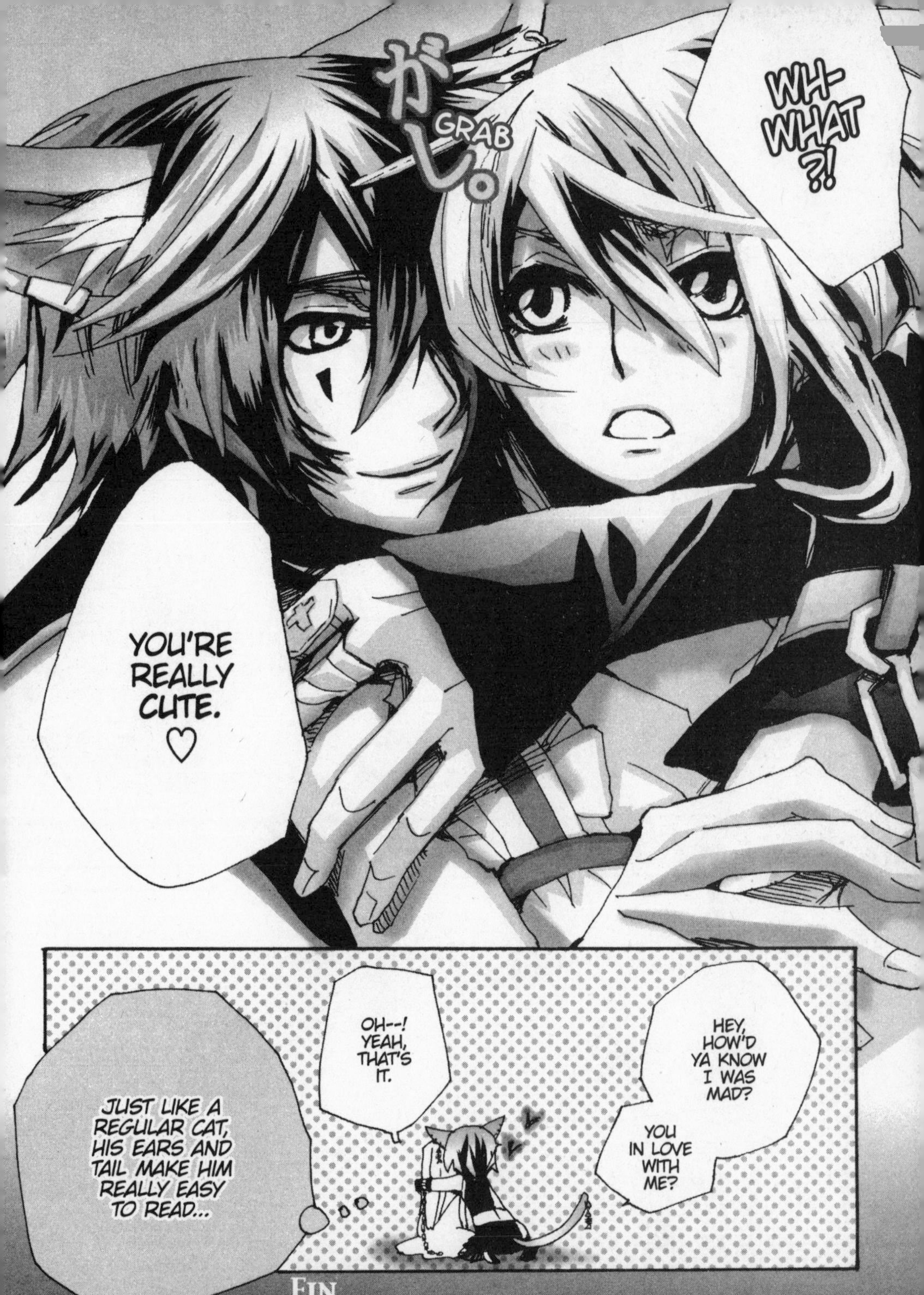
WH-WHAT ?!
がし。
GRAB
YOU'RE REALLY CUTE. ♡
HEY, HOW'D YA KNOW I WAS MAD?
YOU IN LOVE WITH ME?
OH--! YEAH, THAT'S IT.
JUST LIKE A REGULAR CAT, HIS EARS AND TAIL MAKE HIM REALLY EASY TO READ...

FIN.

Alice in the Country of Clover
クローバーの国のアリス
~Wonderful Wonder World~

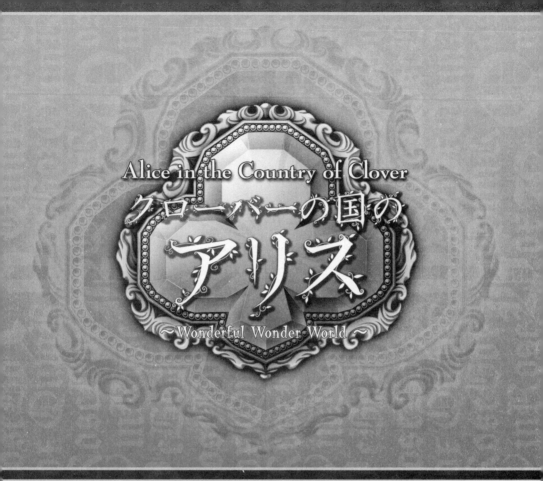

- STORY -

In *Alice in the Country of Clover*, the game starts with Alice having not fallen in love, but still deciding to stay in Wonderland.

She's acquainted with all the characters from the previous game, *Alice in the Country of Hearts.*

Since love would now start from a place of friendship rather than passion with a new stranger, she can experience a different type of romance from that in the previous game. Her dynamic with the characters is different through this friendship—characters can't always be forceful with her, and in many ways it's more comfortable to grow intimate. The relationships *between* the Ones With Duties have also become more of a factor.

In this game, the story focuses on the mafia. Alice attends the suited meetings (forcefully) and gets involved in various gunfights (forcefully), among other things.

Land fluctuations, sea creatures in the forest, and whispering doors—it's a game more fantastic and more eerie than the first.

Will our everywoman Alice be able to have a romantic relationship in a world devoid of common sense?

Alice in the Country of Clover
Character Information

Elliot March
VA: Tsuguo Mogami

Blood's right-hand man has a criminal past... and a temperamental present. But he's not as bad as he used to be, so that's something. Joining Blood has been good(?) for him.

Blood Dupre
VA: Katsuyuki Konishi

The head of the mafia Hatter Family, Blood is a cunning yet moody puppet-master. Alice now has the pleasure of having him for a landlord.

Alice Liddell
VA: Rie Kugimiya

A normal girl with a bit of a chip on her shoulder. Deciding to stay in the Wonderland she was carried to, she's adapted to her strange new lifestyle.

Vivaldi
VA: Yuuko Kaida

The beautiful Queen of Hearts has an unrivaled temper—which is really saying something in Wonderland. Although a picture-perfect Mad Queen, she cares for Alice as if Alice were her little sister...or a very interesting plaything.

Tweedle Dum
VA: Jun Fukuyama

The second "Bloody Twin" is equally cute and equally scary. In *Clover*, Dum can also turn into an adult.

Tweedle Dee
VA: Jun Fukuyama

One of the "Bloody Twin" gatekeepers of the Hatter territory, Dee can be cute when he's not being terrifying. In *Clover*, he sometimes turns into an adult.

Boris Airay
VA: Noriaki Sugiyama

This riddle-loving cat has a signature smirk—and in *Clover*, a new toy. One of his favorite pastimes is giving the Sleepy Mouse a hard time.

Ace
VA: Daisuke Hirakawa

The unlucky knight of Hearts was a former subordinate of Vivaldi and is perpetually lost. Even though he's depressed to be separated from his friend and boss Julius, he stays positive and tries to overcome it with a smile. He seems like a classic nice guy... or is he?

Peter White
VA: Kouki Miyata

The Prime Minister of Heart Castle—who has rabbit ears growing out of his head—invited (kidnapped) Alice to Wonderland. He loves Alice and hates everything else. His cruel, irrational actions are disturbing, but he acts like a completely different person (rabbit?) when in the throes of his love for Alice.

Gray Ringmarc
VA: Kazuya Nakai

Nightmare's subordinate in *Clover*. He used to have strong social ambition and considered assassinating Nightmare... but since Nightmare was such a useless boss, Gray couldn't help but feel sorry for him and ended up a dedicated assistant. He's a sound thinker with a strong work ethic. He's also highly skilled with his blades, rivaling even Ace.

Nightmare Gottschalk
VA: Tomokazu Sugita

A sickly nightmare who hates the hospital and needles. He has the power to read people's thoughts and enter dreams. Even though he likes to shut himself away in dreams, Gray drags him out to sulk from time to time. He technically holds a high position and has many subordinates, but since he can't even take care of his own health, he leaves most things to Gray.

Pierce Villiers
VA: Souichirou Hoshi

New to *Clover*, Pierce is an insomniac mouse who drinks too much coffee. He loves Nightmare (who can help him sleep) and hates Boris (who terrifies him). He dislikes Blood and Vivaldi for discarding coffee in favor of tea. He likes Elliot and Peter well enough, since rabbits aren't natural predators of mice.

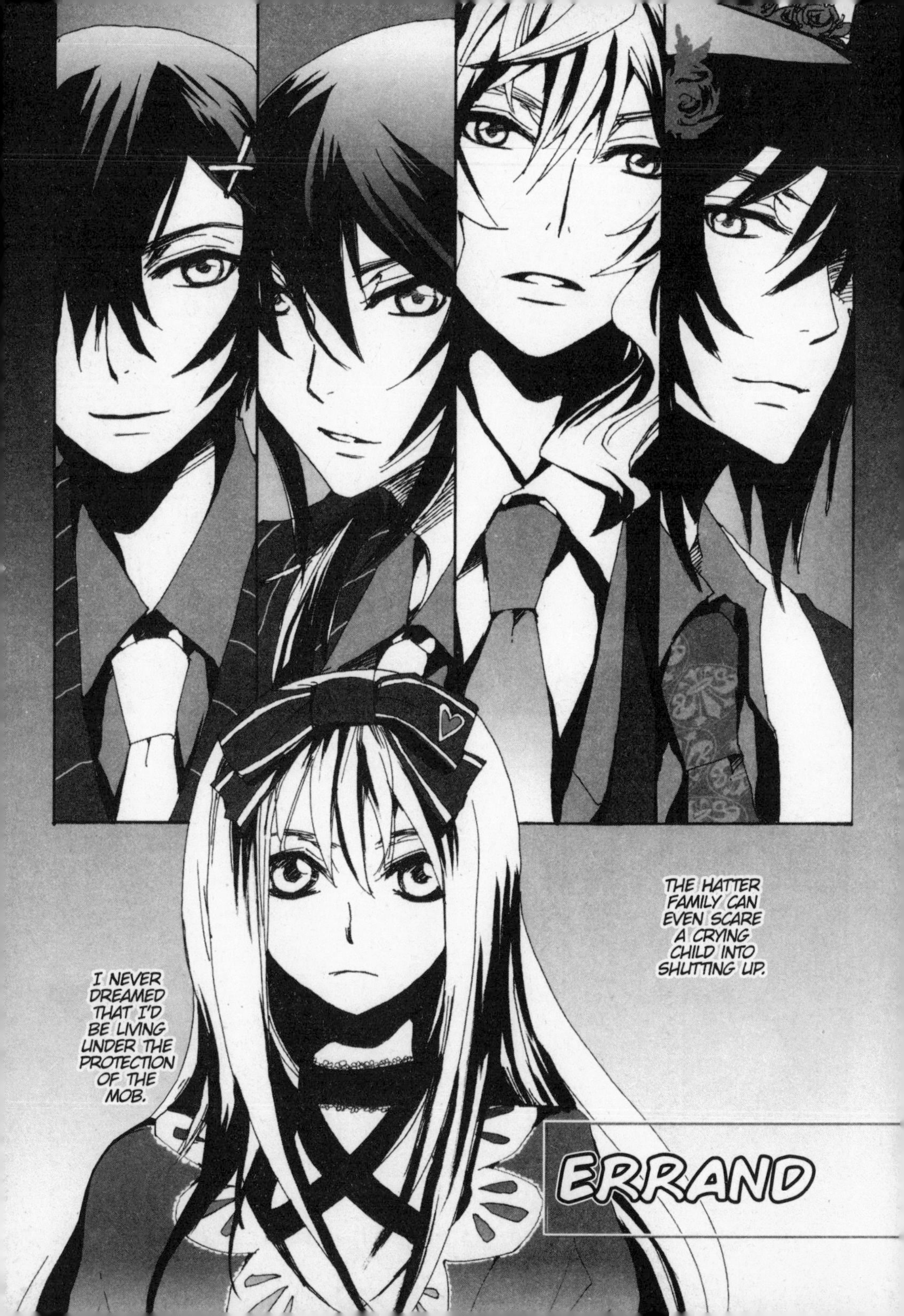
THE HATTER FAMILY CAN EVEN SCARE A CRYING CHILD INTO SHUTTING UP.
I NEVER DREAMED THAT I'D BE LIVING UNDER THE PROTECTION OF THE MOB.
ERRAND

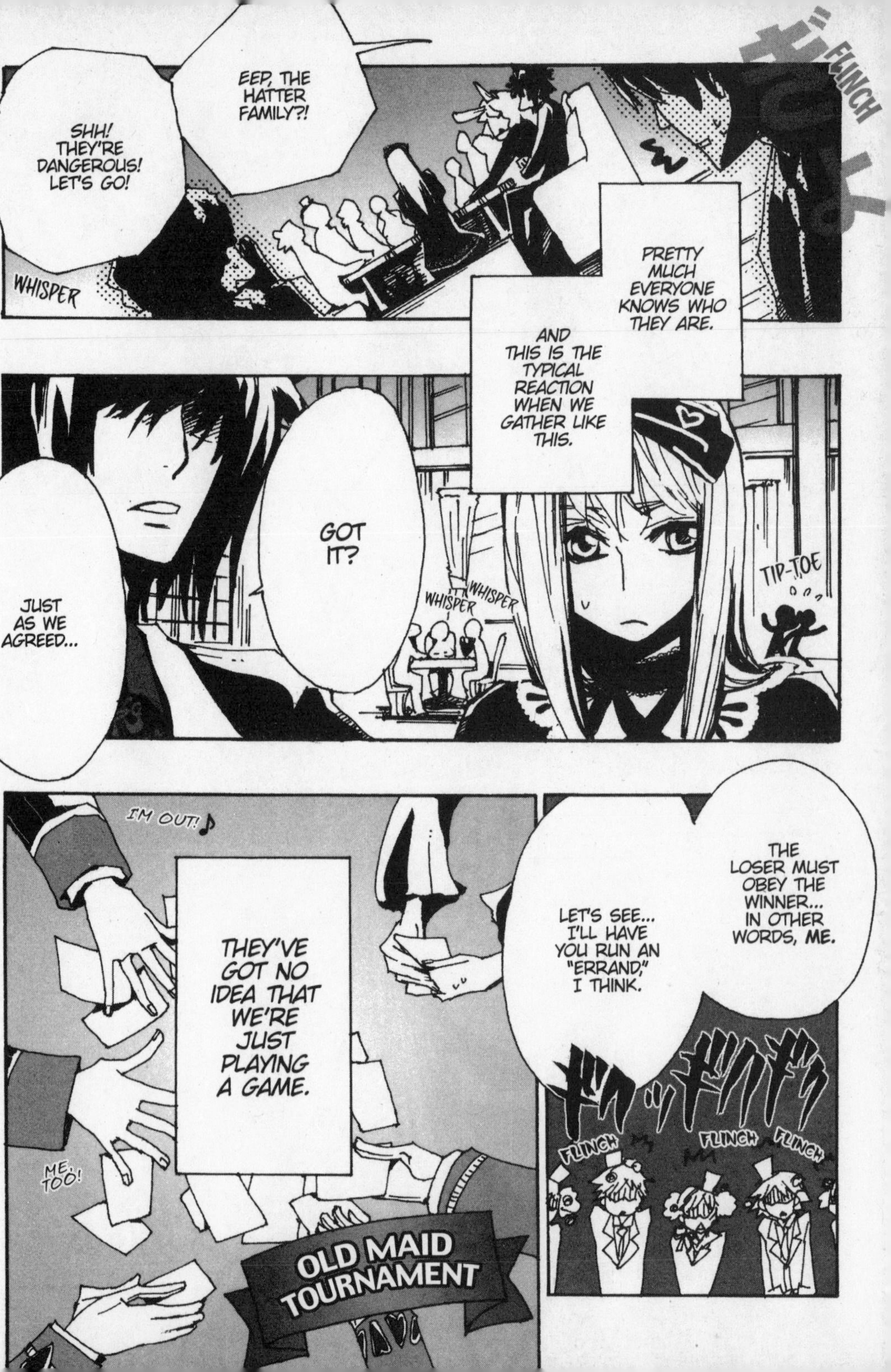
FLINCH
EEP, THE HATTER FAMILY?!
SHH! THEY'RE DANGEROUS! LET'S GO!
WHISPER
PRETTY MUCH EVERYONE KNOWS WHO THEY ARE.
AND THIS IS THE TYPICAL REACTION WHEN WE GATHER LIKE THIS.
TIP-TOE
WHISPER
WHISPER
GOT IT?
JUST AS WE AGREED...
THE LOSER MUST OBEY THE WINNER... IN OTHER WORDS, ME.
LET'S SEE... I'LL HAVE YOU RUN AN "ERRAND," I THINK.
FLINCH
FLINCH
FLINCH
I'M OUT!♪
THEY'VE GOT NO IDEA THAT WE'RE JUST PLAYING A GAME.
ME, TOO!
OLD MAID TOURNAMENT

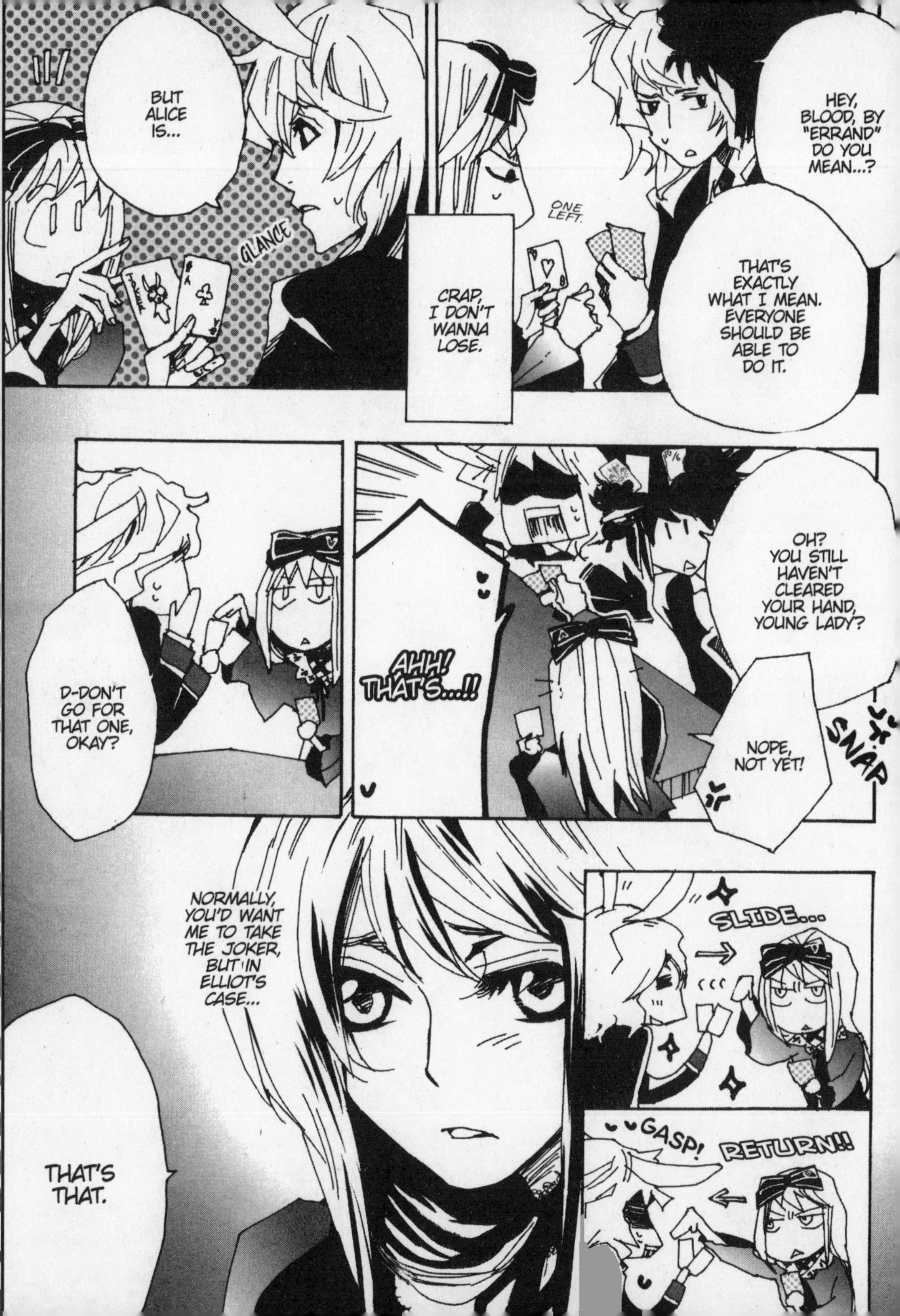
HEY, BLOOD, BY "ERRAND" DO YOU MEAN...?
ONE LEFT.
THAT'S EXACTLY WHAT I MEAN. EVERYONE SHOULD BE ABLE TO DO IT.
CRAP, I DON'T WANNA LOSE.
BUT ALICE IS...
GLANCE
OH? YOU STILL HAVEN'T CLEARED YOUR HAND, YOUNG LADY?
AHH! THAT'S...!!
SNAP
NOPE, NOT YET!
D-DON'T GO FOR THAT ONE, OKAY?
NORMALLY, YOU'D WANT ME TO TAKE THE JOKER, BUT IN ELLIOT'S CASE...
SLIDE...
GASP!
RETURN!!
THAT'S THAT.

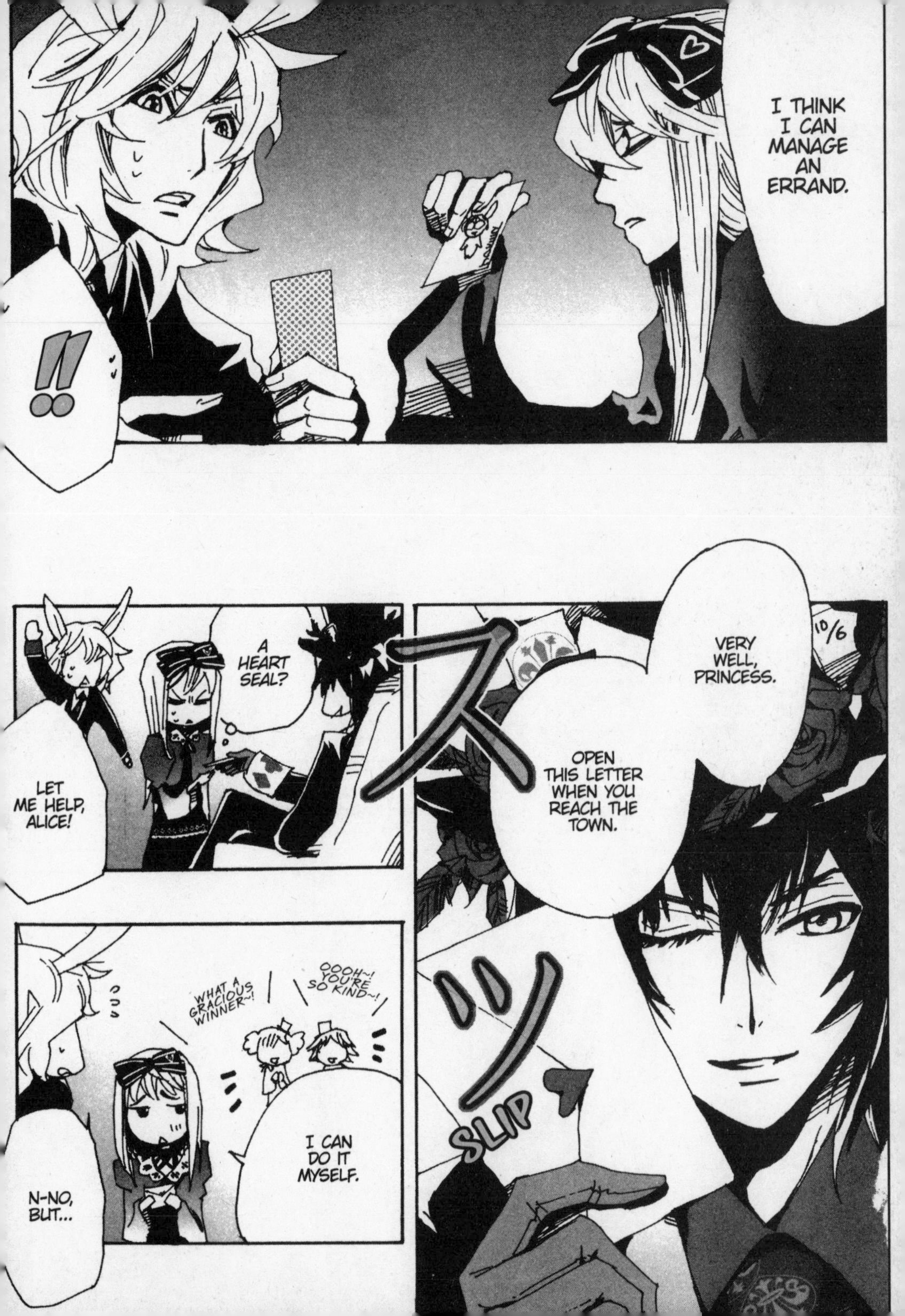
I THINK I CAN MANAGE AN ERRAND.
!!
10/6
VERY WELL, PRINCESS.
スッ
OPEN THIS LETTER WHEN YOU REACH THE TOWN.
SLIP
A HEART SEAL?
LET ME HELP, ALICE!
OOOH~! YOU'RE SO KIND~!
WHAT A GRACIOUS WINNER~!
I CAN DO IT MYSELF.
N-NO, BUT...

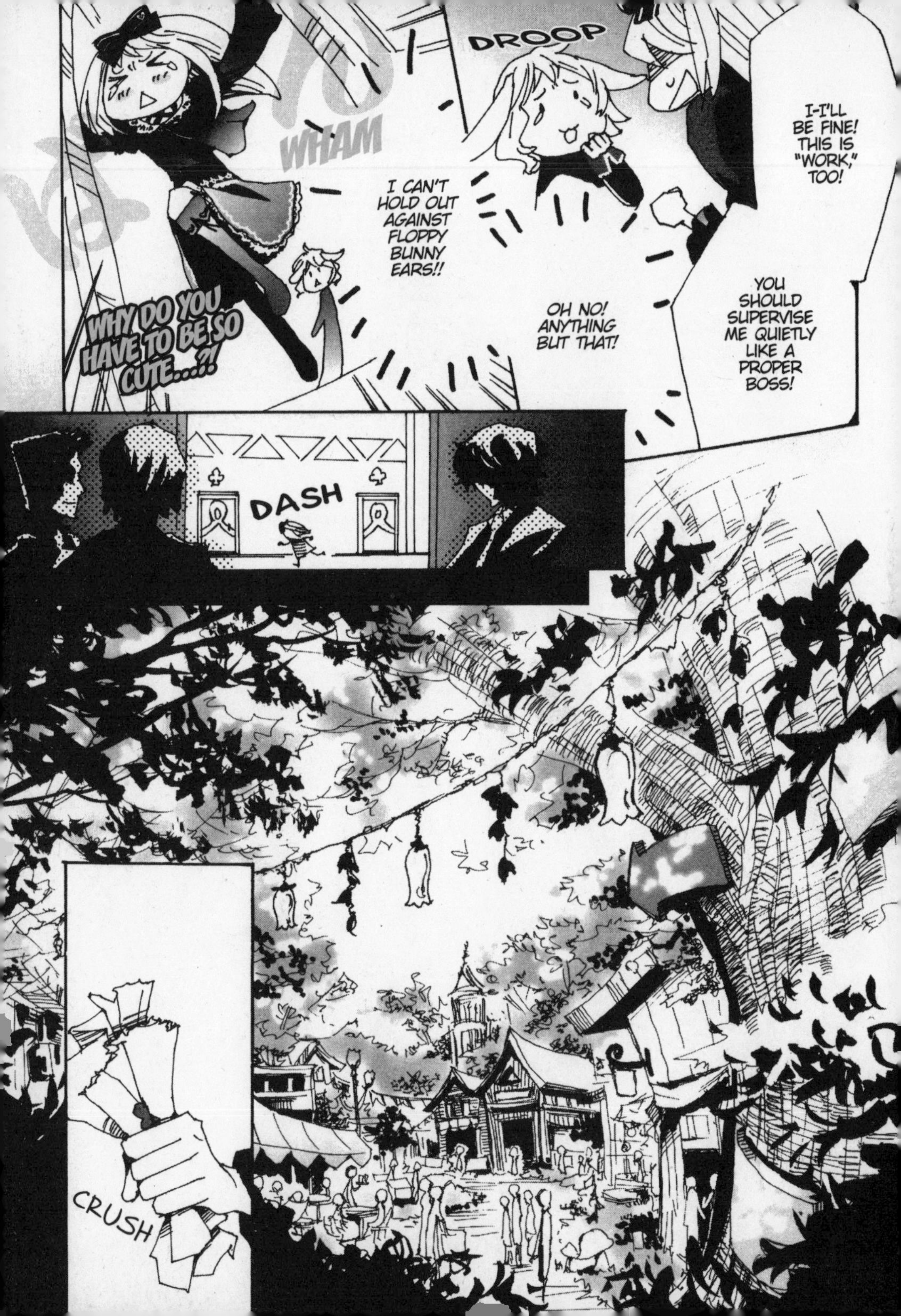
DROOP
I-I'LL BE FINE! THIS IS "WORK," TOO!
YOU SHOULD SUPERVISE ME QUIETLY LIKE A PROPER BOSS!
OH NO! ANYTHING BUT THAT!
I CAN'T HOLD OUT AGAINST FLOPPY BUNNY EARS!!
WHAM
WHY DO YOU HAVE TO BE SO CUTE...?!
DASH
CRUSH

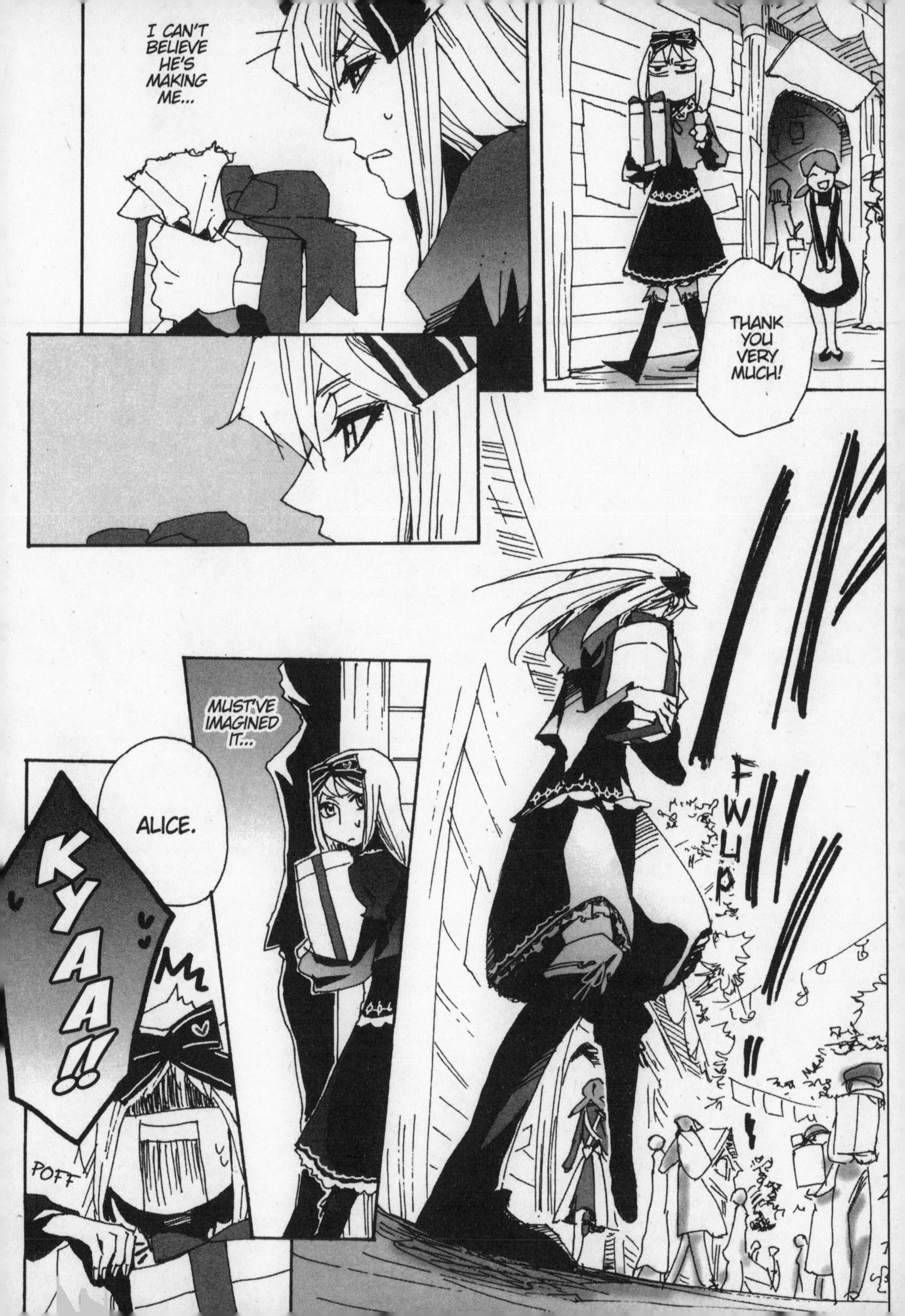
THANK YOU VERY MUCH!
I CAN'T BELIEVE HE'S MAKING ME...
FWUP
MUST'VE IMAGINED IT...
ALICE.
KYAAA!!
MU
POFF

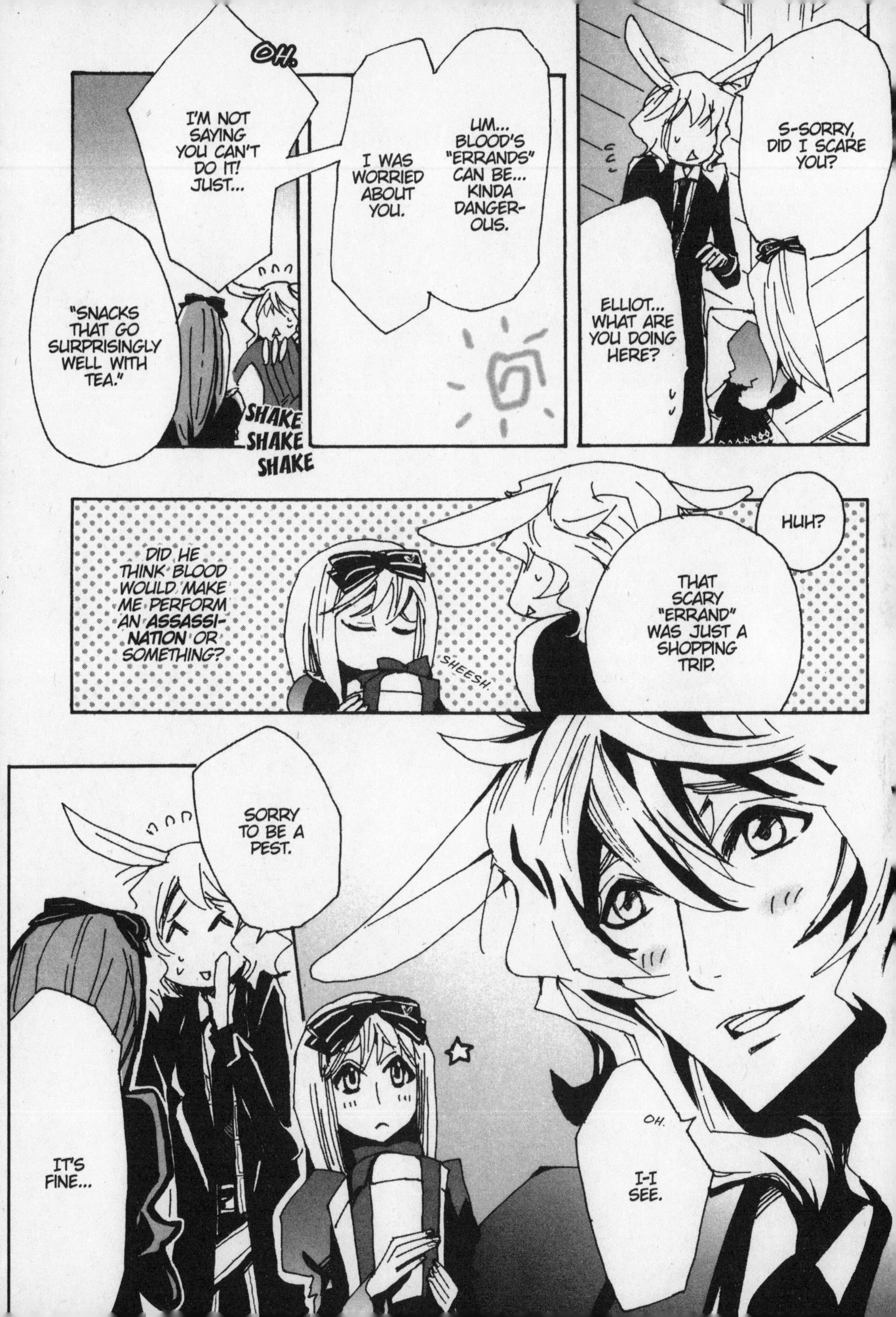
S-SORRY, DID I SCARE YOU?
ELLIOT... WHAT ARE YOU DOING HERE?
UM... BLOOD'S "ERRANDS" CAN BE... KINDA DANGEROUS.
I WAS WORRIED ABOUT YOU.
OH.
I'M NOT SAYING YOU CAN'T DO IT! JUST...
"SNACKS THAT GO SURPRISINGLY WELL WITH TEA."
SHAKE SHAKE SHAKE
HUH?
THAT SCARY "ERRAND" WAS JUST A SHOPPING TRIP.
SHEESH.
DID HE THINK BLOOD WOULD MAKE ME PERFORM AN ASSASSINATION OR SOMETHING?
OH.
I-I SEE.
SORRY TO BE A PEST.
IT'S FINE...

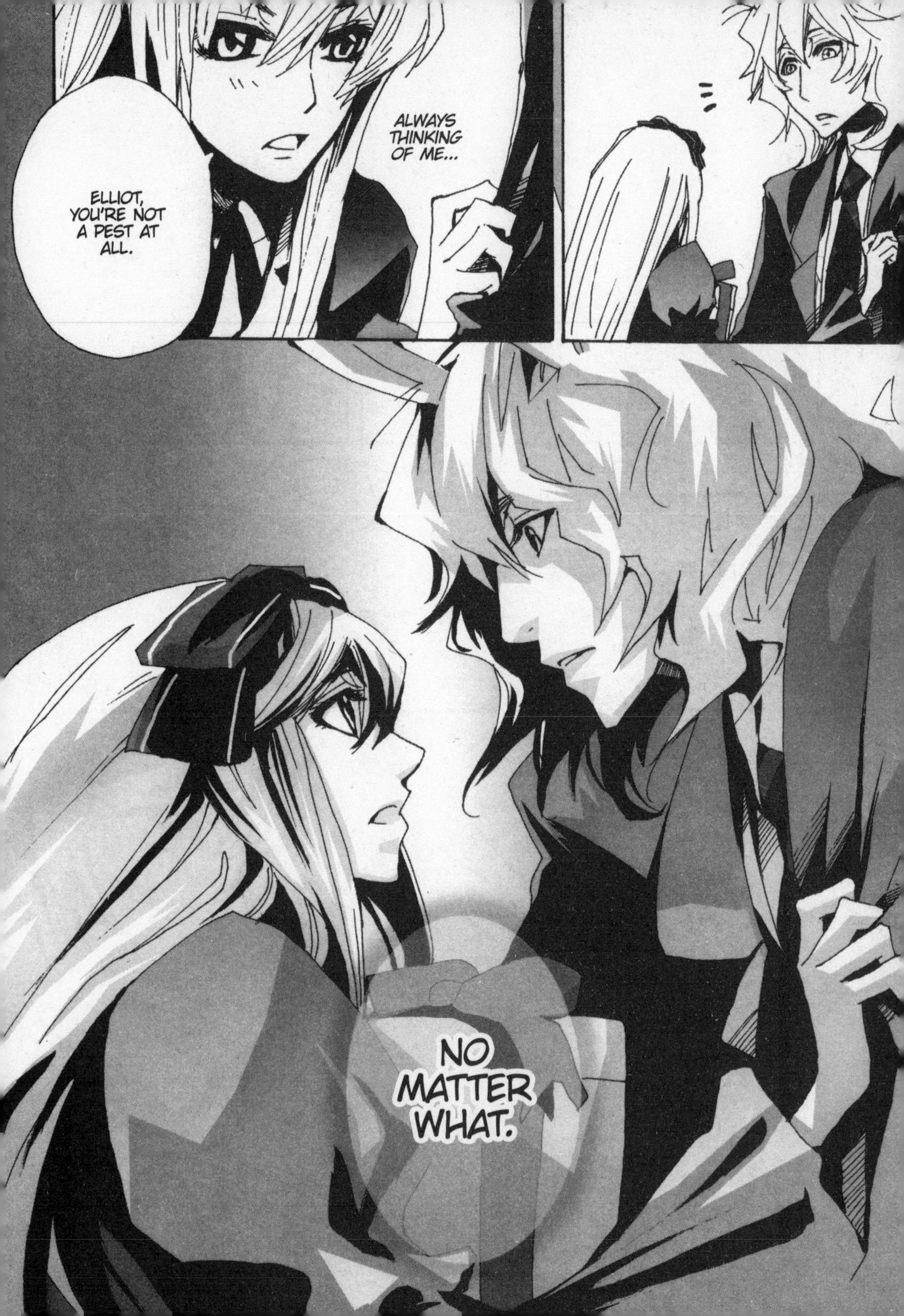
ALWAYS THINKING OF ME...
ELLIOT, YOU'RE NOT A PEST AT ALL.
NO MATTER WHAT.

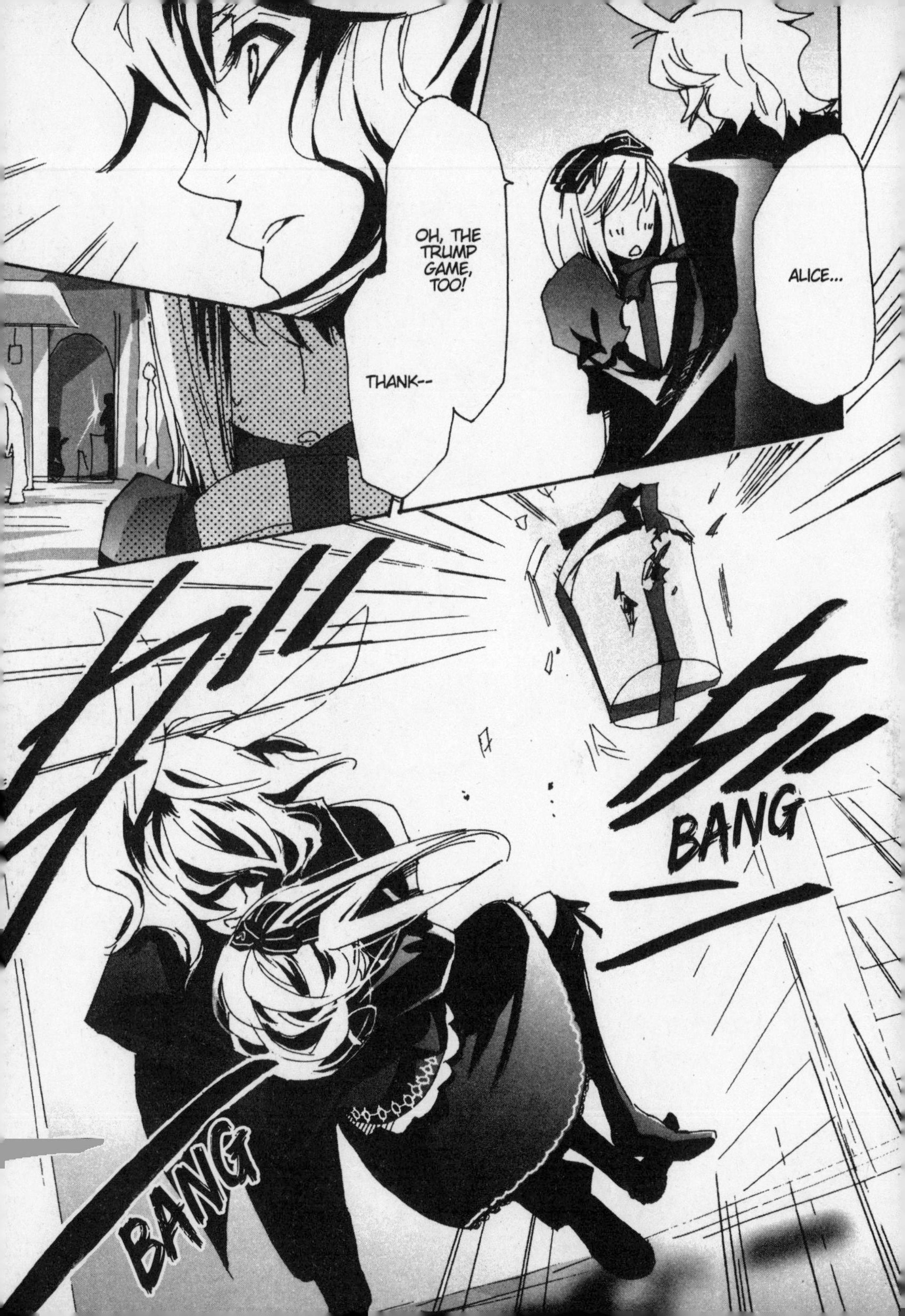
ALICE...
OH, THE TRUMP GAME, TOO!
THANK--
BANG
BANG

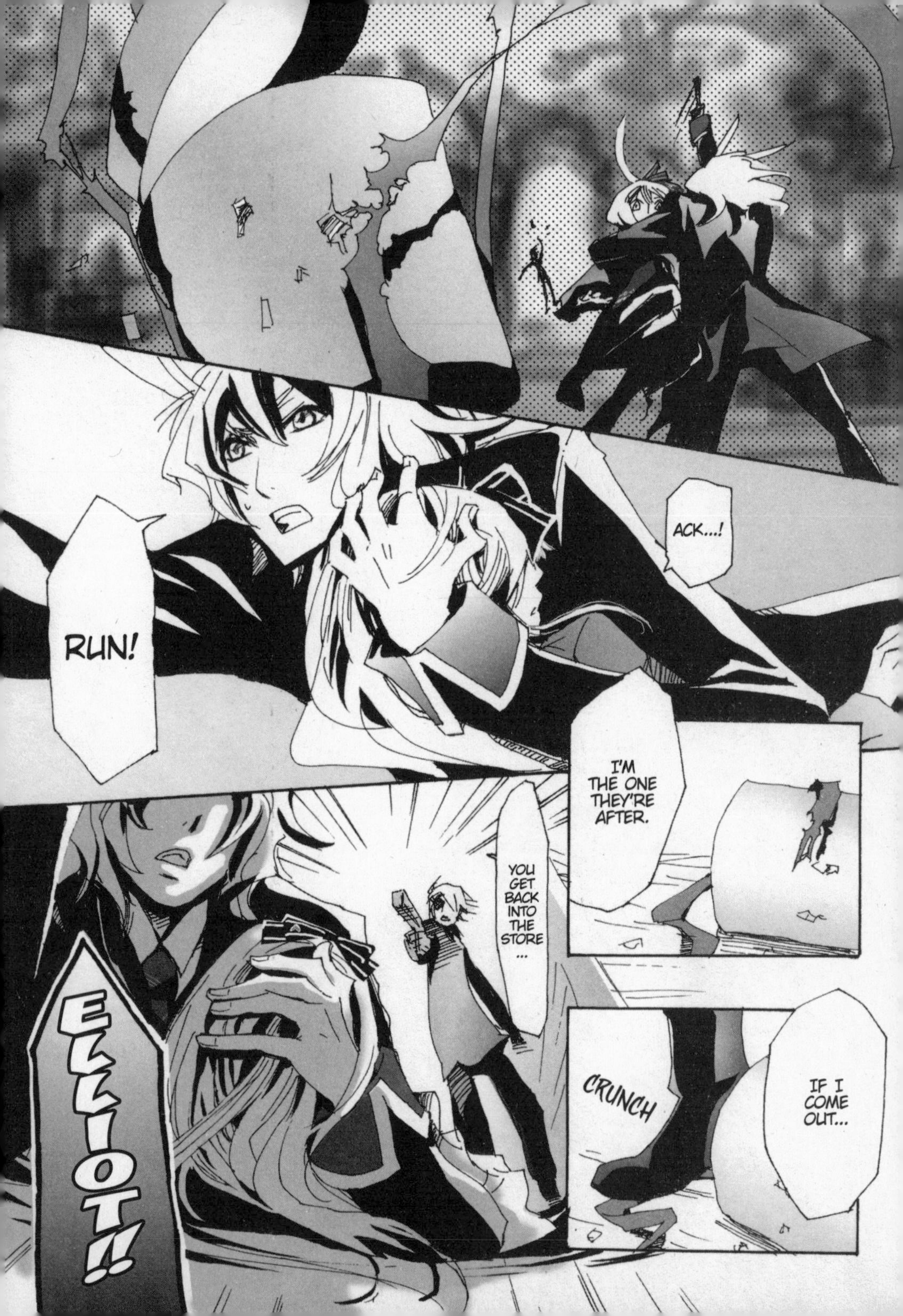
ACK...!
RUN!
I'M THE ONE THEY'RE AFTER.
IF I COME OUT...
CRUNCH
YOU GET BACK INTO THE STORE...
ELLIOT!!

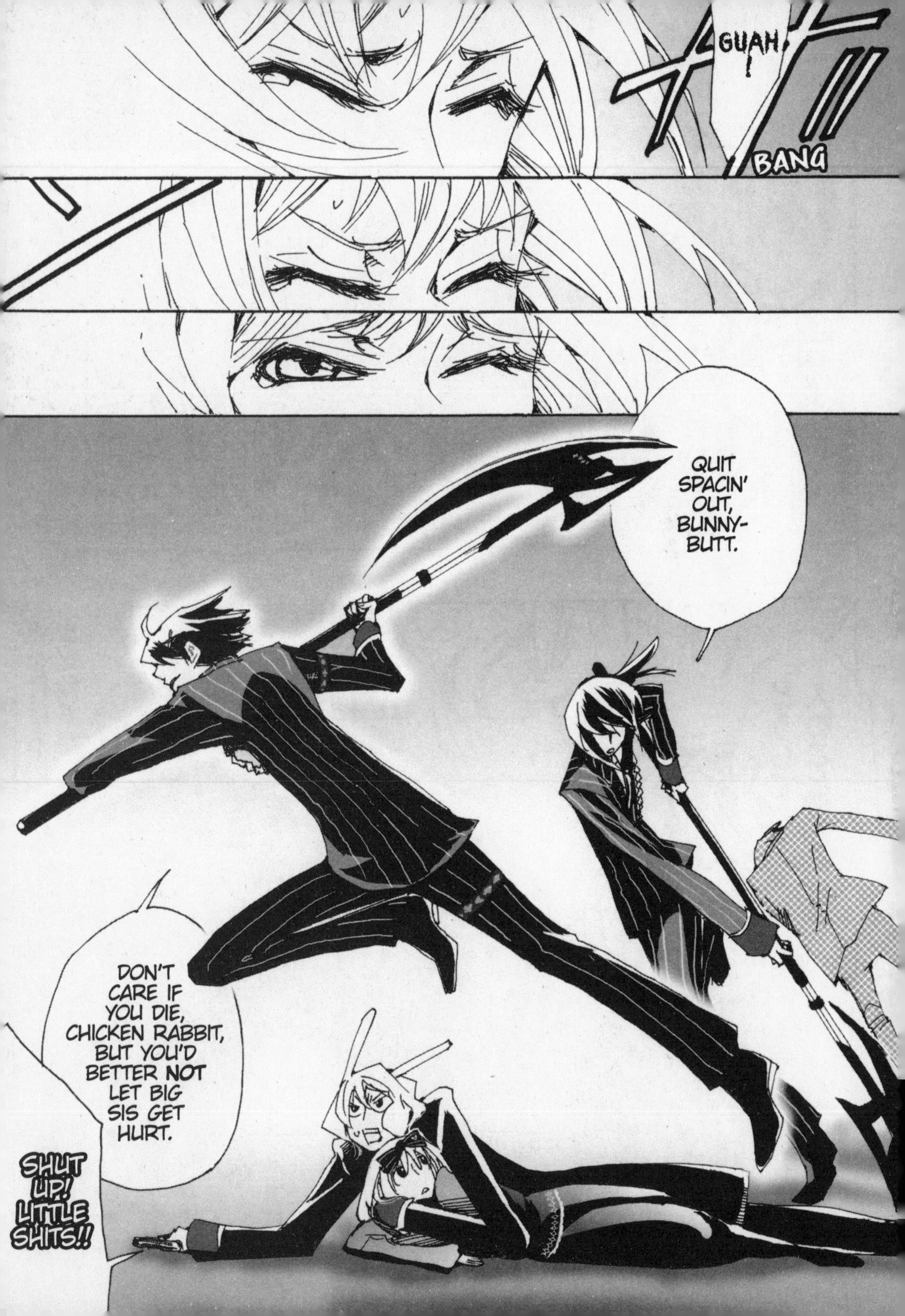
GUAH!
BANG
QUIT SPACIN' OUT, BUNNY-BUTT.
DON'T CARE IF YOU DIE, CHICKEN RABBIT, BUT YOU'D BETTER NOT LET BIG SIS GET HURT.
SHUT UP! LITTLE SHITS!!

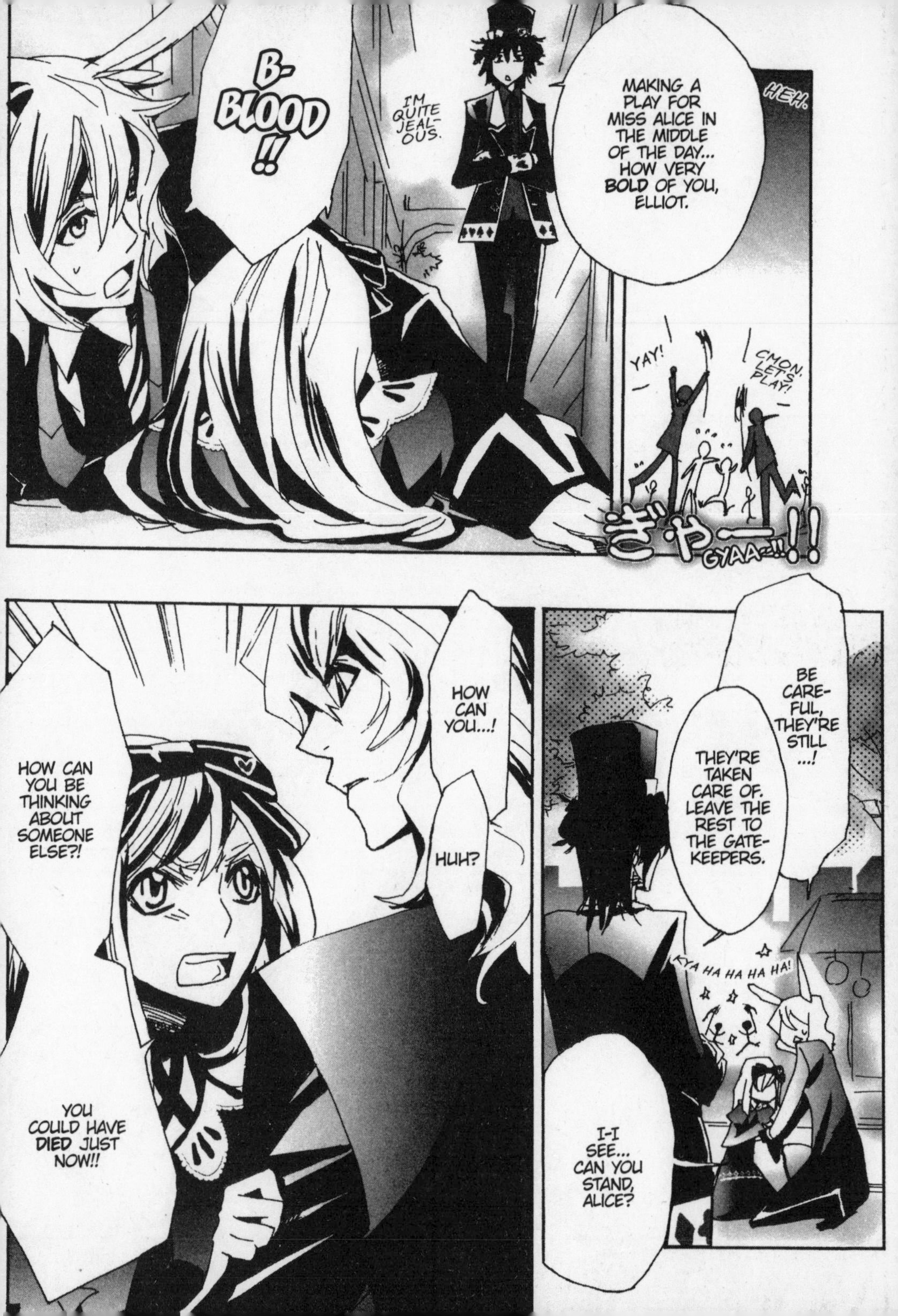
HEH.
MAKING A PLAY FOR MISS ALICE IN THE MIDDLE OF THE DAY... HOW VERY BOLD OF YOU, ELLIOT.
I'M QUITE JEALOUS.
B-BLOOD!!
C'MON, LET'S PLAY!
YAY!
ぎゃーー!!
GYAAA!!
BE CAREFUL, THEY'RE STILL ...!
THEY'RE TAKEN CARE OF. LEAVE THE REST TO THE GATE-KEEPERS.
KYA HA HA HA HA!
I-I SEE... CAN YOU STAND, ALICE?
HOW CAN YOU...!
HUH?
HOW CAN YOU BE THINKING ABOUT SOMEONE ELSE?!
YOU COULD HAVE DIED JUST NOW!!

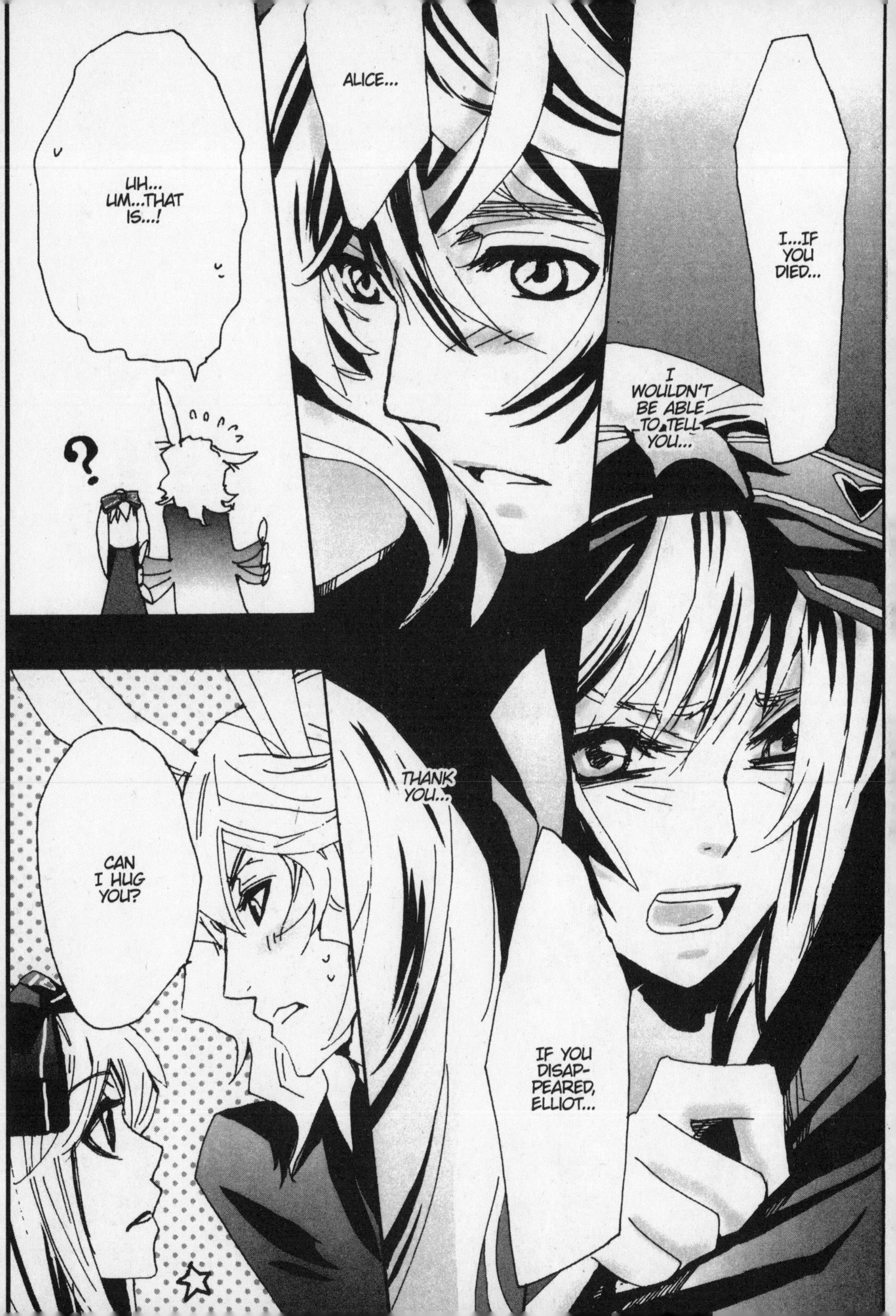
I...IF YOU DIED...
I WOULDN'T BE ABLE TO TELL YOU...
IF YOU DISAPPEARED, ELLIOT...
THANK YOU...
ALICE...
UH... UM...THAT IS...!
CAN I HUG YOU?

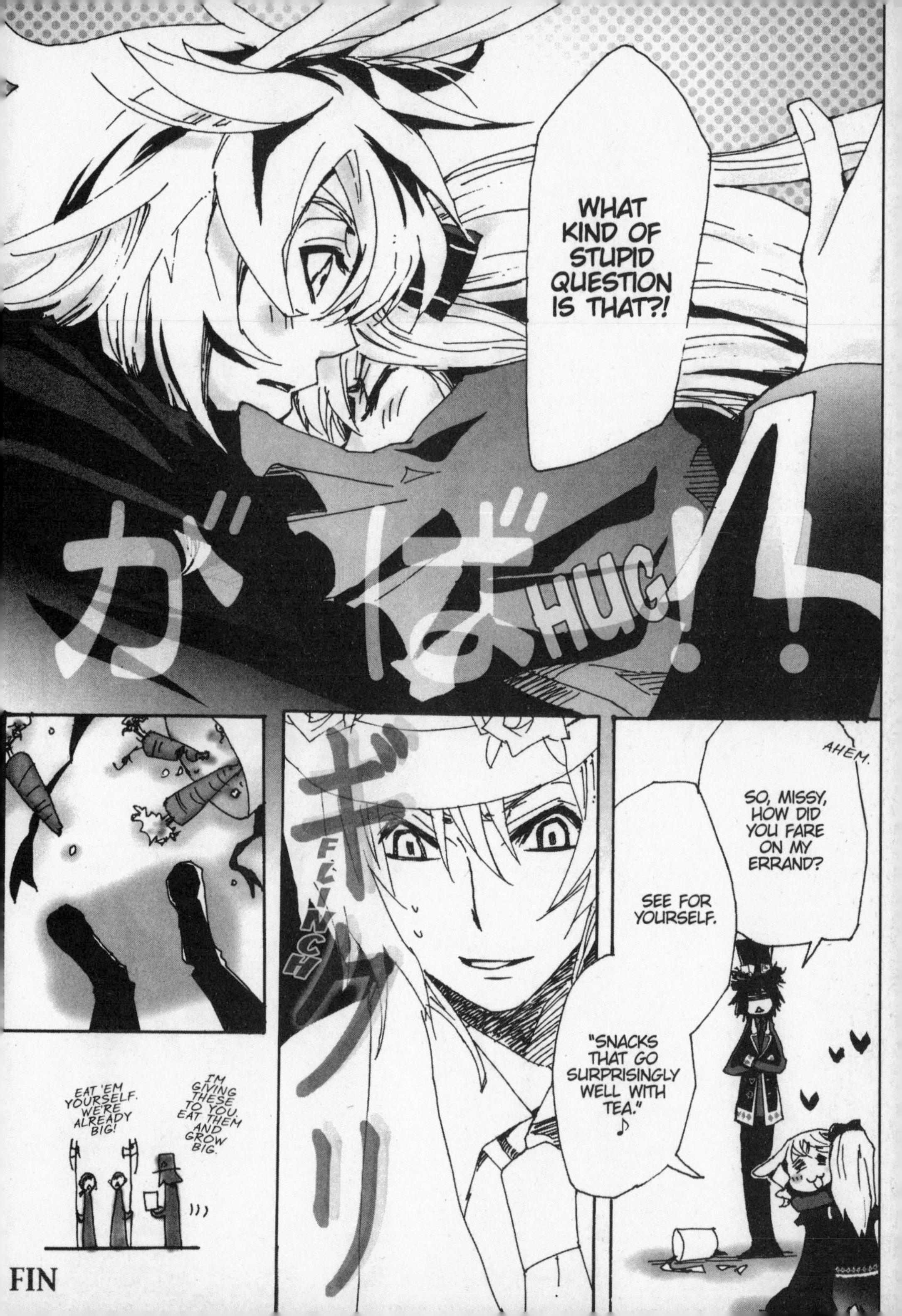
WHAT KIND OF STUPID QUESTION IS THAT?!
HUG!
AHEM.
SO, MISSY, HOW DID YOU FARE ON MY ERRAND?
SEE FOR YOURSELF.
"SNACKS THAT GO SURPRISINGLY WELL WITH TEA." ♪
FLINCH
I'M GIVING THESE TO YOU. EAT THEM AND GROW BIG.
EAT 'EM YOURSELF. WE'RE ALREADY BIG!
FIN

For the direction and coloration, QuinRose-sama, who helps so much with everything.

And the people who read this book.

I appreciate you and thank you all from the bottom of my heart.

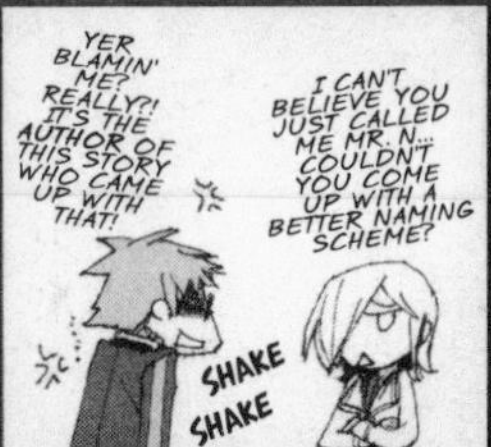
I CAN'T BELIEVE YOU JUST CALLED ME MR. N... COULDN'T YOU COME UP WITH A BETTER NAMING SCHEME?
YER BLAMIN' ME? REALLY?! IT'S THE AUTHOR OF THIS STORY WHO CAME UP WITH THAT!
SHAKE
SHAKE

QuinRoseBox

GOWLAND'S MAGICAL MYSTERY TOUR
CHAPTER 512

[The Story So Far]

"A domain leader who can't play music is no real domain leader." Gowland (voice/violin virtuoso*) goes on a journey to put together a band. After ~~kidnapping~~ recruiting the Nightmare (piano/violin) into his group, he heads to the Hatter mansion.

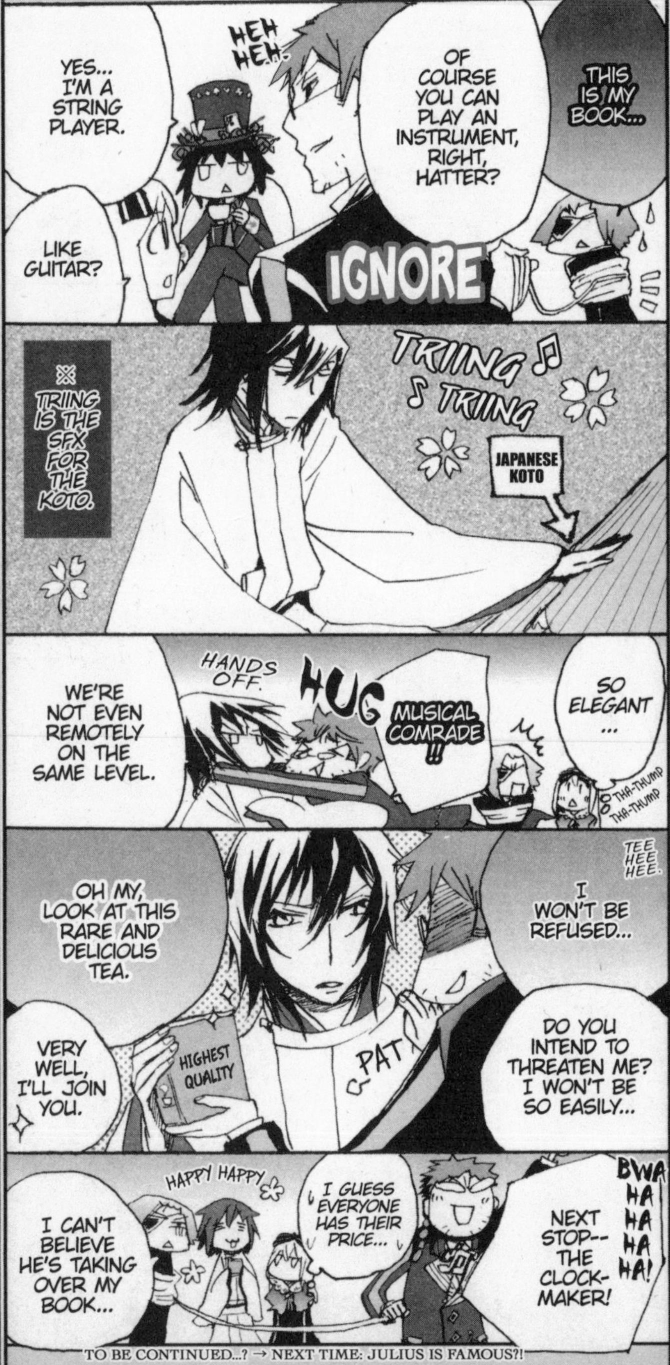
THIS IS MY BOOK...
OF COURSE YOU CAN PLAY AN INSTRUMENT, RIGHT, HATTER?
HEH HEH.
YES... I'M A STRING PLAYER.
LIKE GUITAR?
IGNORE
TRIING ♫ TRIING
JAPANESE KOTO
※ TRIING IS THE SFX FOR THE KOTO.
SO ELEGANT...
MUSICAL COMRADE!!
HUG
HANDS OFF.
WE'RE NOT EVEN REMOTELY ON THE SAME LEVEL.
THA-THUMP THA-THUMP
TEE HEE HEE.
I WON'T BE REFUSED...
OH MY, LOOK AT THIS RARE AND DELICIOUS TEA.
DO YOU INTEND TO THREATEN ME? I WON'T BE SO EASILY...
PAT
HIGHEST QUALITY
VERY WELL, I'LL JOIN YOU.
BWA HA HA HA HA HA!
NEXT STOP-- THE CLOCK-MAKER!
I GUESS EVERYONE HAS THEIR PRICE...
HAPPY HAPPY
I CAN'T BELIEVE HE'S TAKING OVER MY BOOK...

TO BE CONTINUED...? → NEXT TIME: JULIUS IS FAMOUS?!

NOTE: *Gowland's Magical Mystery Tour* is a work of fiction. Many of the statements in this story should be taken with a ~~grain~~ whole heaping handful of salt.

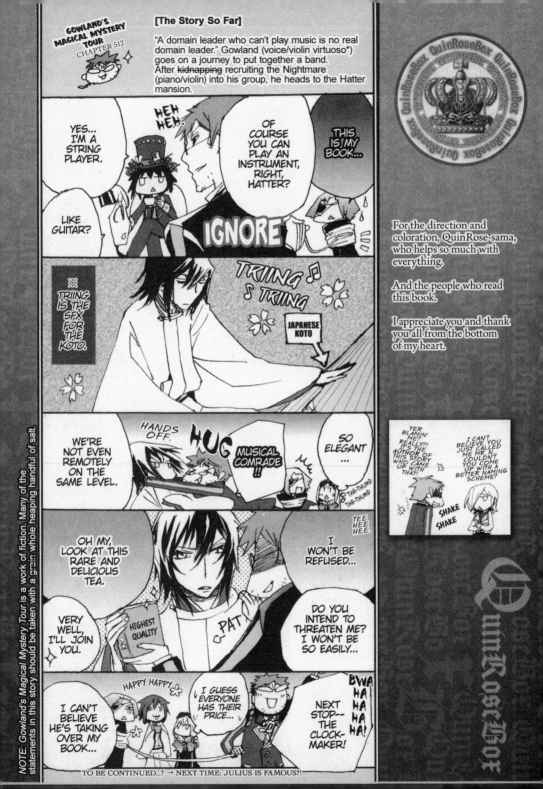

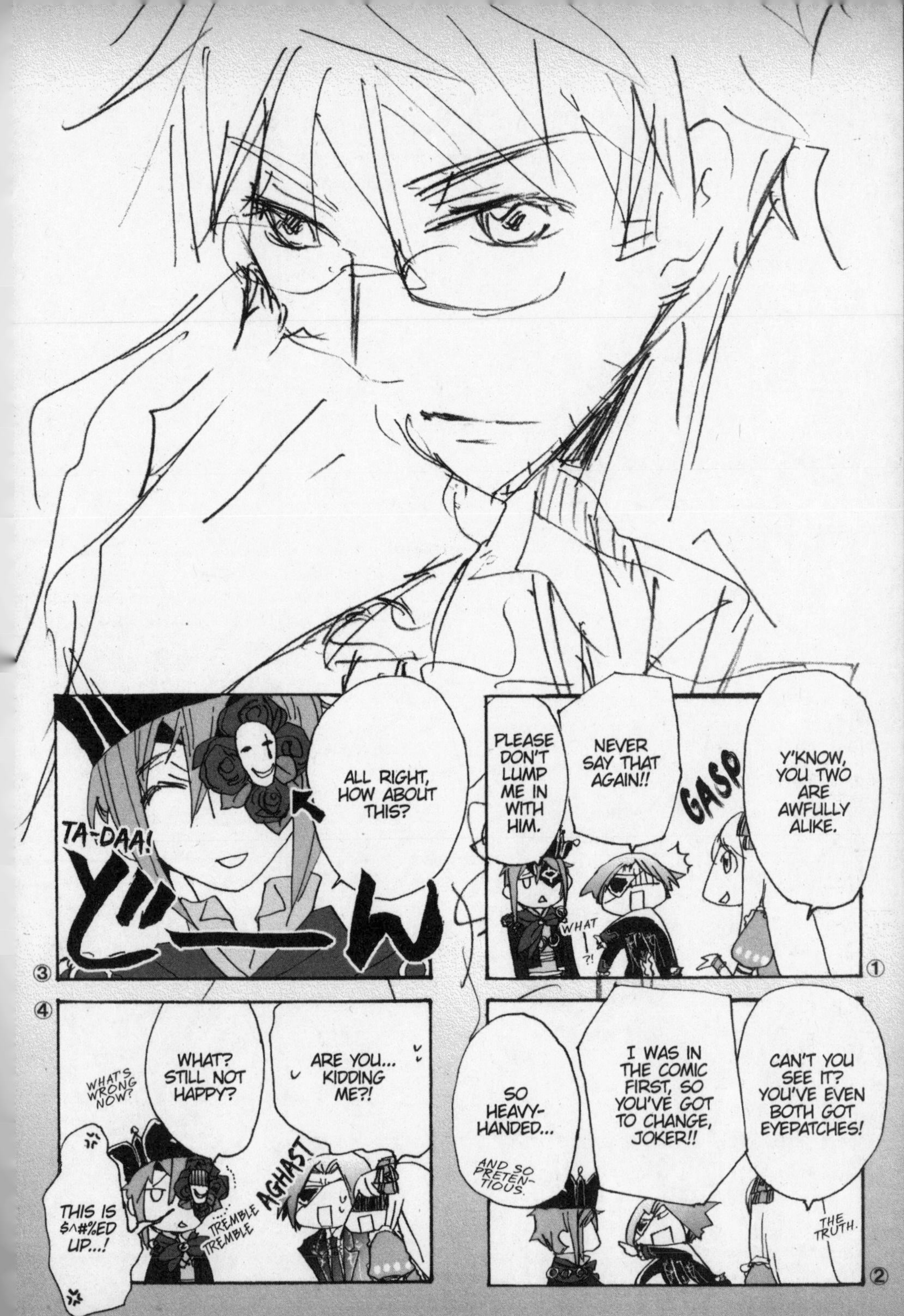
Y'KNOW, YOU TWO ARE AWFULLY ALIKE.
GASP
NEVER SAY THAT AGAIN!!
PLEASE DON'T LUMP ME IN WITH HIM.
WHAT—?!
CAN'T YOU SEE IT? YOU'VE EVEN BOTH GOT EYEPATCHES!
THE TRUTH.
I WAS IN THE COMIC FIRST, SO YOU'VE GOT TO CHANGE, JOKER!!
SO HEAVY-HANDED...
AND SO PRETENTIOUS.
ALL RIGHT, HOW ABOUT THIS?
TA-DAA!
ARE YOU... KIDDING ME?!
AGHAST
TREMBLE TREMBLE
WHAT? STILL NOT HAPPY?
WHAT'S WRONG NOW?
THIS IS $^#%ED UP...!

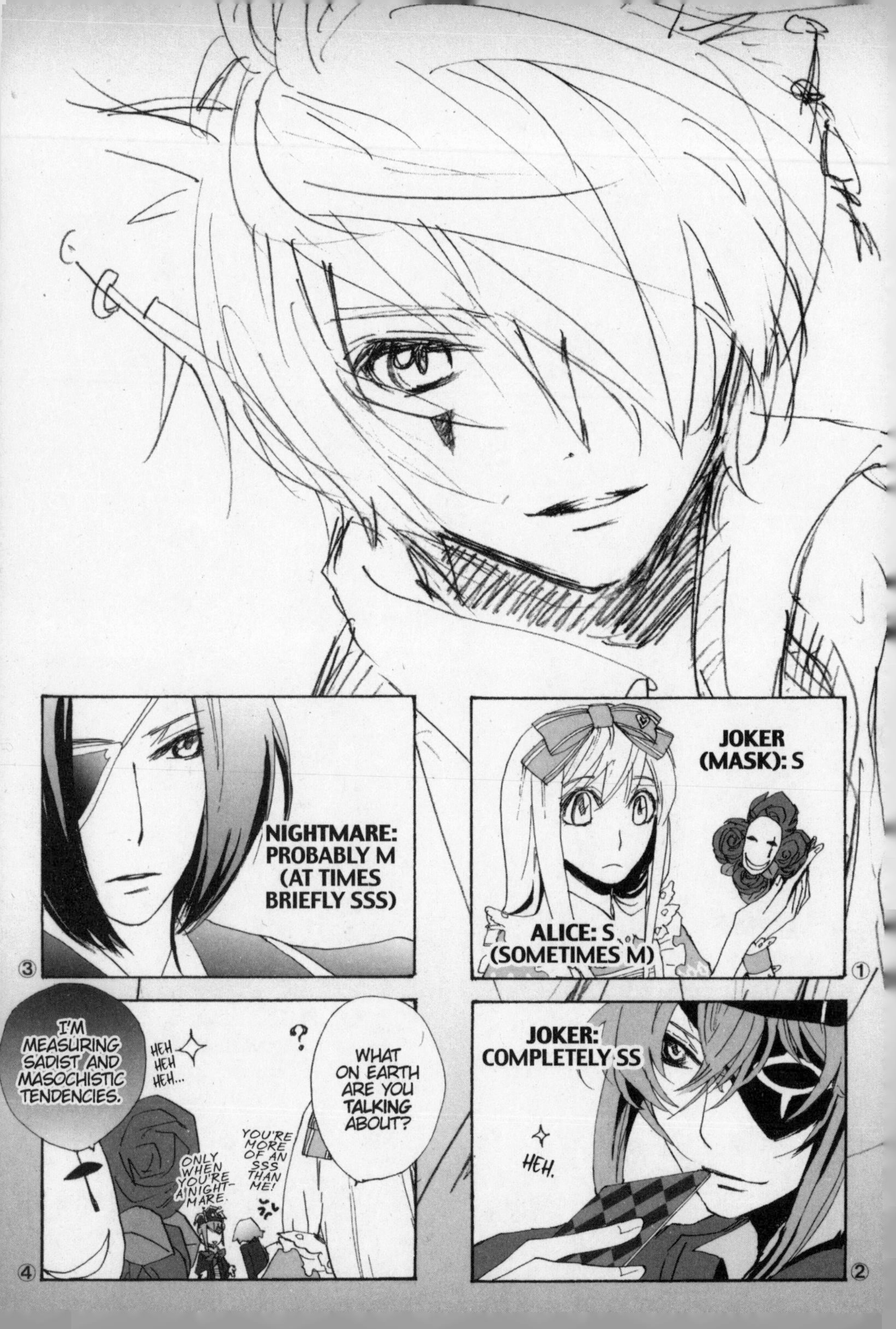
JOKER (MASK): S
ALICE: S (SOMETIMES M)
①
JOKER: COMPLETELY SS
HEH.
②
NIGHTMARE: PROBABLY M (AT TIMES BRIEFLY SSS)
③
?
WHAT ON EARTH ARE YOU TALKING ABOUT?
YOU'RE MORE OF AN SSS THAN ME!
HEH HEH HEH...
I'M MEASURING SADIST AND MASOCHISTIC TENDENCIES.
ONLY WHEN YOU'RE A NIGHTMARE.
④

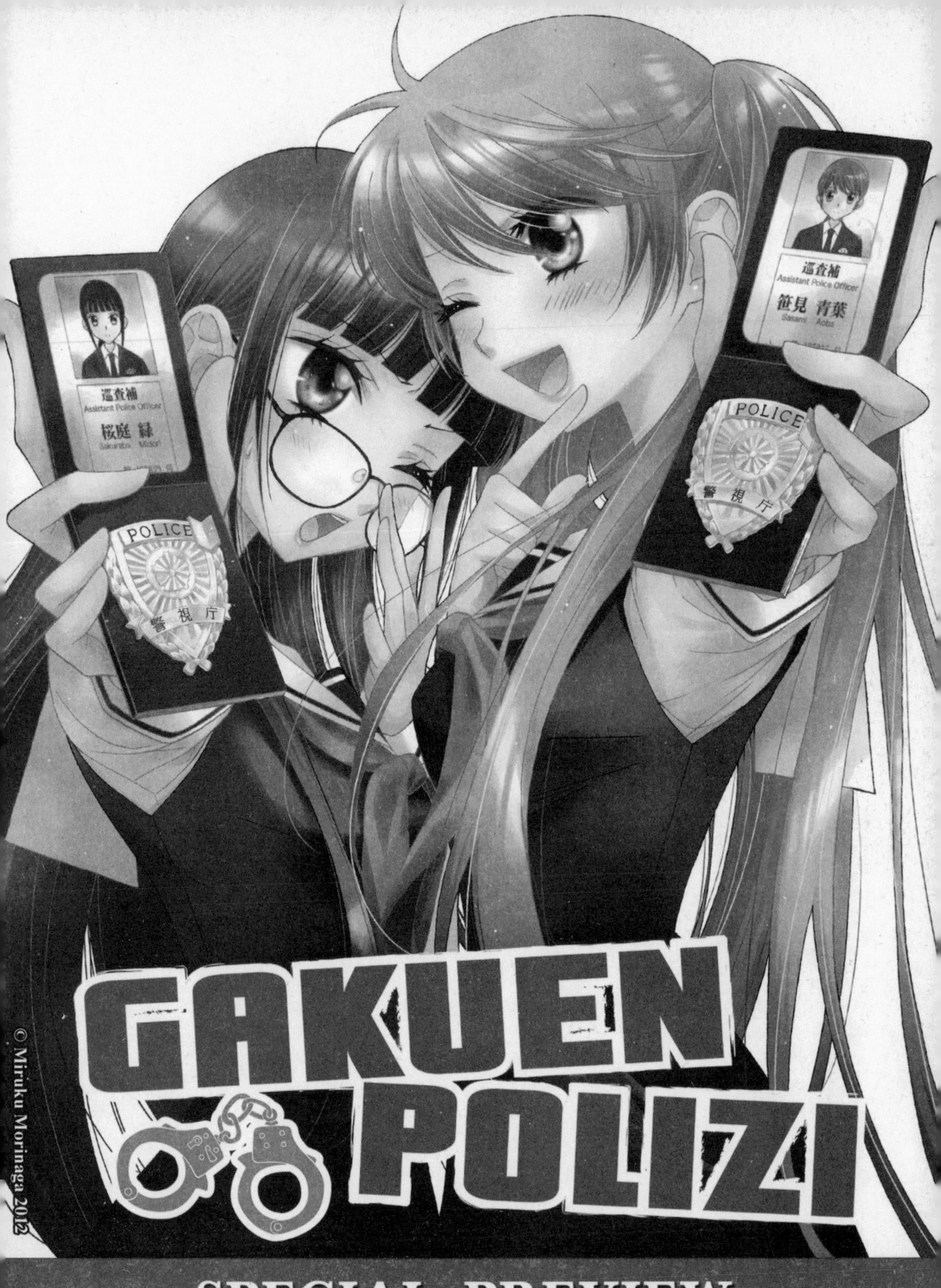
巡査補
Assistant Police Officer
桜庭 緑
POLICE
警視庁
巡査補
Assistant Police Officer
笹見 青葉
POLICE
警視庁
GAKUEN POLIZI

SPECIAL PREVIEW

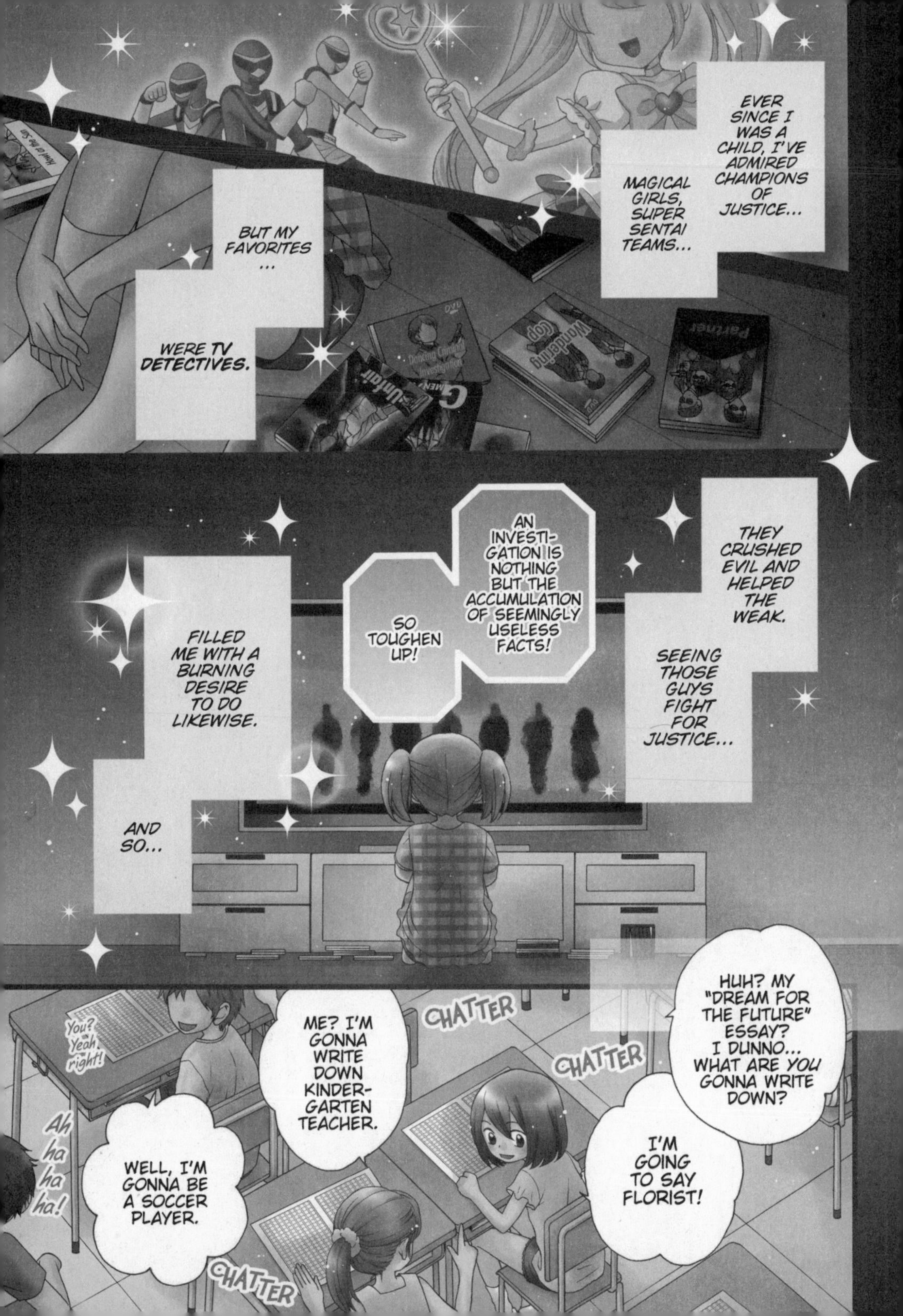
EVER SINCE I WAS A CHILD, I'VE ADMIRED CHAMPIONS OF JUSTICE...
MAGICAL GIRLS, SUPER SENTAI TEAMS...
BUT MY FAVORITES ...
WERE TV DETECTIVES.
Partner
Wandering Cop
DVD
Dancing Candid Investigation
G-MEN
Unfair
Howl at the Sun
THEY CRUSHED EVIL AND HELPED THE WEAK.
SEEING THOSE GUYS FIGHT FOR JUSTICE...
AN INVESTIGATION IS NOTHING BUT THE ACCUMULATION OF SEEMINGLY USELESS FACTS!
SO TOUGHEN UP!
FILLED ME WITH A BURNING DESIRE TO DO LIKEWISE.
AND SO...
HUH? MY "DREAM FOR THE FUTURE" ESSAY? I DUNNO... WHAT ARE YOU GONNA WRITE DOWN?
I'M GOING TO SAY FLORIST!
CHATTER
CHATTER
ME? I'M GONNA WRITE DOWN KINDER-GARTEN TEACHER.
You? Yeah right!
WELL, I'M GONNA BE A SOCCER PLAYER.
Ah ha ha ha!
CHATTER

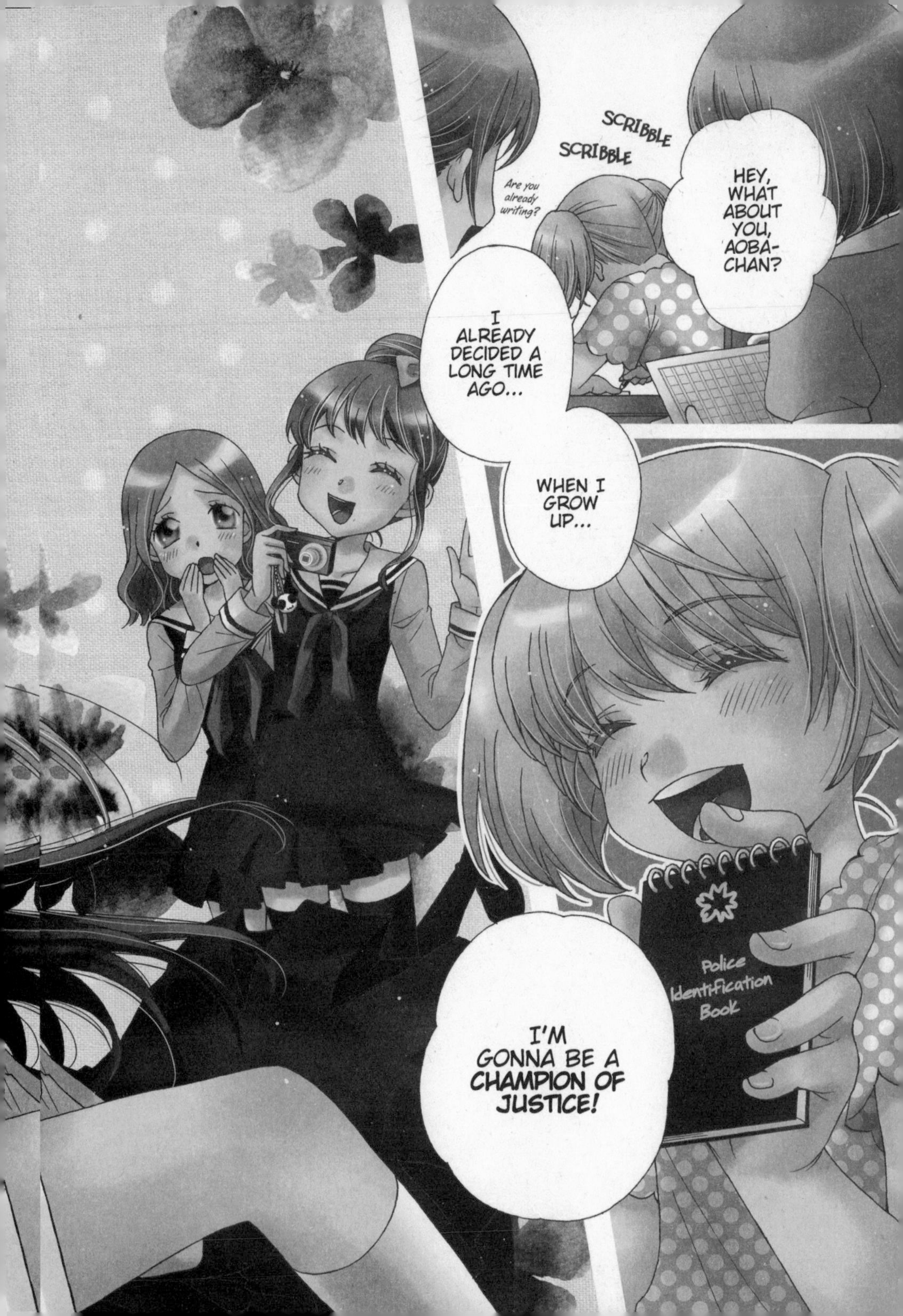
HEY, WHAT ABOUT YOU, AOBA-CHAN?
SCRIBBLE
SCRIBBLE
Are you already writing?
I ALREADY DECIDED A LONG TIME AGO...
WHEN I GROW UP...
Police Identification Book
I'M GONNA BE A CHAMPION OF JUSTICE!

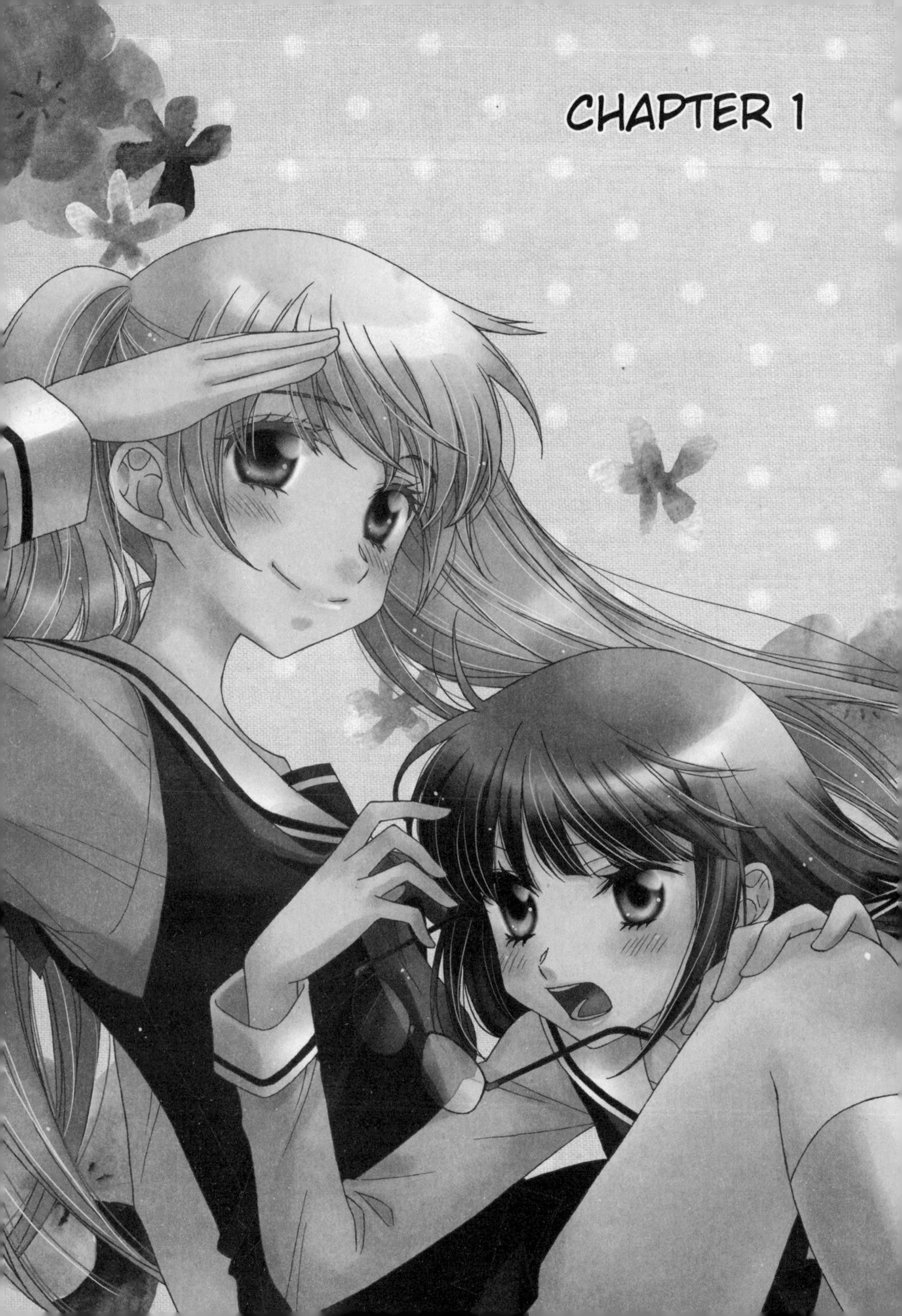
CHAPTER 1

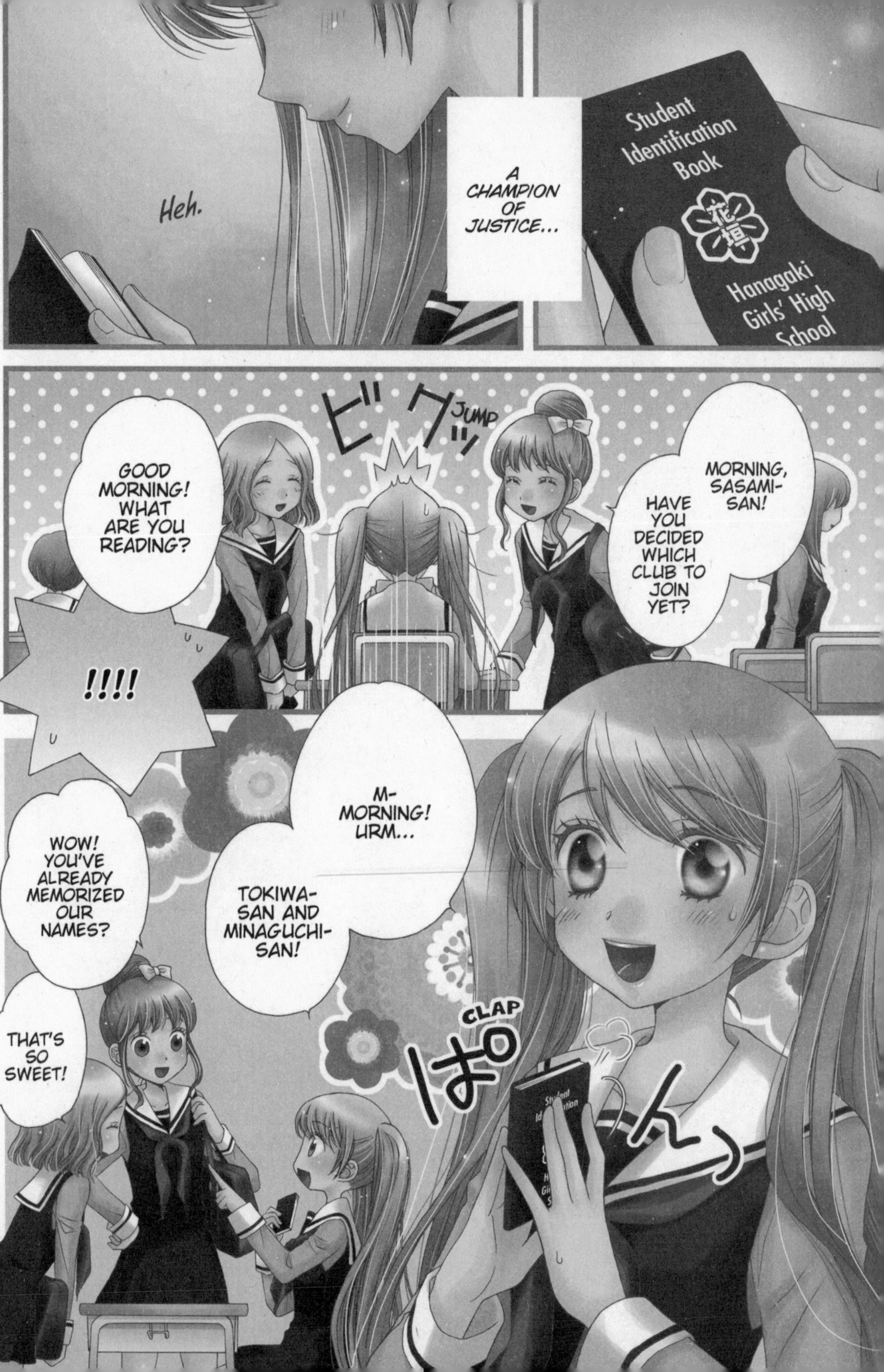
Student Identification Book
花垣
Hanagaki Girls' High School
A CHAMPION OF JUSTICE...
Heh.
MORNING, SASAMI-SAN!
HAVE YOU DECIDED WHICH CLUB TO JOIN YET?
ビクッ
JUMP
GOOD MORNING! WHAT ARE YOU READING?
!!!!
M-MORNING! URM...
TOKIWA-SAN AND MINAGUCHI-SAN!
ぽんっ
CLAP
WOW! YOU'VE ALREADY MEMORIZED OUR NAMES?
THAT'S SO SWEET!

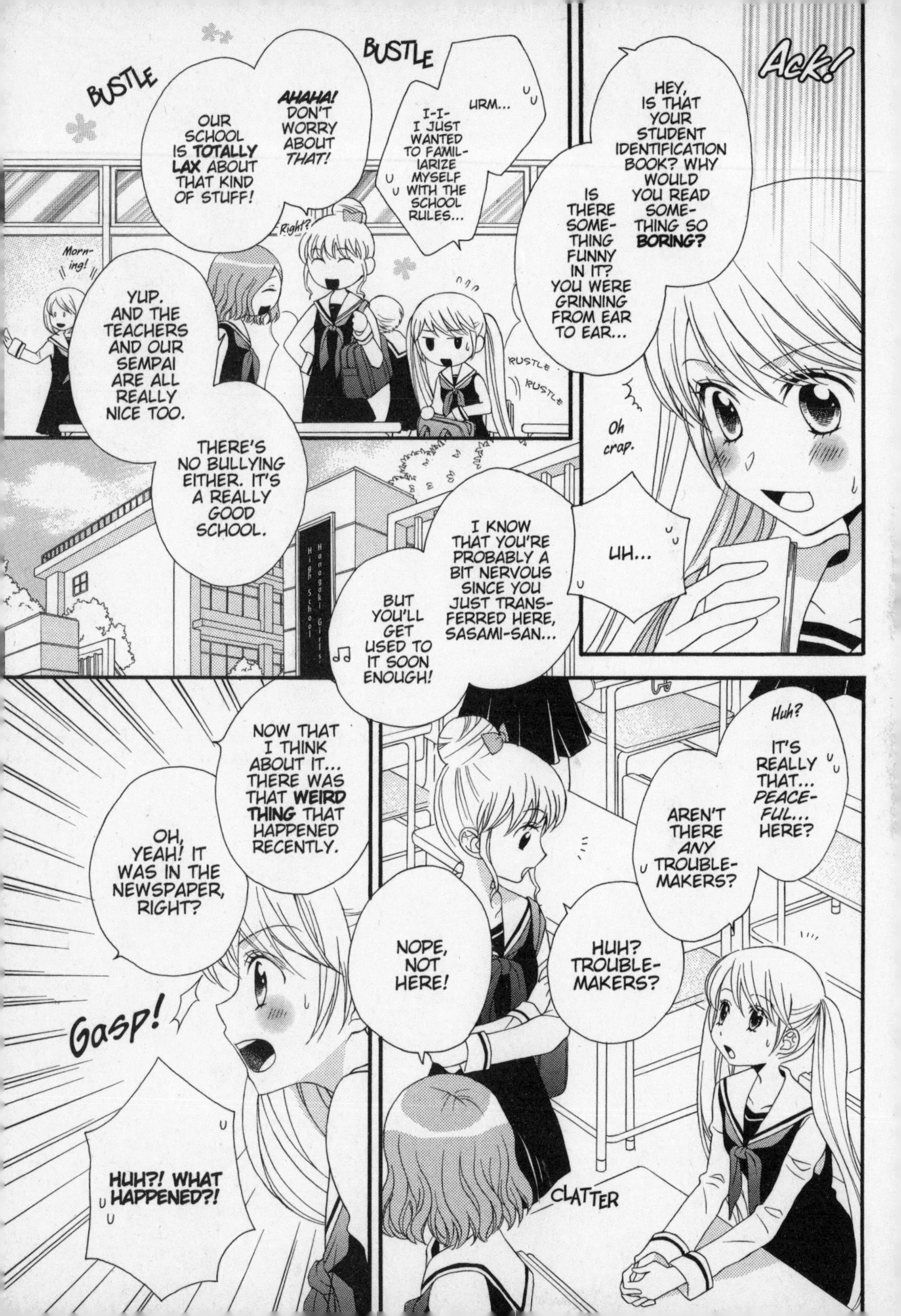
Ack!
HEY, IS THAT YOUR STUDENT IDENTIFICATION BOOK? WHY WOULD YOU READ SOME-THING SO **BORING?**
IS THERE SOME-THING FUNNY IN IT? YOU WERE GRINNING FROM EAR TO EAR...
Oh crap.
UH...
BUSTLE
URM...
I-I- I JUST WANTED TO FAMIL-IARIZE MYSELF WITH THE SCHOOL RULES...
BUSTLE
AHAHA! DON'T WORRY ABOUT *THAT!*
OUR SCHOOL IS **TOTALLY LAX** ABOUT THAT KIND OF STUFF!
Right?
Morn-ing!
YUP. AND THE TEACHERS AND OUR SEMPAI ARE ALL REALLY NICE TOO.
RUSTLE
RUSTLE
THERE'S NO BULLYING EITHER. IT'S A REALLY GOOD SCHOOL.
Hanagaki Girls' High School
I KNOW THAT YOU'RE PROBABLY A BIT NERVOUS SINCE YOU JUST TRANS-FERRED HERE, SASAMI-SAN...
BUT YOU'LL GET USED TO IT SOON ENOUGH!
Huh?
IT'S REALLY THAT... *PEACE-FUL...* HERE?
AREN'T THERE *ANY* TROUBLE-MAKERS?
HUH? TROUBLE-MAKERS?
NOPE, NOT HERE!
NOW THAT I THINK ABOUT IT... THERE WAS THAT **WEIRD THING** THAT HAPPENED RECENTLY.
CLATTER
OH, YEAH! IT WAS IN THE NEWSPAPER, RIGHT?
Gasp!
HUH?! WHAT HAPPENED?!

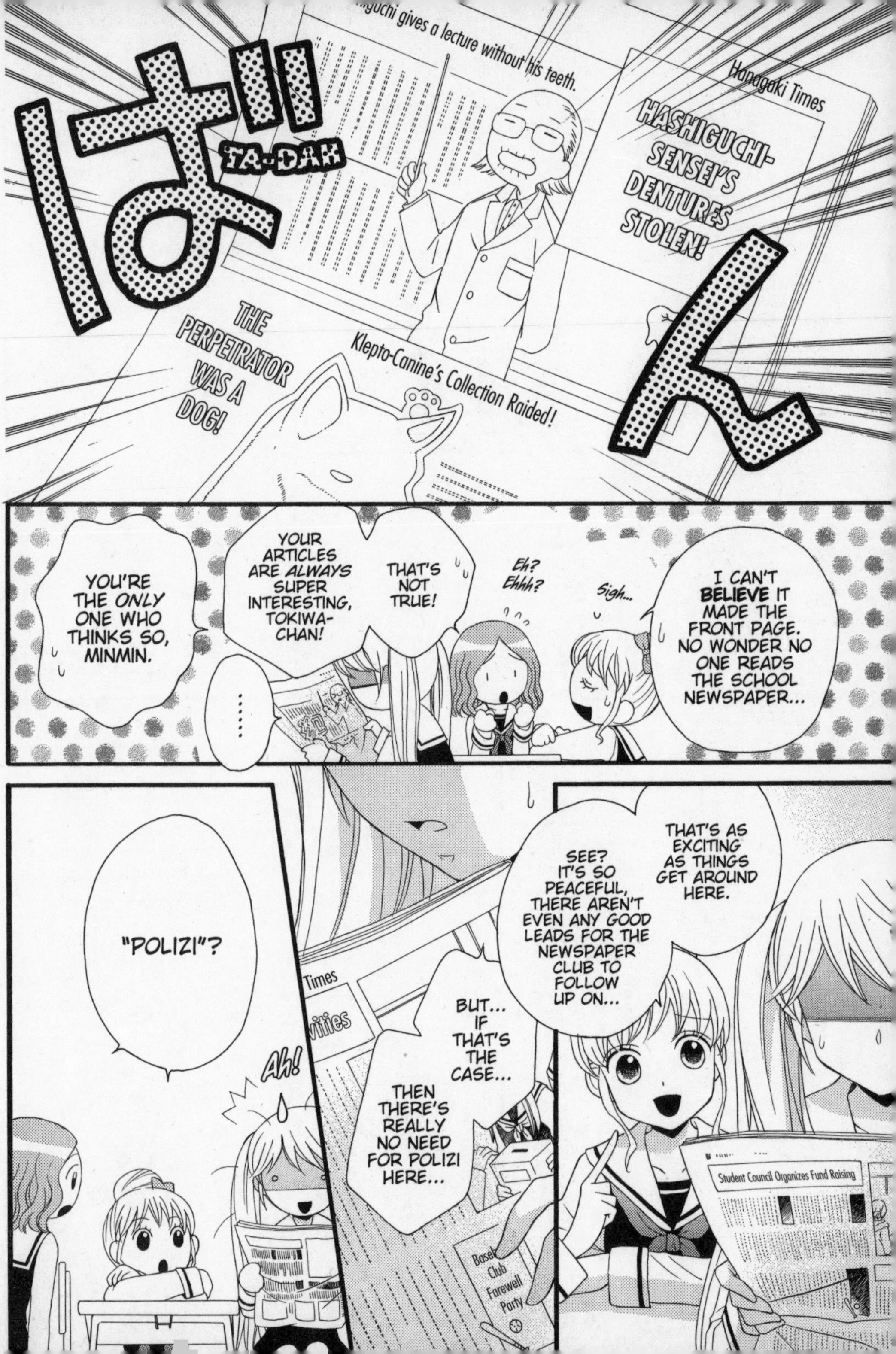
Hanagaki Times
HASHIGUCHI-SENSEI'S DENTURES STOLEN!
ばん
TA-DAH
iguchi gives a lecture without his teeth.
Klepto-Canine's Collection Raided!
THE PERPETRATOR WAS A DOG!
I CAN'T BELIEVE IT MADE THE FRONT PAGE. NO WONDER NO ONE READS THE SCHOOL NEWSPAPER...
Sigh...
Eh? Ehhh?
THAT'S NOT TRUE!
YOUR ARTICLES ARE ALWAYS SUPER INTERESTING, TOKIWA-CHAN!
YOU'RE THE ONLY ONE WHO THINKS SO, MINMIN.
......
THAT'S AS EXCITING AS THINGS GET AROUND HERE.
SEE? IT'S SO PEACEFUL, THERE AREN'T EVEN ANY GOOD LEADS FOR THE NEWSPAPER CLUB TO FOLLOW UP ON...
Student Council Organizes Fund Raising
Club Farewell Party
BUT... IF THAT'S THE CASE...
THEN THERE'S REALLY NO NEED FOR POLIZI HERE...
Times
Ah!
"POLIZI"?

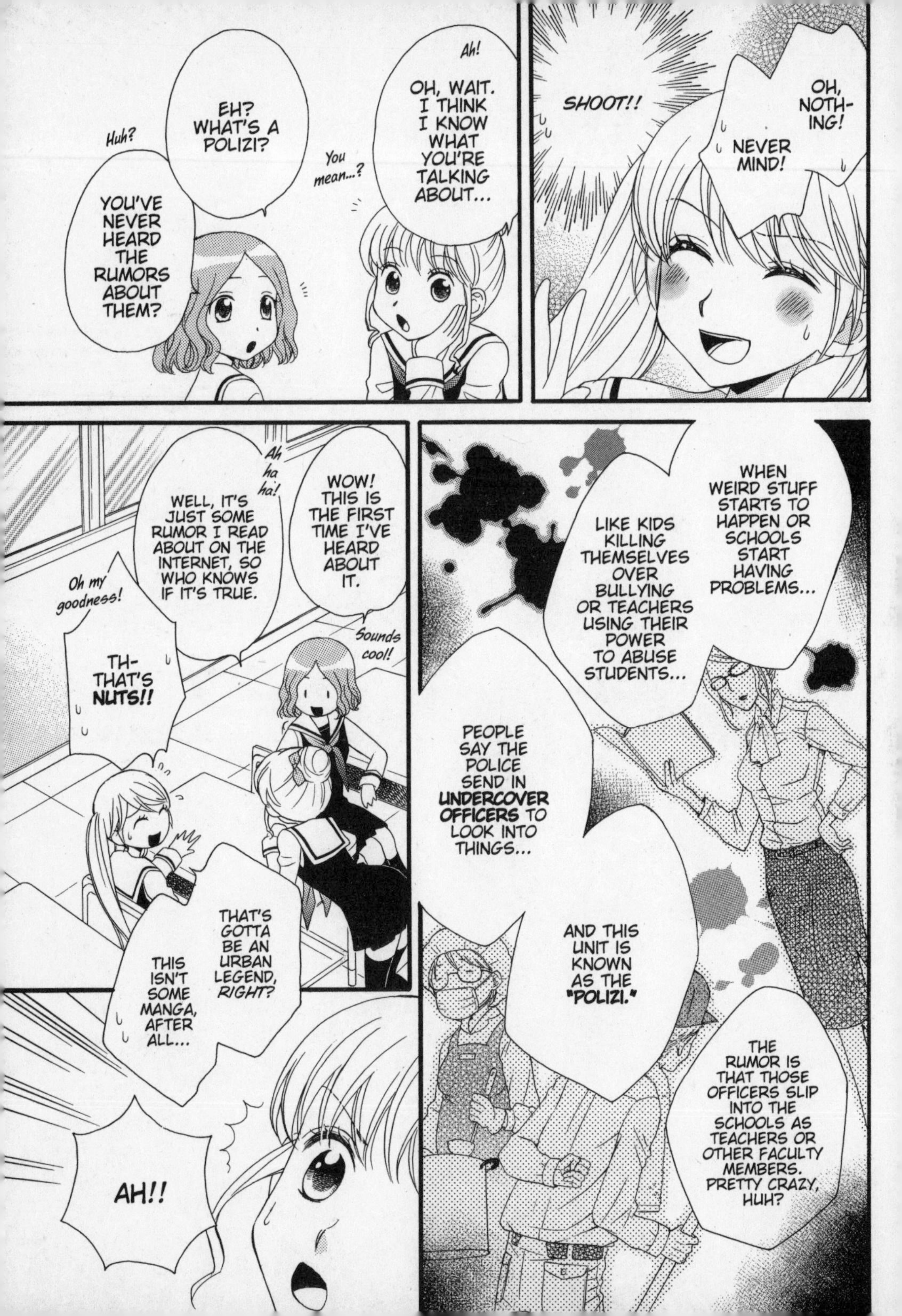
SHOOT!!
OH, NOTHING!
NEVER MIND!
Ah!
OH, WAIT. I THINK I KNOW WHAT YOU'RE TALKING ABOUT...
You mean...?
EH? WHAT'S A POLIZI?
Huh?
YOU'VE NEVER HEARD THE RUMORS ABOUT THEM?
WHEN WEIRD STUFF STARTS TO HAPPEN OR SCHOOLS START HAVING PROBLEMS...
LIKE KIDS KILLING THEMSELVES OVER BULLYING OR TEACHERS USING THEIR POWER TO ABUSE STUDENTS...
PEOPLE SAY THE POLICE SEND IN **UNDERCOVER OFFICERS** TO LOOK INTO THINGS...
THE RUMOR IS THAT THOSE OFFICERS SLIP INTO THE SCHOOLS AS TEACHERS OR OTHER FACULTY MEMBERS. PRETTY CRAZY, HUH?
AND THIS UNIT IS KNOWN AS THE **"POLIZI."**
WOW! THIS IS THE FIRST TIME I'VE HEARD ABOUT IT.
Ah ha ha!
WELL, IT'S JUST SOME RUMOR I READ ABOUT ON THE INTERNET, SO WHO KNOWS IF IT'S TRUE.
Sounds cool!
Oh my goodness!
TH-THAT'S **NUTS!!**
THAT'S GOTTA BE AN URBAN LEGEND, *RIGHT?*
THIS ISN'T SOME MANGA, AFTER ALL...
AH!!

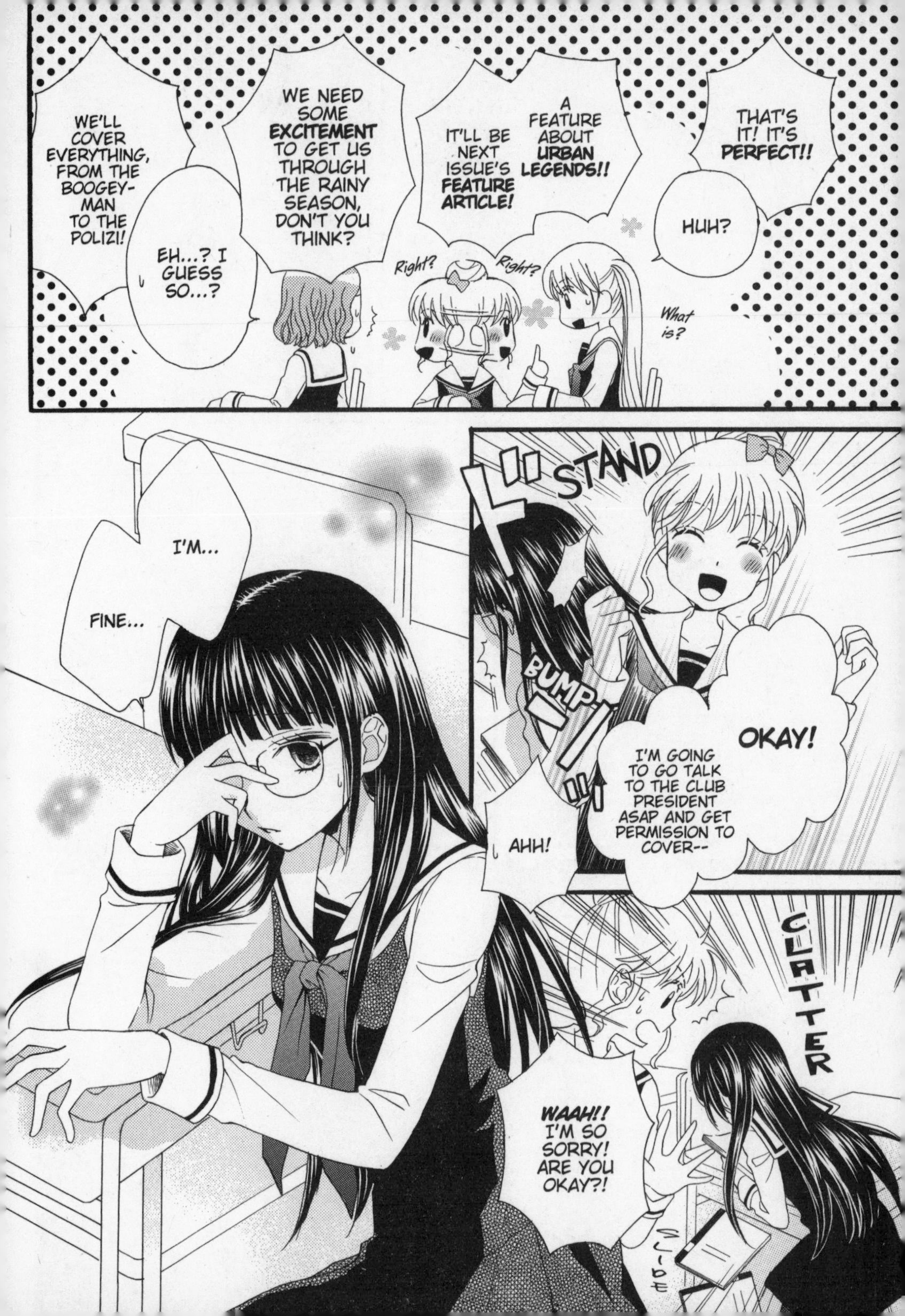
THAT'S IT! IT'S PERFECT!!
HUH?
What is?
A FEATURE ABOUT URBAN LEGENDS!!
IT'LL BE NEXT ISSUE'S FEATURE ARTICLE!
Right?
Right?
WE NEED SOME EXCITEMENT TO GET US THROUGH THE RAINY SEASON, DON'T YOU THINK?
WE'LL COVER EVERYTHING, FROM THE BOOGEY-MAN TO THE POLIZI!
EH...? I GUESS SO...?
STAND
OKAY!
I'M GOING TO GO TALK TO THE CLUB PRESIDENT ASAP AND GET PERMISSION TO COVER--
BUMP
AHH!
CLATTER
WAAH!! I'M SO SORRY! ARE YOU OKAY?!
Slide
I'M...
FINE...

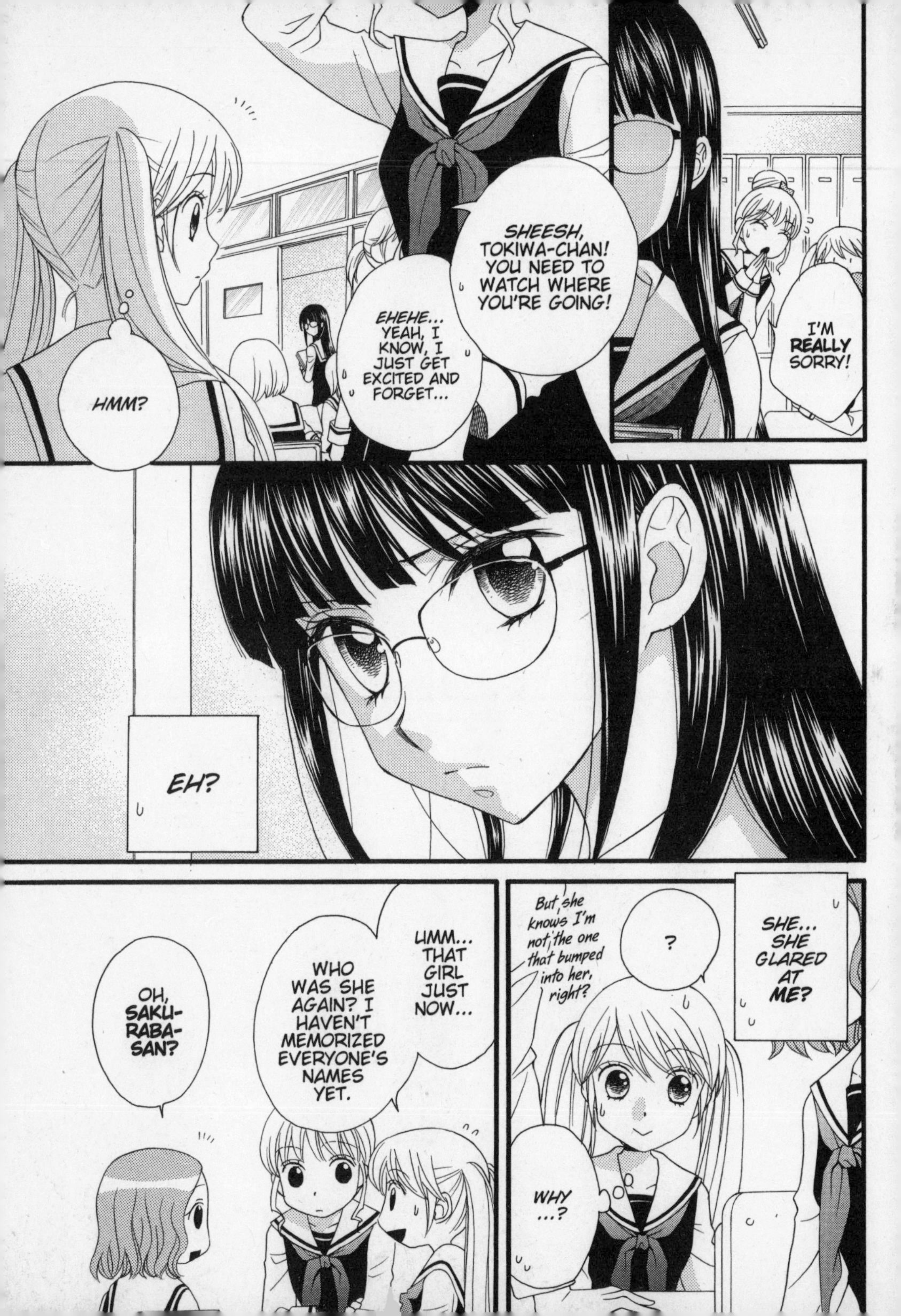
I'M REALLY SORRY!
SHEESH, TOKIWA-CHAN! YOU NEED TO WATCH WHERE YOU'RE GOING!
EHEHE... YEAH, I KNOW, I JUST GET EXCITED AND FORGET...
HMM?
EH?
SHE... SHE GLARED AT ME?
?
But she knows I'm not the one that bumped into her, right?
WHY ...?
UMM... THAT GIRL JUST NOW...
WHO WAS SHE AGAIN? I HAVEN'T MEMORIZED EVERYONE'S NAMES YET.
OH, SAKURA-BA-SAN?

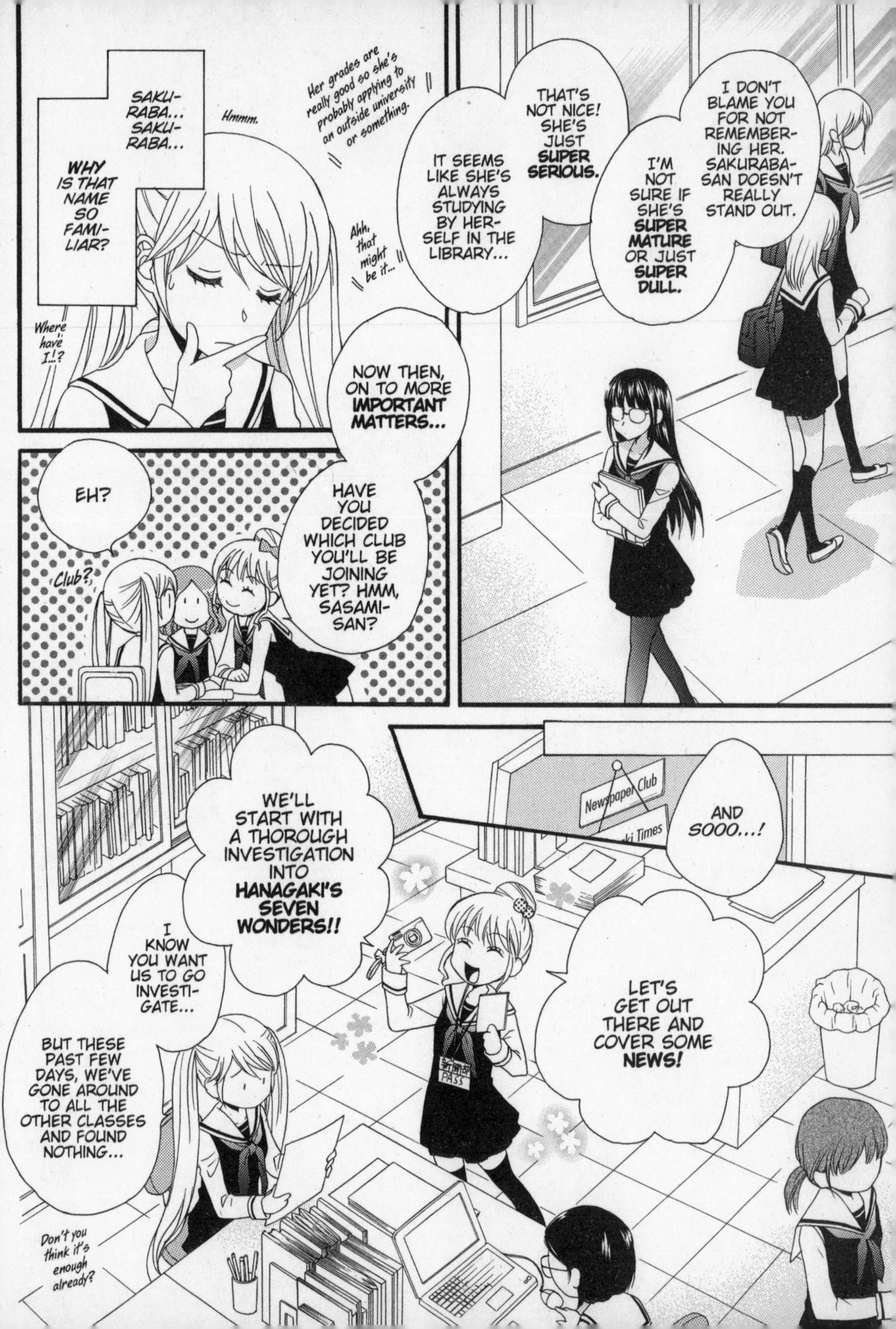
I DON'T BLAME YOU FOR NOT REMEMBER-ING HER. SAKURABA-SAN DOESN'T REALLY STAND OUT.
I'M NOT SURE IF SHE'S SUPER MATURE OR JUST SUPER DULL.
THAT'S NOT NICE! SHE'S JUST SUPER SERIOUS.
IT SEEMS LIKE SHE'S ALWAYS STUDYING BY HER-SELF IN THE LIBRARY...
Her grades are really good so she's probably applying to an outside university or something.
Ahh, that might be it...
Hmmm.
SAKU-RABA... SAKU-RABA...
WHY IS THAT NAME SO FAMI-LIAR?
Where have I...?
NOW THEN, ON TO MORE IMPORTANT MATTERS...
HAVE YOU DECIDED WHICH CLUB YOU'LL BE JOINING YET? HMM, SASAMI-SAN?
EH?
Club?
Newspaper Club
AND SOOO...!
WE'LL START WITH A THOROUGH INVESTIGATION INTO HANAGAKI'S SEVEN WONDERS!!
LET'S GET OUT THERE AND COVER SOME NEWS!
PASS
I KNOW YOU WANT US TO GO INVESTI-GATE...
BUT THESE PAST FEW DAYS, WE'VE GONE AROUND TO ALL THE OTHER CLASSES AND FOUND NOTHING...
Don't you think it's enough already?

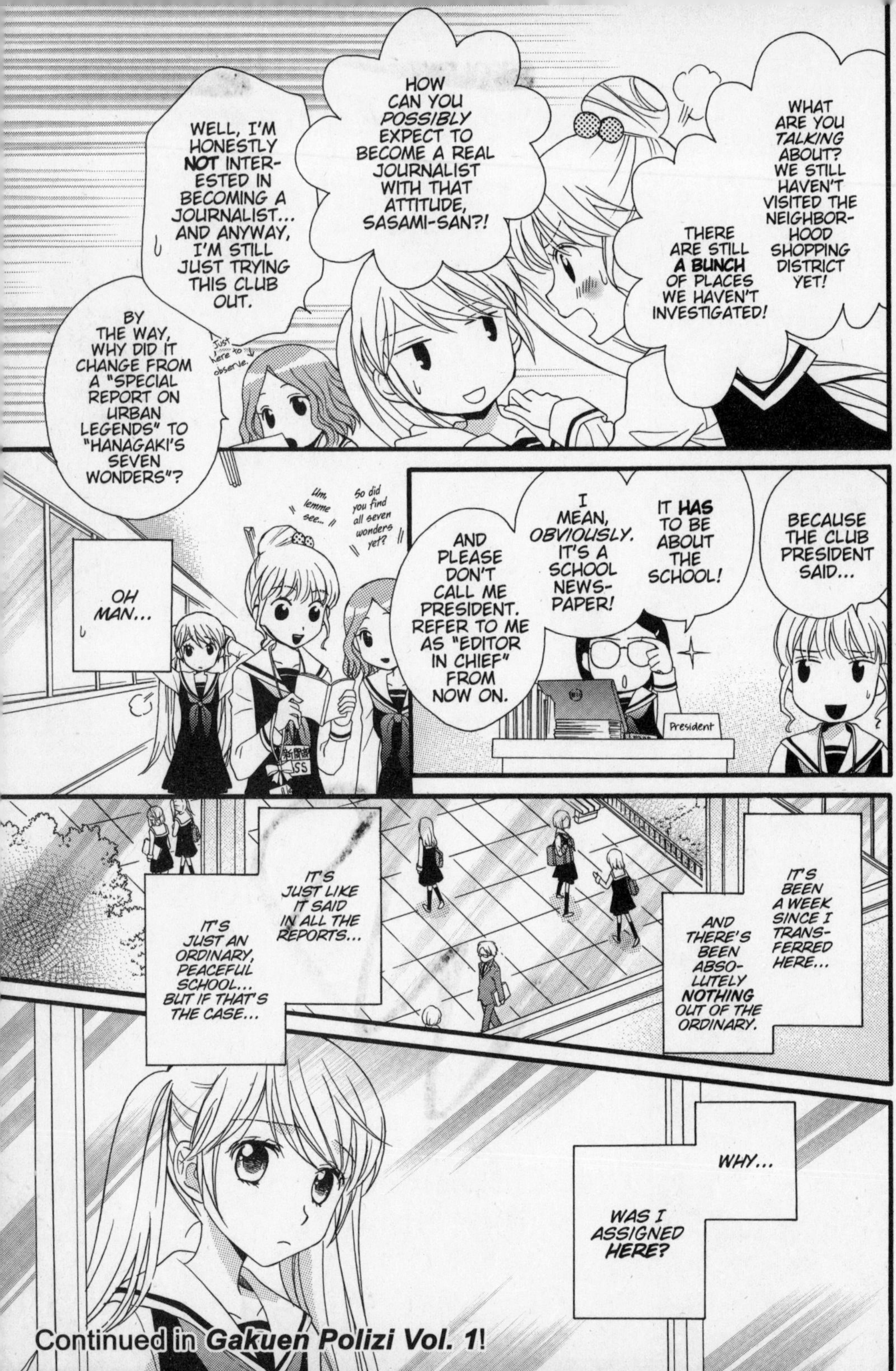
WHAT ARE YOU TALKING ABOUT? WE STILL HAVEN'T VISITED THE NEIGHBOR-HOOD SHOPPING DISTRICT YET!
THERE ARE STILL A BUNCH OF PLACES WE HAVEN'T INVESTIGATED!
HOW CAN YOU POSSIBLY EXPECT TO BECOME A REAL JOURNALIST WITH THAT ATTITUDE, SASAMI-SAN?!
WELL, I'M HONESTLY NOT INTER-ESTED IN BECOMING A JOURNALIST... AND ANYWAY, I'M STILL JUST TRYING THIS CLUB OUT.
Just here to observe.
BY THE WAY, WHY DID IT CHANGE FROM A "SPECIAL REPORT ON URBAN LEGENDS" TO "HANAGAKI'S SEVEN WONDERS"?
BECAUSE THE CLUB PRESIDENT SAID...
IT HAS TO BE ABOUT THE SCHOOL!
I MEAN, OBVIOUSLY. IT'S A SCHOOL NEWS-PAPER!
AND PLEASE DON'T CALL ME PRESIDENT. REFER TO ME AS "EDITOR IN CHIEF" FROM NOW ON.
President
So did you find all seven wonders yet?
Um, lemme see...
OH MAN...
IT'S BEEN A WEEK SINCE I TRANS-FERRED HERE...
AND THERE'S BEEN ABSO-LUTELY NOTHING OUT OF THE ORDINARY.
IT'S JUST LIKE IT SAID IN ALL THE REPORTS...
IT'S JUST AN ORDINARY, PEACEFUL SCHOOL... BUT IF THAT'S THE CASE...
WHY...
WAS I ASSIGNED HERE?
Continued in *Gakuen Polizi Vol. 1*!

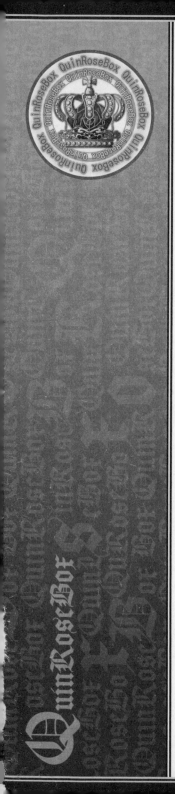

COMING SOON

SEPTEMBER 2, 2014
Alice in the Country of Clover:
Knight's Knowledge Vol. 2

OCTOBER 7, 2014
Alice in the Country of Joker:
Circus and Liar's Game Vol. 6

OCTOBER 21, 2014
Alice in the Country of Diamonds:
Bet On My Heart

NOVEMBER 4, 2014
Alice in the Country of Clover:
Knight's Knowledge Vol. 3

2284 57959